MEMORIALIZING THE GDR

MEMORIALIZING THE GDR

Monuments and Memory after 1989

Anna Saunders

berghahn
NEW YORK · OXFORD
www.berghahnbooks.com

First published in 2018 by
Berghahn Books
www.berghahnbooks.com

© 2018, 2020 Anna Saunders
First paperback edition published in 2020

All rights reserved. Except for the quotation of short passages for the purposes of criticism and review, no part of this book may be reproduced in any form or by any means, electronic or mechanical, including photocopying, recording, or any information storage and retrieval system now known or to be invented, without written permission of the publisher.

Library of Congress Cataloging-in-Publication Data
Names: Saunders, Anna, 1967- author.
Title: Memorializing the GDR : monuments and memory after 1989 / Anna Saunders.
Description: New York : Berghahn Books, [2018] | Includes bibliographical references and index.
Identifiers: LCCN 2017053208 (print) | LCCN 2018017101 (ebook) | ISBN 9781785336812 (ebook) | ISBN 9781785336805 (hardback : alk. paper)
Subjects: LCSH: Germany (East)--History. | Memorials--Germany (East) | Memorialization--Political aspects--Germany (East) | Collective memory--Germany (East) | Germany--History--Unification, 1990--Influence.
Classification: LCC DD282 (ebook) | LCC DD282 .S385 2018 (print) | DDC 943/.1087--dc23
LC record available at https://lccn.loc.gov/2017053208

British Library Cataloguing in Publication Data
A catalogue record for this book is available from the British Library

ISBN 978-1-78533-680-5 hardback
ISBN 978-1-78920-801-6 paperback
ISBN 978-1-78533-681-2 ebook

For David, Scott and Rowan

Contents

List of Illustrations	x
Acknowledgements	xii
List of Abbreviations and Key Terms	xiv

Introduction   1
  Memory Debates and the Built Environment since Unification   5
  'Working Through' the GDR Past   10
  A Shifting Memorial Culture   15

Chapter 1. Memory, Monuments and Memorialization   25
  Notions of, and Problems with, Collective Forms of Memory   27
  Monuments, Memorials and 'Memory Markers'   36

Chapter 2. Socialist Icons: From Heroes to Villains?   55
  The Role of Monuments in the GDR   57
  Transition: October 1989 to October 1990   62
  Eastern Berlin I: From Unification to Lenin's Fall   65
  Eastern Berlin II: From the Commission's Recommendations to
    Thälmann's Survival   72
  Demolition Debates beyond Berlin: Chemnitz's 'Nischel'   77
  Modification: A Modern Makeover for Halle's Flag Monument   85
  Relocation: Finding a New Home for Leipzig's Karl Marx
    Relief   91
  Conclusion: The Ever-Present Narrative of 1989   95

Chapter 3. Soviet Special Camps: Reassessing a Repressed Past — 110

Special Camps and Interrogation Centres — 112
Commemoration without Monumentalization: Representing Silenced Memories at Buchenwald — 117
Emotive Symbolism and Reconciliation at Fünfeichen — 128
Breaking the Silence: Historical Revision in Greifswald — 135
A Monument without Answers? *Haftstätte* Prenzlauer Allee, Berlin — 140
Conclusion: Revoking Silence — 147

Chapter 4. 17 June 1953 Uprisings: Remembering a Failed Revolution — 159

Conflicting Interpretations in Berlin: Katharina Karrenberg, Wolfgang Rüppel and Beyond — 165
Remembering Hennigsdorf's Steelworkers — 174
Tank Tracks in Leipzig — 178
Tank Tracks in Dresden — 181
Conclusion: Diverse Remembrance — 185

Chapter 5. The Berlin Wall: Historical Document, Tourist Magnet or Urban Eyesore? — 194

The Early Post-*Wende* Years: From Commodification to Preservation — 197
Übergänge: Remembering Border Crossings and Transitions — 201
Bernauer Straße Wall Memorial (Part I): Peripheral Remembrance? — 207
Victimhood and Visibility I: Remembering Child Victims in Treptow — 214
Victimhood and Visibility II: White Crosses in Duplicate — 218
Victimhood and Visibility III: The Freedom Memorial, Checkpoint Charlie — 224
Towards Decentralized Remembrance: The *Gesamtkonzept* and Bernauer Straße (Part II) — 231
Conclusion: Shifting Remembrance — 236

Chapter 6. Remembering the 'Peaceful Revolution' and German Unity — 251

Building National Memory? Berlin's Freedom and Unity Monument — 256
Remembering the Leipzig Demonstrations: The Nikolaikirchhof and Beyond — 268

Schwerin's Controversial Remembrance of the Round Table	277
Swords into Ploughshares: Dessau's Peace Bell	281
Transforming the Fortunes of Magdeburg? The Development of a Citizens' Monument	286
A Truly Democratic Project? Plauen's *Wende* Monument	291
Conclusion: The Concrete Legacy of the Peaceful Revolution	296
Conclusion. Beyond the Palimpsest	**314**
What Remains?	315
Dominant Narratives	317
Dialogic Remembrance and Entangled Memories	322
Bibliography	329
Index	351

Illustrations

2.1 Lenin Monument (Nikolai Tomski, 1970) on the former Leninplatz, Berlin (destroyed 1991/92) — 67
2.2 Thälmann Monument (Lev Kerbel, 1986), Greifswalder Straße, Prenzlauer Berg, Berlin — 73
2.3 Karl Marx Monument (Lev Kerbel, 1971), Brückenstraße, Chemnitz — 78
2.4 Flag Monument (original monument by Siegbert Fliegel, 1967 / redesigned by Steffen O. Rumpf, 2004), Hansering, Halle — 90
2.5 Karl Marx Relief (Rolf Kurth, Klaus Schwabe and Frank Ruddigkeit, 1974), now located in the university campus on Jahnallee, Leipzig — 91
3.1 *Waldfriedhof* (installed 1995/96), Buchenwald Memorial Site — 125
3.2 Memorial ensemble at Fünfeichen, including the leaning cross (Uwe Grimm, 1993) and the bell (to the right) from Neubrandenburg's Marienkirche — 131
3.3 Commemorative stele in memory of Greifswald's victims of Soviet special camps (Thomas Radeloff, 1997), between the station and Lange Straße (on the site of the former town walls), Greifswald — 139
3.4 *Denkzeichen* on 'Haus 3' (Karla Sachse, 1997), Prenzlauer Allee, Berlin — 143
4.1 Memorial to 17 June 1953 (Wolfgang Rüppel, 2000), also showing mural by Max Lingner (1953) on the wall of the Federal Ministry for Finance, Berlin — 170

4.2	'17 June 1958 – Autumn 1989' (Heidi Wagner-Kerkhof, 1993), Platz des 17. Juni 1953, Hennigsdorf	176
4.3	17 June 1953 Memorial (Young Social Democrats Forum, 2003), Salzgäßchen, Leipzig	180
4.4	17 June 1953 Memorial (Heidemarie Dreßel, 2008), Postplatz, Dresden	182
5.1	'Stone, paper, scissors' (Thorsten Goldberg, 1997), Oberbaumbrücke, Berlin (*Übergänge* competition)	203
5.2	'Illuminated box' (Frank Thiel, 1998), former Checkpoint Charlie, Berlin (*Übergänge* competition)	205
5.3	Berlin Wall Memorial (Kohlhoff & Kohlhoff, 1998), Bernauer Straße, Berlin	210
5.4	Memorial to Treptow's Wall victims (Jan Skuin and Rüdiger Roehl, 1999), Kiefholzstraße, Berlin-Treptow	217
5.5	White crosses (Cornelia Müller and Jan Wehberg, 2003), Spreeufer, Berlin	220
5.6	White crosses (in this location since 1995), Ebert-/Scheidemannstraße, Berlin (showing wreaths laid on 13 August 2011)	221
5.7	Window of Commemoration (2010), Berlin Wall Memorial Site, Bernauer Straße, Berlin	234
6.1	St Nicholas Column in memory of the demonstrations of 9 October 1989 (Andreas Stötzner, 1999), Nikolaikirchhof, Leipzig	271
6.2	Round Table (Guillermo Steinbrüggen, 1990), Großer Moor/Puschkinstraße, Schwerin	278
6.3	Peace Bell (frame designed by Dieter Bankert, 2002), Platz der Deutschen Einheit, Dessau	285
6.4	Citizens' Monument (Norbert Zagel, 2003), west of cathedral entrance, Magdeburg	289
6.5	*Wende* Monument (Peter Luban, 2010), Melanchthonstraße ('Tunnel'), Plauen	294

Acknowledgements

I am indebted to numerous individuals and organizations, who have all made this book possible in so many different ways. Throughout the course of my research, I have corresponded with and visited archives, local government offices, memorial sites, diverse institutions, artists and memory activists. Time and again, I have been met with generosity, enthusiasm and patience concerning my requests for information, for which I am extremely grateful. I would like to thank all those who spent time providing me with personal insights, showing me sites of interest, and often allowing me to consult their private archives or collections: Lothar and Heidrun Brauer, Ekkehard Brunstein, Norbert Credé, Lothar Ehm, Rudolf Evers, Manfred Fischer, Falk-Thoralf Günther, Wolfgang Hocquél, Andreas Kahl, Martin Klähn, Rainer Klemke, Wolfgang Krause, Egon Kühlbach, Mathias Lindner, Peter Luban, Rita Lüdtke, Thomas Meyer, Max Renkl, Friedrich Riechel, Bodo Ritscher, Rüdiger Roehl, Wolfgang Sachs, Jan Skuin, Guillermo Steinbrüggen, Annette Tietz, Andreas Wagner, Heidi Wagner-Kerkhof, Barbara Wils, Christopher Zenker and Barbara Zibler. In particular, I would like to express my gratitude to Elfriede Müller, whose time and generosity in allowing me access to materials at Berlin's Office for Art in the Public Sphere during the early stages of my research proved immensely helpful, to Axel Klausmeier for many stimulating discussions and insights into developments in Berlin and at Bernauer Straße, and to Joachim Schwend for providing a stream of newspaper cuttings and taking me on an enlightening memorial day trip. My thanks also go to Alan Deighton and Stephanie Bostock, both of whom have allowed me to use their photographs. Many of my research trips were made possible by funding from a British Academy Small Research Grant as well as an Early Career Fellowship from the Arts and Humanities Research Council, which above all enabled me to devote much-needed time to the project. Study leave granted by Bangor University also allowed me the time to finish the manuscript when it was most critical.

I am especially grateful to those who read or commented on all or part of the manuscript at various stages and provided invaluable advice on how it might be improved: Debbie Pinfold, Bill Niven, Dennis Tate, Carol Tully, Andrew Barker and Andrew Hiscock. Colleagues past and present at Bangor University and beyond have also provided support, inspiration, collaboration and friendship throughout the life of this project. In particular, I would like to thank Sara Jones, Joanne Sayner, Linda Shortt, Stefan Baumgarten, Sarah Pogoda, Helena Miguélez-Carballeira, Gillian Jein, Eva Bru-Dominguez and Nicki Frith. Finally, my special thanks go to David Cornwell, whose love, support, patience and humour have accompanied every stage of this project, and to Scott and Rowan, both of whom were born during the course of this book, and who remind me every day of the important things in life. Although – contrary to much advice – this is not a pop-up book of monuments, it is dedicated to them.

Abbreviations and Key Terms

Alltag	the everyday
Aufarbeitung	working through the past
CDU	Christian Democratic Union
CPSU	Communist Party of the Soviet Union
CSU	Christian Social Union in Bavaria
Denkmal	monument
Denkzeichen	memorial mark
DHM	German Historical Museum
DM	Deutsche Mark
FDJ	Free German Youth
FDP	Free Democratic Party
FRG	Federal Republic of Germany
GDR	German Democratic Republic
GPU-cellar	NKVD-controlled interrogation centre
IM	unofficial collaborator of the Stasi
Mahnmal	monument (with a cautionary purpose)
NGBK	New Society for the Visual Arts
NKVD	Soviet People's Commissariat for Internal Affairs (Soviet secret police)
Ostalgie	nostalgia for the GDR
PDS	Party of Democratic Socialism (from 2007: Die Linke)
POW	prisoner of war
SED	Socialist Unity Party of Germany
SPD	Social Democratic Party of Germany
Stasi	Ministry for State Security of the GDR
Wende	period of political change in East Germany in 1989/90

Introduction

'The Wall must go!' was one of the most arresting slogans of November 1989, and arguably of the twentieth century. The concrete scar across Berlin's cityscape came to define world politics, provoking repeated calls for its destruction. Its demolition in the early 1990s was almost unanimously greeted with enthusiasm by politicians, residents and town planners; this hated Cold War edifice was finally to disappear, allowing Germany's new capital city to look to the future. Yet in March 2013, a chorus of demonstrators at Berlin's East Side Gallery chanted 'The Wall must stay!', angered by the removal of a section of wall from one of few remaining historic sites. One protestor highlighted the historical irony of the situation, inscribing onto its concrete base an evocative plea to Berlin's mayor: 'Mr Wowereit – don't tear down this wall'.[1] The removal activity, sanctioned by the district council, enabled access to a building site between the wall and the river Spree, on which a luxury high-rise apartment block was to be constructed. Protesters objected not only to the damage caused to what has become a valuable historical document and unintended monument to the Cold War, but also to the plans to build a high-rise development in the former death strip, which could potentially dwarf the wall and belittle its historical importance. Revelations about the investor's involvement with the Stasi in the 1980s added further grist to the protesters' mill, and brought an extra layer of moral complexity to one of many recent East German memory debates.

As with other controversies in Berlin and the eastern *Länder*, this debate highlights the ever-present tensions between the shifting demands of past and present in the contemporary eastern German landscape. Despite the increasing tendency of recent years to use the term 'site' to refer to non-spatial domains of memory, especially since Pierre Nora's seminal work *Les Lieux de Mémoire*, the built environment remains central to questions of memory and remembrance.[2] One need only recall the 9/11 memorial in New York and the Holocaust memorial in Berlin as recent examples of sites that have become central to a nation's self-understanding. Whereas the centres of European towns and cities in medieval and early modern times were marked by the construction of cathedrals and castles, one could argue that monuments and memorials have taken on this role today.[3] In contrast, the felling of statues of Saddam Hussein in Baghdad or Stalin in Ukraine demonstrates the extent to which concrete structures can come to symbolize entire regimes and provoke highly emotional responses. As this book demonstrates, however, monuments can become invested with multiple meanings and memories that are often far from intended at the moment of their construction.

Physical structures particularly acted as tangible sites and repositories of memory in former East Germany, where the socialist regime placed great importance on monuments and urban space in order to promote a collective socialist consciousness and a cohesive East German identity.[4] Since the demise of the German Democratic Republic (GDR), however, not only have the futures of many such structures become disputed, but new memorial projects have challenged accepted norms and historical narratives. A project in 2011 to erect stelae to victims of the border regime between the GDR and West Berlin, for instance, caused consternation in the village of Sacrow, a quiet suburb on the outskirts of Potsdam, where one victim had also been an unofficial collaborator (IM) for the Stasi. While this compromised his status as a 'victim' in the eyes of some, the project forced residents to rethink any clear-cut divides between the concepts of victimhood and perpetration. Similar questions also surfaced at Buchenwald, where the use of the site first as a Nazi concentration camp and then as a Soviet special camp caused numerous memorial controversies and conflicting understandings of victimhood. At the other end of the spectrum, however, efforts to commemorate the demonstrations of 1989 in concrete form on former East German territory have raised concerns over the potential dangers of heroization, particularly given the monumental socialist realist structures that formerly scattered the GDR landscape. In all such cases, it is the desire to create physical markers to the past, thus sites of memory in the truest sense of the word, that has caused debate and historical re-evaluation in the present. It is this process that forms the subject of this book.

As this introduction demonstrates, the broader context of GDR remembrance is complex and constantly shifting; there are few places where the past impinges on the present quite as much as in contemporary Germany. In this recently reunified nation, twentieth-century history bears heavily on domestic and international policy-making, as well as on the media landscape, cultural production and the built environment. The early 2000s saw a significant increase in the consumption of popular culture that draws on this history: historical films such as *Der Untergang* (*Downfall*, 2004), *Das Leben der Anderen* (*The Lives of Others*, 2006), *Der Baader Meinhof Komplex* (*The Baader Meinhof Complex*, 2008) and *Sophie Scholl – Die letzten Tage* (*Sophie Scholl – The Final Days*, 2005) became box office hits and were awarded prestigious prizes; TV films, dramas and series, otherwise dubbed 'histotainments', such as *Der Tunnel* (*The Tunnel*, 2001), *Die Mauer – Berlin '61* (*The Wall – Berlin '61*, 2006), *Speer und Er* (*Speer and Hitler*, 2005), *Unsere Mütter, unsere Väter* (*Generation War*, 2013) and *Deutschland '83* (2015) saw soaring viewing quotas; autobiographical memoirs topped bestseller lists; and historical exhibitions drew crowds through museum doors. This preoccupation with the past found expression above all in the so-called 'super commemorative year' of 2009,[5] in which numerous anniversaries fell together: twenty years of the fall of the Berlin Wall, sixty years of the Basic Law, seventy years since the start of the Second World War, and ninety years of the Weimar Constitution – not to speak of 160 years of the Frankfurt Constitution. Not only did this unleash a 'medial Tsunami',[6] but it saw Germany host several large-scale commemorative events, in which there was apparently genuine public interest and participation.

The twenty-year celebrations of the fall of the Berlin Wall on 9 November 2009 highlighted above all the significance of the changing physical landscape, with the high point of the evening being marked by the toppling of one thousand giant painted domino stones along part of the former course of the Wall – an area between Potsdamer Platz and the Spree that had changed beyond recognition in twenty years. It is, indeed, in the cityscape that the recent past – or its absence – is most immediately notable, and urban land has often become a battleground for different groups attempting either to overcome a 'divided memory' or to remember specific elements of this past.[7] As Rudy Koshar states, 'Reunification was not only a process of economic and political synchronization but also a struggle over symbols'.[8] Since the changes of 1989/90, Germany has thus witnessed impassioned battles not only over the GDR legacy, but also over elements of the National Socialist past, sites of which have been freed from entrenched Cold War positions. In

Berlin, the rededication of the *Neue Wache* (New Guardhouse) memorial, the building of the Memorial to the Murdered Jews of Europe, the development of the Topography of Terror exhibition on the former site of the SS and Gestapo headquarters, the demolition of the Palast der Republik (Palace of the Republic, the GDR's parliament building), the survival of socialist realist monuments and the proposals for a Freedom and Unity Monument have all filled endless pages of print, and represent only the tip of the iceberg. Other unexpected projects have also aroused a renewed interest in the intersection between art, politics and memory. Building work on a new underground station in central Berlin in 2010, for example, uncovered a considerable number of statues and sculptures that had been buried since the Second World War. As examples of 'degenerate art', spurned and banned in Nazi Germany, they gained heightened recognition, reminding us of the potentially huge political power of art.[9] Other contemporary projects have provoked considerable interest. Concept artist Christo's 'wrapping' of the Reichstag building in 1995, for instance, attracted millions of visitors, making this history-laden building – and future united parliament – paradoxically more visible through its veiling than it had been for years previously. Art projects in and around the Reichstag have also attempted to symbolize the basis of unification: Hans Haacke's installation *Der Bevölkerung* (to the population) in a courtyard of the Reichstag, and Dani Karavan's construction *Grundgesetz 49* (Basic Law 49) on the Spree promenade, for instance, both emphasize the democratic credentials of united Germany, the former deliberately providing a contrast to the inscription *Dem deutschen Volke* (to the German people) on the front of the Reichstag building.[10]

While much attention continues to be focused on Germany's difficult past, such installations suggest that a certain degree of 'normalization' is being achieved, in which identification with the German nation can be positive, while historical responsibility is not forgotten.[11] The seventieth anniversary events of the end of the Second World War, for instance, were not as contentious as those of the fiftieth anniversary, the Holocaust is increasingly being put in perspective alongside other experiences from that period (see below), and a monument erected in 2009 to the Bundeswehr in Berlin – although controversial – would have been unthinkable twenty years previously. Similarly, the proposed Freedom and Unity Monument in Berlin (discussed in Chapter 6) marks an evident break in the tradition of monuments to German shame, seeking to commemorate instead civil courage, freedom and unity. While some interpret the 'normalizing' process to mark a less sustained interest in memory,[12] others see it as indicative of the shift from embodied communicative memories to institutionalized cultural memories, the latter maintaining less 'emotional resonance'.[13] What, then, of GDR memory, where the actors of history are still very present? Has this, too, been subject to 'normalization'? To what extent does this past compete with that of the National Socialist period for our attention today, and how does this manifest itself in the memorial landscape?

Memory Debates and the Built Environment since Unification

Our understanding of the GDR's material legacy must be placed within the broader context of German memory debates since unification, and specifically those that relate to the built environment. Four key areas raise significant questions for this book, and are notable for the fact that they all relate to the National Socialist past, yet also impact on the way in which the GDR is remembered today. The first and most important of these is the way in which unification changed the terms of official memory of National Socialism in both East and West, and placed it within a new context. While German division ensured that each side could regard itself as morally superior and view the other half as a continuation of National Socialism, unification meant that there was no longer a scapegoat: unified Germany as a whole had to take responsibility for the National Socialist past. The West German notion of *Vergangenheitsbewältigung* (mastering the past) increasingly lost currency, in favour of other terms, most notably *Aufarbeitung der Vergangenheit* (working through the past), a term to which Adorno gave preference in his famous 1959 lecture.[14] The shift in public discourse denoted a growing sense of attempting to come to terms with the past through critical self-engagement, rather than the idea of laying it to rest or, as Adorno saw it, silencing the past. The 1990s witnessed a surge of debates and controversies over the National Socialist past, ranging from the reception of Daniel Goldhagen's book *Hitler's Willing Executioners* and the controversial exhibition 'Crimes of the Wehrmacht', to heated debates over author Martin Walser's acceptance speech for the German Booksellers Association's Peace Prize, and deliberations over the Bundeswehr's active involvement in the Kosovo conflict.[15]

However, if unification caused a new sense of responsibility towards the past, it also brought with it two problems. First, how was the new Germany to be built on the foundations of shame for past injustices? As James Young writes, 'no other nation has ever attempted to re-unite itself on the bedrock memory of its crimes or to make commemoration of its crimes the topographical centre of gravity in its capital'.[16] To a certain extent, Helmut Kohl attempted to bring together east and west in a common experience of totalitarian rule in the *Neue Wache* memorial, dedicated in 1993 as Germany's 'national memorial to victims of war and tyranny'. Although there are references to specific victim groups on the text outside the building, the general dedication remembers all victims together – whether, for example, of Nazism, of expulsion from Eastern territories after the war, of Stalinism or of socialism.[17] This highlights the second problem: to what extent should the GDR dictatorship and the National Socialist regime be placed alongside each other? References to Germany's 'double past', or the GDR as the 'second German dictatorship' naturally encourage such comparisons, and while the equation of the Third Reich with the GDR no longer serves the same political function as during division, it can still serve the purpose of devaluing socialist thinking and placing Nazi crimes within a broader European context. Yet, as Claus Leggewie and Erik Meyer state, 'only the comparison could clear up proportions', namely the fact that the crimes of the GDR's leadership were without doubt lesser than those of National Socialism.[18] Indeed, historians are largely of the view that with the passage of time it is still the 'first' dictatorship that has retained most historical focus and commemorative weight in the public domain.[19] This is evidenced by negotiations at some physical sites of memory where conflicts over a 'double past' cannot be avoided, as seen most prominently at Buchenwald Memorial Site (examined in Chapter 3), where a hierarchy of memory is central to its memorial concept. It is, however, the so-called 'Faulenbach formula', after historian Bernd Faulenbach, that is frequently referenced as the standard model for remembering Germany's 'double past', and which attempts to avoid any sense of hierarchy. This is seen above all in the *Gedenkstättenkonzeption* (Memorial Sites Concept) of 2008 and the earlier findings of the Bundestag's second 'special enquiry commission' (see below), which concluded: 'Nazi crimes should not be relativized as a result of addressing the crimes of Stalinism. Stalinist crimes should not be trivialized through reference to Nazi crimes'.[20] This question of comparison and equation is clearly most important at sites where the two pasts lie side by side, such as at Buchenwald, but this book demonstrates its significance for the development of GDR memorials – and GDR remembrance – more broadly, with numerous case studies revealing the entangled memory of these two pasts.

The second key area relating to memory debates since unification concerns an intensification and institutionalization of memory of the Holocaust, one that began in the Federal Republic of Germany (FRG) during the 1980s, but which gained strength during the 1990s. While this can be witnessed in an increasing number of annual commemorative days, such as 27 January (marking the liberation of Auschwitz, which officially became a national day of remembrance in 1996), the intensification of Holocaust remembrance is above all evident in the physical landscape. Berlin, for instance, has not only witnessed high-profile projects such as Daniel Libeskind's Jewish Museum and Peter Eisenman's Memorial to the Murdered Jews of Europe (hereafter referred to as the Holocaust memorial), but a range of other monuments commemorating different persecuted groups, such as homosexuals, euthanasia victims and Sinti and Roma, as well as historical events such as the book burnings of 1933 (Micha Ullmann's 'Library'), the introduction of anti-Jewish laws in the 1930s (Renata Stih and Frieder Schnock's 'Places of Remembrance') and sites of deportation such as Grunewald station (Karol Broniatowski's 'Platform 17'). Outside Berlin, many other cities have also witnessed the erection of monuments to local victims and events, such as Munich (Ulla von Brandenburg's 'Monument to Lesbians and Gays Persecuted during National Socialism'), Frankfurt am Main (Heiner Blum's 'Wollheim-Memorial') and Duisburg (Gerhard Losemann's 'Deportation Memorial'). The proliferation of such projects, and in particular the extended debates over Berlin's Holocaust memorial, has led to the widely recognized argument that no single, central memorial will ever be able to represent the Holocaust in its entirety. Moreover, this is undesirable, for it would create a sense of finality and closure. The centrality of Holocaust remembrance in Berlin has, however, also led to criticism that the 'Holocaust industry' is tailored to tourism as much as to the demands of memory; indeed, Chancellor Schröder's much-cited comment in 1998 that the memorial should be a place where Germans 'like to go' caused much controversy.[21] Inevitably, such issues have influenced commemorative activities relating to other pasts, and as this book shows, questions of centrality, an over-abundance of memorials, the difficult combination of pleasure and commemoration, and the demands of tourism are all issues that challenge concrete memory of the GDR. Some projects, such as the temporary Freedom Memorial erected near the former site of Checkpoint Charlie, or the planned Freedom and Unity Monument in central Berlin, have indeed encouraged direct comparison with the Holocaust memorial, and can, to some extent, be seen as a response to the centrality of Holocaust remembrance (see Chapters 5 and 6).

Holocaust-centred memory appears to have dominated to a lesser extent from the mid-2000s, since other memories relating to the war and immediate post-war period have re-emerged. This change has been identified by Langenbacher, Niven and Wittlinger as a 'paradigm shift', in which memories of German suffering and the period of division have found renewed resonance.[22] Above all, memory of German victimhood has found intensified expression, for as Niven states, growing distance from the Cold War means that German suffering may now be expressed as 'an existential experience – and without being bound up in political functionalisation'.[23] Indeed, such memories may have been labelled as 'nationalist' or 'revisionist' two decades earlier.[24] Although Kohl's *Neue Wache* project already placed victimhood in the foreground in the early 1990s, it was not until later, under Schröder's governments – which placed more emphasis on German perpetration and Jewish victimhood – that the public sphere appropriated the theme of German victimhood more fully.[25] The two main themes to emerge were Allied bombing and expulsion, both of which marked the return of a memory that was culturally hegemonic in the early post-war decades.[26] The former was symbolized by Jörg Friedrich's 2003 bestseller *Der Brand* (*The Fire*), which was serialized in the tabloid newspaper *Bild* and described the Allied bombing campaigns not only in emotive language, but also in terms usually reserved for the Holocaust.[27] Subsequent documentaries, numerous local publications and commemorative events in heavily bombed cities such as Dresden and Hamburg also raised the profile of Germans' plight during this period, and subsequently triggered several monument proposals.[28] The theme of the flight and expulsion of Germans from eastern territories during or after the end of the war was foregrounded above all by Günter Grass's 2002 bestselling novel *Im Krebsgang* (*Crabwalk*), on the sinking of a ship carrying Germans fleeing the Red Army in January 1945,[29] and a long and controversial campaign initiated by the League of Expellees to construct a Centre against Expulsions in Berlin.[30] Renewed memories of German victimhood during the war have, needless to say, cleared the way for other experiences of suffering, namely those connected to division and socialist rule. The re-publication of the anonymous diary *Eine Frau in Berlin* (*A Woman in Berlin*) in 2003, depicting a woman's experiences of rape during the Red Army's occupation of Berlin in 1945, and its subsequent adaptation into a film in 2008, provides one such example.[31] Other experiences of victimhood include those in the hands of the NKVD (Soviet secret police), the SED (Socialist Unity Party of Germany) and the Stasi, as well as victims of the GDR's border regime (as discussed in Chapters 3 and 5). The recent 'paradigm shift' has also, however, significantly blurred the boundaries between victims and perpetrators; while commemoration of victims may have increased, so too has the recognition that many Germans may, at different times, have been both. This book demonstrates that memorialization of the GDR is increasingly contributing to the blurring of such boundaries, and that understandings of the East German regime are moving towards a more complex and less black and white picture.

The final key theme concerning recent German memory debates is the role of Berlin as the united nation's new capital, and particularly the way in which the urban landscape has showcased the concept of *Aufarbeitung*. During division, Berlin clearly held a special position as a divided city, and the display of power through architecture was no new concept, with the GDR's Television Tower, for example, representing the height of architectural prowess in 1969. The 750th anniversary of Berlin in 1987 also saw efforts on both sides to outdo each other, particularly in the East, where the showcasing of Berlin attempted to draw attention away from the dilapidated state of provincial towns.[32] Since unification, however, Berlin has attracted almost unrivalled international attention from architects, artists and town planners, and Andrew Webber suggests that it was the 'capital of the twentieth century', following Benjamin's similar claim for Paris in the nineteenth century.[33] Having previously been the stage of world conflict, the city is now challenged with reconfiguring and reimagining itself as the capital of a new, united Germany, and constructing a more 'normalized' cultural imaginary in the wake of four decades of division and two twentieth-century dictatorships. As the largest building site in Europe, the city authorities even marketed Berlin's *Baustellen* (building sites) as *Schaustellen* (viewing/exhibition sites) between 1995 and 2005, attracting thousands of visitors each year. In the words of its former mayor, Eberhard Diepgen, the city was – and still is – the 'workshop of German unity'.[34] However, the focus on Berlin brings with it two problems. First, the large influx of monuments and memory markers can have the result of diluting their effect and discouraging real engagement with the past; as Andreas Huyssen writes, 'The more monuments there are, the more the past becomes invisible, and the easier it is to forget: redemption, thus, through forgetting'.[35] Any new monuments – some of which are examined in this book – must thus be carefully placed amidst this increasingly cluttered landscape. Moreover, as this book argues, they are likely to respond to existing structures in numerous ways, and become bound up in a network of mnemonic meaning. Second, the focus on Berlin means that little attention has been paid to regional debates since unification, or indeed the relationship between Berlin and the regions.[36] As this book demonstrates, this relationship has become increasingly important in shaping the commemorative landscape of eastern Germany in recent years.

'Working Through' the GDR Past

The broader memory landscape of united Germany provides the essential context for understanding the memorialization of the GDR. The changing political and social landscape of eastern Germany more specifically, however, has presented the immediate impetus for many memorial projects, which not only become embedded in the extensive process of 'working through' the GDR past, but may also provide a means of *Aufarbeitung* themselves. Needless to say, this process is highly complex, and memory of the GDR provides a curious conundrum. On the one hand, research in the field experienced such a boom after 1989 that the extent of the secondary literature is overwhelming; as Wolfgang Thierse states, 'There is no other dictatorship in world history that has been researched so quickly and so thoroughly'.[37] On the other hand, however, there is still little agreement on the place that the GDR should occupy in the memory culture of the Federal Republic, and although the debates of the early 1990s – in which totalitarian paradigms of power and repression were pitted against social history approaches – have become less politically charged, there remains no single historical paradigm.[38] Instead, as historian Martin Sabrow suggested in 2009, the GDR has become a 'battlefield of memories', in which the voices fighting for specific interpretations of the GDR have been much louder and more varied than was ever the case in the first twenty years after the Nazi dictatorship.[39] The numerous media available today doubtless play a role here, for not only are the voices of professional historians and public figures to be heard through official channels, but those of individuals and a wide variety of interest groups are made public through online presences and social media, as well as through popular publications and the mass media; multiple fora allow for a multitude of competing memories. Despite this apparent plethora of voices, popular images of the GDR all too often become polarized into two extremes: on the one hand the grey, uniform police state marked by control and repression, and on the other hand the happy, colourful collective in which employment and social security maintained communal values. All too infrequently are the two connected in the public sphere, and despite the efforts of academics to complicate the picture through studies of everyday life, and through notions such as the 'welfare dictatorship' (Konrad Jarausch) or the 'participatory dictatorship' (Mary Fulbrook), it is rare that such terms are discussed in the media, let alone appropriated by the population at large.[40]

Official, government-led efforts to 'work through' the GDR past have, unsurprisingly, focused largely on control and repression, yet they also reflect the political colours of the ruling coalition. The findings of the Bundestag's first special enquiry commission to examine the East German past (Enquete-Kommission zur 'Aufarbeitung von Geschichte und Folgen der SED-Diktatur in Deutschland', 1992–94) thus served to establish, in Molly Andrews' terms, a 'didactic public history',[41] in which the totalitarian past was used to counter the democratic present.[42] This was perhaps little surprise, given that the commission was dominated by West German experts, members of the CDU/CSU, and members of the GDR's citizens' rights movement, all of whom held an inevitably critical perspective on the GDR. While the second parliamentary commission (Enquete-Kommission 'Überwindung der Folgen der SED-Diktatur im Prozess der deutschen Einheit', 1995–98) was to focus to a greater extent on stories 'from below', it clearly still served to legitimize the contemporary status quo and the politics of the ruling CDU/CSU-FDP coalition (1990–98). One of its direct outcomes was the creation of the Bundesstiftung zur Aufarbeitung der SED-Diktatur (Federal Foundation for the Reappraisal of the SED Dictatorship), which has received substantial financial backing to help rehabilitate former victims of the regime, and to promote research, exhibitions, events and political education on the GDR. Alongside centrally funded museums, its role in strengthening present institutions through the examination of the past is clear. In contrast, an 'expert commission' led by historian Martin Sabrow was appointed by the SPD-Green coalition government (1998–2005) in 2005 to examine the different institutions involved in GDR *Aufarbeitung* and to make recommendations on a decentrally organized network (*Geschichtsverbund*) of such institutions. The commission's report of 2006 unleashed an intensive debate, for although it criticized the 'trivialization of the GDR', it also advocated – among other things – a state-funded museum that would examine everyday life in the GDR dictatorship. The report concluded that the commission hoped its recommendations would set 'new standards for a plural and multi-perspective *Aufarbeitung* of German history in a "century of extremes"'.[43] While critics accused the commission of belittling the GDR and promoting a homeopathic version of the SED dictatorship,[44] it was a clear attempt to go beyond black and white portrayals of the GDR, and to encourage more serious engagement with the daily workings of the dictatorship. Interestingly, however, a new CDU-SPD coalition was in government by the time the report was published, and the Minister for Culture, Bernd Neumann (CDU), was keen to distance himself from it. Clearly, politics has a significant influence over the interpretation of the past.

This is perhaps nowhere more evident than in the debates concerning the role of the successor party to the SED, Die Linke (until 2007 the Party of Democratic Socialism, PDS), which continues to find support in the eastern *Länder*, much to the consternation of the centre-right. Its role as a coalition partner in a number of regional governments – in particular Berlin – has raised concerns that the process of 'reworking' the past is not always given adequate priority. Indeed, the party's opposition to numerous projects concerning the concrete legacy of the GDR – such as the rebuilding of the Prussian City Palace on the site of the former Palast der Republik, the Memorial Sites Concept concerning Germany's 'double past', and the Freedom and Unity Monument – has only confirmed this view in the eyes of its opponents, who see the party to be obstructing a reworking of the past.[45] However, the party has often gained support in the eastern *Länder* as a protest party, for after the initial euphoria of unification wore off, rising unemployment in the region, the loss of certain social benefits and services, as well as a large influx of managers, university professors and other such top-level professionals from the West caused a growing divide between east and west. A sense of colonization – or 'Kohl-onization' – of the east, particularly in the early years, led some to feel like 'second class citizens' and the common usage of derogatory terms such as *Ossis* (easterners) and *Wessis* (westerners) suggested the persistence of a much-cited 'wall in the head'.[46]

Alongside the world of politics, changing attitudes towards the GDR have been particularly evident in the cultural sphere since unification. The early 1990s, for example, were dominated by vociferous debates over the ideological complicity of GDR writers and intellectuals – triggered by the publication of Christa Wolf's *Was bleibt* (*What Remains*, 1990) and widely known as the *Literaturstreit* (quarrel over literature)[47] – as well as subsequent revelations over the alleged activity of some writers, such as Wolf, Sascha Anderson and Heiner Müller, as IMs for the Stasi. The later 1990s and early 2000s, however, saw the growth of a more light-hearted, and often ironic, engagement with the GDR past, typified above all by the phenomenon of *Ostalgie*, a conflation of the German words for 'East' and 'nostalgia'. While this could be seen in literary and filmic portrayals of the past – with box office hits such as *Sonnenallee* (*Sun Alley*, 1999) and *Good Bye, Lenin!* (2003) – it was also evident in the 'comeback' of a range of GDR consumer goods, TV shows, board games, popular publications and humorous glossaries, the iconization of symbols such as the *Trabi* and the *Ampelmännchen* (the GDR's infamous Trabant car and the East German traffic light man), as well as GDR-themed shops, pubs, nightclub evenings, and even a themed hotel in Berlin named the Ostel.[48] While many critics deplored such developments as *Schönfärberei* (whitewashing the past) and endangering a true engagement with the realities of life in the GDR, others have been keen to point out that *Ostalgie* is not necessarily a form of identification with the GDR state per se, or indeed an obsession with this past, but it may rather demonstrate a sense of oppositional solidarity in the present, itself becoming an embattled site of memory in which individual experiences and biographies seek legitimacy.[49] Recent years have seen the growth of a younger generation of east German authors such as Jakob Hein, Jana Hensel and Claudia Rusch, all of whom have drawn on their own experiences of childhood in the east. In contrast to the earlier, more commercial *Ostalgie*, much of their work rather portrays the 'normality' of adolescence in the GDR, for example by interweaving references to the Stasi with humorous recollections of the everyday. The concept of 'normality' is one that has proved fruitful in research terms, as well as in increasing numbers of museum exhibitions that explore aspects of the GDR *Alltag* (everyday experience), for it allows recognition of the fact that the experience of 'normal' life in the GDR does not necessarily match up to western expectations of such.[50] As Paul Cooke highlights, 'inner unity' does not mean homogeneity,[51] thus growing recognition of biographical differences and experiences can only aid the unification project.

Attempts to reckon with the GDR legacy have, of course, been particularly evident in the physical landscape of eastern Germany. Some of the first efforts to do so symbolically concerned the renaming of streets, a decision made by local councils in the early post-*Wende* years.[52] Local authorities were also responsible for making decisions over whether monuments, memorials and commemorative plaques from the GDR should remain or be removed, and while many such decisions were made in the early years, numerous debates continued into the 2000s, only to be resolved almost twenty years after unification (see Chapter 2). Debates over GDR architecture were represented above all by the battle over the aforementioned Palast der Republik, which was finally completely demolished in 2008, in order to make space for a reconstruction of Berlin's City Palace.[53] As an emblem of state socialism, yet also representative of mass culture – housing restaurants, a bowling alley, a theatre and a large hall, at which numerous national and international artists had performed – the Palast became highly symbolic of the debate that pitted preservation against demolition. The complexity of this site was heightened not only because its future was also bound up with the reconstruction of a Prussian palace, and thus the attempt to create continuity with an older past, but also because it was appropriated for creative art projects and displays before its demolition, making it truly a 'palace of the people'. Further high-profile debates concerning the physical legacy of the GDR have included the government's Memorial Sites Concept, originally drawn up in 1999 and revised in 2008 (see Chapter 3) and the Berlin Senate's *Gesamtkonzept zur Erinnerung an die Berliner Mauer* (Integrated Concept for Memory of the Berlin Wall) of 2006, which aimed to coordinate a decentralized memory landscape in Berlin relating to remnants of the Berlin Wall (see Chapter 5).[54]

With the passing of time, however, public debates concerning the built environment have begun to move away from questions concerning the destruction or preservation of GDR heritage towards those of construction: how should the GDR past be remembered through new commemorative structures? Here the memorial landscape differs significantly from that of the broader cultural sphere, for it predominantly highlights instances of state injustice or efforts to resist it. Thus, although the GDR *Alltag* has become a common feature of many national and regional museums – most notably Berlin's DDR Museum – it is thematized in very few monuments, the best-known example being Berthold Dietz's Trabant Monument in Zwickau, where the iconic GDR car was produced. Reception of this privately funded initiative has, however, been mixed, with critics viewing it as little more than an 'ostalgic fan project',[55] and in 2014 it was moved from its public town centre location to the grounds of the town's automobile museum, further out of town and protected from frequent graffiti attacks. Clearly, representations of the *Alltag* – especially those that may be regarded as ostalgic – prove controversial in symbolic concrete form, where contextual or interpretative media may be missing. In contrast, recent years have seen a growing number of plaques and monuments in memory of victims of the SED dictatorship, often marking the sites of former prisons or Stasi headquarters. One of the most striking examples is Sibylle Mania and Martin Neubert's Monument to the Victims of the Communist Dictatorship in Jena, located near the former building of the region's Stasi headquarters, where piles of archive boxes are cast in concrete, symbolizing not only the extensive administrative structures of the Stasi and its violation of victims' human rights through extensive surveillance, but also the challenges that face victims and their families in unified Germany. Other contemporary memorials to victims of state oppression commonly relate to the uprisings of 17 June 1953 and the GDR border regime (see Chapters 4 and 5); while such monuments have often proven controversial, it is notable that they continue a (Western and unified) tradition of memorialization that stresses German crimes of the past. It is for this reason that recent monuments in memory of the demonstrations of 1989 and German unity (see Chapter 6) have frequently provoked heightened debate, for they denote a move away from a memorial culture of regret to one that rather celebrates the achievements of recent German history. Discussions over Berlin's Freedom and Unity Monument, for example, have been ongoing for nearly twenty years, and despite the awarding of a final prize winner in April 2011, it still – at the time of writing in 2017 – remains to be built. Memorialization of the GDR has thus brought Germany to mnemonic crossroads, at which the well-trodden route of commemorating national crimes meets a new path of celebrating more positive achievements. As this book demonstrates, the decisions over future directions have not proven easy.

Whether in politics, culture or the built environment, the number of official, government-funded institutions and projects, as well as independent, commercial or community initiatives whose mission it is to represent elements of the GDR past is overwhelming today, yet their missions are not uniquely about memory. For some it is about recognition, while for others it may be about political influence, moral standing or even financial gain; as Wolfgang Thierse states, 'Scientific institutions, foundations, initiatives and memorial sites battle over the apportionment of the "*Aufarbeitung* cake"'.[56] While it is crucial not to lose sight of such motivations, it is also important to remember that these debates have changed over time. Sabrow identifies growing conflict in recent years to arise from the beginnings of a shift from embodied communicative to culturally codified memory, in which lived experience of the GDR can no longer be taken for granted; he claims that 'the GDR is increasingly disappearing from our natural world of experience. It has transformed into a place of projection, and has consequently become – in a literal sense – more questionable and more contested'.[57] Interestingly, this view contradicts Langenbacher's aforementioned argument that memory of Nazism is becoming less controversial as it passes into cultural form, a view which, since the mid 2000s, does seem to hold water. How, then, should we interpret the passing of time and its effect on memory? Does this depend on the subject matter and the media through which memory is transmitted, or does the cusp between 'communicative' and 'cultural' memory (discussed in Chapter 1) also prove influential?

A Shifting Memorial Culture

In light of the above discussions, this book examines processes of historical re-evaluation since 1990 through a range of monuments and memorials relating to the GDR. Despite East German writer Stefan Heym's famous comment in 1990 that the GDR would become little more than a 'footnote in world history', its legacy continues to occupy a prominent place in the remembrance landscape of many eastern German cities. While symbolic reminders of the past adopt numerous forms in the built environment, ranging from street names and residential buildings to flagship architecture and traffic signals, this book concentrates on deliberate memorial structures, and examines both the creation of new monuments since 1990 and the decision-making processes concerning older socialist structures. The focus on monuments to the exclusion of museums and other memorial media allows for an in-depth examination of this genre and sustained reflection on the way in which memorial forms develop over time. Moreover, as symbolic – rather than functional – structures, they tend to become crystallization points of contemporary political and social concerns, thus functioning as useful prisms through which to view the process of *Aufarbeitung*. The case studies in this book thus shed light on two key areas: the contemporary negotiation of eastern German identities and the dynamics of collective memory and memorialization.

With reference to the first of these, this book demonstrates not only the continuing importance of GDR remembrance in united Germany, but also the role of monuments in aiding local communities to work through difficult pasts. In particular, a number of case studies highlight the role of 'memory activists', individuals who steer a project from its inception through to construction and beyond, with the aim of creating a lasting tradition of memory. Interestingly, many of the memory activists in this book are of a similar generation, having demonstrated for the overthrow of the SED regime in 1989; as such, we see the importance of individual biographies and lived experience in the shaping of the memorial landscape today. Perhaps ironically, this is not dissimilar to patterns witnessed in the early GDR, when memorialization was led by figures who had been active in the antifascist resistance movement. This book thus highlights a number of continuities with GDR memorialization, as well as identifying new memorial patterns and themes. In particular, it asks whether certain historical narratives of the GDR are emerging as more dominant than others in collective remembrance, and why. While it may be too early to speak of a 'canon' of GDR remembrance, the following chapters highlight not only a clustering around a select number of key dates, but also the importance of 1989 as an underlying leitmotif in the construction – and destruction – of monuments. Fundamental to this is the importance of demonstrating democratic narratives in the present, in contrast to the SED dictatorship of the past. Such narratives play out not only in the history of 1989, but also through competition rubrics, efforts to ensure transparent processes, public discussion forums and resulting memorial forms. Moreover, projects that have grown from within a community – rather than being imposed from above – have generally also gained greater acceptance. The emphasis on democracy is thus seeing an increasingly complex and diverse memorial landscape, which challenges commonly accepted narratives. This is particularly evident concerning the interplay between Berlin and the regions, for commemorative activities have been especially prominent in Berlin, in order to help establish the city as Germany's new united capital. However, as other towns and regions seek to put their own histories on the commemorative map, the centrality of some narratives, such as the fall of the Berlin Wall, are beginning to be increasingly challenged. Through the inclusion of regional examples, this book thus also seeks to redress the balance of extant studies, which largely focus on the structures of memory in Berlin.

Second, this book seeks to demonstrate the highly dynamic nature of memory and commemorative practices, and in so doing, shows that existing models of memory (discussed in Chapter 1) relating to memorial structures are often too static in nature. In particular, it highlights the limitations of viewing the built environment as a palimpsest, in which the interaction between different 'layers' of history is largely overlooked. Similarly, the findings show that instances of cultural memory are always subject to the interventions of lived, communicative memory, thus suggesting a much more complex understanding of memory dynamics than is commonly accepted. Indeed, this book contends that we must understand memorial sites within their broader perspective – both diachronically and synchronically – if we are to uncover the complex layers and interconnections at play. On a diachronic level, it pursues the interplay between previous memorial traditions and contemporary structures dedicated to the GDR. Two particular traditions are notable here: the development of a countermemorial aesthetic originating from Holocaust memorial designs from the 1980s onwards, and the tradition of GDR socialist realist monuments (both of which are examined in more detail in Chapter 1). While much literature exists on the history of both – in particular Holocaust memorials and countermonuments – the way in which they have influenced subsequent memorial traditions is only now coming to light, and has hitherto received very little critical attention. On a synchronic level, the influence of the contemporary political sphere on the development of memorial projects, as well as the complex interplay between different and sometimes competing projects, demonstrates the highly dynamic and entangled nature of memorial politics and collective remembrance. This book thus seeks to highlight the polyphony of voices that influence, and are influenced by, evolving sites of memory. As the selection of case studies testifies, monuments evolve over time; they 'become' rather than 'exist'. The extent to which attitudes towards the now largely absent Berlin Wall have changed, for example, demonstrates just how radically residents' relationships to the urban landscape and its history may evolve in a relatively short space of time. The stone or bronze in which they are frequently cast can thus be illusory; the perception of permanence and constancy often belies the dynamism of the memory debates that may begin years before their construction and continue long after their erection.

The broader parameters of the discussion around memory and memorial practices are introduced in Chapter 1, in which the 'memory boom' of recent years is examined alongside a critical overview of the key terms and concepts employed in the study of collective memories and memorial cultures. The following chapters are structured around selected case studies, which relate to five thematic areas: former socialist icons, Soviet special camps, the uprisings of 17 June 1953, the Berlin Wall and the 'peaceful revolution'. While monuments clearly exist that relate to other aspects of GDR history, in particular to local events or sites (as seen above, in the cases of Zwickau and Jena), these five areas have been chosen for the fact that they have provoked considerable debate since the demise of the GDR, and have been the focus of varied styles of monument projects. Moreover, they all relate to themes and events of significance across eastern Germany, enabling a comparison of projects across different regions. The case studies have been chosen for their contrasting natures and spread of geographical locations, and in each chapter care has been taken to examine both high-profile and less well-known examples. As a study that seeks to probe every stage of the memorial process, from the initial planning stages through to the period after construction, the availability of data and sources was also a motivating factor in the choice of case studies. The primary sources used in this study are thus varied, and include a range of archival materials (from local government papers to those of regional organizations, grassroots initiatives and private organizations), information gathered through conversations with artists, local politicians, regional organizations and the initiators of memorial projects, as well as published information, such as newspaper reports, readers' letters and online forums, memorial websites and the newsletters of organizations. As a qualitative study, this book does not aim to be a representative survey that maps broad commemorative trends across eastern Germany, but rather one that uses a selection of in-depth case studies, many of which have hitherto attracted little attention outside of their locality, to examine deeper-rooted shifts in memorial culture and memory of the GDR.

Notes

1. In a speech at the Brandenburg Gate in 1987, President Reagan had challenged Soviet leader Mikhail Gorbachev to 'tear down this wall!'. Stefan Jacobs et al., 'Mr. Wowereit – Don't Tear Down This Wall', *Der Tagesspiegel*, 1 March 2013, http://www.tagesspiegel.de/berlin/bauarbeiten-an-east-side-gallery-eingestellt-mr-wowereit-dont-tear-down-this-wall/7856508.html (accessed 20 August 2013).
2. Pierre Nora (ed.), *Les Lieux de Mémoire*, 7 vols (Paris: Gallimard, 1984–92).
3. Jens Brockmeier, 'Remembering and Forgetting: Narrative as Cultural Memory', *Culture & Psychology*, 8 (2002) 1, 15–43 (19).
4. In order to avoid confusion, 'East'/'Eastern' and 'West'/'Western' will be capitalized throughout to refer to the period of division, but not for the post-unification period.
5. Katrin Göring-Eckardt, 'Für ein kritisches Geschichtsbewusstsein', in *Jahrbuch für Kulturpolitik 2009. Thema: Erinnerungskulturen und Geschichtspolitik*, ed. by Bernd Wagner (Essen: Klartext Verlag, 2009), pp. 95–99 (95).
6. Konrad H. Jarausch, 'Der Umbruch 1989/90', in *Erinnerungsorte der DDR*, ed. by Martin Sabrow (Munich: Beck, 2009), pp. 526–35 (526).
7. Jeffrey Herf, *Divided Memory: The Nazi Past in the Two Germanys* (Cambridge, MA; London: Harvard University Press, 1997).
8. Rudy Koshar, *From Monuments to Traces: Artifacts of German Memory, 1870–1990* (Berkeley, CA: University of California Press, 2000), p. 3.
9. See Matthias Wemhoff, *Der Berliner Skulpturenfund: 'Entartete Kunst' im Bombenschutt*, Staatliche Museen zu Berlin – Stiftung Preussischer Kulturbesitz (Regensburg: Schnell & Steiner, 2011).
10. See Michael Diers and Kasper König, *Der Bevölkerung: Aufsätze und Dokumente zur Debatte um das Reichtagsprojekt von Hans Haacke* (Cologne: Verlag der Buchhandlung Walter König, 2000); Eric Jarosinski, '"Threshold Resistance": Dani Karavan's Berlin Installation *Grundgesetz*', in *Walls, Borders, Boundaries: Spatial and Cultural Practices in Europe*, ed. by Marc Silberman, Karen E. Till and Janet Ward (New York; Oxford: Berghahn Books, 2012), pp. 61–76.
11. The concept of 'normalization' must be treated with caution, for the implication that 'normal' behaviour or standards exist is highly problematic. Reference to this term within the German context usually relates to Germany displaying exemplary western, democratic and liberal credentials while also showing remorse for past crimes. On 'normalization', see Stuart Taberner and Paul Cooke (eds), *German Culture, Politics, and*

Literature into the Twenty-First Century: Beyond Normalization (Rochester, NY: Camden House, 2006) and Gavriel Rosenfeld, Hi Hitler! How the Nazi Past Is Being Normalized in Contemporary Culture (Cambridge: Cambridge University Press, 2014).

12. Gavriel Rosenfeld, 'A Looming Crash or a Soft Landing? Forecasting the Future of the Memory "Industry"', *Journal of Modern History*, 81 (2009), 122–58 (141).
13. Eric Langenbacher, 'The Mastered Past? Collective Memory Trends in Germany since Unification', in *From the Bonn to the Berlin Republic: Germany at the Twentieth Anniversary of Unification*, ed. by Jeffrey J. Anderson and Eric Langenbacher (New York; Oxford: Berghahn Books, 2010), pp. 63–89 (83-84).
14. Theodor W. Adorno, 'Was bedeutet: Aufarbeitung der Vergangenheit?', in *Gesammelte Schriften*, vol. 10/2, Kulturkritik und Gesellschaft II, ed. by Rolf Tiedemann (Frankfurt am Main: Suhrkamp, 1977), pp. 555–72.
15. See Bill Niven, *Facing the Nazi Past: United Germany and the Legacy of the Third Reich* (London; New York: Routledge, 2002); Gavriel D. Rosenfeld, 'The Controversy That Isn't: The Debate over Daniel J. Goldhagen's *Hitler's Willing Executioners* in Comparative Perspective', *Contemporary European History*, 8 (1999) 2, 249–73; Daniel Becker, 'Coming to Terms with *Vergangenheitsbewältigung*: Walser's *Sonntagsrede*, the Kosovo War, and the Transformation of German Historical Consciousness', in *Victims and Perpetrators: 1933–1945: (Re)Presenting the Past in Post-Unification Culture*, ed. by Laurel Cohen-Pfister and Dagmar Wienroeder-Skinner (Berlin: de Gruyter, 2006), pp. 337–61.
16. James Young, 'Berlin's Holocaust Memorial: A Report to the Bundestag Committee on Media and Culture, 3 March 1999', *German Politics and Society*, 17 (1999) 3, 54–70 (56).
17. See Karen E. Till, 'Staging the Past: Landscape Designs, Cultural Identity and *Erinnerungspolitik* at Berlin's *Neue Wache*', *Ecumene*, 6 (1999) 3, 251–83.
18. Claus Leggewie and Erik Meyer, 'Shared Memory: Buchenwald and Beyond', *Tr@nsit online*, 22 (2002).
19. See Charles S. Maier, 'Hot Memory… Cold Memory: On the Political Half-Life of Fascist and Communist Memory', *Tr@nsit online*, 22 (2002); Niven, *Facing the Nazi Past*, p. 7; Leggewie and Meyer, 'Shared Memory'.
20. Deutscher Bundestag, 'Schlußbericht der Enquete-Kommission "Überwindungen der Folgen der SED-Diktatur im Prozess der deutschen Einheit"' (Bonn, 1998), Drucksache 13/11000, p. 240.
21. As Niven points out, Schröder is usually quoted out of context, for he actually said he wished for a place where Germans 'like to go to remember and take issue'. This remark does, however, still reflect the notion that such remembrance should be a pleasurable experience. See Bill Niven (ed.), *Germans as Victims: Remembering the Past in Contemporary Germany* (Basingstoke: Palgrave, 2006), pp. 9–10.
22. Eric Langenbacher, Bill Niven and Ruth Wittlinger, 'Introduction: Dynamics of Memory in Twenty-First Century Germany', *German Politics and Society*, 26 (2008) 4, 1–8. See also Robert G. Moeller, 'Germans as Victims? Thoughts

on a Post-Cold-War History of World War II's Legacies', *History & Memory*, 17 (2005) 1/2, 147–94.
23. Niven, *Germans as Victims*, p. 4.
24. Becker, 'Coming to Terms with *Vergangenheitsbewältigung*', p. 338.
25. Niven, *Germans as Victims*, pp. 7–8.
26. See Malte Thießen, *Eingebrannt ins Gedächtnis: Hamburgs Gedenken an Luftkrieg und Kriegsende 1943 bis 2005* (Munich: Dölling und Galitz Verlag, 2007); Robert G. Moeller, *War Stories: The Search for a Usable Past in the Federal Republic of Germany* (Berkeley, CA: University of California Press, 2001); Gavriel D. Rosenfeld, *Munich and Memory: Architecture, Monuments, and the Legacy of the Third Reich* (Berkeley, CA: University of California Press, 2000).
27. Jörg Friedrich, *Der Brand: Deutschland im Bombenkrieg 1940–1945* (Munich: Propyläen Verlag, 2002). See Robert G. Moeller, 'On the History of Man-Made Destruction: Loss, Death, Memory, and Germany in the Bombing War', *History Workshop Journal*, 61 (2006), 103–34.
28. On the plethora of local publications, see the review by Jörg Arnold, 'Bombenkrieg', for *H-Soz-u-Kult*, 28 June 2004, http://hsozkult.geschichte. hu-berlin.de/rezensionen/2004-2-062 (accessed 26 May 2011); see also Thilo Alexe, 'Neuer Plan für Denkmal zum 13. Februar' and Denni Klein, '"Trauerndes Mädchen am Tränenmeer" soll erinnern und Hoffnung geben', both in *Sächsische Zeitung*, 20 September 2010.
29. Günter Grass, *Im Krebsgang: Eine Novelle* (Göttingen: Steidl, 2002).
30. Federal funding made available in 2008 resulted in the foundation of the Stiftung Flucht, Vertreibung, Versöhnung, administered by the German Historical Museum. Among other things, its task is to establish a permanent exhibition on flight and expulsion, to be housed in the 'Deutschlandhaus'. See the Stiftung's website at: http://www.sfvv.de (accessed 18 July 2016).
31. *Eine Frau in Berlin: Tagebuchaufzeichnungen vom 20. April bis 22. Juni 1945* (Frankfurt am Main: Eichborn Verlag, 2003); Max Färberböck (dir.), *Anonyma – Eine Frau in Berlin* (2008).
32. See Michael Z. Wise, *Capital Dilemma: Germany's Search for a New Architecture of Democracy* (New York: Princeton Architectural Press, 1998), pp. 53–54.
33. Andrew Webber, *Berlin in the Twentieth Century: A Cultural Topography* (Cambridge: Cambridge University Press, 2008), p. 12.
34. Eberhard Diepgen, cited in 'Bananen billiger', *Der Spiegel* (1994) 26, 90–91 (91).
35. Andreas Huyssen, *Present Pasts: Urban Palimpsests and the Politics of Memory* (Stanford, CA: Stanford University Press, 2003), p. 32.
36. On Berlin, see, for example, Karen E. Till, *The New Berlin: Memory, Politics, Place* (Minneapolis: University of Minnesota, 2005); Brian Ladd, *The Ghosts of Berlin* (Chicago, IL: University of Chicago Press, 1997); Wise, *Capital Dilemma*; Elizabeth A. Strom, *Building the New Berlin: The Politics of Urban Development in Germany's Capital City* (Lanham, MD: Lexington Books, 2001); Jennifer Jordan, *Structures of Memory: Understanding Urban Change in Berlin and Beyond* (Stanford, CA: Stanford University Press, 2006); Webber, *Berlin in the Twentieth Century*; Simon Ward, *Urban Memory and Visual*

Culture in Berlin: Framing the Asynchronous City, 1957–2012 (Amsterdam: Amsterdam University Press, 2016). There have been efforts to look beyond Berlin, but such studies tend to focus on the years of division or on efforts to overcome the Nazi past. See, for example, Gavriel D. Rosenfeld and Paul B. Jaskot (eds), *Beyond Berlin: Twelve German Cities Confront the German Past* (Ann Arbor, MI: University of Michigan Press, 2008). The very few studies that examine GDR-related examples are largely efforts to catalogue individual case studies, e.g. Anna Kaminsky (ed.), *Orte des Erinnerns: Gedenkzeichen, Gedenkstätten und Museen zur Diktatur in SBZ und DDR* (Bonn: Bundeszentrale für politische Bildung, 2007) and Leonie Beiersdorf, *Die doppelte Krise: Ostdeutsche Erinnerungszeichen nach 1989* (Berlin: Deutscher Kunstverlag, 2015).

37. Interview with Wolfgang Thierse: '"Hinter den Attacken steckt etwas anderes"', *Der Tagesspiegel*, 19 August 2007, p. 7.
38. For an overview of historical debates, see Mary Fulbrook, 'Historiografische Kontroversen seit 1990', in *Views from Abroad: Die DDR aus britischer Perspektive*, ed. by Peter Barker, Marc-Dietrich Ohse and Dennis Tate (Bielefeld: Bertelsmann, 2007), pp. 41–51.
39. Martin Sabrow (ed.), *Erinnerungsorte der DDR* (Munich: Beck, 2009), p. 16.
40. Konrad Jarausch, 'Realer Sozialismus als Fürsorgediktatur: Zur begrifflichen Einordnung der DDR', *Aus Politik und Zeitgeschichte*, B20 (1998), 33–46; Mary Fulbrook, *The People's State: East German Society from Hitler to Honecker* (New Haven, CT: Yale University Press, 2005).
41. Molly Andrews, 'Grand National Narratives and the Project of Truth Commissions: A Comparative Analysis', *Media, Culture & Society*, 25 (2003), 45–65 (51).
42. See Paul Cooke, *Representing East Germany since Unification: From Colonization to Nostalgia* (New York: Berg, 2005), pp. 34–41. On the Bundestag inquiries, see also Andrew H. Beattie, *Playing Politics with History: The Bundestag Inquiries into East Germany* (New York; Oxford: Berghahn Books, 2008); A. James McAdams, *Judging the Past in Unified Germany* (Cambridge: Cambridge University Press, 2001); Jennifer Yoder, 'Truth without Reconciliation: An Appraisal of the Enquete Commission on the SED Dictatorship in Germany', *German Politics*, 8 (1999) 3, 59–80.
43. 'Empfehlungen der Expertenkommission zur Schaffung eines Geschichtsverbundes "Aufarbeitung der SED-Diktatur"', 15 May 2006, p. 21, https://www.bundesstiftung-aufarbeitung.de/uploads/pdf/sabrow-bericht.pdf (accessed 15 December 2017).
44. On the debate, see Martin Sabrow et al. (eds), *Wohin treibt die DDR-Erinnerung? Dokumentation einer Debatte* (Göttingen: Vandenhoeck & Ruprecht, 2007).
45. On the view of Die Linke, see Lukrezia Jochimsen, 'Die linke Gegenstimme zu: Erinnerungskultur und Geschichtspolitik', in *Jahrbuch für Kulturpolitik 2009*, ed. by Wagner, pp. 89–94.
46. On the concept of colonization, see Cooke, *Representing East Germany since Unification*.

47. Christa Wolf, *Was bleibt: Erzählung* (Munich: Luchterhand, 1990). On the debate, see Thomas Anz (ed.), *Es geht nicht um Christa Wolf: Der Literaturstreit im vereinten Deutschland* (Munich: Edition Spangenberg, 1991).
48. On *Ostalgie*, see Cooke, *Representing East Germany since Unification*; Thomas Ahbe, *Ostalgie: Zum Umgang mit der DDR-Vergangenheit in der 1990er Jahren* (Erfurt: Landeszentrale für politische Bildung Thüringen, 2005); Paul Betts, 'The Twilight of the Idols: East German Memory and Material Culture', *The Journal of Modern History*, 72 (2000) September, 731–65; Martin Blum, 'Remaking the East German Past: Ostalgie, Identity, and Material Culture', *Journal of Popular Culture*, 34 (2000) 3, 229–53; Daphne Berdahl, '"(N)Ostalgie" for the Present: Memory, Longing, and East German Things', *Ethnos*, 64 (1999) 2, 192–211; Patricia Hogwood, 'After the GDR: Reconstructing Identity in Post-Communist Germany', *Journal of Communist Studies and Transition Politics*, 16 (2000) 4, 45–67.
49. See Berdahl, '"(N)Ostalgie" for the Present'; Martin Blum, 'Club Cola and Co.: Ostalgie, Material Culture and Identity', in *Transformations of the New Germany*, ed. by Ruth A. Starkman (New York; Basingstoke: Palgrave Macmillan, 2006), pp. 131–54.
50. Research led by Mary Fulbrook at UCL has led the way in exploring the concept of 'normalization', particularly in the large Arts and Humanities Research Council (AHRC) project *'The "Normalisation of Rule"? State and Society in the GDR 1961–1979'* from 2002 to 2007.
51. Cooke, *Representing East Germany since Unification*, p. 202.
52. *Wende* is the term commonly used to refer to the period of political change in 1989/90.
53. On this debate, see Christos Varvantakis, 'A Monument to Dismantlement', *Memory Studies*, 2 (2009) 1, 27–38; Uta Staiger, 'Cities, Citizenship, Contested Cultures: Berlin's Palace of the Republic and the Politics of the Public Sphere', *Cultural Geographies*, 16 (2009), 309–27; Alexander Schug (ed.), *Palast der Republik: Politischer Diskurs und private Erinnerung* (Berlin: BWV, 2007).
54. See 'Gesamtkonzept zur Erinnerung an die Berliner Mauer: Dokumentation, Information und Gedenken' (Berlin: Senatsverwaltung für Wissenschaft, Forschung und Kultur, 12 June 2006), http://www.berliner-mauer-gedenkstaette.de/de/uploads/allgemeine_dokumente/gesamtkonzept_berliner_mauer.pdf (accessed 15 December 2017).
55. Beiersdorf, *Die doppelte Krise*, p. 186.
56. Interview with Wolfgang Thierse: '"Hinter den Attacken steckt etwas anderes"', *Der Tagesspiegel*, 19 August 2007, p. 7.
57. Sabrow, *Erinnerungsorte der DDR*, p. 20.

Chapter 1

MEMORY, MONUMENTS AND MEMORIALIZATION

Memory, it seems, is everywhere. It gives meaning to the present, shapes our everyday movements and conversations, provides a framework for our communities and ultimately defines where we come from and who we are. In short, memory is at the heart of identity, whether personal or collective. Unavoidably omnipresent in our contemporary lives, it appears to have found new currency in recent years, in the rise of historical documentaries and films, the heritage industry, museum exhibitions, popular biographies and autobiographies, the growth of amateur photography and the huge archiving potential of the internet, to name but a few examples. Scholarly references to the emergence of a 'memory boom', the rise of a 'memory industry' and even the outbreak of a 'memory epidemic' are commonplace today,[1] denoting a trend in which, in Jeffrey Olick's words, 'novelty is associated with new versions of the past rather than the future'.[2] Such is the contemporary interest in memory that no student can keep abreast of all the literature written on the subject. Indeed, critics have warned that the field of memory studies could face a 'crisis of overproduction',[3] and that the term 'memory' is 'depreciated by surplus use'.[4] Yet as recently as the 1970s and early 1980s, the usage of this term in academic discourse was notably absent, apparently on the verge of extinction.[5] What, then, has caused this rapid growth of interest in memory? If memory is core to identity, does this new obsession suggest a modern crisis of identity?

As Astrid Erll highlights, the main causes of the contemporary memory boom are threefold.[6] First, historical transformation processes have caused notable changes in the way we think about the past. Above all, the generation that experienced the Holocaust and World War II first hand is now disappearing, causing subsequent generations to seek cultural forms of memory in order to remember this past. Additionally, the end of the Cold War has not only freed many sites of memory for alternative interpretations, but has also caused Western society to reassess its vision of past and future. As Gavriel Rosenfeld argues, the collapse of Eastern European regimes in 1989 saw not only the death of socialism, but also that of future-orientated projects for political change: 'This death of the future ... helped redirect the attention of Western society toward the past'.[7] Recent times have also witnessed widespread decolonization and migration, resulting in a greater plurality of ethnicities, cultures and religions, and in turn a heightened awareness of different traditions and histories. Second, rapid technological developments have enabled greater storage space for our memories and more varied media for their transmission. Not only has the internet become a 'mega archive',[8] but it has allowed a certain democratization of memory, enabling widespread access to historical data, documents and artefacts, as well as the creation of personal collections, and the reassertion of forgotten pasts. The use of film and television, as well as video games and mobile phone apps, have all contributed to a greater presence of memory.[9] Yet technological progress has, in many ways, produced a commonly cited 'acceleration of history', in which 'the most continuous or permanent feature of the modern world is no longer continuity or permanence but change'.[10] In this respect, the past offers (at least on the surface) a safe haven of stability, and as Bill Niven suggests, 'The more we rush headlong into the future, the greater the need to find an anchor in the past'.[11] A third reason for the memory boom relates to the emergence of postmodernism, which – through the deconstruction of historical narratives – ushered in a more sceptical understanding of history, and challenged the very existence of historical truth. As such, the boundaries between history and memory have been dissipated, and many historians have turned rather to the study of the representation of history, and consequently memory. Most famously, perhaps, this movement led Jean-François Lyotard to pronounce the collapse of the 'grand narrative', and Francis Fukuyama famously to predict the 'end of history'.[12] While the end of history may not have come about, scepticism towards historical objectivity has clearly brought about a growth in memory, to the extent that 'memory', as Confino observes, is often understood to be little different to 'ideology'.[13]

If the boundaries have become increasingly blurred between memory and history, or even memory and ideology, what do we actually understand by the term 'memory'? The burgeoning field of memory studies has not been short of attempts to define and theorize the concept, resulting in numerous terms to denote specific types of memory, such as *communicative, cultural, social, political, prosthetic, official, vernacular, multidirectional, hot* and *cold*, to name but a few. What these terms all share is that they denote collective forms of memory – the subject of this book – as opposed to individual or biographical memory.[14] Yet the very presence of multiple definitions highlights the complexity of any concept of 'collective memory', and indicates that it may be, in Jeffrey Olick's words, an 'over-totalizing' concept, 'obliterating finer distinctions'.[15] This chapter aims to unpack some of the central theoretical understandings of what, for now, we shall call 'collective memory', in order to identify a set of productive theoretical and methodological tools for the following case studies. In a second section, the chapter turns to contemporary debates on monuments and the processes of memorialization, and identifies recent trends – particularly that of the 'countermonument' – which prove central to the examination of developments in eastern Germany.

Notions of, and Problems with, Collective Forms of Memory

In literal terms, collective memory cannot exist: an institution, an organization or a nation does not *have* a memory in the same way that an individual does. Instead, collective bodies *create* memories through signs, symbols, images, monuments, texts and other media, and in doing so, build identities for themselves. In methodological terms, we must therefore be careful not to reify collective memory; it is not a 'thing', but rather a process or a set of mnemonic practices. James Fentress and Chris Wickham, for example, highlight the danger of materializing memory by provocatively asking, 'Do we hunt it with a questionnaire, or are we supposed to use a butterfly net?', and Jay Winter proposes to substitute the term with the notion of 'collective remembrance', in an attempt to specify agency.[16] Any investigation of collective memory must, thus, recognize it as a dynamic process, and understand it to be the outcome of different elements – individuals, organizations, spaces and symbolic media – coming into contact with each other at a specific time. In this sense, this book takes monuments and memorials as a starting point, not an end point, for the examination of memory dynamics in east Germany; the chosen monuments do not embody collective memory, but rather serve as a locus of interaction, discussion and meaning-making.

While the usefulness of the term 'collective memory' is likely to be debated for years to come, it provides a helpful starting point for the discussion of memory here. In particular, its emphasis on 'collectiveness' draws our attention to two central issues. First, collective memory does not, and cannot, function as individual embodied memory, yet this does not mean that individuals are powerless in the process of constructing collective memory.[17] Through case studies of monument projects, this book seeks to examine the role of the individual as well as the collective in shaping shared memories of the past. In doing so, it hopes to highlight the important dynamics between individual action and collective acts of remembrance, in much the same way that Pierre Nora sees his *lieux de mémoire* to be 'enveloped in a Möbius strip of the collective and the individual'.[18] Second, the notion of 'collective' also implies an element of unity, or consensus, within a given group's memory. Yet memory is never monolithic, and in increasingly democratic times, it is clear that multiple, and indeed competing, memories may jostle for position alongside each other. For this reason, Olick distinguishes between *collected* memories, as the aggregated individual memories of members of a group, and *collective* memory, which refers to the collective commemorative representations and traces themselves, concluding that we must remember that '"memory" occurs in public and in private, at the tops of societies and at the bottoms ... and that each of these forms is important'.[19] The notion of collective memory must thus be understood metaphorically rather than in any literal sense, and as Niven suggests, the very vagueness of the concept presents part of its appeal.[20] Its use as an umbrella term may ensure a continued awareness of the interrelationship between different forms of memory – a question which is central to this book – yet these different forms prove, themselves, fraught with conceptual difficulty.

Attempts to refine and differentiate between different forms of collective memory find their roots in the work of sociologist Maurice Halbwachs and art historian Aby Warburg, whose seminal works shifted the discourse concerning collective knowledge out of a biological frame of reference into a cultural context. Indeed, despite their different approaches, their common conclusion that culture and its transmission were the products of human activity marked a significant new departure at the start of the twentieth century.[21] It is above all to Halbwachs that most contemporary studies turn, not only because he introduced the term 'collective memory', but because he highlighted the importance of the social frameworks of memory.[22] In contrast to Sigmund Freud, who believed that memories were stored in the unconscious of the individual, Halbwachs stressed that remembering is always an act of reconstruction, in which individual memories are constituted in communication with others. Memories are thus socially mediated, and shaped by the social context in which they are recalled; what we remember depends on the groups to which we belong. In this sense, Halbwachs' concern was not the memory *of* groups, but rather the construction of memory *within* groups, thus highlighting the dynamic nature of memory construction.[23]

Halbwachs' work remained largely unknown until the 1980s, however, when his work provided inspiration for Pierre Nora's project *Les Lieux de Mémoire*, which in turn initiated a new wave of interest in collective memory.[24] Nora's concern was French national memory, which he saw to be crystallized in 'sites of memory', both mental and physical locations, ranging from places and objects to people and commemorative events. In his oft-cited words, 'There are *lieux de mémoire*, sites of memory, because there are no longer *milieux de mémoire*, real environments of memory', meaning that in the absence of 'true memory' (one which he sees to be spontaneous and embodied), we must create deliberate attempts to remember through symbols such as archives, anniversaries and monuments.[25] Thus, 'the less memory is experienced from the inside, the more it exists only through its exterior scaffolding and outward signs'.[26] While his concept has been highly influential in the field of memory studies, it is clearly not unproblematic. On the one hand, his notion of *milieux de mémoire* is somewhat romanticized, identified by Barry Schwartz as a 'mnemonic garden of Eden'.[27] Moreover, his choice of *lieux* themselves points towards nostalgic tendencies, for the more difficult elements of the French national past, such as its colonial history, have been excluded. On the other hand, the large array of types of *lieux de mémoire*, including 'Vichy', 'The Forest', 'Catholics and Seculars', 'Right and Left', 'Generation', 'Divisions of Time and Space' and 'Gastronomy', lead one to question what is *not* a *lieu de mémoire*.[28] In light of this second criticism, Nora's concept of 'sites of memory' as symbolic representations of the past will provide a useful starting point for this book, yet the focus of the present project will return to the principal physical meaning of the term 'site', underlining the primary importance of the relationship between the built environment and memory.

Other scholars to draw heavily on Halbwachs are Jan and Aleida Assmann, whose theoretical models distinguish between two key areas of collective memory: 'communicative' and 'cultural' memory. The former relates to the recent past, and relies on everyday communication for transmission, reaching back at most three generations, or a period of eighty to one hundred years. In Jan Assmann's view, communicative memory is neither supported by institutions, nor formalized or stabilized through material symbols.[29] In contrast, the concept of cultural memory is characterized by its distance to the everyday, and is 'exteriorized, objectified, and stored away in symbolic forms that, unlike the sounds of words or the sight of gestures, are stable and situation-transcendent: They may be transferred from one situation to another and transmitted from one generation to another'.[30] Following this paradigm, communicative memory is the subject of oral history, whereas cultural memory is represented by more fixed, institutionalized forms of expression. While Jan Assmann's model is most commonly cited, especially within German literature, the distinction between two such types of memory has been identified by others, giving rise to parings such as *vernacular* and *official* memory, *lived* and *distant* memory, *interactional* and *institutional* memory, or *biographical* experience and *cultural* transmission.[31] Aleida Assmann has further developed the bimodal structure, suggesting four 'formats' of memory, and identifying individual and social memory as forms of communicative memory, and cultural and political memory as forms of Jan Assmann's cultural memory. The latter two concepts are both understood to be mediated, transgenerational, top-down constructs, with her concept of cultural memory being anchored in works of art (or 'culture'), which may allow for diverse interpretations and privilege individual forms of assimilation (such as reading, writing, scrutinizing), whereas political memory is found in material forms and performative rites, which address individuals as members of a group, thus invoking a clear message and aiming for a high degree of homogeneity.[32] According to this model, monuments fall into the category of 'political memory', yet as this book demonstrates, such categorizations can be little more than heuristic devices; social or cultural memories may also be highly political, and vice versa. Similarly, in democratic systems, political memory may be far from homogeneous.

The wealth of terms and their various distinctions is overwhelming, yet all recognize the basic existence of two types of memory: one that is based in oral communication and relates to lived, experienced memory, and one that is embedded in a system of symbols, signs and cultural artefacts. For the purposes of this book, Jan Assmann's terms 'communicative' and 'cultural' memory will be used as a point of departure, not only because their broad nature is helpful, but also because much research remains to be done on the question of their interrelationship. Indeed, as critics have often noted, the transition from communicative to cultural memory is not as rigid as suggested by Assmann, who identifies a 'floating gap' between the two forms (i.e. between the event of communicative memory dying out, and cultural memory taking root), which shifts with generational change.[33] While this model was developed for pre-modern societies, it is clearly less appropriate for contemporary times, in which the recent and biographically experienced past often becomes the focus of monuments and commemorative rituals. It was, for example, only a matter of days after 9/11 that memorial structures were being discussed.[34] However, it is the very transformation from communicative to cultural memory that provokes contentious decision-making and often the privileging of one understanding of the past over another. Yet how do these two forms of memory interrelate, and to what extent do they influence each other? This is one of the key questions in this book. Moreover, is the transformation from one to the other always unidirectional? Marianne Hirsch suggests not, arguing that postmemorial work strives to '*reactivate* and *reembody* more distant social/national and archival/cultural memorial structures by reinvesting them with resonant individual and familial forms of mediation and aesthetic expression'.[35] Similarly, Alison Landsberg's notion of 'prosthetic memory' examines the interface between these two areas of activity, and traces the development of 'privately felt public memories', which emerge when mass cultural representations of the past 'come into contact with a person's own archive of experience'.[36] While this book does not examine embodied forms of knowledge in the same way as Hirsch and Landsberg, it draws productively on the interaction and dynamism between the notions of communicative and cultural memories as a key element in contemporary memorial trends.

While the above rehearsal of memory theory reminds us of the fundamental concepts and questions, the discussion of monuments in this study draws on a number of associated debates relating to memory. First and foremost, the dynamic force of memory has often led to an overstated opposition of history and memory. Halbwachs and Nora, for instance, view the two to be fundamentally opposed, highlighting the spontaneity, fluidity and organic nature of collective memory in contrast to the more distant, objectified nature of history. To cite Nora, 'Memory is a perpetually actual phenomenon, a bond tying us to the eternal present; history is a representation of the past', and – more emphatically – 'History is perpetually suspicious of memory, and its true mission is to suppress and destroy it'.[37] Such distinctions are widely viewed today, however, as suspicious, for the writing of history is, in many ways, a form of collective memory itself. As Hayden White has demonstrated, historical narratives are inevitably shaped by their authors, who impose a structure and select sources, often using similar techniques to authors of fiction.[38] Marita Sturken usefully suggests that memory and history are thus *entangled*, rather than oppositional, an approach that is supported by the case studies in this book.[39] While many scholars see the opposition of history and memory to be unhelpful today, it has shaped two different approaches to the study of memory: 'presentist' and 'traditionalist' (or 'essentialist') models. The former approach, often attributed to Halbwachs, supposes that memories are produced in the present for the purposes of the present, and thus cannot be read as a reflection of historical reality. This model has become the most robust over recent years, with studies such as Hobsbawm and Ranger's *The Invention of Tradition* adopting this approach.[40] On the other hand, however, the 'traditionalist' model views memory to be an enduring representation of history, or an 'authentic residue of the past'.[41] While this may appear somewhat naive today, we must ask ourselves whether the past is entirely at the mercy of the present; indeed, is there not some objective element of history that transcends the present? As Barry Schwartz points out, 'the past cannot be literally constructed; it can only be selectively exploited. Moreover, the basis of the exploitation cannot be arbitrary. The events selected for commemoration must have some factual significance to begin with in order to qualify for this purpose'.[42] In this way, we must recognize that while memory is constructed in the present, and for present purposes, it must retain a foothold in the past for it not to become entirely fictional. Implicit to this study is thus the exploration of the conflict between, and interdependence and ambiguity of the concepts of history and memory. Which historical narratives, for instance, are chosen for the subject of monument construction? Conversely, how does the memorial landscape in eastern Germany shape public awareness of GDR history?

Second, the relationship between memories and the media through which they are transmitted constitutes a key area of investigation in memory studies. As Jacques Le Goff highlights, the difference between societies whose memories are essentially oral on the one hand and written on the other is significant.[43] With the development of writing, the storage capacity for memory expands, and allows it to exist in a disembodied form, making it available for future generations. The most important changes in memory patterns have been caused by technological advances, above all from oral to written form, written to printed form, and printed to digital form.[44] Jan Assmann's concept of cultural memory is, indeed, based on the principle that cultural media form our basic mnemonic support system, and act as 'vehicles of memory';[45] there is simply too much information to be held in memory alone. Yet, as Olick highlights, the relationship between memory and medium is highly interactive. Not only do the media of memory influence the particular representation of the past that is created, but as memories change, so too do the media of their transmission: 'The media of memory decisively shape not only specific memories but also memory's mediating functions'.[46] Concerns to preserve memory of the Holocaust, for instance, saw an expansion of certain mnemonic media, such as oral history, video testimony and documentary film. Similarly, as discussed below, efforts to remember the Holocaust in memorial form changed the very concept of the memorial. Central to this book, then, is the question of whether memory of the GDR has also influenced memorial aesthetics, and vice versa.

Third, as memory lies at the very heart of identity, it is closely related to narratives of power. The mobilization of memory within the national arena provides the most obvious example of this; as Yael Zerubavel highlights, 'Nationalist movements typically attempt to create a master commemorative narrative that highlights their members' common past and legitimizes their aspiration for a shared destiny'.[47] In this way, national institutions strive for 'mnemonic socialization', teaching us what to remember and what not, and commemorative events ensure 'mnemonic synchronization', encouraging us to remember events together.[48] Thus, as Schwarz claims, 'remembering comes into view as a control system',[49] particularly at times of instability or national upheaval. In eastern Germany, for instance, the renaming of many streets after unification was not only intended as a measure to erase the communist past, but also to assert a new, unified future. As Huyssen suggests, this was 'a strategy of power and humiliation, a final burst of Cold War ideology, pursued via a politics of signs'.[50] However, mnemonic communities clearly need not be national ones; alternative memories of minority groups may assert themselves against hegemonic narratives in the form of counter-memories.[51] Of course, this is not restricted to authoritarian regimes, for – as Halbwachs recognized – we all belong to numerous social groups that compete for our allegiances, and as Hutton summarizes, 'the problem of memory is also one of social power'.[52] Memory can thus be invoked as a compelling orientating force within society, which carries with it moral and social responsibilities, and sometimes legal implications with very tangible outcomes, such as the restoration of property or financial compensation. The concept of victimhood is particularly central to such claims, and thus the reorientation of societies during periods of transition; in this context, David Lowe and Tony Joel claim that 'the Cold War … has given rise to a burgeoning victim/survivor cult of politicized memory'.[53] Monuments and memorials play a significant role here, for alongside other strategies for dealing with the past, such as truth commissions, lustration laws or criminal trials, they are also regarded as part of a 'transitional justice tool kit'.[54] While they may not bring material advantages to individuals, they can – as in many examples in this book – prove to be a very real political force in the realignment of historical narratives.

Fourth, the relationship between remembering and forgetting remains central to all studies of memory, and the two go hand in hand; as Mary Warnock observes, memory is our only mental faculty that we accept as working normally when it malfunctions.[55] Forgetting is, indeed, the norm and remembering the exception, for total recall would make our lives impossible. Yet the relationship between the two is complex, and as Huyssen asks, 'Is it the fear of forgetting that triggers the desire to remember, or is it perhaps the other way around?'[56] Forgetting can, indeed, be both an active and a passive phenomenon. New memories, as highlighted by Gillis, may require 'concerted forgettings', as demonstrated in the active renaming of socialist streets and the destruction of socialist monuments (discussed in Chapter 3).[57] On the other hand, past events may be unintentionally forgotten simply because there has been no need to recall them; as Fentress and Wickham suggest, memories are subject to the law of supply and demand.[58] Working from the concept of active and passive forgetting, Aleida Assmann highlights active and passive modes of remembering through the notion of the *archive* (where memory is stored, yet lies passive) and the *canon* (where memory is actively circulated).[59] Memories stored in the archive are thus halfway between the canon and forgetting; storage permits them to become part of the canon, but only through active intervention. Conversely, elements of the canon may enter the archive if they are not actively remembered. As this book will demonstrate, efforts to actively remember some elements of the GDR result in both temporary and longer-term acts of forgetting. The case studies will also demonstrate that the memorial landscape is beginning to result in a visible 'canon' of GDR remembrance.

Finally, and most critically, memory never exists in a vacuum; a given memory will always interact with, modify, and be modified by other memories with which it comes into contact. This is true of different forms of memory of the same event (e.g. 'master narratives' and 'counter-memories' constantly influence each other), as much as memories of different events (such as memories of the Holocaust and those of the GDR). As Aleida Assmann states, 'Memories do not exist as self-contained systems, but rather in social reality they always touch, strengthen, cross over with, modify and become polarized with other memories and impulses of forgetting'.[60] This notion has been expanded by Olick, who draws on the work of literary critic Mikhail Bakhtin to demonstrate the value of dialogism within the study of memory.⁶¹ Bakhtin asserted that when we select words to construct an utterance, we do not use them in their neutral dictionary form, but rather take them from other utterances, thus containing memory traces of other utterances. Thus, 'Utterances are not indifferent to one another, and are not self-sufficient; they are aware of and mutually reflect one another. ... Every utterance must be regarded primarily as a *response* to preceding utterances of the given sphere'.⁶² Olick applies this to an investigation of commemorations of 8 May 1945 in the FRG, finding that each responded to and interacted with previous commemorations, creating a cumulative effect. Interestingly, Bakhtin also asserts that 'the utterance is related not only to preceding, but also to subsequent links in the chain of speech communication', as the speaker takes into account possible responses, for which purpose the utterance was originally made.⁶³ This notion clearly relates also to the creation of cultural memories, which are largely produced for future generations. This study thus seeks to show that monuments constructed in the present become entangled with past *and* future memorial traditions. In highlighting the dialogic quality of memory, it also demonstrates that the notion of the palimpsest, brought into currency particularly by Huyssen, and now used widely to refer to city texts, fails to encapsulate this dynamism. Huyssen sees Berlin as palimpsest, for example, as 'a disparate city-text that is being rewritten while previous text is preserved, traces are restored, erasures documented'.⁶⁴ While this captures the notion of layering, it fails to acknowledge fully the extent to which each layer influences and shapes the next, a feature that will emerge as central to many examples in this book. Indeed, the dynamic qualities of the built environment are rarely highlighted in quite the same way as those of other cultural media, such as literature, film, digital media or photography – a trend that this book intends to reverse.⁶⁵

The dialogic quality of memory does not, however, only come into play on a diachronic level, and recent scholarship has increasingly stressed the need to focus also on comparative contexts, the 'travelling' of practices and the significance of synchrony. Jens Brockmeier, for instance, draws on John Dewey's *Experience and Education* to highlight the importance of the interconnection between the principles of continuity (i.e. longitudinal dimension) and interaction (i.e. lateral dimension) in order to understand individual and collective experience. In his words, 'both dimensions open up a symbolic space of meaning that binds individuals to each other';⁶⁶ it is thus not only in dialogue with the past and future that we must study memorial acts, but also in conversation with contemporary trends, current beliefs and apparently competing memories. Similarly, Gregor Feindt et al. stress the importance of examining both the diachronic and the synchronic dimensions of acts of remembering in order to understand the truly 'entangled' nature of memory,[67] and Michael Rothberg's notion of 'multidirectional memory' highlights the interlacing and entanglement of memories in a model that shows them as 'subject to ongoing negotiation, cross-referencing, and borrowing; as productive and not privative'.[68] Drawing on the polyphony of memory in both dimensions – diachronic and synchronic – this study thus rejects more linear models, as represented in concrete form by the notion of the palimpsest, or in more abstract form by Jan Assmann's model of communicative and cultural memory, and reveals a complex web of connections between numerous past traditions, multiple understandings of the present and diverse visions of the future. Memory is, indeed, constantly in flux, and to quote Raphael Samuel: 'Like history, memory is inherently revisionist and never more chameleon than when it appears to stay the same'.[69]

Monuments, Memorials and 'Memory Markers'

The 'memory boom' of recent years has seen an upsurge in the construction of monuments and memorials, despite predictions in the early twentieth century of the death of this form.[70] Erika Doss, for instance, identifies a 'memorial mania' in the United States, whereas Wolfgang Wippermann polemically claims that the words of Germany's national anthem may more accurately be 'Denkmal über alles' ('monument above all else'), or indeed 'Deutschland, einig Denkmalland' ('Germany, united land of monuments').[71] This is not the first time that such pronouncements have been made; around the turn of the past century, Germany was similarly diagnosed with suffering from 'monument rage', a 'monument epidemic' and a 'modern monument cult', with France witnessing 'statuomania'.[72] What, then, has caused the return of the monument in recent times, how has its meaning shifted over time, and to what extent do past aesthetic and conceptual traditions still influence contemporary developments?

Stemming from the Latin verb *monere*, meaning 'to warn' or 'to remind', monuments act as aids to memory, defined by Doss as 'materialist modes of privileging particular histories and values'.[73] While memorials are largely constructed to remember the dead, monuments are more likely to commemorate memorable events and people in history, often designed to perpetuate or construct historical myths. In practice, however, the distinction between the two terms is tenuous and they are commonly used interchangeably. For the purposes of this book, it is useful to observe James Young's more formal distinction, and to consider monuments as a subset of memorials, thus as the material forms, sculptures or constructions that are created with the purpose of memorialization. While a memorial may not be a monument (and could take on diverse forms, such as literature, websites or architecture), a monument will always be a type of memorial.[74] The German terminology introduces a further distinction, for the admonitory term *Mahnmal* ('mahnen', meaning 'to warn') is largely reserved for constructions with a cautionary purpose (such as Holocaust memorials), whereas the word *Denkmal* (which literally translates as a 'mark to think') is used more generally. The latter may, however, carry the sense of the *Kulturdenkmal*, a building, structure or built environment that is preserved due to its historical value, and which has since become the object of preservation efforts (*Denkmalpflege*). Such structures are largely, to use Alois Riegl's term, 'unintended' (*ungewollte*) monuments, thus were not built with memorial status in mind.[75] In contrast, the narrower definition of the *Denkmal* – which is of relevance for this book – refers to 'intended' (*gewollte*) monuments, normally works of art that are built specifically for commemorative purposes. As Dirk Verheyen states, such a structure 'is seen as a deliberate construct, with particular dedicatory and ritual practices attached more or less from the start'.[76] While this book focuses on such deliberate constructions, the boundary between the two is often quite fuzzy. Monuments in memory of the Berlin Wall, for instance, may be structures purposely designed with a memorial function, yet which also serve to preserve sections of the wall (see Chapter 5).

Clearly, monuments are ancient forms of commemoration, and are accessible to both literate and illiterate cultures. As Le Goff highlights, however, inscription made the purpose of commemoration specific, and engravings on stelae and obelisks in the ancient Middle East fulfilled multiple functions in perpetuating memory.[77] Interestingly, these forms have lasted, and stelae and obelisks in their most basic form are still being reproduced today. This does not mean to say that the norms and aesthetics of monuments have not changed; a cursory glance back at the last two centuries demonstrates a significant degree of change. Traditionally reserved for rulers and victorious battles, monuments saw a significant shift with the rise of bourgeois society, in which cultural, intellectual and civic figures also became commemorated, as demonstrated by the famous monument to Goethe and Schiller in Weimar, dedicated in 1857. Around the same time, war memorials began to find their first incarnation, with Hans-Dieter Schmid identifying Hanover's 1832 'Waterloo Column' to be the first instance in which hundreds of names of fallen soldiers were listed, albeit still by order of rank.[78] Above all, however, the nineteenth century saw the rise of the national monument, with the period between German unification in 1871 and the end of the First World War in 1918 witnessing the construction of numerous national monuments of gigantic proportions, such as the Kyffhäuser Monument (1896), the Kaiser Wilhelm Monument near Porta Westfalica (1896), the Kaiser Wilhelm National Memorial in Berlin (1897) and the Battle of the Nations Monument in Leipzig (1913).[79] As Rudy Koshar states, 'The idea of the national monument, reinterpreted and extended to an array of buildings and spaces, became the linchpin of a large framing strategy to enhance national loyalties in an uncertain and still youthful state'.[80] While a 'national monument' can never succeed in representing all members of a nation collectively, the symbolic importance of such a display of national unity was of prime importance; indeed, Lewis Mumford's observation that 'the more shaky the institution, the more solid the monument' resonated strongly with this period.[81] It is thus little surprise that many such monuments exploited an iconographic repertoire of long-standing German patriotic mythology, the Kyffhäuser Monument, for instance, drawing an explicit line between Barbarossa and Wilhelm I. Alongside statues to Wilhelm I, those to Bismarck also adorned cityscapes, developing into a veritable 'Bismarck cult' in which – especially after his death in 1898 – his image 'migrated from the realm of heroic politics to that of timeless mythology'.[82] By 1914, approximately five hundred monuments to the 'Iron Chancellor' existed across the German Reich.[83]

National monuments of this period embodied qualities of permanence, power, grandeur and strong leadership, displaying, in Hobsbawm's words, 'a sort of open-air museum of national history as seen through great men'.[84] While the male dominance of this form (in terms of its creators and subjects) was slow to change – and indeed remains far from balanced today – the advent of two world wars and the growth of modernism changed traditional perceptions, challenging Lewis Mumford's claim that monuments could never be 'modern'.[85] In the wake of the First World War, the emphasis on heroic national leaders gave way rather to war memorials, on which it became widespread practice to name victims – ordinary soldiers – without mention of hierarchy or rank, thus bringing about a certain democratization of remembrance, in which equal honour was given for all dead.[86] This tradition has held strong, as witnessed, for example, in the Vietnam Veterans Memorial in Washington. Around the same time, modernism saw the beginnings of abstract monumental form, marking greater ambiguity and democratic orientation. Walter Gropius's Monument to

Victims of the Kapp-Putsch (1922) and Ludwig Mies van der Rohe's Revolution Memorial (1926), in memory of Rosa Luxemburg and Karl Liebknecht, represent two early examples, in terms of both their avant-garde, cubist-inspired forms and the subjects of their commemorative structures.[87] Under the National Socialist regime, the landscapes of Berlin and other towns and cities were altered through new, monumental architecture and memorial constructions, often bearing symbolic party insignia, as well as the destruction of memorial structures to socialist, Jewish or other groups opposed by National Socialism, such as the two aforementioned examples. While this period inevitably produced a difficult material legacy for the following regimes, and much memorial symbolism was destroyed under the occupying powers, it was the post-war period that left a greater mark on the contemporary memorial landscape.[88]

The period from 1945 onwards was marked above all by reconstruction on both sides of the Cold War divide, as well as the rise of the *Mahnmal*, highlighting tragic loss of life and the concept of 'never again', albeit in different forms in East and West. In the GDR, monumental architecture was quick to resurface, first in the form of huge Soviet war memorials, then in a large variety of antifascist memorials, socialist realist constructions to celebrate the working class and the 'building of socialism', and monuments to Soviet leaders (see Chapter 2 for a more detailed discussion). While the later GDR years saw a revaluation of the concept of 'heritage', and with it a wider source of inspiration for monuments, their construction unequivocally served the political ideology of the SED regime and its oft-stated 'brotherhood' with the Soviet Union. The post-war years in the FRG, however, witnessed an aversion to monumental form, with the initial construction of very modest monuments to the war dead and to victims of the Holocaust.[89] It was not until later years, largely from the 1980s onwards, that the memory landscape became increasingly marked by more significant and challenging commemorative signs. Postmodernism brought with it increasing scepticism of monumental form, representing both nineteenth-century nationalism and twentieth-century totalitarianism, and witnessed an emerging 'aesthetic consensus of antimonumentalism'.[90] Indeed, abstraction became the key language of commemorative form, often seeking precisely the opposite of the widespread appeal and acceptance of earlier monuments. The growth of Holocaust memorials also encouraged a shift towards abstract aesthetics, first because there was a need to avoid traditional Christian imagery to represent a Jewish catastrophe, and second because the constructions were to represent absence rather than presence, not only the physical absence of victims, but also 'the absence of any sense of uplift, of meaning, of purpose in the deaths of the victims'.[91] As such, a wealth of terms emerged in the 1980s to rival the concept of the *Denkmal*, such as the *Denkzeichen* (memory/think mark), *Gedenkmal* (remembrance/ commemoration mark) and *Gegendenkmal* (countermonument), all of which prioritized intellectual reflection over the more victorious messages embedded in the traditional monument, encouraging multiple readings and meanings.[92] As highlighted by Mechthild Widrich, 'performative monuments' also emerged around this time, with some artists bringing radical performance practices to the heart of the commemorative process, in the attempt to harness the potential of the monument as a social force.[93]

Of these new concepts, it is that of the 'countermonument' that has found most currency, invented by Austrian sculptor Alfred Hrdlicka and pioneered above all by James Young.[94] Resisting the very premise of the traditional monument as a permanent, solid, upstanding structure with an emphatic message, countermonuments emphasize rather the ephemeral and the transitory, incorporating absences, voids and ground planes, rather than presences and verticals. In doing so, they are intended to draw attention to the fragility – rather than the constancy – of certain communities.[95] In the same way that Michel Foucault's concept of counter-memory involves resistance towards official versions of history, the countermonument thus resists traditional notions of the heroic, state-serving monument. Given that this form evolved with monuments dedicated to the memory of the Holocaust, Young has argued that the countermonument, as a monument against fascism, is thus also 'a monument against itself'.[96] The countermonument phenomenon was only able to emerge in a democratic state that had developed a degree of self-consciousness and confidence; it is little surprise that the GDR witnessed no such structures. As Koshar surmises, 'Countermonuments made sense only in reference to West Germany's commemorative largesse, just as 1960s hippies made sense only in wealthy and highly materialistic societies'.[97] Today, however, they have infiltrated mainstream culture, and while Young refers to the 'counter-memorial architectural vernacular' of German artists and architects,[98] few contemporary competition organizers expect anything other than proposals based on the premise of the countermonument. Yet this may indicate that the concept has run its course, and as Noam Lupu suggests, 'the word "counter" seems to have vanished entirely from "countermemorial"'.[99] Indeed, the concept has not been without its critics, with many observing that the binary opposition between fascism and monumentality is highly flawed, for monumental forms clearly exist beyond fascism.[100] In terms of aesthetics and lacking contextualization, Richard Crownshaw also argues that in placing Jews beyond representation, countermonuments may mirror the Nazi abstraction of Jewish identity, thus risking 'an unwitting slippage from the representation of fascism into a fascism of representation'.[101]

The countermonument is a key concept for this study not only in terms of its influential aesthetics, but also for our understanding of public engagement. Indeed, one of the distinctive features of the countermonument is the notion of involving passers-by and encouraging active participation, with, in Janet Ward's words, the aim to 'explode any rhetoric of silence' that may surround memory of the Holocaust or fascism.[102] Such structures are intended to demand the active attention of the viewer, who is urged to continue the memory-work that cannot be concluded by the monument, and in doing so, delegate the performance of memory to the audience. Lupu even goes so far as to suggest that 'countermonuments depend almost entirely on their audience to interpret their intent, making the artist a sort of prisoner of his/her audience'.[103] The important point here is that such commemorative action is always a public act, and by its very public nature, becomes politically relevant. With reference to 1980s countermonuments in Germany, Widrich argues that it is not simply this participation that is the hallmark of countermonuments, but rather their attempt to 'recognize and codify this audience reaction', sometimes in the monuments themselves – as in Esther and Jochen Gerz's much-cited Monument against Fascism – or in the documents connected to the monuments, which are preserved in the commemorative action.[104] In recognition of this point, Niven suggests the alternative term of 'mnemorials' for such structures, in order to better capture their preoccupation with the processes of memory.[105]

The active involvement of audiences is part of a wider development since the end of the First World War: the increasing democratization of monuments and memorials, both in terms of their subjects and instigators. As memory of the unnamed soldier or the unknown genocide victim demonstrates, it is clearly no longer only national rulers and heroes who are remembered in stone. However, in democratic societies, the will to remember certain individuals or groups may also lead to competition, in which apparent attempts to monopolize memory may provoke challenges or alternative projects.[106] Berlin's Holocaust memorial is an exemplary case in point, for it sparked subsequent memorials to other victims' groups, such as those to homosexuals, victims of the euthanasia programme and the Roma and Sinti. Similarly, Gunter Demning's *Stolpersteine* project, in which individual Jewish victims are remembered on brass cobblestones outside their former places of residence, is a decentralized and individual response to impersonalized, national projects such as the *Neue Wache* in Berlin.[107] The instigation of memorials is no longer uniquely the domain of kings and governments, but also that of a wide variety of social groups and engaged individuals. As Peter Carrier observes, the function of monuments has shifted from that of representation to that of participation,[108] in terms of both instigation and interpretation. As the examples in this book demonstrate, the notions of plurality and democracy prove to be particularly important for monument projects emerging in post-socialist eastern Germany, and the active involvement of the public is often at the heart of this endeavour.

We must ask, however, what the continuing attraction of monuments and memorials is today, when multiple alternative commemorative media exist. On the one hand, the notion of place has always been central to the process of memorialization; as Frances Yates has notably demonstrated, the art of memory, or *ars memoriae*, essentially consisted of associating images with places in order to commit them to memory.[109] The very concept of physical place has been bound up with that of memory for centuries. On the other hand, it seems that the fast-paced changes of the contemporary world have created a widespread desire for memorialization. As Andreas Huyssen suggests, it may be precisely because of the 'accelerated speed of modernization' that we turn towards the past, and develop a desire to preserve, 'as an attempt to break out of the swirling empty space of the everyday present and to claim a sense of time and memory'.[110] Indeed, the monument offers something that is denied by virtual media: the material quality of the object.[111] In contrast to fleeting screen images, second life personae and the immateriality of modern-day communication, 'we cling intellectually and emotionally to our experiences and memories of the material world that is so reassuringly solid'.[112] This material presence – even if temporary – also distinguishes most monuments and memorials from other art forms, as their scale and physical rootedness resist the process of mass reproduction.[113] Unlike paintings or works of literature, for instance, monuments can largely be viewed only in the original, giving them a sense of 'aura' in the Benjaminian sense: 'that which withers in the age of mechanical reproduction is the aura of the work of art'.[114] In this way, we can read the signs of time on monuments, as seen, for example, in graffiti, the state of repair of a structure, or its surroundings. The original use value of a monument is also often evident, and to quote Benjamin again, 'The uniqueness of a work of art is inseparable from its being imbedded in the fabric of tradition. ... It is significant that the existence of the work of art with reference to its aura is never entirely separated from its ritual function'.[115]

The notion of authenticity relates also to the location of monuments, for they are often built on 'authentic' historical sites, such as the former site of the Berlin Wall, or the locations of the uprisings and demonstrations of 1953 and 1989, thus lending further meaning to the materiality of memory. As Jennifer Jordan highlights, however, the authenticity of a site does not guarantee memorial status; indeed, most authentic locations 'slip into mundane usage'.[116] The limited physical space available in a city often brings to the fore debates over what should, and should not, be remembered in specific locations, for in contrast to the infinite storage space available in digital archives, a cityscape cannot retain all traces of the past. Ultimately it must also remain a functional living and working space, giving rise to Huyssen's notion of 'palimpsests of space', in which cities are written and rewritten to suit the present moment.[117] Yet despite the potential for rewriting city texts, place is often perceived as being stable, and as Karen Till notes, 'we often understand them [places] as having a timeless quality'.[118] Once again, monuments can offer a stable basis often denied by more transient forms of memory. Physical location also strongly influences monumental form, for structures are built with specific locations in mind. In this way, they interact with their surroundings and with other landmarks to add another layer of meaning. As Brockmeier highlights, 'Responding to its material and symbolic environment, it [a monument] is a commentary on a given mnemonic system, a commentary that by its sheer existence in this place has already changed this very system'.[119] In this way, the much-commented Vietnam Veterans Memorial responds directly to the national monuments on and around the Washington Mall, and in doing so, portrays them in a different light. On a diachronic level, we see here the way in which structures of memory respond to past instances of commemoration, but also the two-way direction of mnemonic movement, once again showing the problematic linearity of the model of the palimpsest.

Questions of space and location are, ultimately, political questions, for space is a valuable and limited resource. As Martin Schönfeld highlights, 'Public space is, in this sense, a classic arena of symbolic rivalry, in which only those who possess economic, social or political power prevail'.[120] To erect a monument is to invest urban land with powerful symbolism, and to use Bourdieu's term, the 'symbolic capital' of monuments is extensive, especially at times of transition, when new leaders or groups attempt to assert their power.[121] Indeed, the position of most public monuments as 'non-excludible' and 'non-rival' goods (i.e. which are neither restricted in terms of access, nor limited to one or few consumers at the same time) means that they reach the broadest possible number and variety of people.[122] Their potential for making a public statement is thus great, yet it must be remembered that the reception of monuments cannot be influenced or guided in the same way as in a museum or art gallery.[123] Public engagement in – or objection to – a memorial project may, thus, take its creators by surprise; the London statue erected to Arthur Harris (aka 'Bomber' Harris, Commander of the RAF Bomber Command during the Second World War) in 1992, for instance, was allotted police protection after protesters had covered it in red paint and further damage was feared. Monuments are thus interpreted within the context of the present day, and as such, their meaning may change as rapidly as the world around them. Their apparently permanent qualities of materiality and physical rootedness are, in many ways, deceptive, as monuments are constantly reinvested with meaning. It could indeed be said that monuments 'become' rather than 'exist',[124] and as Erika Doss describes the American memorial, 'Its meaning is neither inherent nor eternal but *processual* – dependent on a variety of social relations and subject to the volatile intangibles of the nation's multiple publics and their fluctuating interests and feelings'.[125] Indeed, memorial projects are bound up in a network of hopes, desires, expectations, demands and emotions, on the part of their creators as well as the public. They are sites not only for power struggles, but also to evoke emotions, provoke moral visions, educate younger generations and encourage popular participation in history. They are places not only at which one is to remember, to mourn or to celebrate, but places at which one is seen to remember, to mourn or to celebrate.[126] As such, this book proposes to view monuments primarily as processes and social spaces, rather than as fixed entities or static objects.

The 'becoming' of a monument is a continuous process, and one that may involve numerous different phases. Among these, Jay Winter has identified three key stages, which will prove useful for this study: first, the construction of a commemorative form; second, the grounding of ritual action in the calendar; third, its transformation or disappearance as an active site of memory.[127] The first of these begins with the initial idea for a monument and ends with its physical construction, a phase that will receive much attention in this book. As Winter and Jordan both highlight, however, the construction process can be marked as much by happenstance and determined individuals, or by questions of land ownership and finances, as by rigorous plans and collective action.[128] Yet two 'social place-making practices' – to use Karen Till's term – prove most common in the planning of monuments: public design competitions and citizen actions.[129] Public competitions are nothing new to monument design, and were particularly prevalent during the apogee of the nineteenth-century nationalist monuments. Today they are often seen as an important part of the democratic process, yet can also be costly, lengthy and controversial. Citizen actions may be initiated by any group of people who have cause to remember a specific event, such as survivors' groups or families, human rights activists, historians or political groups. While such initiatives may make ground more swiftly if they choose not to run a competition, they may also lack the public recognition that results from this process. This first stage is marked above all, however, by the debates that surround the proposed construction, and many a monument may 'exist' discursively in the public sphere long before any material presence is evident. One need only mention the Holocaust memorial in Berlin in this context, which witnessed well over a decade of debates before construction began. Deliberations over public monuments often reveal competing understandings of what parts of the past should or should not be remembered, and as such the constructed nature of the nation – or the relevant collective group – as 'imagined' rather than 'natural' becomes more evident.[130] As Young has argued with reference to the Berlin memorial, the discussion itself became the memorial, playing as important a role as the physical construction.[131] Indeed, it has become widely accepted that the success of a monument can be measured by the extent to which it generates debate, and Gabi Dolff-Bonekämper goes so far as to identify a *Streitwert* (dispute value) in monuments, which can be measured against the ability of monuments to engender debate and discussion.[132] Such debate may not, however, always be documented, and the finished form of a monument may hide the budgetary, political or aesthetic disputes that take place before and during construction; as Feindt et al. highlight, 'competing interpretations are not equally visible at different moments in time', and following the 'hegemonic closure' of an act of memory, there is no need to display this variety: 'Dominant interpretations tend to eradicate their signs of being an action'.[133]

The second stage begins once the monument is constructed, but is concerned with grounding the physical construction in regular ritual activity, and may be instrumental in either completing 'hegemonic closure' or allowing for the existence of multiple narratives. This phase is perhaps the most important for securing the long-term impact of the monument, for in Carrier's words, 'monuments are inherently mute'; as constructions, they are little more than projection surfaces for interpretations of the past.[134] The mnemonic meaning of objects is, indeed, far from intrinsic to the object, and as Koshar surmises. 'Objectively considered, such historical sites are mere constructions of stone, wood, brick, concrete, and steel. Their meanings derive from public action, from attempts to draw together a sequence gone astray'.[135] The social construction of meaning around monuments may take the form of ceremonies, rituals of visitation, wreath-layings, vigils or political gatherings, all of which invest a monument with special meaning; furthermore, if they take place on fixed dates – for example on anniversaries or public holidays – then a tradition of activity is ensured for the immediate future. Such ceremonies also strengthen the sense of community for which the monument was built, by offering its members an image of their membership.[136] This fact was particularly evident to leaders of twentieth-century dictatorships in Europe, with many a monument or historical site being designed specifically to house mass gatherings, military parades and oath-swearing ceremonies; in this way, art under power was organized in Hobsbawm's words as 'public drama'.[137] Sites of memory may also gain recognition through single, even spontaneous, acts; Chancellor Willy Brandt's decision to kneel before the Warsaw Ghetto Monument in 1970, for instance, made headlines across the world, since when other leaders (such as Jimmy Carter in 1977 and John Paul II in 1983) have also paid their respects at this site.[138] The circulation of such images today depends, of course, on the mass media, a central body in the writing of commemorative 'software', which serves to comment upon and shape the urban 'hardware', ultimately keeping it alive.[139]

The third stage relates to the longer life of a monument which, in order to remain 'visible', must remain relevant to the present day; as Huyssen highlights, 'the permanence promised by a monument in stone is always built on quicksand'.[140] If the commemorative 'software' does not continue to be maintained, or a political caesura – such as the end of the Cold War – renders monuments redundant, they may be forgotten, removed or destroyed. Those that are left unattended may stand as symbols of forgetting, reminding us of Robert Musil's famous comment that 'there is nothing in the world as invisible as monuments'.[141] Indeed, as Jordan states, 'any landscape of memory also exists within a shadow landscape of forgetting',[142] yet the apparently concrete rigidity of monuments does not mean that they are necessarily destined to destruction or invisibility. Indeed, the transformation of some into sites of satirical or political commentary may prolong their lives, or raise their profile. In Berlin in 1991, for example, graffiti below the statue of Marx and Engels read 'We are innocent', thus raising important questions about the project of socialism in the GDR. In Warsaw, the hands of the Dzerzhinsky statue were painted red – symbolic of blood – before its removal, and in Prague a Soviet tank (allegedly the first to arrive in Prague in 1945) was painted pink in 1991, setting in motion a long and controversial debate.[143] As the next chapter will demonstrate, politically defunct monuments may die a sudden death, but they may also be revived and imbued with new meaning. In this way, memorial places must be understood in a process of continuous transformation, and in relation to their surrounding environment. Ultimately, as Huyssen states, 'the success of any monument has to be measured by the extent to which it negotiates the multiple discourses of memory provided by the very electronic media to which the monument as solid matter provides an alternative'.[144]

Notes

1. See, for example, Rosenfeld, 'A Looming Crash or a Soft Landing?'; Charles Maier, 'A Surfeit of Memory? Reflections on History, Melancholy, and Denial', *History and Memory*, 5 (1993) 2, 136–52; David Berliner, 'The Abuses of Memory: Reflections on the Memory Boom in Anthropology', *Anthropology Quarterly*, 78 (2005) 1, 197–211; Kerwin Lee Klein, 'On the Emergence of Memory in Historical Discourse', *Representations*, 69 (2000) Winter, 127–50; Jay Winter, 'The Generation of Memory: Reflections on the "Memory Boom" in Contemporary Historical Studies', *Bulletin of the German Historical Institute*, 27 (2000) 3, 69–92.
2. Jeffrey K. Olick, 'Introduction', in *States of Memory: Continuities, Conflicts, and Transformations in National Retrospection*, ed. by Olick (Durham, NC; London: Duke University Press, 2003), p. 3.
3. Rosenfeld, 'A Looming Crash or a Soft Landing?', p. 156.
4. Alon Confino, 'Collective Memory and Cultural History: Problems of Method', *The American Historical Review*, 102 (1997) 5, 1,386–403 (1,387).
5. See Klein, 'On the Emergence of Memory', p. 131; Jeffrey K. Olick, '"Collective Memory": A Memoir and Prospect', *Memory Studies*, 1 (2008) 1, 23–29 (24).
6. Astrid Erll, *Kollektives Gedächtnis und Erinnerungskulturen* (Stuttgart: Metzler, 2005), pp. 2–4.
7. Rosenfeld, 'A Looming Crash or a Soft Landing?', p. 135.
8. Erll, *Kollektives Gedächtnis und Erinnerungskulturen*, p. 3.
9. On television and memory, see Andrew Hoskins, 'Television and the Collapse of Memory', *Time & Society*, 13 (2004) 1, 109–27.
10. Pierre Nora, 'The Reasons for the Current Upsurge in Memory', *Transit – Europäische Revue*, 22 (2002), Tr@nsit online.
11. Bill Niven, 'On the Use of "Collective Memory"', *German History*, 26 (2008) 3, 427–36 (427).
12. Jean-François Lyotard, *The Postmodern Condition: A Report on Knowledge*, trans. Geoff Bennington and Brian Massumi (Minnesota: University of

Minnesota, [1979] 1984); Francis Fukuyama, *The End of History and the Last Man* (New York: Free Press, 1992). The deconstruction of historical narratives was also brought to the fore by Hayden White in his *Metahistory: The Historical Imagination in Nineteenth-Century Europe* (Baltimore, MD; London: Johns Hopkins University Press, 1973).
13. Confino, 'Collective Memory and Cultural History', p. 1,393.
14. It could be argued that communicative memory also contains elements of individual and biographical memory, but it is largely referenced as a collective phenomenon.
15. Jeffrey K. Olick, 'From Collective Memory to the Sociology of Mnemonic Practices and Products', in *A Companion to Cultural Memory Studies*, ed. by Astrid Erll and Ansgar Nünning (Berlin: de Gruyter, 2010), pp. 151–61 (152).
16. James Fentress and Chris Wickham, *Social Memory* (Oxford: Blackwell, 1992), p. 2; Jay Winter, *Remembering War: The Great War between Memory and History in the Twentieth Century* (New Haven, CT; London: Yale University Press, 2006), pp. 4–5.
17. See Wulf Kantsteiner, 'Memory, Media and *Menschen*: Where is the Individual in Collective Memory Studies?', *Memory Studies*, 3 (2010) 1, 3–4.
18. Pierre Nora, 'Between Memory and History: Les Lieux de Mémoire', *Representations*, 26 (1989) Spring, 7–24 (19).
19. Jeffrey K. Olick, 'Collective Memory: The Two Cultures', *Sociological Theory*, 17 (1999) 3, 333–48 (346). See also James E. Young, 'The Memorial's Arc: Between Berlin's *Denkmal* and New York City's 9/11 Memorial', *Memory Studies*, 9 (2016) 3, 325–31 (330).
20. Niven, 'On the Use of "Collective Memory"', p. 436.
21. Erll, *Kollektives Gedächtnis und Erinnerungskulturen*, p. 21.
22. Maurice Halbwachs, *Les cadres sociaux de la mémoire* (Paris: Alcan, 1925) and *La mémoire collective* (Paris: Presses universitaires de France, 1950).
23. James V. Wertsch, *Voices of Collective Remembering* (New York: Cambridge University Press, 2002), p. 22.
24. Pierre Nora (ed.), *Les Lieux de Mémoire*, 7 vols (Paris: Gallimard, 1984–92).
25. Nora, 'Between Memory and History', p. 7.
26. Ibid., p. 13.
27. Barry Schwartz, 'Christian Origins: Historical Truth and Social Memory', in *Memory, Tradition, and Text: Uses of the Past in Early Christianity*, ed. by Alan Kirk and Tom Thatcher (Atlanta: Society of Biblical Literature, 2005), pp. 43–56 (46).
28. Olick, 'Collective Memory: The Two Cultures', p. 336.
29. Jan Assmann, *Das kulturelle Gedächtnis* (Munich: Beck, 1999), pp. 48–56.
30. Jan Assmann, 'Communicative and Cultural Memory', in *A Companion to Cultural Memory Studies*, ed. by Erll and Nünning, pp. 109–18 (110–11).
31. John Bodnar, *Remaking America: Public Memory, Commemoration, and Patriotism in the 20th Century* (Princeton, NJ: University of Princeton Press, 1992); William Hirst and David Manier, 'The Diverse Forms of Collective Memory', in *Kontexte und Kulturen des Erinnerns: Maurice Halbwachs und*

das Paradigma des kollektiven Gedächtnisses, ed. by Gerald Echterhoff and Martin Saar (Konstanz: UVK, 2002), pp. 37–58; Andreas Langenohl, Erinnerung und Modernisierung: Die öffentliche Rekonstruktion politischer Kollektivität am Beispiel des Neuen Rußland (Göttingen: Vandenhoeck und Ruprecht, 2000); Thomas Großbölting, 'Eine zwiespältige Bilanz: Zwanzig Jahre Aufarbeitung der DDR-Vergangenheit im wiedervereinigten Deutschland', in Das Ende des Kommunismus: Die Überwindung der Diktaturen in Europa und ihre Folgen, ed. by Thomas Großbölting, Raj Kollmorgen, Sascha Möbius and Rüdiger Schmidt (Essen: Klartext, 2010), pp. 61–74.
32. Aleida Assmann, Der lange Schatten der Vergangenheit: Erinnerungskultur und Geschichtspolitik (Munich: Beck, 2006).
33. Assmann, Das kulturelle Gedächtnis, p. 48.
34. See Marita Sturken, 'Memorializing Absence', http://essays.ssrc.org/sept11/essays/sturken.htm (accessed 3 December 2010).
35. Marianne Hirsch, 'The Generation of Postmemory', Poetics Today, 29 (2008) 1, 103–28 (111). Emphasis in original.
36. Alison Landsberg, Prosthetic Memory: The Transformation of American Remembrance in the Age of Mass Culture (New York: Columbia University Press, 2004), p. 19.
37. Nora, 'Between Memory and History', pp. 8–9.
38. White, Metahistory and 'The Question of Narrative in Contemporary Historical Theory', History and Theory, 23 (1984) 1, 1–33.
39. Marita Sturken, Tangled Memories: The Vietnam War, the AIDS Epidemic, and the Politics of Remembering (Berkeley, CA: University of California Press, 1997), p. 5.
40. Eric Hobsbawm and Terence Ranger, The Invention of Tradition (Cambridge: Cambridge University Press, 1983).
41. Olick, 'From Collective Memory to the Sociology of Mnemonic Practices and Products', p. 159.
42. Barry Schwartz, 'The Social Context of Commemoration: A Study in Collective Memory', Social Forces, 61 (1982) 2, 374–402 (396). See also Yael Zerubavel, Recovered Roots: Collective Memory and the Making of Israeli National Tradition (Chicago, IL; London: University of Chicago Press, 1995), pp. 4–5.
43. Jacques Le Goff, History and Memory, trans. Steven Rendall and Elizabeth Claman (New York: Columbia University Press, 1992), p. 54.
44. Erll, Kollektives Gedächtnis und Erinnerungskulturen, p. 129.
45. Yosef Hayim Yerushalmi, cited in Alon Confino, 'Collective Memory and Cultural History', p. 1,386.
46. Jeffrey K. Olick, The Politics of Regret: On Collective Memory and Historical Responsibility (New York; London: Routledge, 2007), p. 104.
47. Zerubavel, Recovered Roots, p. 214.
48. Eviatar Zerubavel, Time Maps: Collective Memory and the Social Shape of the Past (Chicago, IL; London: University of Chicago Press, 2003), pp. 4–5.
49. Barry Schwartz, 'Introduction: The Expanding Past', Qualitative Sociology, 19 (1996) 3, 275–82 (278).

50. Huyssen, *Present Pasts*, p. 54.
51. For Foucault's concept of counter-memory, see Michel Foucault, *Language, Counter-Memory, Practice: Selected Essays and Interviews*, trans. and ed. by Donald F. Bouchard (Ithaca, NY: Cornell University Press, 1977). For a useful analysis, see Patrick H. Hutton, *History as an Art of Memory* (Hanover, NH; London: University Press of New England, 1993), pp. 5–6.
52. Hutton, *History as an Art of Memory*, p. 79.
53. David Lowe and Tony Joel, *Remembering the Cold War: Global Contest and National Stories* (New York; London: Routledge, 2013), p. 7.
54. Louis Bickford and Amy Sodaro, 'Remembering Yesterday to Protect Tomorrow: The Internationalization of a New Commemorative Paradigm', in *Memory and the Future: Transnational Politics, Ethics and Society*, ed. by Yifat Gutman, Adam D. Brown and Amy Sodaro (Basingstoke: Palgrave Macmillan, 2010), pp. 66–86 (69).
55. Mary Warnock, cited in Fentress and Wickham, *Social Memory*, p. 39. On forgetting, see Paul Connerton, 'Seven Types of Forgetting', *Memory Studies*, 1 (2008) 1, 59–71 and Brockmeier, 'Remembering and Forgetting'.
56. Huyssen, *Present Pasts*, p. 17.
57. John R. Gillis, 'Memory and Identity: The History of a Relationship', in *Commemorations: The Politics of National Identity*, ed. by Gillis (Princeton, NJ: Princeton University Press, 1994), p. 7; see also Benedict Anderson, *Imagined Communities* (London; New York: Verso, 1983), chapter 11.
58. Fentress and Wickham, *Social Memory*, p. 202.
59. Aleida Assmann, 'Canon and Archive', in *A Companion to Cultural Memory Studies*, ed. by Erll and Nünning, pp. 97–107. Elsewhere, she uses the terms 'Funktions- und Speichergedächtnis' to distinguish between the same concepts.
60. Assmann, *Der lange Schatten der Vergangenheit*, p. 17.
61. Jeffrey K. Olick, 'Genre Memories and Memory Genres: A Dialogical Analysis of May 8, 1945 Commemorations in the Federal Republic of Germany', *American Sociological Review*, 64 (1999) 3, 381–402.
62. Mikhail M. Bakhtin, 'The Problem of Speech Genres', in *Speech Genres and Other Late Essays*, trans. Vern W. McGee (Austin, TX: University of Texas Press, 1986), pp. 60–102 (91).
63. Ibid., p. 94.
64. Huyssen, *Present Pasts*, p. 81.
65. See, for example, Astrid Erll and Ann Rigney (eds), *Mediation, Remediation, and the Dynamics of Cultural Memory* (Berlin; New York: de Gruyter, 2009).
66. Brockmeier, 'Remembering and Forgetting', p. 18.
67. Gregor Feindt, Félix Krawatzek, Daniela Mahler, Friedemann Pastel and Rieke Trimçev, 'Entangled Memory: Toward a Third Wave in Memory Studies', *History and Theory*, 53 (2014) February, 24–44.
68. Michael Rothberg, *Multidirectional Memory: Remembering the Holocaust in the Age of Decolonization* (Stanford, CA: Stanford University Press, 2009), p. 3.
69. Raphael Samuel, *Theatres of Memory*, vol. 1: *Past and Present in Contemporary Culture* (London; New York: Verso, 1994), p. x.

70. See, for instance, Lewis Mumford, 'The Death of the Monument', in *The Culture of Cities* (London: Secker & Warburg, 1938), pp. 433–40.
71. Erika Doss, *Memorial Mania: Public Feeling in America* (Chicago; London: University of Chicago Press, 2010); Wolfgang Wippermann, *Denken statt Denkmalen: Gegen den Denkmalwahn der Deutschen* (Berlin: Rotbuch, 2010), p. 144.
72. See Max Schasler, 'Ueber moderne Denkmalswuth', *Deutsche Zeit- und Streit-Fragen*, 7 (1878) 103, 253–92; Richard Muther, 'Die Denkmalseuche', in *Aufsätze über bildende Kunst*, vol. 2: *Betrachtungen und Eindrücke* (Berlin: J. Ladyschnikow Verlag, 1914), pp. 59–68; Alois Riegl, 'Der moderne Denkmalkultus: Sein Wesen und seine Entstehung', in *Gesammelte Aufsätze* (Vienna: WUV-Univ.-Verl., [1903] 1996), pp. 139–84; Gustave Pessard, *La Statuomanie parisienne: Etude critique sur l'abus des statues, liste des statues et monuments existants* (Paris: H. Daragon, 1912).
73. Doss, *Memorial Mania*, p. 38.
74. James E. Young, *The Texture of Memory: Holocaust Memorials and Meaning* (New Haven, CT; London: Yale University Press, 1993), p. 4.
75. Riegl, 'Der modern Denkmalkultus'.
76. Dirk Verheyen, *United City, Divided Memories? Cold War Legacies in Contemporary Berlin* (Lanham, MD: Lexington Books, 2008), p. 24.
77. Le Goff, *History and Memory*, pp. 58–59.
78. Hans-Dieter Schmid, 'Denkmäler als Zeugnisse der Geschichtskultur', in *Geschichte und Öffentlichkeit: Orte-Medien-Institutionen*, ed. by Sabine Horn and Michael Sauer (Göttingen: Vandenhoeck & Ruprecht, 2009), pp. 51–60 (53).
79. See Thomas Nipperdey, 'Nationalidee und Nationaldenkmal in Deutschland im 19. Jahrhundert', *Historische Zeitschrift*, 206 (1968), 529–85.
80. Koshar, *From Monuments to Traces*, p. 12.
81. Mumford, *The Culture of Cities*, p. 434.
82. Sergiusz Michalski, *Public Monuments: Art in Political Bondage 1970–1997* (London: Reaktion, 1998), p. 72.
83. Ibid., p. 74.
84. Eric Hobsbawm, 'Foreword', in *Art and Power: Europe under the Dictators 1930–45*, ed. by Dawn Ades et al. (London: Thames and Hudson, 1995), pp. 11–15 (12).
85. Mumford, *The Culture of Cities*, p. 438.
86. George L. Mosse, *Fallen Soldiers: Reshaping the Memory of the World Wars* (New York; Oxford: Oxford University Press, 1990), pp. 48–49.
87. See Hans-Ernst Mittig, 'Das Denkmal', in *Kunst: Die Geschichte ihrer Funktionen*, ed. by Werner Busch and Peter Schmoock (Weinheim; Berlin: Quadriga Verlag, 1987), pp. 457–89 (481–85); Johannes Langner, 'Denkmal und Abstraktion', in *Denkmal-Zeichen-Monument: Skulptur und öffentlicher Raum heute*, ed. by Ekkehard Mai und Gisela Schmirber (Munich: Prestel-Verlag, 1989), pp. 58–68.
88. See Karl Arndt, 'Die NSDAP und ihre Denkmäler', in *Denkmal-Zeichen-Monument*, ed. by Mai and Schmirber, pp. 69–81; Michalski, *Public Monuments*, pp. 93–106.

89. See Rosenfeld, *Munich and Memory*, p. 125.
90. See Huyssen, *Present Pasts*, p. 38.
91. Jay Winter, 'Sites of Memory and the Shadow of War', in *A Companion to Cultural Memory Studies*, ed. by Erll and Nünning, pp. 61–74 (69).
92. Michalski, *Public Monuments*, p. 204.
93. Mechthild Widrich, *Performative Monuments: The Rematerialisation of Public Art* (Manchester; New York: Manchester University Press, 2014).
94. See James E. Young, 'The Counter-Monument: Memory against Itself in Germany Today', *Critical Inquiry*, 18 (1992) 2, 276–96 (274) and *The Texture of Memory*. See also Corinna Tomberger, *Das Gegendenkmal: Avantgardekunst, Geschichtspolitik und Geschlecht in der bundesdeutschen Erinnerungskultur* (Bielefeld: transcript Verlag, 2007).
95. See Carolyn Loeb, 'The City as Subject: Contemporary Public Sculpture in Berlin', *Journal of Urban History*, 35 (2009) 6, 853–78.
96. Young, 'The Counter-Monument', p. 274.
97. Koshar, *From Monuments to Traces*, pp. 267–68.
98. Young, 'The Memorial's Arc', p. 327.
99. Noam Lupu, 'Memory Vanished, Absent, and Confined: The Countermemorial Project in 1980s and 1990s Germany', *History & Memory*, 15 (2003) 2, 130–64 (157).
100. See, for example, Brett Ashley Kaplan, '"Aesthetic Pollution": The Paradox of Remembering and Forgetting in Three Holocaust Commemorative Sites', *Journal of Modern Jewish Studies*, 2 (2003) 1, 1–18 (4–5); Richard Crownshaw, *The Afterlife of Holocaust Memory in Contemporary Literature and Culture* (Basingstoke: Palgrave Macmillan, 2010), p. 186.
101. Richard Crownshaw, 'The German Countermonument: Conceptual Indeterminacies and the Retheorisation of the Arts of Vicarious Memory', *Forum for Modern Language Studies*, 44 (2008) 2, 212–27 (224).
102. Janet Ward, *Post-Wall Berlin: Borders, Space and Identity* (Basingstoke: Palgrave Macmillan, 2011), p. 229.
103. Lupu, 'Memory Vanished, Absent, and Confined', p. 132.
104. Widrich, *Performative Monuments*, pp. 160–78 (quotation on p. 161).
105. Bill Niven, 'From Countermonument to Combimemorial: Developments in German Memorialization', *Journal of War and Culture Studies*, 6 (2013) 1, 75–91 (82).
106. See Gert Matenklott, 'Denkmal / Memorial', *Daidalos*, 49 (1993) September, 28–35 (30).
107. See Martin Schönfeld, 'Kritisches Denkzeichen und restauratives Denkmal', in *Vom kritischen Gebrauch der Erinnerung*, ed. by Thomas Flierl and Elfriede Müller (Berlin: Karl Dietz Verlag, 2009), pp. 141–74 (155). It should be noted that such examples also serve as an illustration of multidirectional memory, in which different memories become entangled through ongoing negotiation and cross-referencing.
108. Peter Carrier, *Holocaust Monuments and National Memory Cultures in France and Germany since 1989* (New York; Oxford: Berghahn Books, 2005), p. 221.
109. Frances Yates, *The Art of Memory* (London: Routledge and Kegan Paul, 1966).

110. Andreas Huyssen, *Twilight Memories: Marking Time in a Culture of Amnesia* (New York; London: Routledge, 1995), p. 28.
111. Ibid., p. 225.
112. 'Introduction', in *Textures of Place: Exploring Humanist Geographies*, ed. by Paul C. Adams, Steven Hoelscher and Karen E. Till (Minneapolis, MN; London: University of Minnesota Press, 2001), p. xiii.
113. It should be noted that some countermonuments are immaterial in nature (e.g. acoustic), although the majority involve material elements – including all examples in this book.
114. Walter Benjamin, *Illuminations*, ed. by Hannah Arendt, trans. Harry Zorn (London: Pimlico, 1999), p. 215.
115. Ibid., p. 217.
116. Jordan, *Structures of Memory*, p. 15.
117. Huyssen, *Present Pasts*, p. 7.
118. Till, *The New Berlin*, p. 14.
119. Brockmeier, 'Remembering and Forgetting', pp. 34–35.
120. Schönfeld, 'Kritisches Denkzeichen und restauratives Denkmal', p. 142.
121. Pierre Bourdieu, *Outline of a Theory of Practice*, trans. Richard Nice (Cambridge: Cambridge University Press, 1977), pp. 171–83.
122. Ståle Navrud and Richard C. Ready, *Valuing Cultural Heritage: Applying Environmental Valuation Techniques to Historic Buildings, Monuments, Artifacts* (Cheltenham: Edward Elgar, 2002), pp. 3–4.
123. Karin Schittenhelm, *Zeichen, die Anstoß erregen: Mobilisierungsformen zu Mahnmalen und zeitgenössischen Außenskulpturen* (Opladen: Westdeutscher Verlag, 1996), p. 128.
124. See Koshar, *From Monuments to Traces*, p. 30.
125. Doss, *Memorial Mania*, p. 45. Emphasis in original.
126. See Jay Winter, *Sites of Memory, Sites of Mourning: The Great War in European Cultural History* (Cambridge: Cambridge University Press, 1995), p. 93.
127. Winter, 'Sites of Memory and the Shadow of War', pp. 70–71.
128. See Jordan, *Structures of Memory* and Winter, *Sites of Memory*.
129. Till, *The New Berlin*, p. 18.
130. Karen E. Till, 'Reimagining National Identity: "Chapters of Life" at the German Historical Museum in Berlin', in *Textures of Place*, ed. by Adams, Hoelscher and Till, pp. 273–99 (274).
131. James E. Young, *At Memory's Edge: After-Images of the Holocaust in Contemporary Art and Architecture* (New Haven, CT; London: Yale University Press, 2000), p. 191.
132. Gabi Dolf-Bonekämper, 'Gegenwartswerte: Für eine Erneuerung von Alois Riegls Denkmalwerttheorie', in Hans-Rudolf Meier and Ingrid Scheurmann (eds), *DENKmalWERTE: Beiträge zur Theorie und Aktualität der Denkmalpflege. Georg Mörsch zum 70. Geburtstag* (Berlin; Munich: Deutscher Kunstverlag, 2010), pp. 27–40. See also Leo Schmidt, *Einführung in die Denkmalpflege* (Darmstadt: Wissenschaftliche Buchgesellschaft, 2008), pp. 75–76.
133. Feindt et al., 'Entangled Memory', p. 32.
134. Carrier, *Holocaust Monuments and National Memory Cultures*, p. 161.

135. Koshar, *From Monuments to Traces*, p. 9.
136. 'Introduction', in *Moment to Monument: The Making and Unmaking of Cultural Significance*, ed. by Ladina Bezzola Lambert and Andrea Oschner (Bielefeld: transcript Verlag, 2009), p. 11.
137. Hobsbawm, 'Foreword', p. 12.
138. See James E. Young, 'The Biography of a Memorial Icon: Nathan Rapoport's Warsaw Ghetto Monument', *Representations*, 26 (1989) Spring, 69–106; Michael Diers, *Schlagbilder: Zur politischen Ikonographie der Gegenwart* (Frankfurt am Main: Fischer, 1997), pp. 42–50.
139. For the distinction between 'hardware' and 'software', see Carrier, *Holocaust Monuments and National Memory Cultures*, p. 29.
140. Huyssen, *Twilight Memories*, p. 250.
141. Robert Musil, in *Nachlaß zu Lebzeiten* (Hamburg: Rowohlt, 1957), p. 59.
142. Jennifer Jordan, 'A Matter of Time: Examining Collective Memory in Historical Perspective in Postwar Berlin', *Journal of Historical Sociology*, 18 (2005) 1/2, 37–71 (61).
143. See Gamboni, Dario, *The Destruction of Art: Iconoclasm and Vandalism since the French Revolution* (London: Reaktion Books, 1997), pp. 63–77.
144. Huyssen, *Twilight Memories*, p. 255.

 Chapter 2

SOCIALIST ICONS
From Heroes to Villains?

Revolution, regime change and social upheaval have, in recent times, frequently been symbolized by iconic images of the toppling of monuments. With the dissolution of the Soviet Union in 1991, for example, media images of crowds cheering the felling of Lenin in Riga, Enver Hoxha in Tirana, and Felix Dzerzhinsky in Moscow – among others – were transmitted across the globe. More recently, Saddam Hussein's 'fall' in Baghdad in 2003 became one of the most lasting images of the overthrow of his regime, and the toppling of Lenin in Kiev notably marked the Ukrainian demonstrations of 2013. As previously heroic icons are vilified, monuments that have long since received little popular attention and acquired – in Musil's terms – an air of invisibility suddenly become visible again due to their symbolic potential. Eastern Germany is no exception, having witnessed vociferous debates over the future of numerous iconic GDR monuments. However, in contrast to other countries emerging from socialism, no monuments were brought down by spontaneous popular protest during the demonstrations of 1989 and 1990; it was rather the Berlin Wall that became the target of aggression and symbolically represented the fall of the SED (see Chapter 5). Instead, the removal of socialist monuments was the subsequent act of local governments, often following protracted debates. It is these debates, and their varied outcomes, that form the focus of this chapter.

Iconoclasm is often associated with spontaneous popular revolt, yet the removal of symbolic cultural capital as a formal, administrative act has seen many a historical precedent.[1] The twentieth century alone offers numerous examples, most famously Lenin's decree of 12 April 1918 'On the monuments of the Republic', demanding the removal of monuments to 'the Tsars and their servants' from public squares and streets, as well as the creation of a 'special commission' to decide on the fate of these monuments and to mobilize artists to design new monuments to the socialist revolution.[2] In a similar vein, a directive of the Allied Control Council from 13 May 1946 ordered the removal of monuments that honoured German military traditions and the National Socialist party, an instruction that was widely interpreted in the Soviet zone of occupation to include many Prussian military monuments.[3] The destruction of iconic symbols need not, however, take place at times of regime change. The wave of destalinization triggered by Khrushchev's 'secret' speech at the twentieth party congress of the CPSU in 1956, for instance, saw the organized removal of numerous monuments to Stalin across Eastern Europe; in the GDR, the monument to Stalin on Stalinallee (subsequently renamed Karl-Marx-Allee and Frankfurter Allee) was removed in a swift operation under the cover of darkness in 1961. As historical figures fell in and out of favour, so too did their concrete effigies, and as Svetlana Boym has calculated, 'the average lifespan of a Soviet monument is approximately that of an average Soviet male – a little over fifty years'.[4] It is notable, however, that the end of socialism in Europe witnessed a more differentiated treatment of monuments than previous regime changes. Although some were destroyed, others were maintained as historical documents or adapted to suit contemporary times, and it is particularly significant that Gorbachev issued a decree on 13 October 1990 'On the prevention of the desecration of monuments which are connected to the history of the state and its symbols',[5] evidently seeking to display a contrasting approach to that of Lenin in 1918.

Whether the destruction of a monument is ordained from above or the result of popular protest, it makes a political statement about the past and the future; destruction is part of the natural cycle of remembering and forgetting, for new collective memories may bring with them instances of 'collective amnesia'.[6] When iconoclasm is carried out by those in power, it may take on a more brutal form of 'repressive erasure',[7] with the explicit purpose of casting memory of a specific past into oblivion. In contrast, 'strategic forgetting' may occur when individuals or societies choose to forget events that are too painful or dangerous to maintain in active memory.[8] In both cases, the concept of forgetting the past in order to allow for future development is central, and proves particularly relevant within the cityscape, where urban space is scarce and of high political and monetary value. Political caesuras, such as the revolution of 1989, thus force decisions to be made regarding the use of space for both symbolic and practical purposes, and the potential for demolition often provokes an intense struggle between the forces of past and future. In some former socialist states, efforts to 'cleanse' city centres of socialist icons yet also maintain them as historical documents have resulted in the construction of 'monument parks', such as Budapest's Szoburpark (or Memento Park) and Lithuania's Grūtas Park (unofficially known as 'Stalin World'). Here they are housed, however, in a bizarre mix of statue graveyard and tourist attraction, for their new location divests them of their former ideological power and, in doing so, diminishes their historical weight.

Discussions and decision-making processes concerning the potential demolition of monuments clearly do not always result in demolition. Indeed, as the case studies in this chapter demonstrate, alternative solutions are often sought, and practical considerations sometimes prevail over moral judgements. Interestingly, structures that remain standing today have often – unexpectedly – become symbols of tolerance and democracy, not only symbolizing an inclusive engagement with the past, but also provoking more genuine popular interaction and debate than during socialist times. Even where demolition does take place, this does not necessarily result in amnesia, for as Winfried Speitkamp states, 'memory of the act of destruction extend[s] the tradition'.[9] In this way, it is not so much the act of demolition itself, but rather the debates, actions and memories surrounding its potential that are revealing. This chapter will thus examine five contrasting case studies; the first two highlight the early debates in Berlin, and concern two monuments slated for removal – Lenin and Thälmann – the second of which has survived. Three further case studies exemplify a variety of decisions in regional towns, highlighting three different outcomes: preservation (Karl Marx Monument in Chemnitz), adaptation (Flag Monument in Halle) and relocation (Karl Marx Relief in Leipzig). Despite their contrasting outcomes, all five display common tropes regarding the discourse surrounding debates and the passing of time, with the notion of democracy and the legacy of 1989 proving to be particularly central to decision-making processes. In this way, they become embedded in a broader understanding and *Aufarbeitung* of the recent German past. Before examining these cases, an initial discussion of the role of monuments in the GDR will elucidate their intended functions, and prepare the ground for understanding their relevance in post-unification Germany.

The Role of Monuments in the GDR

Emerging out of the ruins of the Third Reich, the GDR found its prime legitimacy in antifascism, and was presented as part of a longer

German and international socialist tradition. Symbolic representation of this new political order began long before the foundation of the state itself, and numerous streets and squares were renamed in the immediate post-war years, with Nazi or Wilhelmine names being replaced by those of Marx, Engels, Rosa Luxemburg and other antifascist resistance fighters; in Leipzig alone, this reached 113 by August 1947.[10] Enormous Soviet memorials, such as that in Treptower Park, were also completed before the foundation of the GDR, designed to be sites of mourning for the war dead and of triumphant victory over fascist Germany. The first memorial project to be carried out by the SED was the Gedenkstätte der Sozialisten (Socialists' Memorial Site) in Berlin-Friedrichsfelde, built on the former site of Ludwig Mies van der Rohe's memorial to Liebknecht and Luxemburg, which had been destroyed by the Nazis.[11] The newly developed site, completed in 1951, provided an important memorial for the founding fathers (and mothers) of German socialism, as well as a site at which their successors, such as Wilhelm Pieck, Otto Grotewohl and Walter Ulbricht, could be honoured in future. Architecture was also used to demonstrate a strong socialist tradition. Particularly significant, for instance, was the integration of the portal from the Prussian City Palace into the new State Council Building in the early 1960s. This was not to do with its Prussian heritage, but rather with the fact that Karl Liebknecht had announced a 'Free Socialist Republic' from its balcony on 9 November 1918. This was particularly significant in legitimizing the SED and its version of history, for as Peter Reichel notes, the GDR 'purported to have made good the failed socialist Revolution of 1918/19'.[12] Often designed hand in hand with new urban structures, monuments frequently adopted quasi-religious symbolism to promote a positive emotional relationship with the state, and were commonly seen to be little more than symbols of power, for their intended messages were unambiguous and directed from above.[13] Otto Grotewohl made the relationship between art and politics particularly clear in 1951: 'Literature and the visual arts are subordinate to politics, but it is clear that they exert a strong influence on politics. Ideas in art must follow the direction of the political struggle. ... Whatever proves to be right in politics must necessarily also be so in art'.[14] As with all intended monuments, they said more about those who erected them than the past they sought to portray.

The majority of GDR monuments fell into five categories, all of which sought to make a clear link between allegedly 'progressive' elements of the past and the socialist present. The first consisted of monuments to the victims of fascism and the communist resistance movement, in which victims were presented as active, rather than passive; their resistance, rather than their suffering, became the focus of monuments. Fritz Cremer's Buchenwald memorial is one of the best-known examples of this aesthetic, in which the concentration camp victims stand defiantly looking to the future (see Chapter 3). The second group consisted of Soviet memorials (typically *Ehrenmäler* – monuments designed to 'honour' a particular group), largely erected under the Soviet occupation after the end of the war and often on the sites of mass graves of fallen soldiers. At such memorials, the victory of the Red Army over fascism was celebrated in highly symbolic fashion, whether through heroic, quasi-religious soldier figures (such as at Treptow), or the placing of T-34 tanks on pedestals (such as at Berlin's Tiergarten memorial).[15] Third, monuments throughout the GDR were erected to socialist martyrs and hero figures, as well as to the ideological fathers of communism, most notably Lenin, Marx and Ernst Thälmann. Although other figures and local heroes were celebrated, these three figures dominated, with plans for large-scale monuments to Wilhelm Pieck, Otto Grotewohl, Rosa Luxemburg and Karl Liebknecht coming to nothing.[16] Repetition, it seemed, was simpler and more effective than variety, and such monuments were always marked by heroic and formulaic aesthetics. Fourth, reliefs and plaques to the 'progressive' historical heritage of the GDR were erected throughout the GDR in remembrance of events such as the revolutions of 1848 and 1918. Close to the site of the State Council Building, for instance, two reliefs were installed on the north side of the Neuer Marstall building in 1988, in celebration of the seventieth anniversary of the November revolution on 1918, one of which depicts Liebknecht's proclamation from the castle. Monuments relating to the broader socialist heritage also feature in this group, such as the *Spanienkämpfer-Denkmal* (Monument to Fighters of the Spanish Civil War) in Berlin, or monuments dedicated to friendship with other socialist countries. Fifth, monuments and reliefs in honour of collective groups and events in the GDR were erected, largely from the 1960s onwards. Such groups included *Aufbauhelfer* (workers involved in the 'construction of socialism' – two such statues by Fritz Cremer still stand opposite the Rotes Rathaus) and *Betriebskampfgruppen* (workers' militia groups), as well as policemen and border guards killed in action.[17] More generally, however, the figure of the 'worker' featured strongly, often on reliefs and murals, as well as farmers, construction workers and those working in technological or scientific careers. Max Lingner's mural on the (now) Federal Ministry of Finance (see Chapter 4) and Walter Womacka's frieze on the Haus des Lehrers near Alexanderplatz both stand today as striking examples of socialist realist images of working life in the GDR.

In all five areas, a clear historical line linked past and present, as the SED sought to cast socialist communicative memory in stone, in the attempt to instil in younger generations a sense of loyalty to the socialist and antifascist cause. From the mid 1960s onwards, many new monument projects brought together different commemorative strands, not only indicating the future direction of socialism, but also in order to present the GDR as an inevitable and 'natural' outcome of the progression of German history. The SED was all too aware that memorial sites do not carry intrinsic meaning, and that places can only be invested with active memory through human interaction. For this reason, monuments became the locus of ritual acts, such as the laying of wreaths, annual processions, public announcements and commemorative ceremonies, where communicative memories found expression; they became central to the state's symbolic self-representation, and functioned as ritual stages on which the power of the SED was choreographed. One way of ensuring this was to integrate monuments into larger concepts of urban planning, and in later years new housing developments were rarely complete without a monument or prominent wall painting to indicate their socialist roots. Many such projects – including the case studies in this chapter – took on enormous proportions, and were usually directly commissioned by the party. In this way, they served as visual symbols of SED power, rather than promoting or challenging new artistic movements. Many monuments were also strongly influenced by the aesthetics of Soviet visual art, not least because a significant number of the larger commissions in the GDR went to Soviet artists, such as Lev Kerbel and Nikolai Tomski.

On the surface, it seems that the SED may have had some success in instilling in citizens a heroic image of socialism through such images. As Brian Ladd argues, the unfamiliar aesthetics of the Marx Engels Forum in East Berlin, in which the figures of Marx and Engels are not defiantly heroic and Marx is rather unusually sitting down, attracted much criticism before its completion in 1986, largely because 'these new artistic forms did not measure up to expectations'.[18] However, this does not mean that other monumental structures were necessarily popular; criticism of Lev Kerbel's Ernst Thälmann Monument of the same year, for example, focused on its highly formulaic aesthetics, and accompanied widespread resentment that a GDR artist was not chosen for the commission. Indeed, as artist Krzysztof Wodiczko claims, the functionalization of sculpture in the GDR led to 'the petrification of the art of sculpture into depleted pathos formulas',[19] and a survey carried out at four Berlin monuments in July 1990 revealed the ambivalence of the majority of residents towards such structures.[20] Town planner

Dieter Hoffmann-Axthelm even goes so far as to claim that such monuments were intentionally ugly: 'by expressly refusing to communicate with the beholder through beauty, instead cultivating monstrosity in a one-sided manner, they completely fulfil their political goal: that of intimidating and humiliating people'.[21] It is, thus, unsurprising that such structures are viewed to be more than simply aesthetically flawed; as Andreas Huyssen claims, 'The monumental ... is politically suspect because it is seen as representative of nineteenth-century nationalisms and of twentieth-century totalitarianism. It is socially suspect because it is the privileged mode of expression of mass movements and mass politics'.[22]

However, the understanding of GDR monuments as little more than symbols of power is a convenient condemnation that overlooks several complexities. First, activities behind the scenes revealed that a large number of GDR monuments were the result of much political wrangling, and many never came to fruition. Rather than clearly symbolizing a regime's power, Brian Ladd claims that such monuments 'offer murky testimony to the compromises – between regime and artists, regime and populace, or different leadership factions – that brought them into being'.[23] Second, the intended meanings of monuments can never be guaranteed, and a memorial's effects are rarely identical to the intentions of its creators. This was particularly true in the GDR, where the monument landscape and official collective memory were determined by the party leadership, yet correlated very little with the communicative memory of the population at large. In this way, ritual ceremonies often became emotionally empty acts, and as Hubertus Adam observes, 'In place of a remembrance tradition there was ritual; in place of the inwardly convincing monument, there was the authoritarian monument', which was employed in 'strictly organized, redundant memory discourses'.[24] Yet this does not mean that monuments were devoid of meaning for the population, for commemorative ceremonies and monuments need not always be understood as top-down constructs. The visible authority of GDR monuments meant that they could, for instance, become the focus of popular resentment, or function as 'indexes of the unchangingness of everyday life', thus adopting a somewhat more prosaic meaning.[25] It is notable that many monuments also provoked subversive jokes, nicknames and popular stories among the local population. Berlin's Marx and Engels Monument, for instance, was quickly dubbed 'The Pensioners', with the two figures allegedly awaiting an exit permit to the West, as Marx is sitting on what looks like a suitcase.[26] Another popular quip in the mid 1980s pointed towards the huge cost of the monument, with Marx asking,

'How much has all this cost?', and Engels responding, 'You had better sit down before I tell you'.[27] In this way, official monuments also offered space for counter-narratives, sometimes – as the following sections will demonstrate – extending their lives beyond the death of socialism.

Transition: October 1989 to October 1990

It was not until political and social change took place that the popular interpretations of monuments could find public expression or that symbolic structures could become imbued with new meanings. In late 1989, 'intended' monuments in the GDR suddenly became 'unintended', and while their physical form remained unchanged, their symbolic meanings rapidly evolved, allowing them to be appropriated by new groups with new causes. Although the Berlin Wall initially received the brunt of vandalism and popular protest, the early period of November and December 1989 also saw the removal of some plaques, particularly those quoting Erich Honecker, yet most were anonymously handed over to Berlin's Märkisches Museum within a few days.[28] It was not until spring 1990 that some monuments were vandalized and the urban landscape began to change more rapidly, seeing the removal of commemorative structures by local authorities, as well as party insignia, plaques and socialist slogans. At the same time, many street names were vandalized or painted over, and some streets were spontaneously renamed by residents with makeshift signs.[29] Over subsequent months and years, a number were then officially changed by local authorities, alongside the renaming of schools, factories and public buildings, and in 1993 an 'Independent Commission on the Renaming of Streets' was set up to examine street names in the historic centre of Berlin.[30] Due to the course of twentieth-century German history, some long-standing residents saw their street name change for a third or even fourth time.

Debates surrounding the future of monuments swiftly followed the first phase of half-hearted vandalism, and by mid 1990 filled multiple sides of newspaper print. Not only did increasing swathes of graffiti highlight their redundant political status, but the controversial aesthetic quality of many monuments, as well as their sheer quantity – East Berlin reportedly contained some six hundred monuments, including seven of Lenin[31] – provoked the ire of many artists and social commentators. More often than not, their dismantlement was called for in what artist Joachim John controversially referred to as 'a necessary hygiene' and a 'cleaning' of the city.[32] In a year in which East Germans produced three times more rubbish per capita than West Germans,[33] calls for the disposal of the past notably escalated. As artist Joachim Scheel argued, monumental art could be seen as little more than 'un-art on high pedestals' (*hochgesockelte Unkunst*) and 'artistic atrocities', which represented a 'daily deformation of taste' (*tägliche Geschmacksverbildung*) that necessarily provoked 'every citizen of the GDR'.[34] Above all, however, it was the conservative tabloids such as *Bild* that called for demolition, claiming unanimous popular agreement on the matter,[35] a claim that this chapter proves far from accurate. In response to such calls, the 'Political Monuments of the GDR' Initiative was set up by art history students in East and West Berlin, who, together with the New Society for the Visual Arts (NGBK) and the Active Museum of Fascism and Resistance in Berlin, organized an exhibition in the autumn of 1990 about GDR monuments in Berlin, and worked to raise public awareness of their importance as historical documents.[36] As they claimed, lessons had been learned from the removal of monuments in 1945: 'this experience shows that their removal and expulsion leaves behind a gap, which makes historical analysis impossible and creates space for dangerous myths'.[37] The exhibition thus highlighted the existence of alternatives to the binary options of preservation or destruction, and sought to provoke discussion on a number of creative solutions.

It is worth briefly exploring the alternatives that were available in 1990, which consisted of variations on four basic models, each of which will be discussed in the following case studies: preservation, removal, relocation or modification. In some cases the decision to retain a monument was legally binding, most notably in the case of Soviet war memorials and graves, which were protected in article 18 of the German-Soviet agreement of 9 November 1990.[38] As a result, Soviet war memorials have not only been maintained but in many cases renovated; at Treptower Park, renovation also included the erection of explanatory information boards in order to place the memorial site in context, a solution that has been used at many sites where memorials have been retained unchanged. On occasion, mounted plaques may actually serve the purpose of rededicating a preserved monument; the 1972 monument to 'Polish Soldiers and German Antifascists in the Second World War' in Friedrichshain park, for example, gained a plaque in 1995 to dedicate it also to those who fought as soldiers 'in the Polish underground state, the allied forces and the Polish resistance movement', thus recognizing its previous propagandistic purpose and enabling it to serve a broader commemorative purpose, but also – indirectly – turning it into an anti-Soviet memorial.[39] Many monuments have, however, remained uncommented, often becoming increasingly accepted over time. Among these, it is notable that the Marx Engels Monument appears to have found widespread acceptance, becoming a significant tourist magnet in central Berlin, perhaps precisely because of the less heroic stature of its subjects and their more human scale, which allows children to clamber on them and tourists to be photographed on Marx's knees.[40]

The second option – removal – clearly requires a monument to be taken from public view. However, this does not necessarily mean complete erasure; even if the material is fully destroyed, it still remains as a mass that may be recycled or reused, thus continuing a lifecycle open to remembrance. The Berlin Wall, for instance, has been put to many a practical, touristic and commemorative use (see Chapter 5), and where monuments are dismantled but not destroyed – as in the case of Berlin's Lenin Monument, discussed below – they are still available for potential future use. Similarly, the storage of monuments in archives or museums ensures that they may, in future years, be reappropriated. The re-erection of numerous Prussian statues in the 1980s in the GDR – most notably the equestrian statue of Fredrick the Great on Unter den Linden – provides testimony to this. A monument that has been taken down but not destroyed may, thus, also fall into the third category: relocation. The 'monument parks' discussed above provide the most obvious example of this, yet it is not a model found in Germany. While a small collection of fallen monuments briefly existed in Gundelfingen in Bavaria, home of the stonemason and collector Josef Kurz, the collection was not continued following his death in 1994, with most exhibits eventually being passed to the Haus der Geschichte in Bonn.[41] The suggestions in 1990 of artists Rainer Süß and Joachim Scheel to erect a *Monsterkabinett* (literally 'monster cabinet') or *Kuriositätensammlung* ('collection of curios') on the grounds of the former Stasi headquarters at Normannenstraße also came to nothing,[42] and a more recent suggestion in 2012 by Peter Ramsauer (CDU), Federal Minister of Construction, to deposit the Marx Engels Monument at the Socialists' Memorial Site in Berlin met with widespread criticism.[43] Monuments from the GDR have, however, been relocated in recent years for both practical and political reasons, as seen with the Marx Engels Monument in Berlin and the Karl Marx Relief in Leipzig (discussed below).

The final option for monuments after the demise of socialism was the most wide-ranging: modification. This could encompass anything from temporary artistic engagement with a monument to permanent redevelopment. Some artists, such as Sophie Calle, based projects around the absence of monuments,[44] while others worked with their presence, encouraging passers-by to view them through different eyes. The Marx Engels Monument, for instance, has been at the centre of several such projects, with the two figures being eerily cloaked by artist Stefan Moses in August 1990,[45] and surrounded by a 'golden temple' by Herbert Fell in June 1993, which was gradually pulled down over a month, reminding viewers of the fall of the Berlin Wall.[46] The *Betriebsgruppendenkmal* (monument to workers' militias) in Berlin's Prenzlauer Berg Volkspark took on a whole range of guises before finally being removed in February 1992. These ranged from the attempt to train plants to grow over it, to shrouding it in a white cloth and wrapping it in barbed wire from the Wall. Official measures also involved the erection of an information board providing background information on the monument's history, as well as the removal of the bronze figure of a boy handing flowers to the soldiers.[47] While the local authorities had deliberately wanted to encourage discussion, it seemed that the monument was too provocative to remain. Other monuments have undergone a complete facelift, either officially, as in the case of Halle's Flag Monument discussed below, or as a result of street artists, as seen further afield in Sofia in 2011, where soldiers on a Red Army monument were transformed into storybook characters from Superman and Ronald McDonald to Santa Claus.[48]

At different moments in time, a monument may, of course, fall into all of the above four categories, and more than twenty-five years on, the fate of socialist monuments continues to be decided. While the heated nature of debates from the early 1990s may have died down, ongoing discussions over the future of such monuments continue to demonstrate their 'conflict value'. The examples discussed below demonstrate a range of monuments and locations, providing insight into the way these sites of memory have both changed and provoked change over time.

Eastern Berlin I: From Unification to Lenin's Fall

The early 1990s witnessed the largest number of demolition orders, when emotions were raw and the political authorities were keen to demonstrate the beginning of a new era. Two events in 1991 furthered calls for demolition, especially in Berlin. First, the decision was made in June to return the seat of Germany's capital city back to Berlin, thus raising the city's symbolic profile. Chancellor Helmut Kohl is reported to have said that he did not know what to tell foreign guests when he accompanied them along Wilhelm-Pieck-Straße and later past the Lenin Monument.[49] Second, popular responses to the attempted coup d'état in Moscow in August that year included the toppling of socialist monuments, widespread media coverage of which reminded leaders in Berlin of their symbolic potential. Decisions in Berlin remained uncoordinated in the first years, however, as it was not until March 1992 that a commission was formed to investigate the future of the city's monuments. The most high-profile monument to fall in Berlin during these early years was the Lenin Monument in Friedrichshain (see Figure 2.1), one of numerous Lenins to be removed across the country, but the only one of such gigantic proportions.[50]

In honour of Lenin's hundredth birthday, on 19 April 1970, this nineteen-metre-high figure of Lenin, made from Ukrainian red granite and designed by the Soviet artist Nikolai Tomski, was unveiled on Leninplatz in front of 200,000 people. At the unveiling ceremony, Walter Ulbricht spoke of its role as a testimonial to the efforts of the working class to bring about the victory of socialism,[51] and the Soviet ambassador, Pjotr Abrassimov, called it an 'emblem of German-Soviet friendship'.[52] It was designed to stand at the centre of a new housing project, with the sloping line of its top edge mirroring the diagonal outline of the apartment blocks in front of which it stood; its prime position was likened to that of a keystone in an archway.[53] The ensemble was thus to represent the coming together of past and present, placing the GDR within a clear socialist tradition. Although one of many Lenin monuments in the GDR, this one stood in prime position, and was erected at the height of the Federal Republic's *Ostpolitik*, a time during which the SED feared that Bonn wished to isolate the GDR. Like a number of other new monuments at the time, it thus explicitly thematized the bonds of friendship between the GDR and other socialist countries, and its reverse side pictured a relief of German and Soviet workers shaking hands.

As one of the most prominent examples of socialist art, this monument became the focus of much attention after 1989, and entered the political limelight in September 1990 when it featured in the art project entitled *Die Endlichkeit der Freiheit* (The Finiteness of Freedom), a brief but symbolically significant prologue to its demolition. The project, sponsored by the German Academic Exchange Service (DAAD), saw eleven international artists produce installations that highlighted corresponding locations in East and West Berlin. Polish/Canadian artist Krzysztof Wodiczko chose the Lenin Monument and 'Haus Huth' at Potsdamer Platz, also in danger of demolition, as the backdrop for four night-time projections. On two evenings he transformed Lenin into a Polish shopper, wearing a red and white striped pullover and pushing a shopping trolley full of bargains from discount stores such as Aldi.[54] While some residents saw this to represent the defamation

Figure 2.1 Lenin Monument (Nikolai Tomski, 1970) on the former Leninplatz, Berlin (destroyed 1991/92). Photograph by Alan Deighton.

of a prominent historical personality[55] – it should be noted that those who gained apartments around Leninplatz were largely loyal GDR citizens – the installation highlighted the monument's role as a broader symbol of the GDR. On the one hand, the easy transformation of Lenin into a consumer tourist highlighted the formulaic nature of its monumental design, underlining the highly functional nature of propaganda art, which often failed to engage the population emotionally. On the other hand, Wodiczko's installation provided a critique of the demise of socialism, showing it to have sold out to the cheap mass consumerism of capitalism less than a year after the demonstrations of 1989. In this way, the Lenin Monument became a canvas for a range of interpretations.

The monument received considerably more attention immediately prior to its demolition, a lengthy process that began in November 1991 and culminated in the renaming of the square from Leninplatz to Platz der Vereinten Nationen (United Nations' Square) in March 1992 – a name equally notable for didacticism. Despite a variety of alternative suggestions to demolition, such as growing ivy on the monument, allowing Christo to 'wrap' it, setting it crooked or displacing it to a sculpture park,[56] members of the district council of Friedrichshain voted for its removal on 19 September 1991 by forty votes to thirty-three.[57] Within a month, the monument's protected status was controversially removed by Berlin's Senator for Urban Development and Environmental Protection, Volker Hassemer (CDU), and the demolition process began. This was not, however, straightforward: legal challenges from Tomski's widow delayed progress, and the immense size and weight of the monument caused numerous technical problems, resulting in costs of 500,000 DM, a dismantling period of three months, and the contracting of a second building company to complete the job.[58] There was also outspoken resistance from residents, art historians and town planners, in the form of petitions, demonstrations, vigils and human chains. Matthias Matussek, writing in *Der Spiegel*, even compared Leninplatz shortly before the demolition to Lourdes, as a place of pilgrimage and devotion.[59] Media attention reached its height once the head of Lenin was detached, with the image of his suspended head featuring in all major newspapers; according to *die tageszeitung*, the date of this event was journalists' most sought-after piece of information in 1991.[60] In January 1992, while demolition was still underway, the annual procession to the graves of Rosa Luxemburg and Karl Liebknecht took place from Leninplatz, led by a cart carrying stones of the fallen Lenin which were then placed on the graves of Luxemburg and Liebknecht.[61] Organized by the Bürgerinitiative Lenindenkmal (Lenin Monument Citizens' Initiative), this ritual demonstrated that the demolition debate provoked emotional responses from Berliners in a way that the monument had rarely done during GDR times, for it provided a forum for the expression of wider concerns regarding the GDR past and the politics of the present.

Those in favour of demolition – largely representatives of the CDU, FDP and a majority of the SPD fraction – saw Lenin's removal to be a necessary symbolic act in 'overcoming' the socialist past. This represented less an atavistic belief in the power of the monument itself than an assertion of newfound authority and moral standing. Indeed, almost two years after the fall of the Wall, the images of Lenin's head hanging over Berlin represented a symbolic, stage-managed counterpart to those of the spontaneous events of 9 November 1989 – directed this time by the authorities rather than the masses.[62] It is little surprise that Berlin's Mayor, Eberhard Diepgen (CDU), proclaimed this event to represent a continuation – and even completion – of the revolution of 1989;[63] similarly, Senator Hassemer claimed that demolition was justified by the anger of demonstrators in 1989: 'If the world of politics pooh-poohs this anger … it is disregarding honourable emotions … Revolutions don't wait for expert commissions and don't comply with their recommendations'.[64] Demolition clearly allowed the new regime to demonstrate its authority in symbolic fashion at a time when the prosecution of former SED leaders was proving slow and problematic, unemployment was rife and the prospect of Kohl's 'blossoming landscapes' seemed increasingly distant. Interestingly, those against demolition – from art historians and town planners to residents and left-wing parties, such as the PDS and the Alliance '90/Greens (hereafter Greens or Green Party) – called on imagery from 1989 to an even greater extent. A group of demonstrators, for example, draped a banner across Lenin's chest reading *keine Gewalt* (no violence), one of the mottos of 1989;[65] others erected a billboard in front of the site which stated, 'Here the Berlin Senate is disposing of German-German history in the context of a cleansing mission against those who think differently [*Säuberungsaktion gegen Andersdenkende*]',[66] recalling Rosa Luxemburg's famous line about *Andersdenkende* that was used by the opposition movement in the GDR. The Bürgerinitiative Lenindenkmal was founded, a vigil organized, and candles lit: all reminiscent of the desire in 1989 to stage peaceful protests in the face of a regime perceived to be acting in self-interest. Parallels were also drawn between the authorities and the SED, with the demolition being compared to the monument's 'undemocratic' erection in 1970, as well as the demolition of the Berlin City Palace in 1950.[67] Graffiti took the authoritarian nature of the demolition even further, reading *Wann brennen die Bücher?* (When will the books burn?), thus drawing parallels with Nazi policies.⁶⁸ Clearly, both sides of the debate centred their discourse around the slogans and images of 1989, as well as the former actions of the SED, and as Matthias Matussek observed, the debate was less about logical argumentation than 'tribal rituals', with Lenin representing 'the totem pole of the perished GDR'.⁶⁹ Indeed, the monument became, for all concerned, a new symbol of the GDR and, above all, of its democratic deficit.

The battle for and against the Lenin Monument also reflected new power struggles since 1990. It is little surprise that the campaign for demolition, led largely by the parties that had benefitted from unification, was supported by a former West Berlin radio station, Hundert, 6, whose reports in the late 1980s had been highly critical of the GDR. By collecting 42,000 DM for the demolition campaign, the station continued its clear condemnation of the GDR regime.⁷⁰ Those opposing demolition often did so, however, as much out of resistance to the new regime as in defence of the old. As one member of the *Bürgerinitiative* claimed, 'I'm not at all bothered about Lenin himself, but about demonstrating our power and not letting ourselves be monopolized'.⁷¹ Others pointed towards more pressing issues in Berlin, such as rising unemployment, housing poverty and poor infrastructure, with the leader of the PDS, Gregor Gysi, denouncing the demolition as a 'pure demonstration of power and a waste of money'.⁷² Members of the PDS and Green Party also highlighted unsavoury elements of Prussian history that still stood firm in Berlin, some provocatively calling for the demolition of the *Siegessäule* (Berlin's 'victory column' glorifying the Prussian wars);⁷³ in contrast, writer Stefan Heym cynically suggested that the authorities should replace Lenin's head with that of a 'less objectionable' figure, such as Bismarck, who, 'as founder of the Reich', was 'a kind of forerunner of our Dr Kohl'.⁷⁴ Those who sought a more differentiated view made other suggestions: Senator for Construction Wolfgang Nagel (SPD), who likened its demolition to that of the City Palace in 1950, proposed allowing the monument to become overgrown and placing a 'swords into ploughshares' monument next to it; former activist Bärbel Bohley suggested leaving all monuments for at least ten years in order to allow for some emotional distance.⁷⁵

The passing of time has had some interesting effects, and Lenin has not yet vanished from the cityscape. After its eventual piecemeal removal, the monument was buried in 129 pieces in a woodland location in Köpenick – as the authorities hoped, 'out of sight, out of mind'.⁷⁶ In the weeks and months following demolition, however, memories of Lenin continued to mark the newly named Platz der Vereinten Nationen; graffiti on the remaining platform read *Und die Erde war wüst und leer* (Genesis 1:2: And the earth was without form, and void), a large silhouette of the monument was sprayed on its surface, and smaller versions were stencil-sprayed onto the ground in the vicinity, sometimes next to another iconic symbol of East Berlin, the TV tower.[77] Small posters were also stuck to the flagpoles, showing images, texts, poems and caricatures, some of which depicted the replacement of communist symbols with capitalist ones.[78] Once the platform was removed and a fountain installed, graffiti symbols still reappeared; the act of destruction had created a new tradition. Given this trend, it is interesting that the *Berliner Zeitung* reported in 2001 that the former mayor of Friedrichshain would have decided differently ten years on, voting rather to keep Lenin; others, including a representative of the Senate Administration for Urban Development, also claimed that time had softened the views of many.[79]

A recent epilogue to Lenin's destruction has, indeed, demonstrated changing attitudes: in September 2015, his head was exhumed from the Köpenick forest and put on display at the exhibition 'Unveiled: Berlin and Its Monuments' at Spandau Citadel from April 2016. Although initial suggestions to display the monument within a museum context met with positive reactions from the PDS and SPD in 2005, they provoked widespread disapproval from CDU and FDP representatives in the Berlin Senate. Frank Henkel, General Secretary of the CDU in Berlin, for example, claimed that 'left-wing historical ideology belongs exactly where the Lenin Monument is now located – buried deep underground'.[80] Lenin hit the headlines once again in 2014, when the Berlin Senate vetoed the exhuming of Lenin's head, due to an apparent mix of technical, financial and preservational concerns – possibly also ideologically motivated. Above all, however, it was claimed that there were no records to show exactly where the monument was buried, unleashing a wave of interest in the monument's whereabouts and a number of people involved in the demolition process coming forward to provide information. Evidently surprised by the public reaction, the Senate reversed its decision within a month, allowing the head to eventually be unearthed and put on display.[81] On its arrival in Spandau, the town councillor for culture, Gerhard Hanke (CDU), claimed that this was a 'highlight', and as historical witnesses, sculptures should not be destroyed.[82] Increasing historical distance appears to have rendered the monument a more culturally accepted relict of the past, and one that is beginning – twenty-five years on – to lose the political brisance of the early post-unification years. Perhaps the most interesting aspect of this recent debate, however, is that it has resulted in a thorough documenting of the monument's biography. While it was the aim of the exhibition to unveil and document political monuments that had been removed or destroyed over the course of history, the media attention devoted to Lenin resulted in an unexpected number of historical actors coming forward. Documentary evidence of the demolition, such as video footage taken by the then site manager, has now become part of the exhibition alongside documentation concerning the unearthing of the head.[83] As many other examples in this book demonstrate, this is indicative of a wider trend to democratize and record our dealings with the past.

In other parts of eastern Germany, the passing of time also appears to have witnessed a historical re-evaluation of Lenin monuments; Eisleben and Potsdam, for instance, both witnessed debates over the re-erection of their former Lenin monuments in 2003 and 2006 respectively (with intermittently recurring calls), and Schwerin's town council voted in 2007 to keep its surviving Lenin monument, adding to it an information panel that provides context on the history of the monument and, significantly, Lenin's crimes.[84] Interestingly, these and other Lenin monuments have become the subject of several publications, websites and documentary projects, once again with the aim of documenting history.[85] Dresden's Lenin monument, which was taken down in 1992, witnessed a particularly innovative 'comeback' in 2004, in which artist Rudolf Herz exhibited the disembodied Lenin bust, along with those of two anonymous workers, on an open articulated lorry that drove through central Europe for four weeks. The provocative images of the three figures tied to the lorry with heavy ropes triggered memories of socialism and reflections on its icons among those who witnessed this 'mobile monument', thus encouraging dialogue between past and present. Recorded as an exhibition, a film and a book, it has become part of the recent documentary trend.[86]

Eastern Berlin II: From the Commission's Recommendations to Thälmann's Survival

The controversial events in Friedrichshain made the formation of a commission to review Berlin's monuments all the more pressing, and it was only days after the last piece of the Lenin Monument was carried away that the Berlin Senate called for the formation of such a body. Officially constituted on 27 March 1992, the 'Commission for Dealing with Post-war Political Monuments in Former East Berlin' was given the task of documenting all architectural ensembles, sculptures, statues, busts and memorials, as well as determining criteria for the evaluation of such structures and developing 'an initial overall concept for the handling of political monuments'.[87] The ten members came from east and west and were largely artists, art historians, heritage professionals and town planners, although the inclusion of two members of the city council led some to question its independent status.[88] Others, such as art historian Hans-Ernst Mittig, who refused participation in the commission, claimed not only that the formation of the commission was far too late, but that its focus purely on east Berlin represented a missed opportunity.[89] The failure to examine Cold War monuments also in west Berlin indicated that there was a political agenda behind the establishment of the commission. The final report, published in February 1993, recommended the preservation of most monuments, albeit sometimes with modifications or historical contextualization. The small number that were recommended for removal were monuments and plaques in memory of GDR border guards killed in service, reliefs depicting the November revolution on the Neuer Marstall, the Spartakus Monument on Chausseestraße, and most notably the colossal Thälmann Monument in Prenzlauer Berg (see Figure 2.2). It was inevitably the Thälmann Monument that attracted most attention, and which represented the next major battleground after Lenin.

Figure 2.2 Thälmann Monument (Lev Kerbel, 1986), Greifswalder Straße, Prenzlauer Berg, Berlin. Photograph by Anna Saunders.

Monuments to Ernst Thälmann could be found in most sizable towns in the GDR, alongside streets, schools and factories in his name. As a worker who became the leader of the Communist Party during the Weimar Republic and who was then imprisoned by the Nazis in 1933 and killed in Buchenwald concentration camp in 1944, Thälmann became a central antifascist martyr figure in the GDR. Not only did the GDR boast forty memorial sites to Ernst Thälmann, but approximately 350 further sites honoured his name in concrete fashion.[90] Most significantly, his name was given to the children's organization of the FDJ, the Pionierorganisation Ernst Thälmann, where his nickname 'Teddy' was affectionately used. The refrain of the *Thälmann-Lied* perhaps best summarized his status in the GDR: 'Thälmann and Thälmann above all / Germany's eternal son / Thälmann has never fallen / voice and fist of the nation'. Given his status in the GDR, it is little surprise that a colossal monument to the GDR's 'immortal son' was built in Berlin: a fourteen-metre-high and fifteen-metre-wide bronze bust of Thälmann with a raised fist in front of a stylized flag bearing a Soviet star. What is surprising, however, is that the monument was only completed in 1986. Plans for a Thälmann monument in Berlin were initiated as early as 1949, yet due to a long and complicated history of political wrangling, these were eventually shelved in the early 1960s.[91] It was not until the late 1970s that ideas for a monument in Prenzlauer Berg were developed to stand at the heart of a new, high-profile housing programme. Despite proposals by several German artists, it was Soviet sculptor Lev Kerbel who was commissioned by the Politbüro to design the monument, a decision that caused resentment among local artists and a dislike for its aesthetics;[92] indeed, Thälmann's face resembled that of Lenin to such an extent that it was commonly referred to as 'Lehmann'.[93]

Unveiled in honour of Thälmann's hundredth birthday in April 1986 as part of the new housing complex, the monument clearly served the self-legitimization of the SED, bolstering the myth of Thälmann as an antifascist and communist hero; one of the inscribed pillars installed near the monument cited Honecker, who praised Thälmann as a 'bold fighter for freedom, humanity and the social progress of our people'.[94] The square was used for official ceremonies, such as the swearing-in of soldiers or the entry of children into the Young Pioneers, and it was no coincidence that the monument was placed on the daily route of the SED bigwigs' drive from their housing complex in Wandlitz to the centre of Berlin. In the words of Thomas Flierl, the monument stood for a 'profoundly undemocratic relationship between politics, art and the public';[95] it was also somewhat ironic that the monument was to represent the working classes, yet those who lived in the new housing complex were 'hand-picked' citizens.⁹⁶ For these reasons, the inscribed pillars with quotations by Honecker and Thälmann were removed from the monument in June 1990 (and are now exhibited at the Spandau exhibition), in an attempt to distance it from the SED regime.⁹⁷ However, the Prenzlauer Berg district council agreed shortly afterwards that it would not undertake any rash decisions,⁹⁸ and it was only after the commission's report, which labelled the monument a 'mistake' and criticized the 'heroizing, uncritical representation' of Thälmann,⁹⁹ that it narrowly voted in favour of removing the monument in May 1993.¹⁰⁰ The ensuing costs proved, however, to be so prohibitive – at an estimated three to four million DM¹⁰¹ – that the monument was never removed. External offers to relieve the district of its former icon came to nothing, and Berlin's priorities lay elsewhere.

Discussions remained protracted throughout this period, especially in the wake of Lenin's contentious 'fall'. In the summer of 1993, the district's Office for Cultural Affairs and the Prenzlauer Berg Museum held an exhibition about the monument, outlining the different options for its future in order to encourage reflection and prevent a 'premature suppression' of public discussion.¹⁰² Finances aside, the district council was also reluctant to contract a demolition company before plans were in place for the redevelopment of the square – a mistake that was evident from the hole left by Lenin. An external assessor was thus contracted to investigate redevelopment options, and the report presented five variants, only one of which involved complete removal. Although those who had voted for demolition objected that the assessor had not kept to his brief, his suggestions (including 'hiding' the monument behind trees or confining its dominant position) only served to provoke further discussion on its future.¹⁰³

While the outcome of the Thälmann debate was very different to that concerning Lenin, it revealed a similar battleground of interests. Advocates of Thälmann's removal were also largely represented by the CDU, FDP and SPD, yet it is interesting that there were fewer vehement calls for its destruction. These groups largely supported the arguments of the commission, highlighting the monument's authoritarian history and presenting it as politically and aesthetically suspect, especially in light of Thälmann's pro-Stalinist stance and support of the 'social fascist' theory, thus weakening the left wing at the end of the Weimar Republic. Some former GDR artists also opposed the monument due to the SED's abrupt volte-face in favour of Kerbel; sculptress and commission member Ingeborg Hunzinger, for instance, claimed that 'the history of the monument's origins is as violent as the monument', and that attempts to 'hide' it under greenery were 'cowardly'.¹⁰⁴ Among those opposing demolition, however, there were few voices in favour of leaving the monument unchanged, with the PDS and the Greens both proposing a competition to redevelop the area around the monument, thus distancing it from its immediate past. There were three main lines of argument in favour of this option. First, it was claimed to be the most democratic option, with criticism that demolition was analogous to the authoritarian nature of the monument's erection,[105] providing a variant of Hunzinger's argument. The PDS thus pleaded for a 'public, democratic and pluralistic process', attempting to make a decisive break from its SED past.[106] Second, Thälmann's status as – in the words of two residents – an 'important, antifascist resistance fighter' and 'a true workers' leader, not like Honecker', gave rise to claims that his legacy was not so politically contaminated as that of Lenin.[107] GDR propaganda about 'Teddy' had, perhaps, not been entirely ineffective. Third, despite widespread recognition that the monument held little aesthetic appeal, the discussions offered some residents a sense of new-found involvement in the local community and a means through which to counter growing disenchantment with politics and feelings of helplessness at a time when, nearly three years after unification, many East Germans were disillusioned.[108] As in the case of Lenin, the monument thus became reinterpreted from the present perspective, and offered residents and politicians alike a tangible sense of purpose.

Media interest remained high in 1993, yet once demolition became progressively unlikely, attention waned; even in early 1994, a public meeting at which the external assessor's report was presented only attracted twenty-five people.[109] Repeated graffiti attacks on the monument became a regular cause for complaint, highlighted by the large stencilled letters that were sprayed on its base by a residents' group in 1995 that read *eingekerkert, ermordert, beschmiert* (imprisoned, murdered, besmirched).[110] Over time, however, the monument has become an increasingly accepted part of the landscape and even gained protected status in the late 1990s; moreover, in 2014 the whole of the Thälmann Park was placed under a protection order.[111] Despite occasional calls for its demolition from the political right,[112] popular and political will to see it go has clearly declined.[113] There has also been an increasing will to look after it, and the efforts of the left-wing 'Thälmann Monument Action Group', founded in May 2000, to remove graffiti from the monument at regular intervals have met with approval from local residents.[114] From 2006, the district authorities also agreed to take on its cleaning twice a year, and initial approval has been given for night-time illumination of the monument, in order to deter graffiti artists – somewhat ironically for a monument that was listed for demolition fifteen years previously.[115] It is also significant that in 2014 the suggestion was made by district councillors and monument preservation authorities to reinstate (and provide commentary on) the inscribed pillars with quotations by Honecker and Thälmann, in order to return the monument to its original state.[116] Currently located in the high-profile exhibition in Spandau, however, there is no immediate prospect of this happening. The Action Group has also raised significant sums of money to keep the monument in order,[117] and aims to educate local residents, especially young people and graffiti artists, about Thälmann and his politics, and to promote a 'democratic way of dealing with the GDR legacy'.[118] Over the years, the monument has also been appropriated as an anti-war symbol, particularly after the controversial Bundeswehr involvement in the Kosovo conflict,[119] and left-wing groups continue to meet at the monument on occasions such as Thälmann's birthday, as well as for political – largely antifascist – demonstrations. In this way, the monument has been subject to a type of 'vernacular' reframing, in which grassroots initiatives have reinterpreted it for the needs of the present. Although the numbers involved in such demonstrations remain relatively small, the monument has, in a number of ways, provoked very real emotions since unification, and serves as a site of memory that links past and present in a more genuine sense than was ever the case during the GDR.

Demolition Debates beyond Berlin: Chemnitz's 'Nischel'

Discussions in Berlin inevitably influenced decision-making in other eastern German towns, and the fall of Berlin's Lenin was a precursor to dismantlement in other towns, such as Eisleben and Dresden. However, without the same pressures of national symbolism as the new capital, discussions in regional towns often adopted a somewhat different quality, as the following three examples will show. The first of these, the Karl Marx Monument in Chemnitz (see Figure 2.3), bears initial similarities to Berlin's Lenin and Thälmann monuments in both size and function. At 7.1 metres tall, the bronze head of Marx is purported to be the second largest free-standing head in the world, and significantly, the sculptor was once again Soviet artist Lev Kerbel. The monument was also designed to stand at the heart of a new inner-city redevelopment, and to be a central meeting point for official parades and ritual demonstrations. Yet unlike Lenin, the Karl Marx Monument remains standing, and unlike Thälmann, it has become a popular icon of the town.

Figure 2.3 Karl Marx Monument (Lev Kerbel, 1971), Brückenstraße, Chemnitz. Photograph by Anna Saunders.

The post-1989 fate of the Karl Marx Monument is tightly bound up with the post-war history of Chemnitz and local loyalties to the town. As a significant industrial town, Chemnitz suffered devastating destruction during the Second World War, and was rebuilt during GDR times as a modern socialist town with wide streets, large housing blocks and generously sized squares and parks in the inner city. Before redevelopment started, it was renamed Karl-Marx-Stadt in 1953, marking it as an important industrial centre with what was envisaged to be a strong socialist future; the inclusion of an iconic monument to Karl Marx in redevelopment plans was, thus, no surprise. What was surprising, however, was the final design proposed by Kerbel, for it resisted the typically triumphant and heroic poses of other socialist monuments. Instead, Marx's giant head sternly stares forwards with a furrowed brow. As Kerbel explained, 'his influence is global. His ideas and their realization must be visible in his face. Karl Marx doesn't need legs or hands, his head says everything'.[120] Kerbel's main intention was thus to portray Marx as a philosopher, and to link his revolutionary ideas to the redevelopment of the town that carried his name. Many artists and town planners remained unconvinced of this design – commissioned without the legitimacy of a competition – and the regional head of the Association of Visual Arts sent a letter to the district's party headquarters calling it to reconsider.[121] Kerbel's design went ahead, however, and the monument was unveiled to huge crowds on 9 October 1971 in the presence of Honecker. The monument was complemented by a massive tableau on the building behind, designed by graphic artist Heinz Schumann and sculptor Volker Beier, on which the words 'Working men [sic] of all countries unite!' could be read in German, French, English and Russian. This ensemble became a well-known motif, dispatched around the world on the GDR's thirty-five-Pfennig stamp.

Standing in front of a building that housed the district administration of the SED and the district council, the monument stood in a prominent position and soon became a well-known symbol of the town, gaining the local nickname of the 'Nischel', originating from the Saxon dialect for 'head'. Its location also gave rise to derisory jokes, such as the suggestion that Marx should be facing the other way, as laws were being passed behind his back.[122] The gloomy look on his face was also put down to the fact that he could not get to the 'Intershop' across the road – where Western goods were available – despite having to look at it twenty-four hours a day. As a site of official symbolism, yet one that also provoked counter-narratives, the Karl Marx Monument thus became a dual site of memory. Its function was further complicated in the autumn of 1989, when the monument was adopted as the start and end point of the demonstrations. As a figure whose basic principles were upheld by many demonstrators, he served as a 'patron saint' of the demonstrations, wearing at one point a banner that read 'No, I didn't want this socialism!'[123] The chasm between Marxist utopia and 'real existing socialism' – represented by the party headquarters behind the monument – had become all too glaring. Subsequently, the so-called 'House of the Party' became the 'House of Democracy', housing new parties and organizations involved in the restructuring of this period.[124] In March 1990, Willy Brandt also spoke at an SPD rally to 150,000 people in front of the monument,[125] symbolizing its new status as the location of pro-reform ideals.

Around this time, another significant development took place, and in November 1989 the initiative 'For Chemnitz' was founded, with the aim of changing the name of the town back to Chemnitz. This received considerable support, and following the round table's decision to consult residents, a popular vote was held in April 1990, in which nearly three-quarters of all residents took part. Of them, 76.14 per cent voted for reverting to Chemnitz, and only 23.3 per cent for retaining Karl-Marx-Stadt.[126] On 1 June – four months before unification – the town officially took its old name again. This decision was important for two reasons. First, it demonstrated that a large majority of the population felt little emotional attachment to the town's socialist name; inflicted upon them in 1953 by the SED, the new name had represented for many the undemocratic nature of power relations in the GDR.[127] Second, it represented a clear break from the socialist past and a fresh start for the future. Whereas other towns underwent long and controversial decisions on how to symbolically mark this new start – sometimes through the toppling of monuments – the renaming of Chemnitz provided an easy and widely accepted solution to this problem. Subsequently, it seems that the Karl Marx Monument was not as widely attacked as other socialist monuments of similar proportions. Although there was much discussion about its future, no interest groups emerged either for or against demolition, and newspaper surveys in 1990 revealed a balanced range of opinions, with a strong sense of ambivalence among many.[128] The view of one local portrayed the sense that the Marx Monument was not the prime target: 'What has Marx got to do with what happened here? It's others who should be knocked off their pedestals!'[129] Interestingly, the new mayor of Chemnitz, West German Dieter Noll (CDU), also argued in favour of keeping the monument, but 'not as a symbolic figure of a town's name, rather as a nasty memory of past times'.[130] While discussions continued – although without the same urgency as those in Berlin – the monument disappeared from the limelight of the town; postcards picturing the 'Nischel', for example, were almost impossible to find in 1990, with images being deliberately shot away from its view.[131] Similarly, guide books and tourist information skirted around the monument; a thirty-two-page booklet about the town, published as late as 1993/94, fails to mention or picture the monument, even omitting its construction from the chronology of the town.[132] On the one hand, Marx appeared to be an embarrassment to the image of the town; on the other hand, the local population had other immediate concerns, as the once thriving 'Saxon Manchester' became dubbed 'Cinderella of the East', plagued by soaring unemployment rates.[133] In an ironic turn of events, the job centre moved into the building behind Marx's head, only highlighting the failures of the new capitalist system; as one graffiti slogan pointedly read, *Ruinen schaffen ohne Waffen* (make ruins without weapons) – a play on the GDR peace movement's oppositional slogan of *Frieden schaffen ohne Waffen* (make peace without weapons).[134]

With time, however, the monument gradually regained a notable presence. If anything, it was the involvement of outsiders that spurred on locals to be protective of their monument. An early proposition from a Swiss firm wanting to buy the monument, as well as a later offer from the western city of Cologne, for example, both caused consternation, and when Saxony's Minister for Justice, Steffen Heitmann (CDU), called for the monument's removal on a visit to Chemnitz in 1994, he was strongly rebutted by residents, not least because he came from Saxony's more powerful capital of Dresden.[135] Despite recurrent political calls for demolition, largely from the political right, it is significant that no formal plans were considered for this option. An international competition for the redevelopment of the town centre in 1991 saw three prize winners, none of whom proposed demolishing either the monument or the forum around it.[136] In 1994, when the proposal to place the whole forum under monumental protection caused uproar – with many fearing that it would stymie all development in the area and turn the centre into a 'GDR museum' – no-one appeared to question the future of the monument itself.[137] Once again, objections to the proposal were largely targeted at the regional authorities in Dresden, from whom the protection order was issued. As Chemnitz's Head of Town Planning Bela Dören claimed, the decision 'seriously interferes with the autonomous decision-making of the local authority and the people'.[138] The resulting compromise placed certain buildings and elements under protection, including the monument, complete with background tableau and landscaped square immediately surrounding the monument.[139] Subsequently, the monument was cleaned of graffiti more regularly,[140] and lights were once again erected to illuminate the monument – albeit after the Federal Minister of Finance, Theo Waigel (CDU), controversially threatened 'to send no more finances to the East in future, if Chemnitz spends money on something like that'.[141]

By the mid to late 1990s, the Marx Monument had once again adopted a central role within the town, and had been reappropriated by many in light of criticism and challenges from outside. It became particularly prominent in three areas: public protests, tourism and marketing, and art projects. The first of these is perhaps no surprise, for it continues a tradition that began during the *Wende* (the period of transition in 1989 and 1990), and since the demonstrations of 1989 the monument has become a regular meeting point for anti-government protesters rallying against policies regarding social benefits, education cuts, pensions and unemployment.[142] From 2004, protesters against the government's *Hartz IV* reforms concerning unemployment and welfare benefits explicitly appropriated this tradition, staging regular Monday demonstrations much in the same vein as in 1989.[143] While participation was much smaller than in 1989, the monument once again adopted a ritual character, and in objecting to the social cutbacks of a capitalist government, the protests ironically brought the monument close to its intended purpose.

The second area of tourism and marketing has seen the Marx Monument emerge from metaphorical hiding and be reappropriated as a highly visible icon of the town. From the mid 1990s, numerous items of 'Marx kitsch' have been produced for tourists, from confectionary and liqueur bottles bearing Marx's head, to coffee cups, USB sticks, wrist watches, paperweights and *Räuchermännchen* (small figurine incense burners, traditionally made in the nearby Erzgebirge).[144] Some display a humorous relationship to the past; on one liqueur bottle entitled *Denkerschluck* (thinker's shot), for example, the label reads *Trinker aller Länder vereinigt euch* (drinkers of all countries unite).[145] From 1998, the slogan *Stadt mit Köpfchen* (town with brains, a play on the word *Köpfchen*, literally meaning 'little head') was officially used by the town for almost a decade, adorning tourist brochures, information leaflets and posters;[146] and despite adopting a new slogan in 2009, the image of Marx's head still abounds. The symbolic capital of Marx has also been appropriated by numerous companies, with a local car dealership producing an advertising film in which the monument was made to smile.[147] At the time of the World Cup in 2014, the town promoted its welcoming nature by dressing the pedestal in a Germany football shirt and placing black, red and gold stripes on his cheeks, with a trilingual banner behind reading in German, French and English, 'Football fans of all countries, we greet you'.[148] Most spectacular, however, was the erection of a massive Ikea catalogue, measuring just over five metres high and eight metres wide, placed in front of the monument as reading matter for Marx. The installation celebrated the fifteenth anniversary of the local Ikea branch, in return for which the furniture company contributed 25,000 euros to much-needed repairs on the granite pedestal.[149] Perhaps the most ironic engagement with Marx's legacy was the local Sparkasse's decision in 2012 to print bank cards bearing the image of the monument. As one of ten images that clients could choose from, the Marx Monument proved to be the most popular, with roughly half of the first five hundred cards bearing this image.[150] In many ways, these playful marketing initiatives have indicated a more 'normalized' way of dealing with the town's past, and one that demonstrates its arrival in the market economy of unified Germany.

Like local companies and marketing campaigns, artists have also been drawn to the monument. While the majority of suggested projects have not been allowed by the local authorities for fear of damage to the monument, proposed installations have included wrapping it as a Mozartkugel confection (in honour of the forty-fourth German Mozart Festival taking place in Chemnitz), surrounding it with ice, turning it into the largest *Räuchermännchen* in the world, and integrating it into a monument to 1989.[151] The most controversial project was that of Lithuanian artist Deimantas Narkevicius, who had initially hoped to transport the original monument to Münster for the *Skulptur Projekte Münster* 2007, an open-air exhibition of sculptures that takes place in Münster every ten years. When this project was refused by the town, he then proposed making an exact copy of the monument by taking its imprint. While this second suggestion was refused primarily on the grounds that the monument could be damaged in the process of taking an imprint, it seems that other concerns also existed.[152] On the one hand, unofficial sources suggested that representatives from Münster had aggravated officials in Chemnitz through their overly self-confident manner, reminiscent of the *Besserwessi* (know-it all westerner) stereotype of earlier years.[153] On the other hand, the town was clearly reluctant to see the monument exhibited outside its home in Chemnitz; as the SPD mayor Barbara Ludwig claimed, 'The head is unique, and should remain unique'.[154] The leader of the SPD fraction also stated, 'We shouldn't give away the town's emblem simply as a copy – after all, it is part of our town history',[155] indicating the extent to which the identity of Chemnitz had become bound up with the monument. The PDS even feared the lack of influence that the town would have over the copy, concerned that its use or presentation may represent a defamation of Chemnitz, and thus an attack on the town's identity.[156] The monument has, it seems, genuinely become bound up with the town's identity in the way that SED officials could only have hoped for.

One of the few art installations that was granted permission was a project resulting from a student workshop organized by the Neue Sächsische Galerie in Chemnitz, in which students from the Austrian town of Linz worked together with local students from Schneeberg in order to design an artistic installation that engaged with the Marx Monument. For over two months in 2008, a tilted white box was placed around the monument, which visitors could enter and climb up in order to stand eye to eye with Marx. The so-called Temporary Museum of Modern Marx enabled visitors to view him from a different perspective, and to listen to and read *Das Kapital*, copies of which were to be found in the structure.[157] The project attracted approximately ten thousand visitors, and ended with the night-time projection of a film by Hungarian artist Gyula Pauer onto the white canvas, in which in an endless loop the image of Marx was slowly shown to metamorphose into that of Lenin and back again.[158] The film not only demonstrated that Lev Kerbel was responsible for many a Lenin monument, but also highlighted the formulaic aesthetics of Soviet art, provoking viewers to reflect on the history and meaning of the statue. The project as a whole aimed to encourage residents and visitors to see the monument in a different light, and to engage with Marx on his own terms as a serious philosopher, rather than simply as a 'mascot' of the town. In this vein, the students also recorded visitors' views of Marx and the monument, creating a historical document to be made accessible to future generations.[159]

The Temporary Museum of Modern Marx arose from students' serious engagement with the role of the monument in contemporary Chemnitz, finding it to be widely viewed as an asset to the town, yet one that is always seen to be symbolic of the GDR rather than of Marx's philosophy.[160] As Mathias Lindner, initiator of the project, stated of the monument, 'It ranges between being a thorn in the town and a mascot'.[161] Indeed, a survey carried out by the broadcaster MDR in 2008 on the most attractive monuments in Saxony, Saxony-Anhalt and Thuringia found that the Karl Marx Monument ranked highly, even above Dresden's Frauenkirche.[162] The monument is clearly set to stay, and has been adopted by the town as an old icon of new times; significantly, it provided one of the central locations for twentieth anniversary celebrations of the town's name change in 2010.[163] For many, it also represents regional self-assertion, and its role as a site of political protest as well as controversial art projects places the monument in a subversive tradition, rendering it a site of counter-memory. While its survival – in contrast to Berlin's Lenin – may relate to Marx's position as a nineteenth-century philosopher who could not be held responsible for the realities of twentieth-century socialism, this was clearly not its only saving grace. Local circumstances, including the town's symbolic name change and the monument's role in the demonstrations of 1989, were also factors, not to speak of aesthetics. Indeed, Marx's facial expression is significant here, for his unpatriotic pose and gloomy demeanour resisted common notions of GDR symbolism and triggered derisory jokes in the GDR, thus allowing the monument to be invested with a wider panoply of meaning.

Modification: A Modern Makeover for Halle's Flag Monument

The most controversial discussions concerning the future of socialist monuments have largely involved figurative monuments, in which their intended symbolic function is unequivocal. However, abstract monuments were also created in the GDR, such as the Flag Monument in Halle, which was built in honour of the fiftieth anniversary of the October Revolution in 1917, and unveiled on 7 November 1967. At twenty-four metres high and at the cutting edge of architectural design of the time, it was a large-scale iconic construction, not dissimilar in stature to the GDR's larger figurative monuments of that era. As a huge, twisting piece of concrete shaped like an unfurling flag, the Flag Monument is, however, not bound to a specific personality, and thus much more open to interpretation. Furthermore, its extensive concrete surface provides a potentially blank canvas onto which new interpretations can be projected. For these reasons, the debate in Halle has followed slightly different lines, yet still reveals significant similarities concerning the memory of 1989 and party memory politics.

The site on which the monument stands – Halle's Hansering – reveals a longer commemorative history, for it was here that a monument to Kaiser Wilhelm I was unveiled in 1901. With bronze figures of Wilhelm I, Bismarck and the Prussian General Field Marshall Moltke, the monument was subject to an explosive attack by a young communist in the early 1920s, which led to a triumphant rededication of the repaired monument in 1924 by right-wing paramilitary groups.[164] Although the monument survived the Second World War, its history and Prussian symbolism meant that it soon fell victim to the new socialist order, and was demolished in 1947; the site remained a green space for nearly twenty years, until architect Siegbert Fliegel was commissioned by the district party leadership to design a monument to commemorate fifty years of the October Revolution, and to celebrate the GDR's relationship with the Soviet Union and the victory of the working classes.[165] While the choice of location was in part the result of behind-the-scenes machinations,[166] the site of the former Prussian monument lent Fliegel's design greater symbolic gravitas, for a large number of residents still remembered the older monument. The most contentious point concerned the monument's colouring. Gaining inspiration from the 1920s, Fliegel's models all depicted a clean white form, yet the SED's suspicion of formalism, and the then regional leader Horst Sindermann's comment that 'Halle cannot fly the white flag', led to the addition of colour.[167] Reflecting the monument's official title, 'Revolutionary Flame', painter Gottfried Schüler's design of a flame motif, which blended from yellow at the top to red at the bottom, was realized. However, the night before the unveiling, the yellow flames were reddened, for they were the same colour as the emblem on the social democrat flag, an association that the SED leadership was keen to avoid. More worryingly, the combination of red and yellow on top of a dark pedestal evoked the colours of black, red and gold, the colours of the West German flag.[168] Within a year, however, the paint began to peel, and it was freshly painted in plain red,[169] leading the structure to be commonly designated as the Flag Monument, and widely associated with the banner of the working class. Designed as part of a ritual space for ceremonies and political demonstrations, with a speaker's platform, water feature and wall at which wreaths could be laid, the site was used for commemorations on the annual memorial day for the victims of fascism, as well as for swearing-in ceremonies for soldiers to the National People's Army (NVA), parades and other mass demonstrations. Plastic models of the monument were even produced as gifts for dignitaries on important anniversary occasions, such as the thirtieth anniversary of the SED, thus underlining its broader symbolic function.[170]

As in Chemnitz, the Flag Monument rapidly occupied a different position during the autumn of 1989, becoming the end point of demonstrations and the location of opposition rallies.[171] Designed as the 'Revolutionary Flame', its symbolism was extended to another revolution, and the speaker's platform was put to regular use for its intended purpose, albeit for a different cause. Ironically, the quotation by Johannes R. Becher on the back wall, which read *Unser Leben erhalten und schöner gestalten* (nourish our life and make it more beautiful), could also be appropriated for the new times. Representing the ideological repression of the SED, but at the same time becoming a symbol of hope for the future, the monument curiously represented old and new at the same time. At New Year celebrations, eggs filled with coloured paint were thrown at it, breaking up its dominating red, and a variety of slogans were written on and around the monument. While some were not politically motivated, a large number related to the contemporary situation, such as: 'The country needs new colour', 'SED – no thanks' or 'Defend yourselves against the old symbols of the dictatorship. Don't let yourselves be convinced [*Laßt Euch nichts weismachen*], make it colourful yourselves' (this last slogan being a play on the word 'weismachen', which also sounds like 'weiß machen' – to make white).[172] While many newspaper reports put this action down to drunken youths, a subsequent report written by members of the reform party Demokratie Jetzt claimed that it was an organized action by citizens objecting to the formal symbolism of the state and wanting to turn the monument into a 'colourful canvas of the *Wende*'. The statement claimed that 'many people brought about the "October" revolution in our country: a monument was created by everyone for everyone'.[173] Here, of course, the originally intended 'October' of 1917 is turned on its head, and the symbolic language of the past is used for the present.

In the aftermath of unification, the Flag Monument initially slipped away from public attention, despite a local community club giving it a new coat of paint in 1992, in order to mark the third anniversary of the *Wende*.[174] It was not until 1996 that discussions over its future seriously began to occupy residents and politicians alike, when the completion of a Telekom control centre next to the monument placed a question mark over its future. The building, having been granted planning permission in 1994, was placed on part of the memorial site, thus destroying certain elements such as the wall and water feature. Placed within metres of the monument, the building confined it to a small space, rendering it a misfit in its surroundings, and Telekom offered to pay for its removal costs.[175] The FDP subsequently took a proposal for demolition to the town council, which narrowly rejected it in November 1996, with the familiar pattern of the CDU (including Mayor Klaus Rauen) and FDP voting for demolition, the PDS against, and the SPD and Greens divided.[176] Opinion was clearly divided, and letters streamed into the local newspaper objecting to the decision;[177] the Junge Union (youth organization of the CDU) even staged an event where members attempted to pull it down with ropes.[178] However, it was above all the process that caused objection, for the proximity of the new building was frequently given as a reason for demolition, despite the fact that the monument clearly existed first. Inevitably, some critics claimed that this was little more than a ploy to undermine the future of the structure,[179] and the monument came to adopt new meaning as, in the words of one journalist, a 'symbol for poor local politics'.[180]

The decision of 1996 did not secure the monument's future, for in 2000 the CDU brought another proposal for demolition to the town council, once again on the grounds that it no longer stood in its original surroundings. The public outcry was even greater this time, with voices both for and against demolition filling letters pages of local newspapers; a telephone survey in 2000 found that 64.5 per cent of those surveyed were for demolition,[181] but this time, the new mayor, Ingrid Häußler (SPD), was against demolition, and both the planning committee and the town council rejected the proposal in early 2001, with the CDU being the only party showing large support.[182] Arguments in favour of keeping the monument included the high cost of demolition, the structural uniqueness of the monument, and the questionable urban politics of the early 1990s.[183] Only the PDS argued for its importance as a continuing sign of antifascist resistance,[184] yet a significant number of politicians, preservationists and locals once again pointed towards the role of the monument in 1989 as a reason for its contemporary importance. Some saw it as a place of personal recollection, wanting to be able to show their children where they protested, while others saw in it a 'symbol that even concrete relationships can be broken'.[185] Gotthard Voß, head of Sachsen-Anhalt's Office for the Protection of Historical Monuments, described it as a 'document of the pre-*Wende* years, the *Wende* and also the present', which is bound to its location by historical events and represents dynamic historical forces.[186] In this vein, others highlighted its role as a symbol of present and future tolerance in society, as well as a sign of democracy, in which the past is accepted, not discarded.[187] In contrast, a large number of those in favour of demolition argued along aesthetic lines, calling it an 'eyesore', a 'blot on the landscape' and an 'ugly concrete monster',[188] as well as being unsafe and unsightly due to its state of disrepair.[189] Aesthetic pollution was also linked to the idea of political pollution, with the centre-right seeing it as little more than a 'symbol of the old GDR'.[190] Once again, we see how argumentation on both sides attempted to bolster the values of present-day democracy.

Suggestions were also made for familiar alternative options, such as growing plants over the monument, moving it to a different location, or using it as advertising space.[191] The only alternative that gained relatively widespread support among readers' letters was painting it in the colours of the EU flag, Halle's coat of arms, or alternatively with the flags and symbols of the German *Bundesländer*, thus turning it into a symbol of unification and western integration.[192] None of these happened, however, for the town council voted in favour of renovating the monument in 2002, stating: 'The Flag Monument … will not be whitewashed. The events that took place there in 1989/90 will be considered in a design competition'.[193] The specific mention of the *Wende* period is significant here, for the intention was clearly to incorporate this visually into the monument, creating a longer memory tradition. A competition was subsequently launched in which seven local artists were invited to participate. Their designs were publicly exhibited in early 2003, and residents were encouraged to view and formally comment on designs in a visitors' book, which was to play a nominal role in the jury's decision.[194] In this way, the process was intended to be as inclusive as possible, marking itself apart from the monument's GDR construction history. In July 2003, the jury – of which the original architect Siegbert Fliegel was a member – decided on a design by Steffen O. Rumpf, which depicts a pixelated image of the Milky Way against the background of our galaxy and the universe, based on infrared images from the COBE satellite (see Figure 2.4).[195] While this design bears little immediate relevance to 1989, the idea found favour with the jury for two main reasons. First, the arrangement of the colours red, orange and yellow took the monument back to its original design, reminiscent of a flame.[196] Second, the design challenged viewers to reflect upon their place not only within society and the world, but also within the wider universe, and consider the impact of human history on future ways of living.[197] As such, the design is intended to remind viewers of its GDR roots, while pointing to the future, yet refrains from making any overtly political statement; as the chair of the jury stated, 'The flag is thus a memory which offends no one, but which also forgets nothing'.[198] It significantly also forms the end point of a pathway of ten plaques bearing images and slogans relating to the demonstrations of 1989, which was installed in 2006 as the Monument to the Memory of the Monday Demonstrations of 1989. Here we see how its meaning has been augmented by subsequent memory activity, albeit conceived as an independent project.

It is questionable whether passers-by who do not seek out the explanatory plaque near the Flag Monument will understand such connections. However, since being unveiled on 29 October 2004, there have been no more proposals to remove the monument, and it has become a unique symbol of the town, considered by the authorities to be representative of a 'constructive way of dealing with the past'.[199] Its abstract form and above all its role in the demonstrations of 1989 did, it seems, save it from demolition; one need only compare its fate with another of Siegbert Fliegel's projects from a similar era in Halle: the monumental statue of four fists. As the embodiment of unambiguous socialist symbolism, and not having played a part in the events of 1989, this monument was destroyed in 2003 with relatively little discussion.[200] In contrast, the Flag Monument, like Chemnitz's Marx Monument, has gained considerably in meaning since becoming an 'unintended' monument, and has become a canvas for the negotiation of recent history. Significantly, some of its original symbolism has remained, both in its association with revolutionary activity, and in its attempt to encourage reflection on the place of the individual within a broader societal – or cosmic – system.

Figure 2.4 Flag Monument (original monument by Siegbert Fliegel, 1967 / redesigned by Steffen O. Rumpf, 2004), Hansering, Halle. Photograph by Anna Saunders.

Relocation: Finding a New Home for Leipzig's Karl Marx Relief

The final case study, a huge bronze relief measuring over fourteen by six metres, depicting the face of Karl Marx amidst smaller figures fighting for historical progress (see Figure 2.5), is testament to the fact that demolition debates did not necessarily lose intensity with time; having taken on a panoply of meanings, this monument provoked a raging debate in Leipzig throughout the mid to late 2000s. Entitled 'Karl Marx and the Revolutionary, World-Changing Nature of His Work', it was the result of a competition for a piece of artwork to adorn the new buildings of Leipzig's then Karl Marx University. Artists Rolf Kurth, Klaus Schwabe and Frank Ruddigkeit won the competition, and their relief was mounted over the entrance to the main university building in 1974, on the twenty-fifth anniversary of the GDR. Controversially, however, it hung directly above the location of the former altar of the university church, St Pauli (commonly referred to as the Paulinerkirche), which was destroyed in 1968 to make way for the new buildings. In this way,

Figure 2.5 Karl Marx Relief (Rolf Kurth, Klaus Schwabe and Frank Ruddigkeit, 1974), now located in the university campus on Jahnallee, Leipzig. Photograph by Anna Saunders.

it represented a new altar for the regime, akin to 'a type of SED triumphal arc'.[201] Aesthetically, however, it met with little approval, and has been variously described as a *Klotz* and *Trumm* (both bearing the sense of a bulky 'lump'), as well as 'pretentious', 'repellent' and – similar to Thälmann – a 'Marx-Lenin mix'.[202] Although the University Senate unanimously decided in 1992 to remove the relief and erect it as a monument on top of the hill where the remains of the church are buried, technical difficulties and the high cost of removal prevented its relocation.[203] In August 2006, it was finally removed in order to make way for the demolition of the 1970s building, and following much debate was re-erected in August 2008 at the university campus on Jahnallee, just outside the town centre, in a somewhat hidden location behind the canteen of the sports forum. Two months later, an information board was placed alongside the relief, explaining its historical context.

Although this example is somewhat different, with the university rather than the public authorities owning the relief, it still became widely symbolic of the GDR past, and as an iconic monument in the town centre, the ensuing debate involved local political parties, residents and the university alike. Discussions were, however, complicated by the relief's association with a number of other elements. First, it had become widely associated with the university's strong socialist orientation during the GDR, for it had not only worked closely with the SED, but was particularly known for its regime-faithful journalism section, commonly named the *Rotes Kloster* (red monastery), the only university department to train journalists in the GDR. Second, the relief became inextricably bound up with the history of the former Paulinerkirche, the blasting of which had provoked widespread protest in Leipzig. In commemoration of the thirtieth anniversary of this event, a triangular installation of steel girders was erected around the relief in 1998, marking the shape and location of the east end of the church's roof. Although artist Axel Guhlmann had only intended for it to stand for one hundred days, this private initiative in fact remained until 2006 when the relief itself was dismounted.[204] The installation did much to remind residents and politicians of the inextricable link not only between the church and the relief, but also their futures. While debates raged about the removal of the relief, some citizens' groups, most prominently the Pauliner Association, fought for the reconstruction of the church; this never happened, but a modern building has now been constructed that evokes the outline of the church. Third, the relief has become associated with the monumental wall painting 'Working Class and Intelligentsia' (1970–73) by Werner Tübke, which hung inside the university building, back to back with the Karl Marx Relief. Measuring fourteen by three metres, it depicts the historical triumph of socialism at the university and a number of local SED functionaries who were responsible for the blasting of the church. The fact that this picture once again hangs in the university – albeit in the corridor of a teaching building – has angered those who regard it as left-wing propaganda. Writer Erich Loest even commissioned a 'counter picture' by Reinhard Minkewitz, on which victims of former university policies are portrayed.[205] While the fate of Tübke's painting has been treated separately from that of the relief, the two have invariably been mentioned in the same breath by those who oppose their reinstatement. As all three examples show here, the face of the relief became entangled in a much broader nexus of debates about the cultural heritage of the GDR.

After demounting the relief, the university was initially keen to re-erect it in a central location, but the local authorities rejected this option as the proposed park behind the Moritzbastei was public land.[206] The ensuing debate thus related to choice of location as much as to whether it should be mounted at all. The university's principal, Professor Franz Häuser (interestingly a former West German), was one of the monument's most vocal advocates, calling it 'evidence of contemporary history, which we must deal with in an active manner',[207] and seeing it as a *Mahnmal* for a 'dark era', rather than as a *Denkmal*.[208] He countered the sometimes personal tone of the debate by highlighting that decisions had been made 'in a democratically organized discussion at the university',[209] and that the university is above all an institution in which debate about the past should be encouraged.[210] Similarly, Mayor Burkhard Jung (SPD) argued against melting down the relief, stating, 'this is not how a democratic society deals with art',[211] and Frank Zöllner, Professor of Art History, took this imagery one step further, claiming: 'With the destruction of works of art or the burning of books, we find ourselves in very, very bad company. The Nazis did it, the SED and the Taliban'.[212] The predominant argument for keeping the monument – and if possible in a central location – was clearly that of maintaining a democratic approach, in contrast to the SED's actions of 1968. This view was also backed by the university's student council, whose members notably had little or no first-hand memory of the GDR, yet who still regarded it as 'a part of history'.[213]

The campaign against the relief was led by a handful of prominent figures, such as conductor Kurt Masur, former pastor of the Nikolaikirche (St Nicholas Church) Christian Führer, Leipzig's CDU leader Hermann Winkler, and writer Erich Loest, as well as the Pauliner Association. In an open letter to Mayor Jung and Minister Eva-Maria Stange (both SPD), Loest suggested that the relief be stored away until a future generation could come to an unbiased decision on its future. Most significantly, he claimed that any uncritical display of the relief would be 'a disgrace for the town in which freedom erupted in 1989',[214] and in linking its re-erection to the relatively strong support of Die Linke in Leipzig, he claimed that it contributed to the 'trivialization and glorification of the GDR'.[215] Others also underlined the undemocratic nature of the action, with Pastor Führer claiming that the relief stands for '*Unrechtsstaat*, wall, barbed wire and Stasi',[216] and SPD Bundestag member Rainer Fornahl regarding it as a 'symbol of indoctrination, totalitarianism and ... spiritual repression'.[217] The tabloid newspaper *BILD Leipzig* adopted similar imagery, stoking the flames with headlines such as 'Leipzig citizens are still being patronized [*bevormundet*]!', 'The day of shame' and 'Black day for the town of the *Wende*-heroes'.[218] Indirect references to 1989 also abounded, with the newspaper reporting, for example, on a 'sensational *Wende*' when the process began to stumble,[219] and CDU leader Winkler suggesting that a 'round table' should be formed.[220] It is, perhaps, no coincidence that the demonstrations of 1989 took place on Augustusplatz, above which the relief hung. The significant role of the churches in the demonstrations of 1989 also received frequent comment, often aligned with objections that relicts from the Paulinerkirche remained neglected, while 300,000 euros were being made available for 'a piece of pure propaganda';[221] some media reports also highlighted former SED membership – and in one case Stasi involvement – among the relief's protégés.[222] Once again, discussions demonstrated the familiar desire to oppose the dictatorial past with present-day democracy, while often utilizing emotional images and memories from 1989.

The debate received massive media attention between 2006 and 2008, stoked in part by the involvement of outspoken public figures such as Loest. Readers of the *Leipziger Volkszeitung* inundated the paper with letters, and its online discussion attracted 339 posts on the subject.[223] Surveys were also carried out by a variety of media organizations, with their results often reflecting the political views of their readership: 80.2 per cent of *BILD Leipzig* respondents, for instance, were against the re-erection of the relief, whereas the figure was 50.37 per cent for *Leipziger Volkszeitung* readers.[224] Throughout the debate, the link between the Paulinerkirche and the relief was one that persisted, particularly among those opposing the relief, for as Pastor Führer stated, 'It is important that the connection with the destroyed university church is made clear, so that the relief isn't left as a victory monument'.[225] Indeed, many believed that the two should effectively be 'buried' together,[226] and although the idea of a 'memory park' on the edge of town came to nothing, the final decision to mount the monument on the Jahnallee campus represented somewhat of a compromise, and a solution that the university's chancellor has described as 'appropriate for the times'.[227] Although the suggestion of mounting it with the triangular steel girders in memory of the church attracted much approval, the artists' objection – and the fact that the girders had been destroyed in 2006 – ended this discussion.[228] Instead, the information board in front of the relief clearly links it to the demolition of the Paulinerkirche, featuring text and images depicting the church and its destruction, the new university building, the demonstrations of October 1989 and the relief in 2000 with the gable-like installation. For some – such as a speaker for the student council – the text goes too far, failing to see the relief as a piece of artwork in its own right, and reading 'rather like a panel devoted to the destroyed Paulinerkirche'.[229] In this way, the intended function of the new ensemble is very similar to that of the original relief: to strengthen the present-day political status quo, by linking past and present in a clear forward-looking trajectory, this time tracing democratic rather than socialist progress. However, it attempts to do so in a more understated way, and as the text claims, the rehoused relief 'documents both responsibility and detachment, through its spatial distance from the original context'.[230] Through spatial and historical distancing, the bronze has thus literally and metaphorically been 'brought down to earth'.

Conclusion: The Ever-Present Narrative of 1989

Whether situated in Berlin or elsewhere, these examples reveal a number of significant tropes. It should first be noted that the post-1990 future of socialist icons has not fallen solely in the domain of memory politics. Practical considerations, such as the cost of demolition and the technical difficulties resulting from the sheer size and weight of some monuments, have necessarily influenced procedures, either prolonging decision-making processes or preventing removal. It is no coincidence that the early 1990s, when many such decisions were being made, was a tumultuous period in eastern Germany, with rising unemployment, environmental and social problems often requiring more urgent attention and resources. The passing of time thus constitutes another important factor, for the political brisance of such structures appears to have waned over time and calls for demolition have become less vocal. As the Leipzig example demonstrates, however, this does not mean that debates have become less controversial, but rather that – in most cases – recognition of the role of such monuments as historical documents has grown. Similarly, it seems that the typical party-political divides of post-*Wende* years have lessened on such issues, and while parties on the right of centre are more likely to support the demolition of socialist structures, this is no longer such a dominant trope. The significance of local politics remains, however, central to the fates of socialist monuments, and as the above examples demonstrate, decisions rarely relate directly to the subject of the monument (Lenin was removed in Berlin, yet remains in Schwerin; Marx has become an icon in Chemnitz, yet was moved out of the centre in Leipzig). Instead, the circumstances of their erection and their interrelationship with the surrounding environment of the past, present and future have proven to be decisive.

Most significantly, the discourse surrounding these monuments reveals how they became important vehicles for the embedding of popular motifs and traditions relating to 1989. It is notable that those for *and* against demolition drew on slogans and interpretations of 1989, with those on both sides eager to demonstrate the democratic value of their arguments in contrast to the authoritarian nature of SED rule. Often this involved comparison with other events or traditions in history, from the SED's destruction of the Berlin City Palace and Leipzig's Paulinerkirche to ostentatious Prussian symbolism and the Nazi book burnings. In this way, we see how GDR history becomes entangled in a broader understanding of the recent German past, and how these monuments have often provoked more genuine social interaction and debate than during socialist times. In a somewhat unexpected turn of events, the structures that remain standing have often become symbols of tolerance and democracy, standing as examples of a positive and inclusive engagement with the past, as well as resistance towards previous techniques of repressive erasure or strategic forgetting. The emphasis on democratic narratives has had two unexpected effects. First, it seems that over time, debates have become increasingly protracted. In the case of the Lenin Monument, for instance, the decision-making process and demolition took place relatively swiftly, still being carried along by the immediate emotions of the post-*Wende* period. Discussions in later years, however, allowed greater time for debate and discussion, with leaders wishing to avoid accusations of acting undemocratically. At times, this has also involved broader consultation, such as the attempt to draw on popular opinion in the Halle competition. Second, the tendency to document and contextualize the fate of these monuments appears to have grown as part of this democratization process. The Spandau exhibition is, itself, testimony to this, for its very aim is to exhibit and document monuments that have become the victims of history, Lenin being the most famous of these. Other examples of this process include the information board installed next to the Karl Marx Relief, and the suggestion to restore the Thälmann Monument to its original state, along with a commentary. In a somewhat different way, the Museum of Modern Marx in Chemnitz also resulted in an audio documentation of residents' views of Marx and the monument, as a snapshot of opinion in 2008. All these examples point towards a concern with documenting the past and present for future generations, as well as demonstrating a democratic concern for our dealings with history in the present.

Not only do we see here how the interpretation of monuments shifts as different layers of meaning build and interact over time, but also how the division between communicative and cultural memory is much more fluid than often assumed. While the monuments discussed in this chapter were all built as durable and fixed forms of cultural memory in which the socialist past was to be incarnated, they also reflected socialist communicative memory of the time. Since unification, however, they have become sites that have triggered new communicative memories of socialism and its demise, which in turn have fed into discussions over their future survival. At a local level, such discussions have often provided inhabitants with a sense of purpose and local pride, demonstrating how monuments are not simply subject to change, but can also become agents of change themselves. The remaining structures represent neither heroes nor villains, but have become platforms – at least temporarily – for public debate and the assertion of democratic rights.

Notes

1. For a comprehensive study of iconoclasm, see Gamboni, *The Destruction of Art*.
2. Lenin, 'Dekret "Über die Denkmäler der Republik"', in *Demontage... revolutionärer oder restaurativer Bildersturm? Texte und Bilder*, ed. by Götz Aly et al. (Berlin: Karin Kramer Verlag, 1992), p. 11.
3. Hans-Ulrich Thamer, 'Von der Monumentalisierung zur Verdrängung der Geschichte', in *Denkmalsturz: Zur Konfliktgeschichte politischer Symbolik*, ed. by Winfried Speitkamp (Göttingen: Vandenhoeck & Ruprecht, 1997), pp. 109–36 (127).
4. Svetlana Boym, *The Future of Nostalgia* (New York: Basic Books, 2001), p. 88.
5. Michail Gorbatschow, 'Über die Unterbindung einer Schändung von Denkmälern, die mit der Geschichte des Staates und seinen Symbolen verbunden sind', in *Demontage...*, ed. by Aly et al., p. 13.

6. John Gillis, 'Memory and Identity: The History of a Relationship', in *Commemorations*, ed. by Gillis, pp. 3–24 (7).
7. Connerton, 'Seven Types of Forgetting'.
8. See Sturken, *Tangled Memories*, p. 7.
9. Winfried Speitkamp, 'Denkmalsturz und Symbolkonflikt in der modernen Geschichte: Eine Einleitung', in *Denkmalsturz*, ed. by Speitkamp, pp. 5–21 (18).
10. Koshar, *From Monuments to Traces*, p. 144.
11. Eberhard Elfert, 'Monumentalplastik im Widerstreit der politischen Systeme in Ost- und West-Berlin', in *Enge und Vielfalt – Auftragskunst und Kunstförderung in der DDR*, ed. by Paul Kaiser and Karl-Siegbert Rehberg (Hamburg: Junius, 1999), pp. 353–72 (354).
12. Peter Reichel, *Politik mit der Erinnerung: Gedächtnisorte im Streit um die nationalsozialistsiche Vergangenheit* (Frankfurt am Main: Fischer, 1999), p. 22.
13. Schmid, 'Denkmäler als Zeugnisse der Geschichtskultur'.
14. Otto Grotewohl, 'Die Kunst im Kampf um Deutschlands Zukunft', *Neues Deutschland*, 2 September 1951, cited in Hubertus Adam, 'Zwischen Anspruch und Wirkungslosigkeit: Bemerkungen zur Rezeption von Denkmälern der DDR', *kritische berichte*, 19 (1991) 1, 44–64 (45).
15. See Michalski, *Public Monuments*, pp. 126–31; Koshar, *From Monuments to Traces*, pp. 190–93.
16. See Brian Ladd, 'East Berlin Political Monuments in the Late German Democratic Republic: Finding a Place for Marx and Engels', *Journal of Contemporary History*, 37 (2002) 1, 91–104 (104).
17. See Peter Feist, 'Denkmalplastik in der DDR von 1949 bis 1990', in *Denkmale und kulturelles Gedächtnis nach dem Ende der Ost-West-Konfrontation*, ed. by Akademie der Künste (Berlin: Jovis Verlag, 2000), pp. 189–98; Hubertus Adam, 'Erinnerungsrituale – Erinnerungsdiskurse – Erinnerungstabus: Politische Denkmäler der DDR zwischen Verhinderung, Veränderung und Realisierung', *kritische berichte*, 20 (1992) 3, 10–35; Aktives Museum Faschismus und Widerstand in Berlin and NGBK (eds), *Erhalten – Zerstören – Verändern? Denkmäler der DDR in Ost-Berlin: Eine dokumentarische Ausstellung* (Berlin: Aktives Museum Faschismus und Widerstand in Berlin, 1990).
18. Ladd, 'East Berlin Political Monuments', p. 102.
19. Krzysztof Wodiczko, 'Leninplatz-Projektion', in *Die Endlichkeit der Freiheit: Berlin 1990. Ein Ausstellungsprojet in Ost und West*, ed. by Wulf Herzogenrath, Joachim Sartorius and Christoph Tannert (Berlin: Hentrich, 1990), pp. 205–11 (207).
20. Dirk Schumann, 'Marx geht, die Monumente bleiben?', *die tageszeitung*, 4 August 1990, pp. 15–16 (16).
21. Dieter Hoffmann-Axthelm, 'The Demise of Lenin Square', *Daidalos*, 'Denkmal/Monument', 49 (1993), 122–29 (126).
22. Huyssen, *Present Pasts*, p. 38.
23. Ladd, 'East Berlin Political Monuments', p. 104.
24. Adam, 'Erinnerungsrituale – Erinnerungsdiskurse – Erinnerungstabus', p. 30.

25. Maya Nadkarni, 'The Death of Socialism and the Afterlife of Its Monuments: Making and Marketing the Past in Budapest's Statue Park Museum', in *Memory, History, Nation: Contested Pasts*, ed. by Katherine Hodgkin and Susannah Radstone (New Brunswick, NJ: Transaction Publishers, 2007), pp. 193–207 (196)
26. Régine Robin, 'Das Verschwinden der DDR im kollektiven Gedächtnis', in *Vom kritischen Gebrauch der Erinnerung*, ed. by Thomas Flierl and Elfriede Müller (Berlin: Karl Dietz Verlag, 2009), pp. 49–66 (59).
27. Wise, *Capital Dilemma*, p. 53. For similar quips, see Jon Berndt Olsen, *Tailoring Truth: Politicizing the Past and Negotiating Memory in East Germany, 1945–1990* (New York; Oxford: Berghahn Books, 2015), p. 230.
28. Eberhard Elfert, 'Die politischen Denkmäler der DDR im ehemaligen Ost-Berlin und unser Lenin', in *Demontage...*, ed. by Aly et al., pp. 53–58 (53). On commemorative plaques, see Martin Schönfeld, *Gedenktafeln in Ost-Berlin* (Berlin: Aktives Museum Faschismus und Widerstand in Berlin e.V., 1991) and Holger Hübner, *Das Gedächtnis der Stadt: Gedenktafeln in Berlin* (Berlin: Argon, 1997).
29. Maoz Azaryahu, 'Zurück zur Vergangenheit? Die Straßennamen Ost-Berlins 1990–1994', in *Denkmalsturz*, ed. by Speitkamp, pp. 137–54 (143).
30. Ibid., p. 147.
31. Peter Schubert, 'Kunst? Oder doch nur monumentaler Schrott?', *Berliner Morgenpost*, 18 October 1990, p. 9.
32. Interview with Joachim John, 'Die Reinigung der Hauptstadt', *die tageszeitung*, 4 August 1990, pp. 16–17.
33. Blum, 'Club Cola and Co.', p. 139.
34. Joachim Scheel, 'Tägliche Geschmacksverbildung', *Der Tagesspiegel*, 15 April 1990, p. 5.
35. 'Reißt die roten Denkmäler ab!', *Bild-Zeitung*, 1 November 1990.
36. The exhibition was entitled *Erhalten – Zerstören – Verändern?* ('Preserve – Destroy – Modify?').
37. Aktives Museum Faschismus und Widerstand in Berlin and NGBK, *Erhalten – Zerstören – Verändern?*, p. 7.
38. Hans Maur, *Sowjetische Ehrenmale: Schutz und Erhalt – Abriss und Verfall* (Berlin: Gedenkstättenverband, 1999), p. 7.
39. An anti-Soviet message is clearly evident here, considering the Soviet failure to aid the Warsaw Uprising and the battle to preserve the Polish state. On the rededication, see Andreas Mix, 'Die Losung aus dem Völkerfrühling', *Berliner Zeitung*, 11/12 August 2007, p. 29.
40. Due to work on the extension to the U5 underground line, the monument was moved in September 2010 to a nearby site closer to the Karl-Liebknecht-Brücke. At the time of writing, it is unclear whether it will be moved back to the original site. See Olsen, *Tailoring Truth*, for a discussion of the politics and aesthetics of this monument.
41. Miriam Zißler, 'Stalin und Lenin ziehen ins Haus der Geschichte', *Augsburger Allgemeiner*, 24 November 2008, http://www.augsburger-allgemeine.de/dillingen/Stalin-und-Lenin-ziehen-ins-Haus-der-Geschichte-id4599096.html (accessed 4 June 2011).

42. Interview with Irana Rusta, 'Ideologisch belastet – und nun ab in den Fundus der Kunstgeschichte?', *Neues Deutschland*, 8 October 1990, p. 5.
43. For further discussion, see Olsen, *Tailoring Truth*, pp. 230–33.
44. Sophie Calle, *Die Entfernung* (Dresden: Verlag der Kunst, 1996).
45. Koshar, *From Monuments to Traces*, pp. 3 and 5.
46. Herbert Fell, 'Tempel des Goldenen Traumes', *kunststadt – stadtkunst*, 38 (1993), 10–11.
47. See Paul Kaiser and Andreas Kämper, 'Gestützte Helden, gestützte Welten', in *Enge und Vielfalt*, ed. by Paul Kaiser and Karl-Siegbert Rehberg (Hamburg: Junius, 1999), pp. 375–82 and Gamboni, *The Destruction of Art*, pp. 74–75.
48. Tom Parfitt, 'Is It a Purge? Red Army Statue Gets Cartoon Makeover', *The Guardian*, 23 June 2011, p. 24.
49. Eberhard Elfert, 'Die Chronologie zum Abbau des Lenin-Denkmals', *Kunst am Bau. Kunst im Stadtraum*, 35–36 (1992), 60–62 (62).
50. Some material in this section, and also with reference to the Karl Marx Relief in Leipzig and the Marx Monument in Chemnitz, has appeared in Anna Saunders, 'The Ghosts of Lenin, Thälmann and Marx in the Post-Socialist Cityscape', *German Life and Letters*, 63 (2010) 4, 441–57, reproduced with permission of John Wiley and Sons.
51. 'Lächelndes Gesicht', *Der Spiegel*, (1991) 41, 154–55 (154).
52. Eberhard Elfert, 'Monumentalplastik im Widerstreit der politischen Systeme', p. 362.
53. Dieter E. Zimmer, 'Was tun mit Lenin?', *Die Zeit*, 18 October 1991, p. 93.
54. See Herzogenrath, Sartorius and Tannert, *Die Endlichkeit der Freiheit*; André Meier and Ludwig Rauch, 'Kulturbetrieb im Niemandsland', *Bildende Kunst*, 10 (1990), 19–26.
55. Martin Schönfeld, 'Erhalten – Zerstören – Verändern? Diskussionsprozess um die politischen Denkmäler der DDR in Berlin', *kritische berichte*, 19 (1991) 1, 39–43 (42).
56. See Ingvild Kiele, 'Ein Denkmal in Ehren. Lenin – Was tun?', *Kommune*, 11 (1991), 62–64; 'Lächelndes Gesicht'.
57. Honika Gerlach and Ute Mirea (eds), *denk' mal! Eine Dokumentation zum Lenin-Denkmal* (Berlin: Kulturverein Prenzlauer Berg e.V., 1992), p. 3.
58. In the *Berliner Zeitung*, figures as high as two million DM were mentioned. See Maria Rüger, 'Das Berliner Lenin-Denkmal', *kritische berichte*, 20 (1992) 3, 36–44 (36).
59. Matthias Matussek, 'Lenins Stirn, fünfter Stock', *Der Spiegel* (1991) 46, 341–43 (341).
60. 'Lenins Abbau immer komplizierter', *die tageszeitung*, 2 January 1992.
61. 'Getrennt zu Rosa und Karl', *FAZ*, 11 January 1997, p. 4.
62. Adam, 'Erinnerungsrituale – Erinnerungsdiskurse – Erinnerungstabus', p. 10.
63. See Thomas Flierl, 'Denkmalstürze zu Berlin: Vom Umgang mit einem prekären Erbe', *kritische berichte*, 20 (1992) 3, 45–52 (47).
64. Hassemer's speech to the Kulturausschuss on 30 September 1991, cited in Michael S. Falser, *Zwischen Identität und Authentizität: Zur politischen*

Geschichte der Denkmalpflege in Deutschland (Dresden: Thelem, 2008), p. 225.
65. 'Lächelndes Gesicht', 155.
66. Petra Roettig, 'Sprechende Denkmäler', kritische berichte, 20 (1992) 3, 75–82 (75).
67. Annette Leo, 'Spuren der DDR', in Demontage…, ed. by Aly et al., pp. 59–66 (61); Ludwig Rademacher, 'Lenin bringt Berlins Bausenator ins Wackeln', Berliner Morgenpost, 19 October 1991.
68. Roettig, 'Sprechende Denkmäler', 76.
69. Matussek, 'Lenins Stirn, fünfter Stock', p. 341.
70. Elfert, 'Die Chronologie zum Abbau des Lenin-Denkmals', p. 61.
71. Erika Biskup, cited in Sascha Adamek and Sigrid Averesch, 'Lenin fällt – der Streit geht weiter', Berliner Zeitung, 6 November 1991, p. 1.
72. Gregor Gysi, cited in 'Abriß des Denkmals ist Demonstration der Macht', Neues Deutschland, 18 November 1991, p. 7.
73. See 'Abriß des Denkmals ist Demonstration der Macht'; Mia Lee, 'GDR Monuments in Unified Germany', in Memorialization in Germany since 1945, ed. by Bill Niven and Chloe Paver (Basingstoke: Palgrave Macmillan, 2010), pp. 308–17 (312).
74. Stefan Heym, cited in Günter Herlt, Birne contra Historie (Berlin: Spotless Verlag, 1993), p. 52.
75. 'Wer hat Angst vor Wladimir Iljitsch?', Der Morgen, 25/26 May 1991.
76. Bettina Ritter, 'Wurde Lenin geklaut', Der Tagesspiegel, 15 May 2003, http://www.tagesspiegel.de/berlin/wurde-lenin-geklaut/414786.html (accessed 19 December 2017).
77. Hans-Ernst Mittig, 'Politische Denkmäler und "Kunst am Bau" im städtischen Kontext', in Verfallen und vergessen oder aufgehoben und geschützt? Architektur und Städtebau der DDR – Geschichte, Bedeutung, Umgang, Erhaltung, Schriftenreihe des deutschen Nationalkomitees für Denkmalschutz, vol. 51 (Bonn: Deutsches Nationalkomitee für Denkmalschutz, 1997), pp. 23–32 (26).
78. Gamboni, The Destruction of Art, pp. 84–85.
79. Stefan Strauss, 'Lenin's Fall', Berliner Zeitung, 13 November 2001, https://www.berliner-zeitung.de/vor-zehn-jahren-kippte-das-denkmal-des-revolutionaers--aber-ueber-den-abriss-denken-heute-viele-anders-lenins-fall-16563962 (accessed 19 December 2017).
80. Cited in Claudia Stäuble, 'Comeback für Lenin?', Spiegel Online, 1 August 2005, www.spiegel.de/kultur/gesellschaft/0,1518,367826,00.html (accessed 9 August 2016); see also CDU press release: 'Wellmann: Mit Lenin zurück in die sozialistische Zukunft', 5 August 2005, www.cdu-fraktion.berlin.de/Aktuelles/Presseerklaerungen/Lenin-Denkmal (accessed 19 March 2010).
81. See Anja Reich, Silvia Perdoni and Corinne Plaga, Kopf hoch, Lenin!, https://berlinerverlag.atavist.com/lenin (accessed 9 August 2016).
82. '3900 Kilo fürs Museum', Die Welt, 10 September 2015, http://www.welt.de/regionales/berlin/article146230813/3900-Kilo-fuers-Museum.html (accessed 9 August 2016).

83. See Reich, Perdoni and Plaga, *Kopf hoch, Lenin!*.
84. See Kerstin Decker, 'Wiedersehen mit Lenin', *Der Tagesspiegel*, 8 January 2003, p. 3; 'PDS will Lenin in Potsdam wieder aufstellen', *BZ*, 1 August 2006, https://www.bz-berlin.de/artikel-archiv/lenin-statue-2 (accessed 19 December 2017); Maren Ramünke-Hoefer, 'Anschlag auf das Lenin-Denkmal?', *Schweriner Volkszeitung*, 27 October 2010, https://www.svz.de/lokales/anschlag-auf-das-lenin-denkmal-id4909661.html (accessed 19 December 2017).
85. See, for example, *Lenin is still around...*, https://leninisstillaround.com (accessed 9 August 2016); Andreas Stedtler, *Die Akte Lenin: Eine Rettungsgeschichte mit Haken* (Halle: Mitteldeutscher Verlag, 2006); MDR Zeitreise, http://www.mdr.de/zeitreise/ns-zeit/gmd-eisleben104.html (accessed 9 August 2016).
86. Rudolf Herz, *Lenin on Tour* (Göttingen: Steidl, 2009).
87. Kommission zum Umgang mit den politischen Denkmälern der Nachkriegszeit im ehemaligen Ost-Berlin, 'Bericht' (Berlin, 15 February 1993), p. 2.
88. See letter from Prof Hardt-Waltherr Hämer to Senator für kulturelle Angelegenheiten, 28 March 1991, in *Denk Mal Positionen: Dokumentation zur Ausstellung vom 14. Juli – 13. August 1993 im Prenzlauer Berg Museum* (Berlin: Kulturamt Prenzlauer Berg / Prenzlauer Berg Museum, 1993), pp. 30–31.
89. Eberhard Elfert, 'Unsere Fachkommission für "Sozialistische Denkmäler"', *Kunst am Bau. Kunst im Stadtraum* 35/36 (1992), 63; Hans-Ernst Mittig, 'Gegen den Abriß des Berliner Lenin-Denkmals', in *Demontage...*, ed. by Aly et al., pp. 41–45 (44).
90. Hans Maur, *Arbeiterbewegung–Gedenkstätten* (Berlin: Gedenkstättenverband e.V., 1999), p. 43.
91. See Thomas Flierl, '"Thälmann und Thälmann vor allen": Ein Nationaldenkmal für die Hauptstadt der DDR. 1996', in *Berlin: Perspektiven durch Kultur. Texte und Projekte* (Berlin: Theater der Zeit, 2007), pp. 37–98.
92. Heidi Kuphal, 'Künstler kontra "Kolossiges"', *Berliner Morgenpost*, 11 May 1993; Eberhard Elfert, 'Was wird aus dem Thälmann-Denkmal?', *Kunst + Stadt. Stadt + Kunst*, 37 (1993), 6–8 (7).
93. Conversation with Wolfgang Krause, former head of Amt für Umwelt und Natur, Bezirk Pankow, 20 August 2007.
94. Eberhard Elfert, 'Monumentalplastik im Widerstreit der politischen Systeme', p. 365.
95. Flierl, 'Denkmalstürze zu Berlin', p. 51.
96. Kommission zum Umgang, 'Bericht', p. 35.
97. Eva-Maria Klother, *Denkmalplastik nach 1945 bis 1989 in Ost- und West-Berlin* (Münster: LIT, 1998), p. 156.
98. Beschluß der Bezirksverordnetenversammlung, 5 September 1990, in *Denk Mal Positionen*, p. 20.
99. Kommission zum Umgang, 'Bericht', pp. 34–35.
100. 'Beschluss der Bezirksverordnetenversammlung Prenzlauer Berg', 12 May 1993, Drucksache 273/93.

101. Conversation with Wolfgang Krause.
102. Bernt Roder, Museumsleiter, in *Denk Mal Positionen*, p. 3.
103. Bernd Kammer, 'Vom Sockel geholt, aber nicht entsorgt', *Neues Deutschland*, 10 December 1993; Andrea Scheuring, 'Thälmann versteckt hinter Pappeln?', *Berliner Zeitung*, 10 November 1993, p. 22; Rolf Lautenschläger, 'Laubwald mit Thälmann-Lichtung', *die tageszeitung*, 10 February 1994.
104. Ingeborg Hunzinger, 'Behutsamer Abriß', under 'Stimmen zu Thälmann-Denkmal', *Neues Deutschland*, 18 February 1993.
105. See, for example, letter from Thomas Flierl to resident Gisela N., dated 23 May 1991, in 'Diskussion um Thälmann-Denkmal nach 1990', Museum Pankow Archiv.
106. 'Gerechtigkeit für Thälmann', press release, PDS Prenzlauer Berg, 16 April 1993, in *Denk Mal Positionen*, p. 12.
107. Anke Meyer, 'Die Sockel der "roten Riesen" wackeln', *Berliner Morgenpost*, 9 August 1990; Regina Mönch, 'Den sozialistischen Koloß im Gebüsch verstecken?', *Der Tagesspiegel*, 19 February 1993; see also letters from residents, in 'Diskussion um Thälmann-Denkmal nach 1990', Museum Pankow Archiv.
108. Annette Tietenberg, 'Wohin mit Thälmann', *Der Tagesspiegel*, 9 June 1993.
109. BW, 'Zukunft mit oder ohne Thälmann?', *Wochenblatt*, 10 February 1994.
110. See Russel Lemmons, '"Imprisoned, Murdered, Besmirched": The Controversy Concerning Berlin's Ernst Thälmann Monument and German National Identity, 1990–1995', in *Memory Traces: 1989 and the Question of German Cultural Identity*, ed. by Silke Arnold-de Simine (Bern: Lang, 2005), pp. 309–34.
111. Anwohner-Initiative Ernst-Thälmann Park, 'Wir sind Denkmal!', 14 February 2014, https://thaelmannpark.wordpress.com/2014/02/14/wir-sind-denkmal/ (accessed 9 August 2016).
112. Karin Nölte, 'Verbaler Dreck', *Neues Deutschland*, 11 July 2003, https://www.neues-deutschland.de/artikel/38293.verbaler-dreck.html (accessed 19 December 2017).
113. See, for example, the readers' survey in 'Soll das Thälmann-Denkmal abgerissen werden?', *Berliner Kurier*, 11 July 2003, www.berlinonline.de/berliner-kurier/archiv/.bin/dump.fcgi/2003/0711/lokales/0074/index.html (accessed 15 July 2007); see also 'Was uns Leser schreiben und sagen', *Berliner Kurier*, 11 July 2003, http://www.berlinonline.de/berliner-kurier/archiv/.bin/dump.fcgi/2003/0711/berlinbrandenburg/0077/index.html (accessed 15 July 2007).
114. Conversation with Max Renkl, 'Aktionsbündnis Thälmann-Denkmal', 10 August 2007.
115. Stefan Strauß, 'Thälmann im Rampenlicht', *Berliner Zeitung*, 11 May 2009, www.berlinonline.de/berliner-zeitung/archiv/.bin/dump.fcgi/2009/0511/berlin/0051/index.html (accessed 15 March 2010); conversation with Max Renkl.
116. Stefan Strauß, 'Honecker-Zitate sollen zurück zum Thälmann-Denkmal', *Berliner Zeitung*, 8 April 2014, http://www.berliner-zeitung.de/berlin/

prenzlauer-berg-honecker-zitate-sollen-zurueck-zum-thaelmann-denkmal-1544398 (accessed 10 August 2016).
117. akl, 'Wieder vorzeigbar', *Der Tagesspiegel*, 22 September 2001, p. 14.
118. Conversation with Max Renkl.
119. Interview with Carsten Pfennig, 'Wie Ernst Thälmanns gedenken?', *Junge Welt*, 12/13 August 2000, p. 2.
120. Kerbel, cited in Karl Joachim Beuchel, *Die Stadt mit dem Monument: Zur Baugeschichte 1945-1990*, Aus dem Stadtarchiv Chemnitz, vol. 9 (Chemnitz: Druckerei Dämmig, 2006), p. 128.
121. Beuchel, *Die Stadt mit dem Monument*, p. 129.
122. Ulrich Hammerschmidt, 'Kerbels kapitaler Kopf für Karl-Marx-Stadt', *Freie Presse (Chemnitz)*, 7 November 1997, p. 9.
123. 'Stille Ehrung am Marx-Monument', *Freie Presse (Chemnitz)*, 6 May 1991.
124. Jens Kassner, *Chemnitz. Architektur. Stadt der Moderne* (Leipzig: Passage-Verlag, 2009), p. 66.
125. Stadtarchiv Chemnitz (ed.), *Karl-Marx-Stadt 1989 – Chemnitz 2009. Eine Stadt im Wandel. Chronik in Wort und Bild* (Erfurt: Sutton Verlag, 2009), p. 51.
126. Ibid., p. 57.
127. Barbara Ludwig, '20 Jahre Rückbenennung', *Chemnitz Inside*, Summer 2010, p. 6.
128. See 'Muß Marx ins Exil', *Blick (Chemnitz)*, 27 June 1990, p. 3.
129. Joachim Oehme, cited in 'Muß Marx ins Exil'.
130. 'OB für Erhalt des Marx-Monuments', *Freie Presse (Chemnitz)*, 4 August 1990.
131. Ulrich Hammerschmidt, 'Kerbels kapitaler Kopf für Karl-Marx-Stadt', *Freie Presse (Chemnitz)*, 7 November 1997, p. 9; Gabi Thieme, 'Streit um Marx fast ausgestanden', *Freie Presse (Chemnitz)*, 18 March 1994.
132. Stefan Weber, *Chemnitz: Ein Stadtzentrum sucht sein Gesicht* (Limbach-Oberfrohna: Bildverlag Thomas Böttger, no date [prob. late 1993/early 1994]).
133. 'Aschenputtel des Ostens', *Der Spiegel* (1993) 44, 56–63 (56).
134. Ibid.
135. Thieme, 'Streit um Marx fast ausgestanden'.
136. Gerhard Glaser, 'Das Karl-Marx-Forum in Chemnitz', in *Verfallen und vergessen oder aufgehoben und geschützt?*, pp. 52–60 (57).
137. See 'Innenstadt als DDR-Museum?', *Freie Presse (Chemnitz)*, 27/28 August 1994; 'DDR-Architektur ist ein Stück Stadtgeschichte', *Freie Presse (Chemnitz)*, 30 August 1994; 'City zum DDR-Museum erklärt', *Freie Presse (Chemnitz)*, 30 August 1994.
138. 'DDR-Museum: Nun ist Minister gefragt', *Freie Presse (Chemnitz)*, 24/25 September 1994; see also 'Der Leser hat das Wort', *Freie Presse (Chemnitz)*, 3/4 September 1994.
139. Glaser, 'Das Karl-Marx-Forum in Chemnitz', p. 60.
140. See 'Steinerne Marx von Schmierereien befreit', *Freie Presse (Chemnitz)*, 23 December 1994 and '"Kunstwerke" kosten Städte viel Geld', *Freie Presse (Chemnitz)*, 10 February 1998.

141. 'Jetzt wird's völlig verrückt – Nischel soll ins Aquarium', *Chemnitzer Morgenpost*, 9 August 1996.
142. See Stadtarchiv Chemnitz, *Karl-Marx-Stadt 1989*, pp. 72 and 76; 'Studenten verhüllen aus Protest den Philosophen Marx', *Freie Presse (Chemnitz)*, 15 May 2001; 'Lehrer streiken und demonstrieren', *Freie Presse (Chemnitz)*, 24 May 2005; 'Demonstration am Montag', *Freie Presse (Chemnitz)*, 12 March 2005.
143. See 'Dritte Montagsdemo heute Abend', *Freie Presse (Chemnitz)*, 30 August 2004; 'Montagsdemo am Marx-Monument', *Freie Presse (Chemnitz)*, 24 June 2005.
144. ULI, 'Wie man aus Marx Kapital schlägt', *Freie Presse (Chemnitz)*, 9/10 May 1998; Gabi Thieme, 'Marx statt Mozart als süßeste Versuchung', *Freie Presse (Chemnitz)*, 12 January 1999.
145. 'Karl Marx als ewiges Vermarktungsobjekt', *Die Welt*, 31 January 2008, http://www.welt.de/reise/article1606343/Karl_Marx_als_ewiges_Ver marktungsobjekt.html (accessed 9 February 2011).
146. ULI, 'Wie man aus Marx Kapital schlägt'; information from Chemnitz Tourist Office.
147. Gudrun Müller, 'Marx grinst – und sollte wohl weinen', *Freie Presse (Chemnitz)*, 14 January 1998.
148. dpa/mpu/chg, 'Wirbel um WM-Trikot vom Chemnitzer "Nischel" – geklaut und besprüht', *Leipziger Volkszeitung*, 6 June 2014, http://www.lvz.de/Leipzig/Polizeiticker/Polizeiticker-Mitteldeutschland/Wirbel-um-WM-Trikot-vom-Chemnitzer-Nischel-geklaut-und-besprueht (accessed 23 July 2015).
149. Grit Baldauf, 'Marx liest ab morgen Ikea-Katalog', *Freie Presse (Chemnitz)*, 28 October 2009, p. 11.
150. 'Karl Marx ziert jetzt die Sparkassen-Kreditkarte', *Die Welt*, 15 July 2012, http://www.welt.de/wirtschaft/article108297022/Karl-Marx-ziert-jetzt-die-Sparkassen-Kreditkarte.html (accessed 10 August 2016).
151. See 'Monumentale Mozart-Kugel', *Freie Presse*, 12 January 1995; 'Auch der geplante "Eismarx" ist noch nicht vom Tisch', *Chemnitzer Morgenpost*, 9 August 1996; 'Marx-Monument sollen die Ohren qualmen', *Freie Presse (Chemnitz)*, 26 August 2003; Marianne Schultz, 'Der blaue Stuhl kommt später', *Chemnitzer Stadtjournal*, 26 May 1997; Torsten Kohlschein, 'Gläserner "Kragen" für das Marx-Monument', *Freie Presse (Chemnitz)*, 26/27 October 1996.
152. Robert Reuther, 'Marx-Kopf soll kopiert werden', *Sächsische Zeitung*, 21 April 2007, http://www.sz-online.de/nachrichten/artikel.asp?id=1469750 &newsfeed=rss (accessed 8 February 2011).
153. Swen Uhlig, 'Absage für den Doppel-Kopf', *Freie Presse (Chemnitz)*, 25 April 2007, p. 11.
154. Dennis Kittler, 'Chemnitz duldet keinen zweiten Marx-Kopf', 25 April 2007, p. 2.
155. Uhlig, 'Absage für den Doppel-Kopf'.
156. Ibid.

157. See http://www.marxmonument.de/projekt.html (accessed 10 January 2011); Reiner Burger, 'Auf Augenhöhe mit Karl Marx', *Frankfurter Allgemeine*, 17 June 2008, http://www.faz.net/aktuell/gesellschaft/chemnitz-kopflos-auf-augenhoehe-mit-marx-1547155.html (accessed 19 December 2017).
158. Conversation with Mathias Lindner, Neue Sächsische Galerie, 15 March 2011; Katharina Leuoth, 'Film wird auf Marx-Plane gezeigt', *Freie Presse (Chemnitz)*, 27 August 2008.
159. Sandra Czabania, 'Marx-Tonbänder: "Unschätzbares Dokument"', *Freie Presse (Chemnitz)*, 12 September 2008.
160. Conversation with Mathias Lindner.
161. 'Marx ist dann mal weg', *Focus online*, 16 June 2008, http://www.focus.de/kultur/musik/kunstprojekt-marx-ist-dann-mal-weg_aid_311367.html (accessed 9 February 2011).
162. H. Jancke and M. Wiegers, 'Marx attraktiver als Frauenkirche', *BILD Chemnitz*, 3 May 2008.
163. Katharina Leuoth, 'Open-Air-Party feiert Namens-Jubiläum', *Freie Presse (Chemnitz)*, 26 May 2010; see also *Chemnitz Inside*, Summer 2010.
164. Hans Schwan, '"Deutscher Tag" mit Denkmalseinweihung und blutigem Straßenkampf in Böllberg', *Hallesches Tageblatt*, No. 109, 11 May 1995.
165. *Die "Fahne der Revolution" in Halle* (Bezirksleitung und Stadtleitung Halle der SED, no date), Stadtarchiv Halle, Häuserarchiv, No. 69.
166. See Volker Neumann, 'Ein "Kunst-Werk", das seine Geburtswehen nie los wurde', *Hallesches Tageblatt*, No. 195, 22 August 1995.
167. See Hubertus Adam, 'Rotes Tuch für die Telekom', *Frankfurter Allgemeine Zeitung*, 27 July 1996, p. 33; Claudia Hofmann, 'DDR-Monumentalkunst – am Hansering in Halle', Spiegel der Heimat Seminar, Universität Halle-Wittenberg, 20 May 1998, http://www.burg-halle.de/~jstahl/ksa99_9/ting/tp_hansa.html (accessed 9 February 2011).
168. Hofmann, 'DDR-Monumentalkunst'.
169. 'Monument in leuchtendem Rot', *Der Neue Weg*, No. 1254, 28 May 1968.
170. Adam, 'Zwischen Anspruch und Wirkungslosigkeit'.
171. Sebastian Stude, 'Halle/Saale 1989', *UTOPIE kreativ*, 201/202 (2007), 764–82 (780).
172. See Hanna Winkler, 'Anzeige gegen Unbekannte', *Der Neue Weg*, 3 March 1990; 'Silvesterscherz?', *Liberal-Demokratische Zeitung*, 2 January 1990.
173. Demmig/Wendt, 'Die Flamme der Revolution zum bunten Segel der Wende...!', *Reformzeitung Halle, Stimme der neuen demokratischen Bewegungen und Parteien*, 23 January 1990, http://www.ddr89.de/ddr89/dj/DJ33.html (accessed 12 November 2010).
174. dlo, 'Bunte Farbtupfer für Monumentalbauwerk', *Mitteldeutsche Zeitung*, 10 November 1992.
175. Bernd Martin, 'Telekom bringt Stadt in Zugzwang', *Mitteldeutsche Zeitung*, 25 October 1996.
176. See 'Stadtrat: "Fahne" soll stehen bleiben', *Mitteldeutsche Zeitung*, 21 November 1996; Bernd Martin, 'Brigt Brief von Vos Entscheidung?', *Mitteldeutsche Zeitung*, 18 November 1996.

177. See 'Leser-Kritik am Beschluß', *Mitteldeutsche Zeitung*, 26 November 1996.
178. 'Halles Junge Union will Fahne zu Fall bringen', *Mitteldeutsche Zeitung*, 24 May 1997.
179. See, for example, Bernhard Ax, 'Bilderstürmerei sollte vermieden werden', *Mitteldeutsche Zeitung*, 22 November 2000, p. 12; U. Rühlmann, 'Erneute Debatten um die Fahne am Hansering', *Hallesche Blätter*, 16 December 2000, pp. 20–21.
180. Walter Zöller, 'Die "Fahne" als Symbol', *Mitteldeutsche Zeitung*, 21 November 1996.
181. 'Häußler ist gegen Abriss', *Mitteldeutsche Zeitung*, 13 December 2000.
182. Andreas Lohmann, 'Ausschuss stimmt gegen den Abriss', *Mitteldeutsche Zeitung*, 10 January 2001; 'Die Fahne soll stehen bleiben', *Mitteldeutsche Zeitung*, 22 February 2001.
183. See, for example, 'Abriss ist umstritten', *Mitteldeutsche Zeitung*, 18 November 2000; Andreas Lohmann, 'Fahne wird herausgeputzt', *Mitteldeutsche Zeitung*, 9 October 2001.
184. Lohmann, 'Ausschuss stimmt gegen den Abriss'.
185. msp, 'Die Diskussion bleibt heftig und kontrovers', *Mitteldeutsche Zeitung*, 6 December 2000; see also Sven Triepel, cited in 'Abriß der "Fahne" weiter umstritten', *Mitteldeutsche Zeitung*, 16 May 1996.
186. Heidi Pohle, 'Fahne erregt die Gemüter', *Mitteldeutsche Zeitung*, 22 November 2000, p. 12; Horst Hartmann, 'Eine Fahne im politischen Winde', *Der Kunsthandel*, (1996) 11, Häuserarchiv der Stadt Halle, 'Hansering Allgemein Denkmale', Nr. 69.
187. See, for example, Frank Noack, 'Etwas mehr Toleranz könnte nicht schaden', *Mitteldeutsche Zeitung*, 22 November 2000, p. 12; Hans Schwan, '"Deutscher Tag" mit Denkmalseinweihung und blutigem Straßenkampf in Böllberg', *Hallesches Tageblatt*, 11 May 1995.
188. See, for example, msp, 'Die Diskussion bleibt heftig und kontrovers'.
189. Katja Pausch, 'Abfall dümpelt unter der Fahne', *Mitteldeutsche Zeitung*, 27 May 1999.
190. See, for example, Hartmann, 'Eine Fahne im politischen Winde'.
191. 'Voß schlägt neue Farbe vor', *Mitteldeutsche Zeitung*, 27 October 1997; msp, 'Kaiser stand weiter südlich', *Mitteldeutsche Zeitung*, 23 November 2000.
192. 'Die "Flamme" künftig als Fahne Europas?', *Mitteldeutsche Neueste Nachrichten*, 15 January 1990; go, 'Fahnen-Denkmal in Stadtfarben kleiden?', *Mitteldeutsche Zeitung*, 28 November 2000.
193. 'Beschluß des Stadtrates der Stadt Halle (Saale)', 27 March 2002, excerpt provided by Kulturbüro der Stadt Halle/Saale.
194. Conversation with Andreas Kahl, Kulturbüro der Stadt Halle/Saale, 8 March 2011. See also 'Fahne strahlt kosmisch rot', *Super Sonntag*, 2 March 2003.
195. 'Fahnenmonument ist neu gestaltet', *Amtsblatt*, 27 October 2004.
196. Detlef Färber, 'Neue Flamme am Hansering', *Mitteldeutsche Zeitung*, 30 October 2004.

197. 'Die "Fahne" erhält jetzt ein neues Gesicht', *Wochenspiegel*, 7 July 2004; Detlef Färber, '"Fahne" soll wieder richtig rot werden', *Mitteldeutsche Zeitung*, 1 March 2003.
198. Prof. Ludwig Ehrler, cited in 'Rückt die "Fahne" mit neuem Anstrich in weite Ferne?', *Mitteldeutsche Zeitung*, 2 July 2003.
199. Färber, 'Neue Flamme am Hansering'.
200. See David Johst, 'Entleerung der Geschichte', *die tageszeitung*, 30 July 2003, http://www.taz.de/1/archiv/archiv/?dig=2003/07/30/a0175 (accessed 15 July 2011).
201. Alexander Wendt, 'Lenins Comeback', *Fokus*, 24 April 2008, www.focus.de/politik/deutschland/tid-9731/ostdeutschland-lenins-comeback_aid_297254.html (accessed 15 March 2010).
202. Christoph Titz, 'Charly ist zurück an der Uni', *Spiegel Online*, 18 August 2008, www.spiegel.de/unispiegel/studium/0,1518,572440,00.html (accessed 15 March 2010); Wendt, 'Lenins Comeback'; Steffen Honig, 'Ärger mit dem 33-Tonnen-Marx', *Leipziger Volkszeitung*, 14 April 2008.
203. '"Einstimmig beschlossen"', *Leipziger Volkszeitung*, 16/17 February 2008, p. 20; Daniel Hechler and Peel Pasternack, *Deutungskompetenz in der Selbstanwendung: Der Umgang der ostdeutschen Hochschulen mit ihrer Zeitgeschichte* (Halle-Wittenberg: Institut für Hochschulforschung Wittenberg, 2011), p. 60.
204. See Thomas Mayer, '"Installation Paulinerkirche" als Symbol – Geschichte soll transparent und erfahrbar gemacht werden', *Leipziger Volkszeitung*, 12 May 1998; Thomas Mayer, 'Stehenlassen oder abreißen? Streit um Installation der Paulinerkirche', *Leipziger Volkszeitung*, 16 October 1999.
205. See Uta Baier, 'Leipzig hängt Tübke's DDR-Propaganda-Bild auf', *Die Welt*, 25 August 2009, http://www.welt.de/kultur/article4393010/Leipzig-haengt-Tuebkes-DDR-Propaganda-Bild-auf.html (accessed 15 July 2011); 'Erich Loest: Warum ich von Leipzig nach Halle emigriere', *Frankfurter Allgemeine Zeitung*, 9 May 2009, p. 40.
206. Sabine Kreuz, 'Ein Denkmal fällt', *Leipziger Volkszeitung*, 22 August 2006.
207. 'Marx-Relief wird fertiggestellt – Aufstellung der Schautafel', Universität Leipzig, Pressemeldung, No. 2008/209, 15 October 2008, http://www.zv.uni-leipzig.de/service/presse/pressemeldungen.html?ifab_modus=detail&ifab_id=3136 (accessed 15 March 2010).
208. Wendt, 'Lenins Comeback'.
209. A. Rau, 'Rektor reagiert auf erneute Loest-Kritik', *Leipziger Volkszeitung*, 22 February 2009, p. 17.
210. Thomas Mayer, 'Marx ist wieder da', *Leipziger Volkszeitung*, 18/19 October 2008, p. 3.
211. Klaus Staeubert, 'Kirchengrab wird Gedenkort', *Leipziger Volkszeiung*, 20 February 2008, p. 17.
212. Thomas Mayer, '"Ich hätte es lieber am Bildermuseum"', *Leipziger Volkszeitung*, 16/17 February 2008, p. 20.
213. Christoph Seidler, 'Viel Knatsch um Marx', *Spiegel Online*, 28 February 2008, www.spiegel.de/unispiegel/wunderbar/0,1518,538321,00.html (accessed 15 March 2010).

214. 'Offener Brief von Erich Loest', *BILD Leipzig*, 8 February 2008.
215. 'Erich Loest: Warum ich von Leipzig nach Halle emigriere', *FAZ*, 18 April 2009.
216. Klaus Staeubert, 'Paulinerinstallation soll über Bronzemonument thronen', *LVZ-Online*, 7 April 2008, www.lvz.de/aktuell/content/59147.html (accessed 15 March 2010).
217. K.S., 'Denkmal für die Opfer', *Leipziger Volkszeitung*, 14 February 2008, p. 20.
218. 'Dresdner Ministerin klebt am Marx-Relief', *BILD Leipzig*, 7 March 2008; 'Der Tag der Schande', *BILD Leipzig*, 15 August 2008; 'Schwarzer Tag für die Stadt der Wende-Helden', *BILD Leipzig*, 2 April 2008.
219. Erik Trümper, 'Marx bleibt liegen!', *BILD Leipzig*, 6 March 2008.
220. Thorsten Hinz, 'Runder Tisch ist Winklers letzte Hoffnung', *Leipziger Volkszeitung*, 29/30 March 2008, p. 17.
221. Press release, Paulinerverein, 'Zur Wiederaufstellung des Marx-Monuments', 27 February 2008, in *Leipziger Zeitung*, 18/19 October 2008, p. 3.
222. Jackie Richard, 'Uni bettelt um Pauliner-Spenden', *BILD Leipzig*, 11 March 2008; Hinz, 'Runder Tisch ist Winklers letzte Hoffnung', p. 17; Wendt, 'Lenins Comeback'.
223. http://forum.lvz-online.de/lvz-ted-diskussionen/962-wo-soll-das-karl-marx-relief-aufgestellt-werden.html (accessed 23 March 2010).
224. Jacki Richard, 'Mehrheit gegen Marx-Comeback bestätigt', *BILD Leipzig*, 25 February 2008; '"Es muss eingelagert werden"', *Leipziger Volkszeitung*, 25 February 2008, p. 17.
225. Klaus Staeubert, 'Marx-Relief: Fünf Leipziger ändern Jungs Meinung', *LVZ-Online*, 7 April 2008, http://www.lvz.de/aktuell/content/59147.html.
226. See Klaus Staeubert, 'Trümmergrab mit Marx-Relief', *Leipziger Volkszeitung*, 18 February 2008, p. 17; Staeubert, 'Kirchengrab wird Gedenkort', p. 17.
227. Wendt, 'Lenins Comeback'. There is, however, in the southeastern suburbs of Leipzig, a 'Gedenkort' in the 'Park an der Etzoldschen Sandgrube' in memory of the Paulinerkirche, where its ruins were deposited.
228. Thomas Meyer, '"Die Installation gibt es nicht mehr"', *Leipziger Volkszeitung*, 15 April 2008, p. 17; Klaus Staeubert, 'Uni stellt Marx "oben ohne" auf', *LVZ-Online*, 9 June 2008, www.lvz.de/aktuell/content/64703.html.
229. Annika Schindelarz, press release, 'Information am Marx-Relief verkürzt historische Einordnung', Leipzig Student Council, 17 October 2008, downloaded from http://www.stud.uni-leipzig.de (accessed 24 March 2010).
230. nle, 'Marx-Relief auf Campus Jahnallee ab Freitag mit Schautafel', *LVZ-Online*, 15 October 2008, www.lvz-online.de/aktuell/content/76019.html (accessed 20 October 2008).

Chapter 3

SOVIET SPECIAL CAMPS
Reassessing a Repressed Past

The demise of the GDR not only brought about a widespread desire to eliminate parts of the socialist landscape, but it also allowed hidden or repressed sites to be rediscovered and reassessed. Most prominently, the discovery in early 1990 of mass graves of German internees who had died in Soviet special camps (*Speziallager*) at Buchenwald, Sachsenhausen and Fünfeichen (near Neubrandenburg) between 1945 and 1950 broke forty years of silence surrounding this subject in the GDR. Former internees finally felt able to speak out about the terrible conditions and brutal interrogations to which they had been subjected, with many claiming their innocence and lack of involvement in the National Socialist regime. Memorial signs were erected by survivors and families of deceased internees, with 1989/90 witnessing the emergence of nearly fifty different commemorative sites to instances of injustice in the immediate post-war years.[1] The following years saw the publication of a plethora of memoirs and reports about the special camps, with seventeen published in the first five years, and a further forty-one by 2007, alongside at least thirty-six edited volumes of collected reports and memories.[2] The history of the special camps and Soviet-run interrogation centres not only became representative of wider abuses of power and repression in the GDR, but was also incompatible with the official historical narrative of the GDR and severely discredited the cornerstone of East German legitimacy: antifascism.

This chapter examines the efforts at four sites after 1990 to commemorate the victims of Soviet imprisonment between 1945 and 1950, and reveals a complex web of conflicting memories. The sites, chosen for their contrasting natures, demonstrate a number of different mnemonic challenges: how, for example, should a new monument be erected within an established memorial site that has for years been a GDR national memorial to antifascism (Buchenwald), and to what extent does such a memorial need to interact with existing symbolism at the site? Conversely, to what extent should a new memorial site be created if all physical remnants have been erased from the landscape (Fünfeichen), and how does a town commemorate its former citizens who never returned from this camp, yet whose fates have almost been forgotten (Greifswald)? Finally, how should a Soviet interrogation centre that was subsequently used by the Stasi be marked today (Prenzlauer Allee)? Despite their different histories, discussions over the design and location of the new monuments have, in all cases, caused debate over Germany's 'dual past' and the comparison of two dictatorships, highlighted frictions between eastern and western modes of remembrance, and raised the question of how one should remember this past without commemorating Nazi perpetrators as victims.

The central conclusions of this chapter all relate to the fact that memorialization of this period is embedded within broader understandings of, and engagement with, twentieth-century German history. Indeed, while the sites in question are dedicated to specific events and locations, debates surrounding their evolution have highlighted much broader ethical concerns, in which the remembrance of past dictatorial regimes is linked to the democratic credentials of the present. Memorial work at these sites has thus often become an ongoing process of learning, in which a number of interest groups have had to review their understandings of the past. Such memorial negotiations have highlighted the blurring of boundaries between those previously considered 'victims' and 'perpetrators', thus demanding the need for a more complex and nuanced understanding of both dictatorships. The memorial aesthetics found at these sites are also best understood within the context of broader traditions of remembrance, for they are all united in their efforts to break the silence surrounding this past, and shaped by the absent remembrance history relating to this past in eastern Germany. In most cases, this has resulted in traditional and often religious memorial symbols, which carry immediate emotional resonance for victims' groups and their families, as well as denoting resistance to the SED's atheist policies. Although 1990 marked a historical caesura, the mnemonic language of new remembrance thus emerged very much in conversation with the past.

Special Camps and Interrogation Centres

On 18 April 1945, the Soviet People's Commissariat for Internal Affairs (NKVD) formed a department for special camps.[3] Subsequently, ten camps were set up within the Soviet zone of occupation, some on the sites of existing prisons (e.g. Torgau and Bautzen), and others on the sites of either former prisoner of war camps (e.g. Mühlberg and Fünfeichen) or former concentration camps (e.g. Sachsenhausen and Buchenwald). A system of camps for the internment of Nazi functionaries and state office holders was not unique to the Eastern zone; camps were set up in the Western zones too, sometimes also on the grounds of former concentration camps. However, differences between the two were marked by the longevity of the camps, the living conditions and death rates. In the American zone, for instance, half of the internees in such camps had been released by the summer of 1946, by which time the camps were already under German administration.[4] Those who remained were awaiting trial and tried according to the rule of law. Internees were also allowed to correspond with relatives from the end of 1945, and later even receive visits; the death rate approximately corresponded to that of the civilian population.[5] In contrast, those in Soviet camps were not allowed any contact with the outside world, and many were held without trial (giving rise to the difference between *Internierte* [those who were interned without trial] and *SMT-Verurteilte* [those who had been put on trial at Soviet military tribunals, and often given long sentences]). Death rates constituted approximately one-third of all camp inmates, a figure estimated to be around 44,000; the majority died of hunger and illness, although Soviet figures from 1990 reveal that 756 German prisoners were shot.[6] The exact death toll and the total number of internees are unknown, and while Soviet data suggest that 122,671 Germans were imprisoned in special camps, these figures are widely contested. Although estimates vary, it is now generally accepted that approximately 154,000 German prisoners were interned, alongside 35,000 foreigners, making a total of 189,000.[7] Early 1947 saw the largest death toll across most camps as a result of hunger, before the food rations were increased. Seven camps were closed in 1948 (although many of the inmates were transferred to other camps), with the three remaining camps at Bautzen, Buchenwald and Sachsenhausen closing in early 1950. While just over half of the remaining 29,632 prisoners were freed at this point, just under half were handed over to the GDR's Ministry for the Interior, either to complete their sentences or to be put on trial in Waldheim; a smaller proportion were sent to the Soviet Union.[8]

Alongside the system of camps, a large number of NKVD-controlled interrogation centres also existed across the country, otherwise known as 'GPU-cellars'.[9] Frequently housed in makeshift cells in the basements of public buildings, prisons or confiscated private houses, prisoners were subjected to extremely unsanitary conditions, violence and torture.[10] Often prisoners did not know why they had been arrested or how long they would be held for; most were then sent on to special camps or deported to the Soviet Union.[11] The exact number of such prisons is unknown, but research has shown that most built-up areas would have at least one building in which a cellar had been provisionally turned into a prison.[12] In many cases, the brutal interrogations forced prisoners into what may have been false confessions, and the Soviet interrogators often showed little interest in establishing whether prisoners were genuinely guilty or innocent.

From April 1945, members of specific groups were arrested to ensure the liquidation of the Nazi Party, a large proportion of whom ended up in GPU-cellars and/or special camps. In the first instance, these consisted of active members of the party, leaders of the fascist youth organizations and members of the Gestapo and security services, as well as regional and local council leaders and newspaper editors. However, other groups also affected included those operating illegal radio stations, printing presses or producing anti-Soviet publications, as well as individuals deemed to be spies, saboteurs or terrorists – commonly young people accused of so-called *Werwolf* activities.[13] Questions concerning the relative guilt or innocence of those interned often remain unanswered, yet it is clear that by no means all prisoners were Nazis, and of those who were, many were small fry; those who were more heavily implicated, such as members of the SS, had largely been sent to POW camps in the Soviet Union. Visual evidence of the conditions and methods of torture in the camps is also limited, for unlike the documentation of concentration camps, there is practically no such record of the Soviet special camps. Evidence is thus often reliant on eyewitness accounts, many of which were written years after the events themselves, and few of which were published before unification due to the difficult status accorded to former internees.

It was particularly in the East that victims of special camps experienced difficulties, for the camps became taboo during the GDR. While there was newspaper coverage of the closure of the last camps in 1950, in order to demonstrate the success of denazification, reporting on this topic was both short-lived and decidedly partial. Reports from January 1950, for instance, depicted those leaving the camps as cheerful, well fed and well dressed, and complimentary about the sanitary conditions in the camps and their treatment by the Soviets.[14] The reports also made clear that the camps were explicitly not concentration camps, and that those interned had either been 'small Nazis' or criminals who had been democratized and no longer posed a danger to society.[15] After such press reports, however, there was no further mention of the camps in *Neues Deutschland* or other GDR media until 1989.[16] Their very existence proved highly problematic to a state that was attempting to build a clear tradition and sense of legitimacy based on antifascist resistance. As such, former internees were forced to remain silent about their experiences; while some were required to sign declarations stating that they would keep silent, others were made aware of professional or familial disadvantages should they decide to speak out.[17] The camps thus became known as *Schweigelager* (camps of silence), not only because internees had no form of communication with the outside world during their internment, but also because they were subjected to silence until 1989. The discovery of mass graves in the early 1950s and 1980s was also covered up, only coming to light once again under new political circumstances. Following Paul Connerton, GDR society was thus encouraged to forget through a process of 'repressive erasure'.[18]

This process became an integral part of the SED's efforts to build a strong antifascist tradition through clear symbolic language. The high point of this development was the opening of the three central 'National Sites of Warning and Memory' in Buchenwald (1958), Ravensbrück (1959) and Sachsenhausen (1961). At all three sites, members of the communist resistance were presented as active heroes rather than passive victims of fascism, and memorial statues such as Fritz Cremer's group of figures at Buchenwald, or Willi Lammert's The Carrier at Ravensbrück captured this active struggle. As Niven observes, these memorials 'transformed misery and death into a kind of muscular spiritual energy focused on defiant mutual support and solidarity'.[19] Yet these sites barely mentioned non-communist resistance groups, and the presentation of Jews was negligible. At Buchenwald, the antifascist myth was taken to its height in the exaggerated narrative of self-liberation that was developed around the liberation of the camp on 11 April 1945, and was clearly represented in the defiant stance of Cremer's figural group, in which heroic resistance rather than suffering is the dominant theme.[20] The memorial site at Buchenwald became a site of pilgrimage for youth groups and school classes, adopting almost quasi-religious characteristics; its symbolic importance for the moral legitimacy of the GDR and as a motive for peace and socialism was hard to trump. There was clearly no space for special camps within this narrative.

In West Germany, the situation was clearly different, although surprisingly few published accounts documented the special camps. While former internees who fled to the West after their release were called upon as important witnesses in the Cold War against the Soviet Union, many were fearful of speaking out in case it endangered relatives in the East. By the late 1960s and early 1970s, however, even fewer were willing to speak publicly, due to growing concerns that they may be condemned as former Nazis, or as inveterate 'cold warriors' at a time of detente between East and West. Some even feared the reactions of their own children and remained silent, believing that no-one would understand what they went through.[21] A few notable accounts and research findings on special camps were published in the West, although it is significant that the first in-depth research to appear dated from 1979, and constituted little more than thirty pages of a much longer book.[22]

The scant treatment of special camps in both East and West German traditions inevitably led to a need to rework this past (or, especially in eastern Germany, to rework the reworking of the past: *die Aufarbeitung der Aufarbeitung*); not only was there a lack of information, but a web of taboos, legends and prejudices had accumulated over the years. Above all, numerous questions were raised by the fact that many special camps lay on the grounds of former concentration camps. How, for instance, should these two pasts be remembered on the same site? Should they be given equal status, or should the remembrance of certain periods and victims be given precedence over others? Should they be compared and remembered alongside each other, or maintain distance from one another? Such questions inevitably re-stoked the much broader debate about the desirability of comparing the Nazi and communist legacies, and harked back to the historians' debate of the 1980s about the singularity of Nazi crimes. Talk of Germany's 'dual past', its 'two dictatorships' or of the GDR as the 'second German dictatorship' brought the two regimes into close proximity, with the totalitarian paradigm often being employed to evoke clear parallels. Not only do a number of sites share a brutal history from these two pasts,[23] but certain formulations – such as Hubertus Knabe's description of the former Stasi prison at Hohenschönhausen as the 'Dachau of communism'[24] – have deliberately sought to compare the two.

The juxtaposition of these pasts at special camps inevitably led to tensions and rivalry between victims' groups. On the one hand, victims of Nazi concentration camps feared that the historical revision of special camps would lead to a relativization of Nazi crimes and ultimately a degradation in the status of their memorial sites. Moreover, they viewed those interned in special camps not as victims, but rather as their perpetrators, and often refused to share sites of memory with them. On the other hand, many former special camp internees – especially those who were interned as young people – demanded equal status to those held in concentration camps, and often claimed that they were treated as 'second-class victims' and unfairly stigmatized as former Nazis. The reluctance of many memorial sites to place both pasts on an equal footing and to follow a certain 'hierarchy of memory' only served to strengthen such sentiments, with victims' groups once again feeling that their history was being marginalized. The critical question in this rivalry concerned above all the composition of the special camp internees. While it is widely recognized that not all internees were Nazi criminals, research suggests that the majority were low-level functionaries of National Socialism, without whom the system would not have worked.[25] Due to the fact that most internees had been responsible adults by 1933, however, the majority of eyewitnesses who were still alive after 1990 fell into the much smaller category of younger internees, many of whom had been incorrectly suspected of *Werwolf* or other subterfuge activities. It is thus little surprise that many of this group felt an acute need to see justice addressed, often through the erection of symbolic markers of remembrance.

Official processes of working through this 'dual past' on a national level and addressing questions of comparability were, of course, examined in the two special enquiry commissions carried out by the Bundestag, at which it was recognized that the comparison – rather than the equation – of Nazi and communist regimes was legitimate. Following the so-called 'Faulenbach formula' (after historian Bernd Faulenbach), the recommendation was thus made that while Nazi crimes should not be relativized, neither should communist crimes be trivialized. The second commission was particularly significant for sites with 'dual pasts', for it was tasked with developing recommendations for a 'comprehensive concept for memorial sites', and recognized the critical role of both Buchenwald and Sachsenhausen in the process of developing an 'anti-totalitarian consensus and democratic remembrance culture in Germany'.[26] Following on from this report, a federal concept was drawn up in 1999 with the aim of systematizing and centralizing federal support for such memorial sites.[27] Subsequently, the coalition treaty of 2005 between the CDU, CSU and SPD committed itself to updating this concept, 'with the goal of giving appropriate consideration to both dictatorships in Germany'.[28] A draft was made public in 2007, which provoked outspoken criticism from historians and directors of memorial sites, who saw the document as not differentiating adequately between the two dictatorships, and equating them too strongly under the paradigm of totalitarianism, thus evoking a sense of parallelism.[29] Criticism was also directed towards the report's tendency to reduce both dictatorships to systems of repression, without recognizing the existence of 'normality' and multiple experiences of life in these systems, especially bearing in mind the 'expert commission' headed by Sabrow from the previous year.[30] A final and revised version of the document was published in June 2008, in which these criticisms were addressed, in particular the question of how unified Germany should responsibly deal with the legacy of both dictatorships. Notably, the 'Faulenbach formula' was once again repeated: while National Socialist crimes were not to be relativized, neither was the SED dictatorship to be trivialized.[31]

The Memorial Sites Concept of 2008 not only ascribes a heightened meaning to memorial sites as 'places of learning', but also highlights the importance of authenticity at such sites, which are expected to display concrete reference to the victims or to the methods of persecution.[32] The concepts of authenticity and materiality are, indeed, central to definitions of memorial sites, in contrast to monuments, which may be erected in any symbolic space.[33] The materiality of authentic buildings, objects or clothing at such sites clearly provides the past with an auratic presence that cannot be replicated through monuments, and which invests memorial sites with a 'truth-value' that can make them sites of strong emotional engagement.[34] Difficulties thus inevitably emerge when there are few traces of authentic remnants left on a site, as is the case with the two special camps examined in this chapter. Should the authenticity of location be marked by new memorial structures? If so, how should the inauthentic interact with the authentic, and how should it correspond to the existing usage of the site? As the following examples show, such questions become further complicated by the differing expectations of conflicting victims' groups, whose demands for representation clashed not only with each other, but often with the desire of historians and memorial site authorities to adopt a more 'scientific' approach.

Commemoration without Monumentalization: Representing Silenced Memories at Buchenwald

Commemoration at Buchenwald has a long history, on which much has already been written. The following discussion aims to move beyond existing scholarship, by focusing on successful and unsuccessful attempts to install symbolic memorial structures in memory of the special camp. These can only be understood, however, within the broader context of the evolution of the site since 1945, which has taken many twists and turns. The memorialization of concentration camp victims began almost immediately, with a temporary wooden obelisk erected in the camp itself on 19 April 1945, only eight days after the arrival of American troops at the camp; it formed the centre-point of a ceremony to remember the dead, organized by the prisoners' camp committee, consisting largely of German communists. Others followed, including a large, red, upturned triangular pyramid erected on Weimar's central Goetheplatz for the second anniversary of liberation on 11 April 1947.[35] The use of the red triangle – the symbol of political prisoners – in this and other monuments highlighted the increasing dominance of communist ideology in interpreting and commemorating the camp. The apogee of this trend came eleven years later with the completion of Cremer's long-awaited and much revised memorial. Dedicated in 1958, it forms part of a massive memorial arena, which takes the visitor down steps flanked by stone stelae, past mass ring graves, along a 'Street of Nations' flanked by a series of pylons, and up a long flight of steps to the memorial and a bell tower. The whole complex constitutes a 'path of learning',[36] for the visitor emerges from the depths of fascism and rises towards the monument, which depicts the prisoners as heroic resistance fighters in charge of their own destiny; they are seen not as victims, but as actors in the battle against fascism, thus celebrating the myth of communist self-liberation.[37] Due to its national importance in the GDR, Buchenwald has been variously called 'the major jewel in the GDR's commemorative crown', the 'Kyffhäuser of the GDR' and a 'Red Olympus';[38] it was without doubt central to the state's myth-building apparatus.

Since 1990, however, the GDR's central Buchenwald myths have been challenged by the emergence of marginalized and silenced memories. The narrative of heroic self-liberation, for instance, became increasingly questioned in view of the arrival of American troops on the same day, and claims over the privileged treatment of communist 'Kapos' – those who were preferred by the SS for the camp's self-administration – to the detriment of other inmates cast a shadow over the heroic role in which they had previously been presented. The discovery of mass graves from the Soviet special camp in early 1990, however, provided one of the most severe blows to the GDR narrative of antifascism, and unleashed the floodgates for personal memories of survivors and their families.[39] Moreover, revelations that bones had already been uncovered in 1983 during the laying of a water pipe, but rapidly covered up, cast aspersions on the management of the memorial complex at the time. Accusations that personnel at the site continued to suppress the history of the camp persisted into the mid 1990s, with a tabloid press campaign claiming that several employees had worked for the Stasi.[40] Against this background, however, questions concerning appropriate commemoration of the special camp became increasingly prominent: should it be remembered on the same site as the concentration camp, and how should its victims – many of whom were Nazi members – be remembered without resulting in heroization?

The first step towards answering such questions was the establishment of a Historians' Commission by Thuringia's Ministry for Science and Art. Chaired by historian Eberhard Jäckel, the commission consisted only of west German experts, and met three times between September 1991 and February 1992. The predominance of western experts echoed the composition of the Bundestag's first special enquiry commission from 1992 to 1994, demonstrating not only the political distrust of former East German experts in these early years, but also the common desire to repurpose the site to western 'norms'. This was of particular significance at Buchenwald given its prominence in the memory landscape of the GDR, and as the 'jewel in the GDR's commemorative crown', the site doubtless retained heightened symbolism (particularly in contrast to other such sites – see the section on Fünfeichen below), this time for the reworking of GDR history. The commission recommended that the site should remember both camps, but that the memory of the special camp should be secondary to that of the concentration camp, and that the sites should be spatially separated.[41] The recommendations were to be realized in three phases through the development of three new exhibitions, relating first to the concentration camp (opened in 1995), second to the special camp (opened in 1997) and third to the history of the memorial complex between 1950 and 1990 (opened in 1999), which would relate especially to the 1958 memorial. The special camp exhibit was to be housed in a flat building opening onto the mass graves – separated from and located below the concentration camp site, thus denoting its secondary status.

While much work has already been done on the evolution of these three phases at Buchenwald, there has been little nuanced reflection on various attempts to install symbolic memorial structures in memory of the special camp. In addition to the above-mentioned exhibition building, plans for the development of the area dedicated to the special camp featured three key elements, all of which involved aspects of memorialization: early spontaneous commemorative gestures, a symbolic *Trauerplatz* (square of mourning) associated with the exhibition building, and the *Waldfriedhof* (woodland graveyard). The first of these began soon after the discovery of mass graves in the wooded area just outside the former camp, for on 4 February 1990 the memorial site authorities erected a provisional wooden cross to the victims of the special camp, to which it cleared a path through the woods.[42] During the following weeks and months, the relatives of deceased internees began to place their own crosses and memorial stones around this cross. Later that year, the Initiativgruppe Buchenwald 1945–1950, a group founded in February 1990 for former internees and their relatives, took charge of building a proper signed path to the graves, which went around the camp grounds rather than across the memorial complex, to which former concentration camp internees had objected. The number of crosses and stones grew rapidly, although not always without controversy. A cross in memory of Otto Koch, mayor of Weimar from 1937 to 1945, for instance, caused notable unrest. The wording on the cross erected by his son, which claimed that he had 'saved' Weimar, had to be removed, for despite being one of the first to wave the white flag when the Americans arrived, he was also responsible for the ghettoization of Weimar's Jews, among other crimes, during the Third Reich.[43] The merging of private and public memories proved difficult here, for this site grew spontaneously as a result of the desire to finally commemorate loved ones in a public way, yet as it grew, it increasingly adopted the aura of an official site of memory, making any attempts to rehabilitate or heroize former Nazis clearly unacceptable. The increasing number of crosses and stones also meant that space in this makeshift memorial became crowded, and following the recommendations of the Historians' Commission, steps were eventually taken to mark the graves in a more systematic way, creating the *Waldfriedhof*, and providing families with a more sizable *Trauerplatz*. These elements, however, were closely bound up with the controversial competition for an exhibition building and associated memorial space.

In November 1993, the *Land* of Thüringen launched a competition for an ensemble that was to consist of an exhibition building and an area to remember the victims of the special camp (the so-called *Trauerplatz*). This second element was to be linked to the *Waldfriedhof*, where the mass graves had been discovered, and to provide space for up to fifty people for commemorative ceremonies and the laying of wreaths and flowers. As the competition brief stated, 'An artistic design for the square is desirable (sculpture, obelisk, cross or similar). All forms of monumentalization should be avoided in this endeavour'.[44] Contrary to the more prescriptive brief for the exhibition building, relative freedom thus existed for the design of an appropriate and symbolic memorial space. However, this found heightened resistance among former concentration camp survivors and their supporters. Most vocal of these was the German-Jewish communist survivor Emil Carlebach, vice-president of the International Buchenwald Committee, who published a damning article entitled 'Reich Flag over Buchenwald? Preparations for a Second Rudolf Hess Valhalla', in which he argued that Buchenwald would become a new pilgrimage site for neo-Nazis.[45] Romani Rose, chair of the Central Council of German Sinti and Roma, claimed that he would not 'bow down to the perpetrators', and would not allow the victims to be 'forced to merge' (*zwangsvereinigt*).[46] Similarly, French communist and president of the International Committee of Buchenwald-Dora (IKBD), Pierre Durand, insisted on one single antifascist tradition, claiming, 'Buchenwald has become a worldwide symbol for suffering and for our struggle against fascism. Dare not desecrate this!'[47]

Despite such objections, a winning design was recommended by the jury in May 1994, which incorporated several symbolic elements. The design by architects Frese and Kleindienst, in conjunction with artist Klaus Eichler, proposed an exhibition building in front of which a memorial space facing onto the mass graves would include several elements: thirty shoulder-high beechwood pillars, a wall extending beyond the end of the exhibition building containing a 'window' that would be visible from the main concentration camp building and would focus visitors' gazes towards the woodland graves, a free-standing wall at right angles to this, which would mark the steps leading to the lower level, and a bridge-like structure that would lead from the exhibition building towards the mass graves, ending in mid-air over the boundary fence. The ensemble of building and memorial space was to draw attention towards the mass graves and create a link towards the concentration camp above. For the architects, this space was to portray the inhumanity of imprisonment of all kinds: 'For this reason we renounce all signs of allegiance, such as emblems or symbols, and instead [present] a design which – beyond national pathos, political contests or religious smokescreens – conveys the feeling of a special place to every single visitor'.[48] The jury saw the design to form 'an exciting dialogue with the *Waldfriedhof*', recommending only that the original plan to burn victims' names into the pillars be dropped.[49] The jury's recommendation was taken forward by the Board of Trustees of the Buchenwald and Mittel-Dora Foundation, with whom the final decision lay. The Board recommended, however, that caution be exercised regarding the memorial space at this stage, and that the beechwood pillars should be withdrawn, at least until the building was completed.[50] As demonstrated by this recommendation, the need to balance the symbolism of this space with existing commemorative structures already at the memorial complex was becoming increasingly clear.

After construction work on the documentation building began in June 1995, the project became the subject of a bitter dispute between the memorial site's new director, Volkhard Knigge, and victims' associations. Following extensive research into Soviet files on the special camps, Knigge asserted that approximately 80 per cent of prisoners had been 'civil functionaries' of the National Socialist regime, meaning that they had held low and middle-ranking offices within the party or its associated organizations.[51] In light of these findings, he became increasingly wary of any form of heroization of the special camp's prisoners through symbolic memorialization, and of drawing parallels with victims of the concentration camp. Consequently, Knigge and the Thuringian Ministry of Science, Research and Culture decided to divorce the exhibition building from the associated memorial elements, causing architects Frese and Kleindienst to withdraw from the project.[52] Knigge argued that historical work at Buchenwald followed 'scientific' principles, and thus he did not wish to mix documentation with memorial elements that could influence visitors' perceptions. For him – and in clear contrast to the architects – these symbols were 'unambiguously interpretative of history' and carried the 'function of a memorial', most problematically calling on 'a very general, victim-focused language of form'.[53] Most significantly, he felt that they harked back to specific memorials to victims of National Socialism, thus potentially drawing dangerous parallels between the victims of the two camps. Not only did he view the bridge-like structure to be a citation of the ramp at Auschwitz, but it also reminded him of a similar monument at Yad Vashem in Jerusalem.[54] Moreover, he felt that the pillars recalled numerous other monuments to victims of the Holocaust, most specifically the recently completed monument to Sinti and Roma at Buchenwald itself, and he controversially warned that the memorial site should not become the home of 'the most beautiful Nazi monument'.[55] For him, this ensemble would have damaged not only the memory of innocent prisoners of the special camp, but also the pedagogical work of the memorial site, for it would have harboured historical misunderstandings and potentially exonerated former Nazi perpetrators of their moral responsibility, thus relativizing the National Socialist past. What is interesting here, above all, is the fact that certain plastic forms appear to have adopted such strong association with the commemoration of Holocaust victims that they have become symbolically replete, rendering them potentially dangerous or damaging in other contexts. While the architects had deliberately attempted to avoid associative emblems or symbols, with the aim of freeing the site from such associations, it is clear that abstract forms may also be imbued with strong symbolic meaning through repeated association, and in the process become highly politicized.

There were widespread objections to Knigge's arguments, particularly among groups representing victims of the special camp and their families. First, they objected to the claim that the large majority of prisoners were guilty, feeling that Knigge was making unfounded moral judgements based on files that sometimes contained information provided by prisoners under torture, or were the result of mistranslations from the German. In this context, he was reproached for acting as a 'judge', while the local *BILD* newspaper polemically accused him of 'classifying corpses'.[56] Second, they objected to the removal of memorial elements from the design, claiming that this left little more than a bunker, which resulted in this part of history being hidden from the main camp. In direct response to Knigge, the Initiativgruppe thus argued that the proposal was as 'historically interpretative' as any memorial elements themselves.[57] In protest against these decisions, the prisoners' advisory board for the special camp refused to work with the memorial site's authorities for a period, and the Initiativgruppe withdrew support for the donation of historical artefacts to the exhibition. In more spectacular fashion, Manfred Wettstein, chair of the Thuringian association 'Victims of Stalinism' (OdS) – and ex-Stasi officer – formally pressed charges against Knigge for 'incitement of the people, defamation and vilification of the memory of the deceased'.[58] While the proceedings were eventually dropped, this action led to a high-profile debate within the local and national press on the management of Germany's 'double past'.

Much of the debate drew on the broader discussion of life in a dictatorship, and as in other monument debates discussed in this book, arguments on both sides called on personal experience of the GDR to provide ammunition. The Initiativgruppe, for instance, objected strongly to Knigge's failure to consult with them, accusing him of acting in a dictatorial fashion rather than democratically,[59] and the regional Association of Victims of Stalinism (VOS) claimed that this treatment of history was 'worse than it was during GDR times'.[60] The Initiativgruppe also questioned Knigge's understanding of what life was like in a dictatorship, for as a former West German he lacked personal experience and was not in a position to judge. As former GDR citizens themselves, they claimed to better understand the constraints and norms of life in a dictatorship, and noted that at least 80 per cent of the GDR population would have been involved in official party-related organizations at some point in their lives.⁶¹ Interestingly, however, Knigge also drew on GDR history in order to justify his actions, claiming that the use of emotional and symbolic elements in order to influence the interpretation of history, particularly before being fully historically informed, was 'a sign of paternalistic [*bevormundenden*] GDR memorial site pedagogy, and is thus no longer to be found in the new permanent exhibition on the history of Buchenwald concentration camp'.⁶² Similarly, he also claimed that official interpretations of National Socialism in the GDR were partly to blame for current conflicts: not only were the histories of special camps suppressed, but in his eyes a societal history of National Socialism that examined the everyday lives of Germans had never been written. Instead, the focus on the upper echelons of power and those deemed 'capitalists' acquitted the large majority of the population from any responsibility; the 'fascists' were always presented as the 'other'.⁶³ For him, the current debate was thus in part about deconstructing the myths and legends of the past, but for both sides, this specific memorial debate concerned the much broader issue of understanding what life was like under the SED dictatorship, and – as seen in debates in Chapter 2 – contrasting the dictatorial past with the democratic present.

While former prisoners and their families continued to lament decisions to withdraw the memorial concept, former victims of the concentration camp conversely expressed their ongoing dissatisfaction with the profiling of this history at the memorial site. At a meeting of the Bundestag's special enquiry commission at Buchenwald in October 1996, where the attempt was made to bring the victims of both dictatorships together to discuss the 'work of memorial sites for later generations', Pierre Durand walked out with two colleagues, announcing, 'We won't sit together at one table with the representatives of our executioners'.⁶⁴ As this incident demonstrated, the presence of eyewitnesses from both pasts gave rise to heightened emotions throughout, only deepening Knigge's belief that a strictly 'scientific' route was the only one that could be pursued by the memorial site. The building and exhibition were duly opened in 1997 without any associated memorial space.

Although former internees and their families were not provided with a formal memorial space, two other developments at the site have helped to assuage their disappointment, and have subsequently been accepted as appropriate commemorative symbols. First, following the discovery of mass graves beyond the perimeters of the camp, methodical searches began in 1991 to identify the locations of the graves. More were found in subsequent years, and by 1994 it was believed that approximately 845 mass graves existed, containing more than four thousand bodies, in the area directly north of the site of the future

Figure 3.1 *Waldfriedhof* (installed 1995/96), Buchenwald Memorial Site. Photograph by Anna Saunders.

exhibition building, as well as a further four hundred graves with an estimated three thousand bodies on a second site to the east of the former station.[65] From 1992, wooden posts were erected as temporary markers for each mass grave, in order to prevent them from being disturbed by forestry workers or vehicles. The land was bought by the memorial site, and the German War Graves Commission was called in at an early stage to provide help and support. They also financed what has become known as the *Waldfriedhof*, in which the wooden poles on the first site were replaced in 1995–96 by 880 taller stainless steel poles, each measuring 1.75 metres, which are numbered and bear the inscription 'unknown', in accordance with the law on war graves; the same procedure was followed at a later date on the second site. The design for the steel poles was inspired by the temporary wooden posts, yet due to their polished metallic surface, they are much more visible amidst the trees (see Figure 3.1).

The decision to erect the steel poles as a memorial to the dead was not, however, uncontroversial. On the one hand, some of the victims' families wished to see crosses, representing a more prominent and symbolic type of grave marker. On the other hand, antifascist groups saw the poles to be 'a mythological, excessive exaltation [*Überhöhung*] of the dead of the special camp'.⁶⁶ The Board of Trustees of the memorial site also came to the conclusion that the poles were too prominent, even recommending that they be removed and replaced once again by shorter wooden poles.⁶⁷ While the steel poles have remained, and become increasingly accepted by victims' groups such as the Initiativgruppe, the debate highlighted the tensions of the time and the battle over visibility and public recognition. In Knigge's eyes, this was intended to be a place of individual mourning and reflection, rather than a public memorial.⁶⁸ Indeed, the completion of the exhibition building in 1997 reflected this stance, with only a very narrow vertical window opening onto the mass graves, allowing visitors to see only a few poles at once, thus reflecting on the fate of individuals rather than the mass nature of their deaths. Others, however, such as Niven, view the poles rather as 'precisely the kind of dubious memorialization that Knigge was keen to avoid', pointing out that the inscription 'unknown' on the poles could be 'construed as heroization and distortion' of the historical facts, for it could read as if the victims fell in battle.⁶⁹ This was also the view of an antifascist group from Aachen, which covered a number of the poles with black bin bags during the fifty-second anniversary of the liberation of the concentration camp in April 1997;⁷⁰ the bags bore the slogans 'No monument for Nazis' and 'NS-stelae must go [auf den Müll]'.⁷¹ Ironically, however, it has been battles such as these that have raised the profile of the mass graves in the public consciousness, thus unwittingly increasing their status as a mass memorial.

The final symbolic area to be completed was the so-called *Trauerplatz*. With the planned memorial space having been erased from the initial plan, pressure from the Initiativgruppe and the prisoners' advisory board ensured that a square was created as a space for services and commemorative events by the time the building was completed. This was largely because the area that had been used until that point – the collection of individual crosses and remembrance stones in the woods – had grown since 1990 to such an extent that there remained little standing space, the ground was unstable for elderly visitors, and it was located directly on top of some of the graves. The new area, located at the edge of the woods across the path from the documentation centre, was marked by the small wooden cross that had first been placed on the mass graves in 1990. However, the Initiativgruppe and the prisoners' advisory board deemed this inadequate, and felt that the space would be more appropriate if marked by a 'central monument'.⁷² The prisoners' advisory board suggested a 3.5-metre-high cross made of steel tubes – reflecting the steel poles in the woods – that was deemed too ostentatious by Buchenwald's Board of Trustees, who instead agreed to a 1.8-metre-high wooden cross.[73] The victims' groups still viewed this second cross to be too small, and following further consultation, a third one was agreed upon, at a height of 2.4 metres, along with the installation of a ground inscription reading *Die Toten des sowjetischen Speziallagers 1945–1950* (The dead of the Soviet special camp, 1945–1950). The square did not reach its present state, however, until 2005, when a fourth and final cross was erected at a height of 4.5 metres, and the square was redesigned to fit its proportions, funded by the memorial site and through donations from members of the Initiativgruppe. In conjunction with this development, the original space on which families had erected crosses and stones was extended and given a border, in order to provide a suitable space for individual mourning. The fact that this site has returned to its original function as a site of private remembrance is the result of numerous compromises over a fifteen-year period regarding public symbolism. As negotiations over the size of the memorial cross demonstrate, a major concern for victims and their families was one of visibility and public recognition; having had to conceal this history throughout the GDR, they desired above all a visible and concrete sign that unequivocally marked this past. Contrary to contemporary countermemorial trends of ground planes, voids or more ephemeral monuments – many of which have developed out of an established tradition of Holocaust remembrance – the traditional symbol of the cross has been prevalent in discussions here from the start. With no specific memorial tradition on which to build, the cross provided immediately accessible emotional symbolism, and evolved to its final form following negotiations and compromises over a number of years. In contrast, deliberate decision-making over memorial symbolism here was driven as much by what it should *not* do (e.g. evoke parallels with Yad Vashem or Auschwitz, or overshadow Holocaust remembrance on the same site) as what it should positively aim to do.

It took approximately fifteen years to reach agreement on an appropriate commemorative space with which both the victims' groups and the memorial site were happy; as Lothar Brauer of the Initiativgruppe stated, 'everything that we have achieved to the present day is a result of many small steps'.[74] On the one hand, it seems that these small steps have been aided by the passing of time, and increasing distance from the heady days of the early 1990s has aided relations and improved understanding on both sides. On the other hand, these steps have largely been driven forwards by former prisoners or their offspring, and the commemorative structures have resulted from their efforts to mark in permanent fashion their communicative memories. However, with very few eyewitnesses now remaining – and indeed many of their children aging – the parameters of this memory landscape are changing. The Initiativgruppe, for instance, changed the format of its annual meetings in 2011 to include sessions with schoolchildren, in order to communicate these memories to future generations.[75] They feel that now the bulk of research on the camp has been carried out and appropriate commemorative symbolism is installed, their duty is to address the changing structures of memory in society, and to ensure that their memories are not lost in years to come. The apparent resolution of these memory contests, alongside the death of a generation, has focused attention in a different direction in order to promote continued engagement with this past; physical memory markers alone will not ensure that the historical silence surrounding these camps is broken. The process of 'working through' this history on the ground can, however, be seen as an important step in engaging future generations, and it is significant that such workshops have been supported by the Konrad Adenauer Foundation, a political organization associated with the CDU; this is a past that will doubtless remain politicized for generations to come.

Emotive Symbolism and Reconciliation at Fünfeichen

While all GDR citizens would have been very familiar with the (state-ordained) history of Buchenwald, very few had ever heard of Fünfeichen, home to Soviet special camp Nr. 9 and located just outside the town of Neubrandenburg. Although the conditions of the camp and the social composition of its prisoners were in many ways similar to Buchenwald, its remembrance in post-*Wende* Germany has been strikingly different, precisely because the site itself carried fewer associations during the GDR than the national memorial site at Buchenwald. This is not to say that the site of special camp Nr. 9 had no pre-history during the war; in 1938 the estate was purchased by the Wehrmacht, and from the following year was used as a prisoner of war camp (known as Stalag II A; the neighbouring officer camp, Oflag II E2, was destroyed in 1946–47). The camp held prisoners of war from ten different nations until it was freed by the Red Army on 28 April 1945. After being temporarily used to house displaced persons and former prisoners, the NKVD began to use the barracks to intern Germans from July 1945. More than fifteen thousand prisoners went through the camp before its closure in November 1948. Of these, approximately one-third died, one-third were sent to other camps (many to Buchenwald) or deported, and one-third were released.[76] As in Buchenwald, historians estimate that approximately 80 per cent of prisoners had had some kind of formal involvement with the National Socialist regime, especially those interned during the first year. The majority of these, however, could be classed as 'followers', and only 2 per cent of prisoners were interrogated about their previous involvement in the regime; the large majority could only guess as to why they had been arrested.[77] While approximately 10 per cent were arrested due to activity in the police, Gestapo, judiciary or as concentration camp guards, others were suspected of being 'spies', 'saboteurs' or *Werwölfe*, the numbers of which increased from approximately 4 per cent in September 1945 to 20 per cent in March 1947, an indication that increasing numbers were being arrested for their suspected opposition to the new order.[78]

After its closure in 1948, the camp was destroyed by 1950; all the wooden huts were razed to the ground and only a few stone houses remained, which soon fell into disrepair. During the GDR, only the POW camp was remembered, and from 1958 to 1960, the town of Neubrandenburg created a memorial site at the POW graves, erecting a bell tower and sculpture by Albert Braun in 1961, surrounded by a green area. However, the site was never officially inaugurated, for the area was used by the army for military practice and became increasingly inaccessible. From 1979, it was classed as a prohibited zone and the site became forgotten and neglected. While research carried out in the 1980s by Neubrandenburg's district history museum uncovered some details of the area's post-1945 history, the special camp inevitably remained a taboo topic until the *Wende*. Alongside the high security of the area, the local party leadership's politically conditioned reluctance to investigate meant that the history of both camps remained largely forgotten.[79]

The process of unearthing the history of the special camp was led by historian Dieter Krüger from the Neubrandenburg History Museum in early 1990, and in March of that year, two mass graves were found in the woods at Fünfeichen, in which thousands of corpses were interred.[80] Having made local and national headlines – particularly as this was around the same time that mass graves were being found in Buchenwald and Sachsenhausen – these findings triggered much local interest, and on 8 July 1990, an ecumenical service was held at the graves, reportedly attracting several thousand people.[81] On 28 April 1991, the working group, or Arbeitsgemeinschaft (AG) Fünfeichen, was subsequently founded, the aims of which were threefold: to create a 'dignified memorial site' for those who died in the special camp; to contribute towards uncovering the history of the camp; and to support former prisoners.[82] With membership largely consisting of survivors and their relatives, numbers grew considerably over the years, from 135 in 1991 to over 750 members by 2010, making it the largest victims' association of all special camps.[83] The association normally organizes two meetings a year at Neubrandenburg, in April (marking the freeing of the POW camp) and November (for the National Day of Mourning), which have regularly attracted several hundred visitors. The success of the association in maintaining a strong memory tradition lies in several elements discussed below, as well as the strong personal engagement of the present chair, Rita Lüdtke. However, this does not hide the fact that the personal histories of those involved often caused internal tensions, especially in the early years, and those who had previously been active in the SED and its organizations found that their pasts compromised the way they were viewed by others. Unlike in Buchenwald, however, such tensions remained largely behind closed doors, enabling the public work on the historical reappraisal of the camp to be rather less dogged by political scandal. It is also significant that Krüger, Lüdtke and others involved in reworking the camp's history were former East Germans, and thus that Fünfeichen was not subjected to the same level of western influence after the *Wende* as Buchenwald, largely because it did not hold the same status in the GDR's commemorative landscape.

The AG Fünfeichen put much time and effort into developing a concept for a memorial site, for which it succeeded in gaining substantial amounts of public funding from both the federal and regional governments. Logistical problems initially concerned public access to the area, as the site was owned by the Bundeswehr after unification. With the backing of the town administration, however, necessary agreements were made to ensure that a public memorial site could be constructed and visited. The more controversial issue concerned whether there should be one single site dedicated to both camps, or whether the POW camp and the special camp should be remembered separately. After much debate, it was decided that one integrated site was preferable, and that any design for a commemorative structure should also incorporate the bell tower constructed during GDR times. In contrast to debates at Buchenwald, the emphasis from the early 1990s was thus the incorporation of both pasts, rather than the separation of their memorial spaces; as the first chair of the AG Fünfeichen, Ingrid Friedlein, stated, 'Through the creation of a memorial site in Fünfeichen, it was our fundamental concern to remember all victims of war and violence'.[84]

Over time, the ongoing construction of various commemorative structures has created more of a 'memorial complex' than a single monument. This process began in early 1992, when a competition was launched for a design to mark the entrance to the memorial site, funded by the regional government.[85] Eleven of fifteen invited artists submitted designs, resulting in a winning design by artist Uwe Grimm, which consisted of three elements: first, an eleven-metre-tall oak cross at the entrance, leaning to one side and supported by a stainless steel pole; second, two rows of stelae, seven to the left (representing the years 1939–45) and four on the right (representing 1945–48), leading into the memorial ground, the tops of which slope upwards towards broken points; third, a horizontal three-metre square of stones – to which visitors can add – framed by oak beams and leading the viewer's gaze towards the existing bell tower and sculpture for POW victims (see Figure 3.2). Grimm intended the leaning cross to stand as a symbol of suffering and death, and of the fragility of a world threatened by forces such as fascism and Stalinism; the steel pole was to represent resistance to such destruction, hope for the future and a humanization of the world.[86] The symbolism of oak was also significant, for not only does the name 'Fünfeichen' translate as 'five oaks' (and a 120-year-old oak tree was chosen by the artist for the cross), but the oak has been used as

Figure 3.2 Memorial ensemble at Fünfeichen, including the leaning cross (Uwe Grimm, 1993) and the bell (to the right) from Neubrandenburg's Marienkirche. Photograph by Anna Saunders.

an emblem of German identity, survival and rebirth since the early nineteenth century, featuring strongly in Romantic poetry, as well as state symbolism.[87] In this sense, the leaning oak cross could be interpreted as a symbol of the rebirth of a united, yet more self-aware Germany. The jury commented on the heightened emotions called forth by the cross, and its recommendation for this design was adopted unanimously.[88] However, the public exhibition of the three winning entries in the town hall in July 1992 gave rise to criticism. Some viewers, for instance, felt that the oversized cross was too monumental in proportion – not, as in Buchenwald, because it was deemed to overshadow other victims' groups, but rather because of an unhealthy tradition of monumentalism. As one letter to the local newspaper read, 'An eleven metre high cross is … above all, a German symbol, because it demonstrates yet again the inclination of the Germans towards grandiosity'.[89] For others, the symbolism of the cross was too strongly Christian, and one that was already overloaded at the site through other crosses in remembrance of the dead.[90] Indeed, the cross particularly evokes West German symbolism of the 1950s, when numerous crosses were erected in memory of the flight and expulsion of Germans from eastern territories. Once again, we see here how the symbolism of remembrance carries strong associations with past remembrance traditions.

Grimm's design was inaugurated in April 1993 at the official opening of the memorial site, along with an inscribed bronze tablet by Walter Preik, which explains the history of the two camps. The site also housed eleven newly erected granite crosses in two groups, each one marking the years 1945–48 and 1939–45 in remembrance of the victims of both camps, alongside the pre-existing bell tower ensemble. Later that year, further searches at the sites of the mass graves in the nearby woods were conducted, in order to ascertain the boundaries of the grave fields, after which fences were erected around the perimeters and new paths were laid in order to allow visitors easy access.[91] In November 1999, fifty-nine bronze plaques bearing the names of over five thousand victims of the special camp were inaugurated on the southern grave field. The act of naming victims, and thus raising them out of anonymity, was one that had been ongoing since the early 1990s,[92] and continued even after the installation of these plaques, with three correction plaques being installed on the graves in 2005 and updated lists being published sporadically.[93] The opportunity to publicly name the camp's victims was seen to be the high point of the memorial development, and the erection of the plaques was noted by the town council to represent the completion of the memorial site.[94] Although a book of victims' names exists for Buchenwald, it is interesting that the act of publicly naming victims on a monument was explicitly taken out of the concept, for fear that this would provoke the criticism of honouring former Nazis. The 'dual pasts' at Fünfeichen were apparently much less contentious than those at Buchenwald – a point to which we will return.

While the existing memorial symbols – crosses, plaques and stelae – became an integral part of the site, the efforts of the AG Fünfeichen to further develop the site did not halt. In 2003, a fifth oak tree was planted, once again raising public awareness of the site,[95] and in 2007, two further elements were added to the complex. First, two smaller replicas of the leaning cross were erected on the road below the memorial site, in order to mark the boundaries of the two camps and make the presence of the site more visible to the public. Second, a two-part model of the camp was unveiled on the site, along with a mounted site plan, financed by donations from political organizations, individual donations to the AG Fünfeichen and local businesses.[96] The following year, a bell from Neubrandenburg's Marienkirche was mounted on a frame and inaugurated at the site as part of the annual meeting in April. Financed via donations, this was the brainchild of the AG's chair, Rita Lüdtke, who herself admits that the opportunity to acquire one of the church's former bells simply presented itself, rather than this being a long-term plan of the AG.[97] At the inauguration, however, its symbolic meaning was highlighted by those who spoke, including a former prisoner who recollected how the church bells from Neubrandenburg could be heard in the camp when the wind blew in the right direction, and represented the free world outside the camp.[98] Furthermore, the ringing of the bell was associated with breaking the silence that had surrounded the camp for so many years. In 2012, a bilingual (German/ English) 'history trail' was established across the site, with information boards documenting the history of the site, and in 2015, bronze plaques were also installed with the names of those POWs who had lost their lives at Fünfeichen. All these symbols not only work together to create an emotive site for the visitor, but the regularity with which new elements have been unveiled has helped to maintain publicity and interest in the site. The symbol of the supported cross has also become central to the memorial site and provides the logo for the AG, as well as the distinctive background to numerous brochures, images and publicity materials associated with the site.

There are notable differences between the remembrance cultures at Buchenwald and Fünfeichen, which stem from the pre- and post-*Wende* engagement with history on these sites. Most prominent is the way in which Buchenwald's national significance during the GDR conditioned the way in which it was developed after 1989 and harnessed as an exemplary, national case for the reworking of GDR history. In contrast, Fünfeichen's obscurity during the GDR has led to less open controversy after 1989 and a more 'bottom-up' redevelopment, which has been managed largely by local teams. The decisions and organizational structures of the post-1990 period have thus also been central to the way in which the special camps have been commemorated in physical form. There appear to be two key influential factors here: the history of the 'dual past' and the emphasis on 'scientific' versus emotional features. Germany's 'dual past' clearly affects both sites, as both special camps occupied previous camp grounds. Tensions between former concentration camp prisoners and special camp prisoners at Buchenwald have, however, been much stronger than between former POWs and special camp prisoners at Fünfeichen, not least because ideological differences were not so prominent, but also because the POWs – often coming from further afield – had no specific interest group acting on their behalf. While tensions between the two groups of victims in Buchenwald meant that joint symbols and commemorations were impossible, the emphasis in Fünfeichen has been a common memorial site from the start, as symbolized in Grimm's design. Indeed, as Ingrid Friedlein highlighted in her speech at the opening in 1993, this was to be a place that brought together the two groups as 'victims of terroristic violence' and fostered the younger generations' respect and engagement for 'human dignity, justice and freedom'. In promoting tolerance, she even claimed that 'the inner difficulties that East and West Germans have had in coming together can only be overcome in peace and freedom, with tolerance and without prejudice'.[99] The events of 1989 were still very present, and some of the rhetoric of this period continued to resonate; her claim, for instance, that 'freedom without tolerance towards those who think differently [Andersdenkende] is not freedom' clearly echoed Rosa Luxemburg's famous comment.[100] The site as a symbol of reconciliation is one that frequently emerges in discourse about the memorial and at public events, and the desire to overcome political extremism is often expressed as a common movement against both fascism and Stalinism.[101] Indeed, since 2008 the order of ceremony at the annual April commemoration involves laying wreaths first at the POW graves, and then remembering special camp victims afterwards – a schedule that would still be unthinkable at Buchenwald. It should be noted, however, that all such events are led by the AG Fünfeichen, which is ultimately the interest group for special camp prisoners; as such, there is a lead party and inevitably a stronger emphasis on this past.

The second main difference between the two memory cultures relates also to the relationship between the two victims' groups, and the apportioning of guilt and responsibility for the past. Whereas in Buchenwald, much was made of Knigge's claim that 80 per cent of special camp prisoners had been Nazi functionaries at some level – which led to his emphasis on a 'scientific' approach and the removal of symbolic elements from the original design – such findings have been much less central to the remembrance tradition at Fünfeichen. Indeed, in heightened contrast to Knigge, Lüdtke claimed that 'the memorial site does not answer the question of guilt or innocence, it commemorates human suffering'.[102] As such, the emphasis on emotional symbolism is much stronger at Fünfeichen, with the combination of crosses, stelae, inscribed names and bells producing precisely the type of 'interpretative' symbolism that Knigge was keen to avoid. These differences may, in part, result from the fact that remembrance in Buchenwald was led largely by professionals and historians, whereas in Fünfeichen it has been led primarily by the AG Fünfeichen, engaged individuals and local personalities with a keen interest in this history. It is also significant that there is less detailed documentation at Fünfeichen itself, although part of the regional museum is dedicated to this history, and as a result, visitors to the memorial site are likely to have a more emotive experience that is less rooted in historical enlightenment. While the regular unveiling of new memorial elements has maintained interest in the site over a number of years, this strategy is necessarily coming to an end. As in Buchenwald, the AG Fünfeichen is thus also concerned with the question of how to maintain this memory in the future, and similarly works with the young generations on a regular basis. As the next example shows, it is precisely this element that proves essential in ensuring that material symbolism does not retreat into longer-term 'invisibility'.

Breaking the Silence: Historical Revision in Greifswald

The history of the special camp at Fünfeichen affected many families in the region, as prisoners were often sent there from local towns. Greifswald, approximately sixty-five kilometres north of Fünfeichen, was one such town, in which a stele was erected in 1997 in memory of locals who lost their lives at Fünfeichen. While this case study is much smaller in scale than the two previous ones, and is not integrated into a memorial site, it demonstrates once again how commemoration of the special camps must be understood within the broader context of local history – this time, the events that unfolded during the final days of the Second World War in Greifswald, and which subsequently became a central part of the town's legacy. At the same time, this example also demonstrates how commemorative markers may simply serve the needs of a specific generation, without necessarily aspiring to the creation of a long-term memory tradition.

The starting point for understanding the broader context in Greifswald is marked by 29 April 1945, when a delegation from the town headed towards the front line in order to negotiate with the advancing Red Army. The result was that the town was handed over to the Soviets without any fighting, which is believed to have saved thousands of lives, prevented the destruction of the town – unlike nearby Anklam – and allowed civilian life to continue as normally as possible. Regarded as a unique event in Germany, the celebration of this date has become a long-standing tradition in Greifswald, especially on round anniversaries. In 2005, for instance, Mayor Arthur König proclaimed at a commemorative event, 'What happened back then in Greifswald was a tremendously strong symbol of civility and humanity, amidst the confusion of those dark days. And we cannot remember this enough!'[103] During the GDR, remembrance of this event was particularly prominent, with the story being inscribed onto the large bronze doors of the town hall in 1966 by artist Jo Jastram. However, it was the story of one man that dominated during the GDR: that of the town's commanding officer, Colonel Rudolf Petershagen, who was presented as the initiator of the delegation and the saviour of Greifswald (and whose post-war status differs notably from the aforementioned mayor of Weimar, Otto Koch). It is no coincidence that his post-war history was also one that bolstered the GDR's cause: having returned to Greifswald after being taken prisoner of war by the Soviets, he became actively involved in building the fledgling GDR state, becoming town councillor of Greifswald in 1950, and shortly after a regional councillor. The following year, however, he was arrested by the American secret service on a visit to Munich, suspected of spying for the Soviet Union, and following trial in an American military court, he was imprisoned in the FRG until 1955. On his release, he returned to Greifswald, where he was awarded the status of honorary citizen of the town, and in 1957 published his autobiography *Gewissen in Aufruhr* (Conscience in Turmoil), which became known across the GDR and was subsequently made into a five-part TV film by DEFA in 1961.[104] As a result, he was widely celebrated as a pacifist and democrat.

The focus on Petershagen in the GDR overshadowed the involvement of other key players in negotiations, such as the group of peace envoys: the rector of the university, Carl Engel, the director of the university clinic, Gerhardt Katsch, and Petershagen's deputy, Max Otto

Wurmbach. Of these, Carl Engel and a number of others were sent to Fünfeichen, where they lost their lives and became a taboo topic during the GDR.[105] The process of uncovering the history of these men was clearly still difficult after unification, since their high-profile positions in 1945 necessarily also meant involvement with the Nazi Party, yet at the same time their actions in April that year were crucial to the future of the town.[106] The need to redress the GDR narrative of this past was clear, and the erection of a stele to the Greifswald victims of Fünfeichen forms an essential part of this revision. Indeed, the initial drive to achieve historical justice came from Walther Gätke, a survivor of Fünfeichen, who claimed that his imprisonment had resulted from his unfair denunciation by Hermann Lindgreen, a communist and police inspector who was active in building the new communist regime. Gätke demanded that, in order to rebuild a just society after 1990, Lindgreen should have his status as 'honorary citizen' of Greifswald (awarded in 1965) revoked due to his actions at the time, an act to which the town assembly agreed in December 1990.[107] Having achieved an element of personal justice, Gätke then set out to collect the names of all those from Greifswald who had perished in the camp, and together with Egon Kühlbach, whose father died in Fünfeichen, worked to make the history of this period better known.

Alongside survivors and family members of victims, Gätke and Kühlbach initiated a movement for a physical commemorative marker for Greifswald's victims of Fünfeichen. They approached the town council for support, and subsequently a proposal for a memorial plaque was passed in June 1995 by a majority of votes. This was not, however, without controversy, for the PDS voted against the motion, claiming that a memorial should not be erected until historical research into this period had been completed.[108] The party also objected to the proposed inscription on the plaque, a quotation from a letter written by the widow of Carl Engel to a former colleague of his in 1949: '... hopefully the times will come, when this Calvary [Golgatha] will be respectfully recognized as such'. This was deemed inappropriate due to its religious connotations,[109] with party representatives suggesting the alternative inscription of 'Never again fascism, never again war',[110] a formulation that harked back to GDR inscriptions, and presented a certain interpretation of this history. While the original inscription was approved, the following two years witnessed discussions over a variety of alternative locations and forms for the plaque. In the summer of 1996, for instance, a motion was passed that would see a commemorative plaque erected at the town's 'Old Cemetery', next to two recently installed commemorative stones in memory of councillor Siegfried

Remertz (1891–1945) and Mayor Richard Schmidt (1882–1946), both of whom had been involved in the peaceful negotiations of April 1945 and subsequently died in Fünfeichen.[111] Interestingly, there appeared to be little concern that this proposal would explicitly link the lives of former Nazi functionaries with the victims of Fünfeichen more generally, an association that the special camp victims' group in Buchenwald was keen to avoid. Once again, the specific circumstances of the local history here conditioned the nature of historical revision. In this instance, the fates of these men were primarily bound up with unearthing the GDR's Petershagen myth and the revision of this history. However, this proposal was never realized, as a fundraising campaign raised sufficient sums to build a more visible structure without burdening any public funds.[112] While many individuals, groups and political parties made donations, it is notable that the CDU, which was particularly engaged in the matter, was a significant contributor – demonstrating similar party-political affiliations to Buchenwald.

Local artist Thomas Radeloff was commissioned by the town council and designed a 3.5-metre-high bronze stele with two commemorative inscriptions: a slightly shortened version of Irmgard Engel's quotation, and a second one that reads, 'In memory of Greifswald's victims of the internment camps 1945–1950. The assembly [*Bürgerschaft*] of the Hanseatic town of Greifswald' (see Figure 3.3). It was erected on a public green area marking the former town fortifications, a central and visible location that would be passed by numerous pedestrians, and a space that would have been visible from the prison building where inmates were held before being taken to Fünfeichen.[113] Perhaps most significantly, the unveiling ceremony in 1997 took place on 17 June, a date deliberately chosen for its historical connotations, and one that represented the remembrance of victims of Stalinism more broadly. Those present, including approximately thirty former prisoners, were not asked to partake in the traditional minute's silence usually integrated into such events, due to the forty years of silence that had already surrounded the camp. Instead, they were encouraged to hold hands and say together 'Crimes against humanity: never again!'.[114] As with the date of the unveiling, this demonstrated a concern with abuses of human rights in a broader sense than simply the historical facts concerning Fünfeichen, thus showing a similar trend to commemoration at Fünfeichen itself.

While the development of the stele took place on a smaller scale than the structures discussed at Fünfeichen and Buchenwald, it is interesting that considerably less effort has been made to maintain a tradition of memory here. While it was a burning issue in the 1990s and engaged

Figure 3.3 Commemorative stele in memory of Greifswald's victims of Soviet special camps (Thomas Radeloff, 1997), between the station and Lange Straße (on the site of the former town walls), Greifswald. Photograph by Anna Saunders.

many who had been personally affected by events, its broader resonance in the town appears to have been limited. Even those who were involved in its erection readily admit that it plays little role in the town today. While wreaths are still laid at the stele on round anniversaries, the circle of those who attend is decreasing and becoming increasingly aged; few of the younger generation attend or indeed are aware of the stele.[115] Moreover, as it is not located at an 'authentic' site, unlike the previous two examples, it holds less potential as a pilgrimage site for victims and families wanting to mourn loved ones, thus becoming less engrained in a regular ritual or tradition. As such, it is an example of a marker that served an important function at the time of its creation, and encouraged an active *Aufarbeitung* both individually and collectively; in terms of meeting the needs of former prisoners and their relatives, as well as revising the GDR narrative around Petershagen, it thus proved central to the town's self-understanding in the 1990s. As in previous examples, we see here how an instance of 'cultural' memory became central to reinvigorating 'communicative' memory within the town, showing how the two can work hand in hand and be mutually reinforcing. Once the latter subsides, however, the concrete structure itself becomes increasingly obscure.

A Monument without Answers? *Haftstätte* Prenzlauer Allee, Berlin

The final case study in this chapter concerns a less traditional *Denkzeichen* (memorial mark) in memory of a GPU-cellar in the Berlin district of Prenzlauer Berg. As with the previous examples, the question of commemoration is complicated not only by a period of silence surrounding this history during the GDR, but also by subsequent Stasi activity on the site. The *Denkzeichen* marks a building – known as 'Haus 3' – just off Prenzlauer Allee, which stands as part of a complex on Fröbelstraße that was built and used as a hospital and care home from 1889 to 1934, after which it was used by the district administration of Prenzlauer Berg until 1945.[116] From 1945 to 1950, the building was then used by the NKVD to house an interrogation centre, commonly known as a 'GPU-cellar' or 'inner prison'. As one of the largest of approximately sixty such buildings in Berlin, it housed around forty cells. Due to a lack of historical records, research on this period has largely been dependent on eyewitness reports of former prisoners, the majority of which reveal that a large number of prisoners were young people, often under the age of twenty. While a proportion of the prisoners in

1945 and 1946 were nominal members or supporters of the Nazi Party, this was by no means consistent. A large number were also arrested on suspicion of opposing the Soviet occupying forces and the new regime; social democrats and Christians, for example, were often among them. Many were sent from here to other prisons or special camps, such as Hohenschönhausen or Sachsenhausen. Within the prison, physical and psychological methods of torture were regularly used; prisoners were beaten, starved, deprived of sleep, subjected to constant electric light or sometimes punished in a 'water cell', and none were allowed contact with the outside world. Many did not know why they had been arrested, and their relatives were rarely informed of their whereabouts; many were simply deemed 'missing'. Interrogations regularly took place at night, when other inmates were subjected to the cries of those being tortured.[117]

In 1950, the building was taken over by the Stasi, which used it as a remand prison until 1956, after which it housed the district Stasi administration until 1985 and then a kindergarten. During its time as a Stasi prison, the extreme violence against prisoners ended; however, techniques of torture continued, such as a 'standing cell', where some prisoners were kept for several days; isolation, disorientation and night-time interrogations also remained common.[118] After 1985, the whole complex was used by the district council and the local SED leadership. Today the building is still used by the district authorities and primarily houses offices belonging to the social services and youth services; many visitors come through its doors to use their services, including parents with young children, asylum seekers and those receiving social security.

After unification, the building was still widely associated with the Stasi, but very few residents knew anything of the pre-1950 history of 'Haus 3'. Only a few older residents who recollected hearing screaming in the building before 1950, or who remember having been summoned to the building themselves, associated it with a much darker history.[119] This history thus only came to light gradually, once survivors began to track down the building and recount their experiences. It was subsequently these reports that spurred on the call for a *Denkzeichen*. Although the district council of Prenzlauer Berg passed a resolution put forward by the CDU in 1998 to erect a plaque outside 'Haus 3' and to research the history of the building,[120] little further happened until 2001, when a former prisoner's recollection of his time in 'Haus 3' at a local discussion evening prompted the formation of a citizens' initiative.[121] The initiative called for the resolution of 1998 to be realized, but also underlined the importance of local involvement, calling for donations from residents and stating, 'We want to make it clear that this is about an initiative of engaged citizens from our municipality'.[122] While the group consisted of local residents, from both the East and the West, it included a number of influential members, such as Marianne Birthler (then Federal Commissioner for the Stasi Files) and Ulrike Poppe (GDR civil rights activist), who doubtless helped raise the profile of their cause.

In February 2002, the initiative, together with the 'Berlin-Brandenburg History Workshop', erected an information board outside the building, informing locals of its forgotten history and the work of the initiative. Over a decade after unification, this was still deemed controversial by some, and it disappeared a month later, only to be found vandalized nearby, requiring another to be erected. The knock-on effect was that numerous eyewitnesses contacted the Prenzlauer Berg museum, which was carrying out research into this period.[123] The following year, the newly formed 'Pankow large district' (resulting from the fusion of the districts of Prenzlauer Berg, Weißensee and Pankow) voted to realize the resolution of 1998, and to launch a competition for 'a memorial sign in honour of victims of the NKVD and the Stasi'.[124] This went ahead with the financial backing of the Berlin Senate, and in December 2004 the jury announced the winner to be Karla Sachse. Following a public exhibition of all seven invited entries in March 2005, the winning design was unveiled in October 2005. During the days preceding the inauguration, a number of public events were held, to which eyewitnesses and their relatives were invited, such as podium discussions, a tour of the building and sessions in schools for eyewitnesses to recount their experiences.

Sachse's design consists of approximately sixty questions, inspired by her reading of two eyewitness reports. These are written in white on a black band measuring 320 metres long, which stretches round the building (see Figure 3.4). The following provides a selection of her questions:

> who shut the iron door? how heavy was the weight of uncertainty? who disappeared into the cellar? what did they know? what did a sip from the bowl taste like? how many nails protruded from the wooden bed? how much silence did the ear endure? how cold was the wall? what did the shorn head feel? when did a poem help? who heard the screams in the night? where did the first blow strike? who looked for the missing people? when did hunger set in? why? how long was a day without light? where was the bucket?

Intrigued pedestrians will find some initial answers on the two information boards placed in front of the building, produced in conjunction

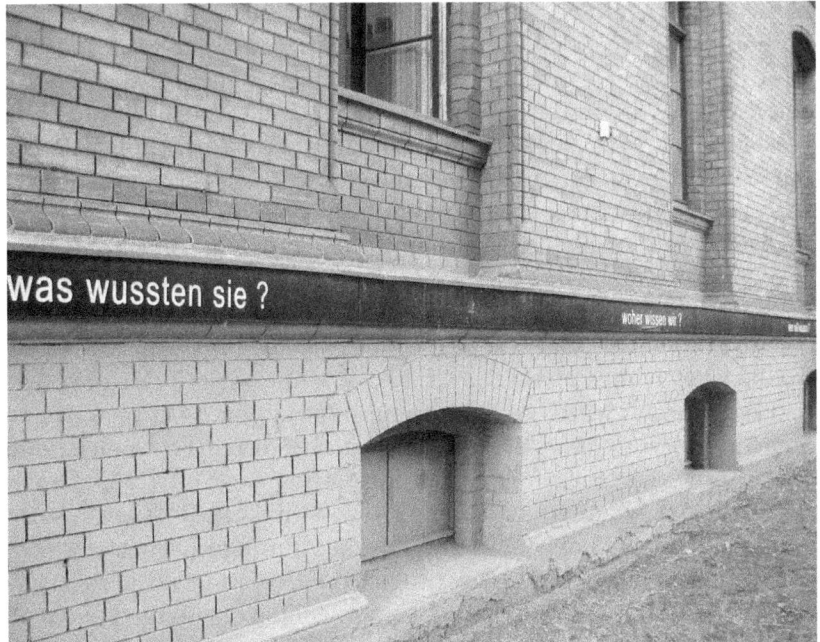

Figure 3.4 *Denkzeichen* on 'Haus 3' (Karla Sachse, 1997), Prenzlauer Allee, Berlin. Photograph by Anna Saunders.

with the district council. However, the questions themselves also offer some historical information about the conditions for prisoners, thus educating those passers-by who stop to read. Above all, however, it aims to enter into dialogue with residents, encouraging them to investigate further and reflect on this past.

Although the design may not have received large-scale press attention, it proved highly controversial in the local community, largely because the project was implemented in a district in which the PDS was dominant. Not only was this the largest party in the district (in both 1998 and 2003), but both the mayor (Burkhard Kleinert) and the councillor for culture (Almuth Nehring-Venus) of the new, larger district were PDS members, the latter becoming the key negotiator with the initiative. Difficulties emerged primarily in two areas. First, there were divisions within the PDS itself, with the party's old guard objecting to the actions of the reform wing, and wishing to see the SED past defended. These objections came largely from former SED and Stasi functionaries, many of whom wrote to Thomas Flierl (PDS), Berlin's Senator for Culture, asking him to intervene and stop the project, regarding it to be a 'political provocation'.[125] One such letter from representatives of the

'Society for Legal and Humanitarian Support' (GRH), an association uniting many former Stasi functionaries, defended the actions of the Stasi in the early 1950s, claiming that it was protecting the country against western attempts to liquidate the GDR at the height of the Cold War. Moreover, it objected to any comparison between the GDR and the Nazi era, regarding this to be a falsification of history, and claiming that 'anti-antifascists and anticommunists' have caused new support for brown politics in united Germany.[126] This line of argument was clear in other protests staged by the group, particularly at the opening of the exhibition displaying the competition entries and at the inauguration of Sachse's design. At both events, the group claimed that the *Denkzeichen* masked the crimes of the Nazis, and that the majority of prisoners had been former Nazis. At the inauguration, at which between twenty and fifty demonstrators appeared, the group displayed banners with slogans such as '*Honou*rable commemoration for *Nazis*?', 'Do Nazis recognize the suffering of others?', 'Do you think the Russians wanted war?' and 'Is this how the past is worked through [*aufgearbeitet*]?'[127] Interestingly, such protests only provoked the reform wing of the party to pursue its goal and to highlight the need for historical enlightenment. As Flierl claimed in his response to the GRH:

> The PDS is wise to take an active part in this discussion, to break taboos and to confront its own past with historical facts, even if it hurts. Such action is consistent with the founding consensus of the PDS. ... Your demands to stop this process contradict my understanding of democracy, because it is democratically entirely legitimate.[128]

As in other case studies, the desire to demonstrate democratic intentions in the present was a prime motivation for its supporters. In this case, it was not only about preventing a repetition of history, but became integral to the PDS's attempt to reposition itself as an enlightened and democratic party in the political climate of united Germany – and to distance itself from its undemocratic SED roots.

Difficulties also emerged in the negotiations between the citizens' initiative and the PDS-led district. Although relations were surprisingly good considering that many members of the initiative had actively protested against the SED in 1989, discussions were at times fractious, and the involvement of the PDS proved controversial for many in the initiative. Above all, the written set of 'basic principles' for the monument took months of writing and rewriting before they were agreed upon, as did the text for the information boards. The main question in both cases concerned the issue of *what* should be remembered – was this a monument about the punishment of Nazi crimes, or the repression of those who opposed Soviet occupation? Was it about antifascist politics, or the erection of a new dictatorship? Was it about legitimate rights, or the breaking of Allied rights? The most controversial passage in both texts concerned the role attributed to prisoners in the early years of 1945–46, many of whom had connections to the Nazi Party. The initial text drafted by Almuth Nehring-Venus, for example, placed the prisoners who were Nazi members or sympathizers in a more prominent position than desired by the initiative, which believed that this suggested a continuation of the GDR's 'antifascist legend'.[129] Although the final version of the text published in the competition brief recognizes this group of prisoners until 1946, the emphasis lies much more strongly on those who were arrested under false evidence, and those who suffered because of their opposition to the Soviet regime.[130] A second point of controversy concerned the initial document's focus on the Stalinist era, which members of the initiative claimed 'masked important historical continuities' and represented 'a cultural code from the PDS's version of history, which evaluates the period after Stalin as positive'.[131] Once again, the final text represented a compromise, but demonstrated willingness on the side of the local authorities and the PDS to listen to and incorporate the views of the initiative. On this point, the final text of the competition brief read:

> In the years and decades that followed Stalin's death, the political environment of the GDR changed significantly, and had to change in order to maintain the existing power structures. But it remained the dictatorship of one party, in which political opposition was eliminated and basic rights were denied, such as the right to free elections, the freedom of movement and the protection of the private sphere.[132]

Lengthy discussions and disagreements over the competition text and the information boards both came to compromises, but illustrated above all the willingness of the PDS in this district to work through the GDR past, and to make an effort to deal constructively with its own political history.

From the start, such discussions revealed three key principles that guided the project and shaped the resulting design. First, a clear aim on all sides was to bring together past and present, in order to mobilize memory for contemporary purposes; as the competition guidelines stated, the *Denkzeichen* was to strengthen 'the power of judgement for political debates in the present' and to promote 'responsibility for human rights' and 'respect for life and the freedom of every individual'.[133] Moreover, the monument was also to reflect the lack of any common remembrance concerning this history, seen most notably in the 'ambivalence surrounding the topic, which stems from the historical, as well as diverse, usage of the prison cellar'.[134] With this in mind, interviews were carried out not only with eyewitnesses from the time, but also with current authority employees working in 'Haus 3', as well as their clients. These revealed mixed reactions, but generally a curiosity on the part of locals to find out more about the history of the building, and the presence of asylum seekers and refugees in the corridors only highlighted the ongoing abuse of human rights elsewhere in the world and the need to link past and present more strongly.[135] Indeed, Sachse's questions aim to bring the past of the building into dialogue with its present users, in order to bring about a learning process. On the one hand, the questions are historically unspecific, allowing them to be read with other abuses in mind – at the time of the competition, for example, there was much public discussion about methods of torture at Abu Ghraib – yet they also invite visitors to engage with the specific circumstances. The physical placing of some questions furthers this dialogue: the question that is likely to first catch the visitor's eye, for instance – to the left of the main entrance – reads 'who wants to know?', thus inviting the observer to explore further. The eye may then wander to the adjacent question, 'what do we know?', offering a communicative 'we' to the observer, and drawing him/her in further. A third question, however, asks 'what did they know?', changing the perspective, and indicating that those incarcerated – or indeed living nearby – may have had limited knowledge of their situation.[136] The incessant nature of the questions also reflects a sense of desperation, mirroring the unanswered questions of those who were detained, but also highlighting those that remain unanswered today. Whether answered or not, it is the act of engagement with this past that initiators hope will bring greater moral responsibility in the present.

The second principle was to call on the power of art, rather than historical reconstruction, to bring past injustices to light. As the competition explicitly stated, 'A recreation of the prison cell is not desired. As the interrogation and remand cellar no longer exists in the layout that it did back then, it is rather art that should render the no longer visible once more noticeable and discernible'.[137] In this way, individual interpretation and recourse to imagination were recognized as powerful tools and reflected in Sachse's design. This was, however, by no means evident from the start of the project, for the overriding vision for a monument among members of the initiative was initially that of a traditional 'bronze victim sculpture' that would stand outside the building, largely in line with the aesthetic norms of GDR memorial culture.[138] Similar to the process of self-examination in the PDS, however, the process of discussion, debate and historical enlightenment shifted the group's expectations of memorial art in favour of a less interpretive design that would say as much about the present as the past.

Finally, and perhaps most significantly, the initiators of this project recognized that the uncovering of the history of this building is an ongoing process. As stated in the competition rubrics, the *Denkzeichen* was to be seen as an 'intermediate step in a debate concerning the still unfinished process of working through German history'.[139] The emphasis on public relations activities was thus central from the start, and it was repeatedly stated that a monument was not desired 'from above', but rather 'by citizens for citizens'.[140] Regular discussion circles took place, alongside sessions at schools, information evenings and dialogue with eyewitnesses, as well as the erection of temporary information boards to inform residents of the project, thus ensuring constant engagement. In order for such events to take place, the promotion of research into this history was key, and was commissioned and carried out by the Prenzlauer Berg museum. While the research triggered a process of historical reassessment within the PDS and provided evidence to dismiss the protests of former Stasi officials, it highlighted above all the historical complexities of this period, and the need to continue carrying out such research. This, in turn, was reflected in the open-ended artistic form of Sachse's design. Indeed, entries that displayed restricted perspectives or drew on established motifs were rejected by the jury, which feared that viewers' perceptions might be skewed by preconceived ideas.[141] As Thomas Flierl stated at its unveiling, 'The historical investigation of the site is not complete. There are historical witnesses who talk and remember. There are few material remnants and some archives are still closed. And because of this, there are still questions'.[142] Contrary to the Greifswald stele, which served a clear historical purpose in the 1990s, this is an exploratory monument to the hitherto unknowns of history, yet one that has also prompted the reassessment and self-examination of several political and social groups. As such, the *Denkzeichen* is thus best understood as just one of many stages in a process of historical enlightenment and contemporary political engagement.

Conclusion: Revoking Silence

The case studies in this chapter highlight perhaps more clearly than in any other the complex juxtaposition of memories, for the history of all four sites both before and after the period of Soviet occupation has been integral to their conception and development. At the same time, contemporary expectations regarding the political function and aesthetic form of monuments have also shaped negotiations over the size, shape and purpose of the resulting structures. Discussions over appropriate forms of memorialization have invariably led to difficult decisions and muddied the waters regarding categories such as 'victims' and 'perpetrators', or accusations of guilt and blame. As Knigge has claimed, the situation at Buchenwald 'shows in exemplary fashion, that *the* victims – as they are so often referenced – do not exist'.[143] Instead, the multiple shades of grey between the poles of victims and perpetrators highlight the limits of the totalitarian paradigm. Moreover, as demonstrated by the heavy silence that stifled the victims of the special camps due to the GDR's policy of repressive erasure, it is also clear that one may not only be a victim *in* history, but also a victim *of* history. It is above all in response to this silence that these sites have developed. In both Buchenwald and Fünfeichen, for instance, the size of the monumental crosses was of great significance, for they made this history once again visible. Perhaps unsurprisingly, the importance of auditory elements also emerged in several locations – the bell at Fünfeichen, the desire not to have a minute's silence in Greifswald, and the incessant nature of the questions on 'Haus 3' – all serving to counter the silence of the past and overturn GDR commemorative traditions.

The historic silence surrounding special camps and the brutality of the NKVD has influenced two further elements at these sites of memory. First, the largely traditional and often religious choice of symbolism (crosses, stelae, bells) and commemorative acts (ecumenical services, laying of wreaths) marks three of the four sites: those where victims and their families were directly involved in the initiation and development of commemorative structures. On the one hand, the high frequency of religious imagery could be seen as a response to the GDR's anti-church policies. On the other hand, however, recourse to traditional symbolism created emotional sites that carried immediate resonance for victims and their families, and recalls the Christianization of memory in 1950s West Germany. Emotional immediacy became particularly important in the post-*Wende* years given the absence of historical sites of remembrance for this past, and not only could individual mourning take place at such sites, but also public performances of remembrance, which proved central to countering the silence of the past. As in the 1950s, however, this was not without its problems, particularly at sites with 'double' pasts, where the lines between victims and perpetrators were blurred. Even at Buchenwald, where the memorial site has advocated a clear 'scientific' approach, the resulting memorial is doubtless highly emotive, with much traditional symbolism. As in the early years of Holocaust remembrance, when classical forms such as obelisks, stelae and tall pylons were most commonly used to mark sites,[144] the absence of a tradition of established aesthetics has also meant that recourse to familiar and widely recognized symbolism was more likely. This is not to say that these sites were not influenced by other aesthetic traditions; in Buchenwald, for instance, the established aesthetics of Holocaust remembrance both on the same site and elsewhere prevented certain structures from being built, and in Fünfeichen the emphasis on naming individual victims (also seen at other sites, such as the former special camp at Mühlberg), reflects a widespread tradition that began after the First World War.

The GDR's silence surrounding special camps also appears to have led to a strong desire among interest groups to see memorial work as an ongoing process of learning and understanding. Indeed, heated discussions over monumental form and location have often led to an element of reconciliation and sometimes a shift in thinking on the part of those involved; in Prenzlauer Berg, for instance, the involvement of the PDS led to a positive working relationship between groups that had previously been ideologically opposed and a reworking of history on the part of the PDS; in Buchenwald, communication between the two victims' groups also reached a level of tolerance. The notion that uncovering and working through history is an ongoing process has also been reflected in most discussions concerning monumental form, for designs have been modified, documented and challenged on a regular basis. The unanswered questions on 'Haus 3' present perhaps the most evocative call for ongoing engagement with an unfinished history, but the seemingly never-ending development of the site at Fünfeichen also displays the desire not to let this memory rest. In Greifswald, however, where the monument served a specific purpose at a specific time, concern over the future of the monument has been minimal; it is perhaps significant that this is the only one of the four examples not placed in an authentic location. While authentic sites may be criticized for buying into 'tragic tourism', in which a 'grim fascination with the deaths of innocents and unfortunates is accompanied by feelings of grief, guilt, and gratitude',[145] these examples show their important role in engaging the community and serving a cathartic function. Indeed, the interplay between communicative and cultural memory is at its strongest here, for it is the desire to produce cultural forms of memory that triggers greater activity on the communicative level, and is often the driving force, especially where there is no widely accepted consensus. Once again, the relationship between these two memory forms is clearly far from unidirectional.

Finally, we see a common element between these memorial sites and the monuments featured in the previous chapter. While on the one hand they stand as reminders of specific periods and events in East German history, on the other hand they have been used to highlight much broader moral questions, in which the democracy of the present is pitted against the dictatorship(s) of the past. Indeed, in debates at several of these sites, a common line of argumentation – employed both for and against memorial structures – was to accuse the opposition of acting in an undemocratic manner typical of the SED. Other common tropes at unveiling ceremonies also highlighted the inclusion of broader themes from the GDR: the unveiling of the Greifswald monument on 17 June, for example, emphasized the need to remember victims of Stalinism more broadly; and the inclusion of rhetoric from 1989 in speeches at Fünfeichen served to demonstrate wider ideals of reconciliation. In this way, such structures stand as much for the promotion of the global values of human rights, freedom and democracy in the present as for the remembrance of specific Soviet and GDR crimes in the past, and demonstrate a more complex web of historical associations than can be typically portrayed through the linear notion of the palimpsest.

Notes

1. Anna Kaminsky, 'Gedenkstätten für die Opfer des Stalinismus als "Stiefkinder" der deutschen Erinnerungskultur?', in *'Asymmetrisch verflochtene Parallelgeschichte?' Die Geschichte der Bundesrepublik und der DDR in Ausstellungen, Museen und Gedenkstätten*, Geschichte und Erwachsenenbildung, vol. 19, ed. by Bernd Faulenbach and Franz-Josef Jelich (Essen: Klartext, 2005), pp. 93–110 (100).
2. Bettina Greiner, *Verdrängter Terror: Geschichte und Wahrnehmung sowjetischer Speziallager in Deutschland* (Hamburg: Hamburger Edition, 2010), p. 32.
3. Alexander von Plato, 'Zur Geschichte des sowjetischen Speziallagersystems in Deutschland: Einführung', in *Sowjetische Speziallager in Deutschland 1945 bis 1950*, vol. 1, *Studien und Berichte*, ed. by Sergej Mironenko, Lutz Niethammer and Alexander von Plato (Berlin: Akademie Verlag, 1998), pp. 19–75 (29).
4. Hans-Peter Ehrentraut-Daut, Daniel Gaede, M. Gräfe et al., *Das sowjetische Speziallager Nr. 2. Buchenwald 1945 bis 1950*, 'Materialien' Series, vol. 61 (Bad Berka: ThILLM, 2001), p. 149.
5. Ibid.

6. Greiner, *Verdrängter Terror*, pp. 10–11.
7. Ibid., p. 10; Alexander von Plato, 'Sowjetische Speziallager', in *Erinnerungsorte der DDR*, ed. by Martin Sabrow (Munich: Beck, 2009), pp. 90–97 (92).
8. Plato, 'Sowjetische Speziallager', p. 95.
9. GPU was the acronym of the former Soviet secret police, which was the forerunner of the KGB.
10. Alexander von Plato, 'Sowjetische Speziallager in Deutschland 1945 bis 1950: Ergebnisse eines deutsch-russischen Kooperationsprojektes', in *Speziallager in der SBZ: Gedenkstätten mit 'doppelter Vergangenheit'*, ed. by Peter Reif-Spirek and Bodo Ritscher (Berlin: Links, 1999), pp. 124–48 (131–32).
11. Greiner, *Verdrängter Terror*, pp. 162-63.
12. Jan Lipinsky, 'Gefängnisse und Lager in der SBZ/DDR als Stätten des Terrors im kommunistischen Herrschaftssytem', in *Materialien der Enquete-Kommission: 'Überwindung der Folgen der SED-Diktatur im Prozeß der deutschen Einheit'*, vol. VI, ed. by Deutscher Bundestag (Frankfurt; Baden Baden: Nomos Verlagsgesellschaft, 1999), pp. 490–566 (496).
13. Greiner, *Verdrängter Terror*, pp. 65–66.
14. See, for example, '"Die Feststellungen von Dibelius und Grüber sind wahr"', *Neues Deutschland*, 20 January 1950, cited in Ehrentraut-Daut et al., *Das sowjetische Speziallager Nr. 2.*, pp. 99–100.
15. Greiner, *Verdrängter Terror*, p. 340.
16. Karl Wilhelm Fricke, '"Konzentrationslager, Internierungslager, Speziallager": Zur öffentlichen Wahrnehmung der NKWD/MWD-Lager in Deutschland', in *Instrumentalisierung, Verdrängung, Aufarbeitung: Die sowjetischen Speziallager in der gesellschaftlichen Wahrnehmung 1945 bis heute*, ed. by Petra Haustein, Anna Kaminsky, Volkhard Knigge and Bodo Ritscher (Göttingen: Wallstein, 2006), pp. 44–62 (48–49).
17. Hasko Zimmer (ed.), *Der Buchenwald-Konflikt* (Münster: agenda Verlag, 1999), p. 123.
18. Connerton, 'Seven Types of Forgetting', p. 60.
19. Niven, *Facing the Nazi Past*, p. 21.
20. Bruno Apitz's novel, *Nackt unter Wölfen* (Halle: Mitteldeutsche Verlag, 1958) became the best-known version of the narrative of self-liberation in the GDR.
21. Plato, 'Sowjetische Speziallager in Deutschland 1945 bis 1950', p. 147.
22. Karl Wilhelm Fricke, *Politik und Justiz in der DDR: Zur Geschichte der politische Verfolgung 1945–1968* (Cologne: Verlag Wissenschaft und Politik, 1979). For an earlier work, see also Gerhard Finn, *Die politischen Häftlinge in der Sowjetzone 1945–1959* (Pfaffenhofen: Ilmgauverlag, 1960).
23. Other than Buchenwald and Sachsenhausen, examples of other sites that now document these two pasts include the Dokumentations- und Informationszentrum Torgau, the Gedenkstätte Münchner Platz Dresden and the Gedenkstätte 'Rote Ochse' in Halle.
24. Gilbert Schomaker and Jens Stiller, 'Der neue Leiter über die Gedenkstätte Hohenschönhausen "Das Dachau des Kommunismus"', *Berliner Zeitung*,

1 December 2000, http://www.berliner-zeitung.de/archiv/der-neue-leiter-ueber-die-gedenkstaette-hohenschoenhausen--das-dachau-des-kommunismus-,10810590,9856710.html (accessed 18 March 2012).

25. Volkhard Knigge, 'Zweifacher Schmerz: Speziallagererinnerung jenseits falscher Analogien und Retrodebatten', in *Instrumentalisierung, Verdrängung, Aufarbeitung*, ed. by Haustein, Kaminsky, Knigge and Ritscher, pp. 250–64 (259).
26. Schlußbericht der Enquete-Kommission 'Überwindung der Folgen der SED-Diktatur im Prozeß der deutschen Einheit', Bundestag Drucksache 13/11000, pp. 227, 240–41.
27. 'Konzeption der künftigen Gedenkstättenförderung des Bundes', 27 July 1999, Bundestag Drucksache 14/1569.
28. Cited in 'Fortschreibung der Gedenkstättenkonzeption des Bundes', 19 June 2008, Bundestag Drucksache 16/9875, p. 3.
29. See Marc-Dietrich Ohse, 'Aufarbeitung und Gedenken', *Deutschland Archiv*, 40 (2007) 6, 965–67; 'Stellungnahme zur Fortschreibung der Gedenkstättenkonzeption durch den Beauftragten der Bundesregierung für Kultur und Medien', *Gedenkstättenrundbrief* 139, 22 June 2007, http://www.gedenkstaettenforum.de/nc/gedenkstaetten-rundbrief/rundbrief/news/stellungnahme_zur_fortschreibung_der_gedenkstaettenkonzeption_durch_den_beauftragten_der_bundesregie/ (accessed 29 March 2012).
30. Hans-Hermann Hertle, 'Stellungnahme zur BKM Gedenkstättenkonzeption', *H-Soz-u-Kult*, 16 July 2007, https://www.hsozkult.de/article/id/artikel-910 (accessed 19 December 2017); 'Stellungnahme zur Fortschreibung der Gedenkstättenkonzeption'.
31. 'Fortschreibung der Gedenkstättenkonzeption des Bundes', p. 2.
32. Ibid., pp. 2–3.
33. See, for instance, Bert Pampel, *'Mit eigenen Augen sehen, wozu der Mensch fähig ist.' Zur Wirkung von Gedenkstätten auf ihre Besucher* (Frankfurt; New York: Campus Verlag, 2007), pp. 25–26; Wolfgang Benz, 'Authentische Orte: Überlegungen zur Erinnerungskultur', in *Der Nationalsozialismus im Spiegel des öffentlichen Gedächtnisses: Formen der Aufarbeitung und des Gedenkens*, ed. by Petra Frank and Stefan Hördler (Berlin: Metropol Verlag, 2005), pp. 197–203.
34. See Jörg Skriebeleit, '"Orte des Schreckens": Dimensionen verräumlichter Erinnerung', in *Der Nationalsozialismus im Spiegel des öffentlichen Gedächtnisses*, ed. by Frank and Hördler, pp. 205–20.
35. For these examples and a broader discussion of early commemoration of Buchenwald concentration camp, see Volkhard Knigge, 'Buchenwald', in *Das Gedächtnis der Dinge: KZ-Relikte und KZ-Denkmäler 1945–1995*, ed. by Detlef Hoffmann (Frankfurt; New York: Campus, 1998), pp. 94–173.
36. Susanne Scharnowski, 'Heroes and Victims: The Aesthetics and Ideology of Monuments and Memorials in the GDR', in *Memorialization in Germany since 1945*, ed. by Niven and Paver, pp. 267–75 (270).
37. As Volkhard Knigge suggests, this monument was conceived as a response to the Treptower Park monument, and aimed to symbolize a German

victory that was parallel to that of the Soviets. See Debbie Pinfold, '"Das Mündel will Vormund sein": The GDR State as Child', *German Life and Letters*, 64 (2011) 2, 283–304 (293). On the history of the memorial, see also Bill Niven, *The Buchenwald Child: Truth, Fiction, and Propaganda* (Rochester, NY: Camden House, 2007).

38. Koshar, *From Monuments to Traces*, pp. 208, 213–14; Reichel, *Politik mit der Erinnerung*, p. 101.
39. The special camp at Buchenwald existed from August 1945 until it was officially dissolved on 1 March 1950.
40. See Zimmer, *Der Buchenwald-Konflikt*, pp. 81–122.
41. 'Zur Neuorientierung der Gedenkstätte Buchenwald: Die Empfehlungen der vom Minister für Wissenschaft und Kunst des Landes Thüringen berufenen Historikerkommission' (Weimar-Buchenwald, 1992)
42. 'Nationale Mahn- und Gedenkstätte Buchenwald, Speziallager 2 1945–1950', Rundbrief No. 1, 1990, p. 2.
43. Conversation with Lothar and Heidrun Brauer, Initiativgruppe Buchenwald 1945–1950 e.V., 24 March 2011.
44. 'Realisierungs-Wettbewerb "Gedenkstätte Buchenwald" (Internierungslager)', 1993, p. 9, in 'Speziallager Nr. 2 – Buchenwald – Eine Dokumentation der Initiativgruppe Buchenwald 1945–1950 e.V.', kindly made available by Heidrun and Lothar Brauer.
45. 'Reichtagsflagge über Buchenwald? Eine zweite Rudolf-Heß-Walhalla in Vorbereitung', in *Die Glocke vom Ettersberg*, Mitteilungsblatt der Lagergemeinschaft Buchenwald-Dora/Freundeskreis e.V., IV/1993.
46. Bettina Markmeyer, 'Verbrechen nicht gleichsetzen, aller Opfer gedenken', *die tageszeitung*, 13 April 1992.
47. Ibid.
48. Letter from Frese and Kleindienst to Herr Dr. Knigge, dated 27 September 1995, in 'Speziallager Nr. 2 – Buchenwald – Eine Dokumentation'.
49. 'Rahmenprotokoll des Preisgerichtsverfahrens', 5–6 May 1994, p. 11, in folder 'Wettbewerb Gräberfelder', kindly made available by Bodo Ritscher (curator for the history of the Soviet special camp, Stiftung Gedenkstätten Buchenwald und Mittelbau-Dora).
50. 'Protokoll des Kuratoriums der Stiftung Buchenwald und Mittel-Dora', 15–16 July 1994, p. 4, Archiv der Stiftung Gedenkstätten Buchenwald und Mittelbau-Dora.
51. Zimmer, *Der Buchenwald-Konflikt*, p. 23.
52. Letter from Frese and Kleindienst to Knigge, 27 September 1995.
53. Letter from Volkhard Knigge to Minister Dr. Schuchardt, Prof. Dr. Jäckel and Gerhard Finn, 19 October 1995, in 'Speziallager Nr. 2 – Buchenwald – Eine Dokumentation'.
54. Ibid.
55. Ibid.
56. See letter from VOS Landesvorsitzender Sachsen to Knigge, 9 April 1996, in 'Speziallager Nr. 2 – Buchenwald – Eine Dokumentation'; 'Thüringen heute', *BILD Thüringen*, 4 December 1995.

57. Letter from Initiativgruppe Buchenwald 1945–1950 e.V. to Volkhard Knigge, 10 December 1995, in 'Speziallager Nr. 2 – Buchenwald – Eine Dokumentation'.
58. 'Anzeige gegen Leiter der KZ-Gedenkstätte', *Thüringer Allgemeine*, 5 December 1995.
59. Letter from Initiativgruppe Buchenwald 1945–1950 e.V. to Knigge, 10 December 1995.
60. See letter from VOS Landesvorsitzender Sachsen to Knigge, 9 April 1996.
61. *Rundbrief*, Initiativgruppe Buchenwald 1945–1950 e.V., Weimar, 30 December 1995. This point was also raised in conversation with Lothar and Heidrun Brauer, 24 March 2011.
62. *Jahresinformation der Gedenkstätte Buchenwald 1995* (Weimar-Buchenwald, 1996), p. 8.
63. Volkhard Knigge, 'Die Umgestaltung der DDR-Gedenkstätten nach 1990: Ein Erfahrungsbericht am Beispiel Buchenwalds', in *Woran erinnern? Der Kommunismus in der deutschen Erinnerungskultur*, ed. by Peter März and Hans-Joachim Veen (Cologne: Böhlau, 2006), pp. 91–108 (104).
64. Klaus Hartung, 'Wer behält recht in Buchenwald?', *Die Zeit*, 25 October 1996.
65. 'Gräberfelder werden Waldfriedhof', *Mitteldeutsche Allgemeine*, 21 May 1994.
66. 'Sechs-Punkte-Erklärung von IVVdN, BDA, VVN/BdA', published in *antifa*, April 1996, in *Der Buchenwald-Konflikt*, ed. by Zimmer, p. 161.
67. 'Protokoll der Sitzung des Kuratoriums der Stiftung Gedenkstätten Buchenwald und Mittelbau-Dora', 7–8 July 1995, p. 4.
68. Rainer Jogschies, 'Ein Wessi in Weimar', *Das Sonntagsblatt*, No. 38, 20 September 1996, p. 9.
69. Niven, *Facing the Nazi Past*, p. 48.
70. Reports on the number of poles covered up vary between sixty and three hundred. See 'Gräber geschändet', *Thüringische Landeszeitung*, 14 April 1997 and Alfred Stoffels, 'Keine Störung der Totenruhe', *an-online* (in Archiv der Stiftung Gedenkstätten Buchenwald und Mittelbau-Dora).
71. '4500 Mark für die Müllsäcke-Aktion', *Thüringische Landeszeitung*, 13 February 1999.
72. Lothar Brauer, cited in *7. Buchenwaldtreffen*, ed. by Initiativgruppe Buchenwald 1945–1950 e.V. (Weimar, 1998), p. 38.
73. 'Protokoll der Sitzung des Kuratoriums der Stiftung Gedenkstätten Buchenwald und Mittelbau-Dora', 12–13 July 1998, p. 4.
74. Lothar Brauer, cited in *12. Buchenwaldtreffen*, ed. by Initiativgruppe Buchenwald 1945–1950 e.V. (Weimar, 2003), p. 42.
75. Conversation with Lothar and Heidrun Brauer.
76. Tobias Baumann, 'Das Speziallager Nr. 9 Fünfeichen', in *Sowjetische Speziallager in Deutschland*, ed. by Mironenko, Niethammer and von Plato, pp. 426–44 (427).
77. Jörg Morré, 'Geschichte des NKWD-Speziallagers Nr. 9 in Fünfeichen', in *Streng verboten: Das Tagebuch des Pastors Bartelt*, ed. by AG Fünfeichen (Neubrandenburg: Henryk Walther, 2008), pp. 5–15 (10–12).

78. Ibid., p. 11.
79. Dieter Krüger and Gerhard Finn, *Mecklenburg-Vorpommern 1945 bis 1948 und das Lager Fünfeichen* (Berlin: Verlag Gebr. Holzapfel, no date [1990/91?]), p. 95.
80. Ibid., p. 96.
81. Ingrid Friedlein, 'Die Arbeitsgemeinschaft Fünfeichen – eine Rückbesinnung', in *Die Opfer von Fünfeichen: Gedanken und Erinnerungen*, ed. by Sprecherrat der Arbeitsgemeinschaft Fünfeichen (Bozen: Athesiadruck, 2000), pp. 55–64 (55).
82. Ibid., p. 56.
83. *Informationsblatt Nr. 19*, December 2010, Arbeitsgemeinschaft 'Fünfeichen', p. 2.
84. Ingrid Friedlein, 'Arbeitsgemeinschaft Fünfeichen', in *Die Opfer von Fünfeichen: Erlebnisberichte Betroffener und Angehöriger*, ed. by Sprecherrat der Arbeitsgemeinschaft Fünfeichen (Schwerin: Stock & Stein Verlag, 1996), pp. 10–47 (23).
85. 'Beschluß' D-Nr 1/0136, 10 January 1992, Stadtarchiv Neubrandenburg.
86. Uwe Grimm, 'Kurzbeschreibung: Gestaltung Eingangsbereich Gedenkstätte "Fünfeichen"', no date [1992?], in folder 'Mahn- und Gedenkstätte Fünfeichen', kindly made available by Rita Lüdtke, Chair of the AG Fünfeichen.
87. See Neil MacGregor, *Germany: Memories of a Nation* (London: Allen Lane, 2014), pp. 120–22.
88. 'Protokoll: Juryberatung zum offenen Ideen- und Realisierungswettbewerb', Neubrandenburg, Rathaus, 6 May 1992, in folder 'Mahn- und Gedenkstätte Fünfeichen'; 'Beschluß Nr. 274/31/92: Entscheidung zur Realisierung der künstlerischen Gestaltung des Eingangsbereiches der Mahn- und Gedenkstätte Neubrandenburg-Fünfeichen', 18 August 1992, in folder 'Mahn- und Gedenkstätte Fünfeichen'.
89. Manfred Buller, 'Leserbriefe', *Neubrandenburger Rundschau*, 3 June 1992, p. 11.
90. 'Jury entschied sich für ein Kreuz aus Eiche', *Nordkurier*, 12 May 1992.
91. 'Holzzaun soll Gräberfelder umfrieden', *Neubrandenburger Rundschau*, 17 August 1993.
92. Dieter Krüger and Egon Kühlbach, *Schicksal Fünfeichen – Versuch einer Ermittlung: Stand 1991* (Neubrandenburg: Regionalmuseum Neubrandenburg, 1991).
93. See, for example, Arbeitsgemeinschaft Fünfeichen (ed.), 'Korrekturen und Ergänzungen zum Buch der Namen der Verstorbenen des NKWD-Speziallagers Nr. 9 Neubrandenburg-Fünfeichen', March 2010.
94. 'OB-Bericht: Sitzung d. Stadtvertretung am 4.11.1999', folder entitled 'Fünfeichen' in Stadtarchiv Neubrandenburg, p. 9.
95. 'Fünfte Eiche am Denkmal gepflanzt', *Neubrandenburger Zeitung*, 22/23 November 2003.
96. *Informationsblatt Nr. 16*, December 2007, Arbeitsgemeinschaft 'Fünfeichen', pp. 5–6.

97. Conversation with Rita Lüdtke, Neubrandenburg, 10 January 2011.
98. 'Lager Fünfeichen: 60 Jahre danach', DVD (2009), by www.videomagic-gmbh.de.
99. Friedlein, 'Arbeitsgemeinschaft Fünfeichen', p. 31.
100. Ibid.
101. For example, 'Gedenkstätte in Fünfeichen eingeweiht', *Nordkurier*, 26 April 1993; conversation with Rita Lüdtke; 'Ansprache Generalmajor Friedrich Riechmann', in *Die Opfer von Fünfeichen: Gedanken und Erinnerungen*, ed. by Sprecherrat der Arbeitsgemeinschaft Fünfeichen (Bozen: Athesiadruck, 2000), pp. 26–30 (27).
102. Matthias Wyssuwa, 'Stimme aus dem Schweigelager', *FAZ*, 21 October 2008, http://www.faz.net/aktuell/politik/tagebuch-eines-sowjetischen-haeftlings-stimme-aus-dem-schweigelager-1709294.html (accessed 31 July 2012).
103. *Greifswald 1945. Kampflose Übergabe und Kriegsende. Reden und Beiträge anlässlich des 60. Jahrestags am 29. und 30. April 2005* (Greifswald: Universitäts- und Hansestadt Greifswald, 2005), p. 16.
104. Rudolf Petershagen, *Gewissen in Aufruhr* (Berlin: Verlag der Nation, 1957).
105. See Norbert Buske (ed.), *Die kampflose Übergabe der Stadt Greifswald im April 1945: Dokumentation* (Schwerin: Landeszentrale für politische Bildung Mecklenburg-Vorpommern, 2000); Joachim Mai (ed.), *Spurensicherung. Greifswald 1945. Neue Dokumente und Materialien* (Berlin: FIDES Verlag, 1995).
106. Alongside Carl Engel, others to die in Fünfeichen were Ernst Lohmeyer, Siegfried Remertz and Richard Schmidt; Hans Lachmund survived imprisonment there.
107. '"Fünf Eichen war die Hölle"', *Greifswalder Tageblatt*, 5 December 1990, p. 4; 'PDS: "Zutiefst betroffen". Lindgreens Ehrenbürgerschaft beendet', *Greifswalder Tageblatt*, 9 December 1990, p. 3.
108. 'Niederschrift des öffentlichen Teiles der 11. Sitzung der Bürgerschaft der Hansestadt Greifswald vom 22.06.1995', p. 8, kindly made available by Ekkehard Brunstein, Leiter des Büros des Oberbürgermeisters.
109. Conversation with Ekkehard Brunstein and Thomas Meyer, Greifswalder Rathaus, 14 January 2011.
110. 'Niederschrift des öffentlichen Teiles der 11. Sitzung'.
111. Hansestadt Greifswald, Drucksachen-Nr. 2117, Beschluß-Nr. HA-152/96, 13 August 1998.
112. 'Einweihung einer Gedenkstele', *Ostsee-Zeitung (Greifswald)*, 16 June 1997, p. 11.
113. Conversation with Egon Kühlbach, 17 January 2011.
114. 'Gedenkstele am Wall eingeweiht', *Ostsee-Zeitung (Greifswald)*, 18 June 1997, p. 13.
115. Conversations with Ekkehard Brunstein and Thomas Meyer, as well as Egon Kühlbach.
116. For the early history of the building, see Berlin-Brandenburgische Geschichtswerkstatt (ed.), *Prenzlauer, Ecke Fröbelstraße* (Berlin: Lukas Verlag, 2006).

117. See Reinhard Fuhrmann, 'Die Haftstätte in der Prenzlauer Allee (1945–1956)', in *Prenzlauer, Ecke Fröbelstraße*, ed. by Berlin-Brandenburgische Geschichtswerkstatt, pp. 97–120; Reinhard Fuhrmann, 'Manuskript eines Vortrages', 18 May 2004, BVV Pankow, kindly made available by Elfriede Müller, Büro für Kunst im öffentlichen Raum, Berlin (hereafter Kiör-Büro).
118. Fuhrmann, 'Die Haftstätte in der Prenzlauer Allee', p. 115.
119. Ulrike Gentz, 'Hinter vorgehaltener Hand', in *Prenzlauer, Ecke Fröbelstraße*, ed. by Berlin-Brandenburgische Geschichtswerkstatt, pp. 164–75.
120. Bezirksverordnetenversammlung Prenzlauer Berg von Berlin, 30 September 1998, Drucksache 494/97.
121. Volker Wild, 'Die Geschichte des Denkzeichen-Projekts', unpublished draft manuscript, 5 August 2008, p. 5, Kiör-Büro.
122. 'Gedenkzeichen für die Opfer des NKWD und der Staatssicherheit in der Haftstätte Prenzlauer Allee', flyer produced by citizens' initiative, Berlin, 8 July 2001, Kiör-Büro.
123. Wild, 'Die Geschichte des Denkzeichen-Projekts', p. 7.
124. Drucksache der Bezirksverordnetenversammlung Pankow von Berlin, V-0459/03, 21 May 2003.
125. Karin Schmidl, 'Fragen über Fragen', *Berliner Zeitung*, 18 October 2005, p. 21.
126. Letter from Siegfried Mechler, Wolfgang Schwanitz and Siegfried Hähnel to Thomas Flierl, 7 April 2005, kindly made available by Annette Tietz, Kunst im öffentlichen Raum, Pankow (Kiör Pankow).
127. See Stefan Strauss, 'Einst bei der Stasi, heute bei der Demo', *Berliner Zeitung*, 24 October 2005, p. 20; Wild, 'Die Geschichte des Denkzeichen-Projekts'. Emphasis in original.
128. Letter from Flierl to Mechler, Schwanitz and Hähnel, 22 August 2005, Kiör Pankow.
129. E-mail from Christian Sachse to the initiative, dated 17 February 2004, Kiör Pankow.
130. See 'Grundsätze zur Auslobung eines künstlerischen Wettbewerbs', version by Fr. Nehring-Venus, Kiör, Pankow; 'Denkzeichen. Für die Opfer der ehemaligen Haftstätte Prenzlauer Allee, Berlin-Pankow. Auslobung', Berlin, October 2004, pp. 3–5.
131. E-mail from Volker Wild to Fr. Nehring-Venus, dated 16 February 2004; E-mail from Christian Sachse to the initiative, dated 17 February 2004, both Kiör Pankow.
132. 'Denkzeichen. Für die Opfer der ehemaligen Haftstätte Prenzlauer Allee', p. 4.
133. Ibid., p. 5.
134. Ibid., p. 16.
135. See Volker Wild, '"Haus 3 heute"', parts I and II, September 2004, Kiör Pankow.
136. Volker Wild, 'Der Wettbewerb', unpublished document, 1 May 2008, p. 13, Kiör-Büro.

137. 'Denkzeichen. Für die Opfer der ehemaligen Haftstätte Prenzlauer Allee', p. 16.
138. E-mail from Volker Wild to Elfriede Müller, 16 May 2004, Kiör-Büro.
139. 'Denkzeichen. Für die Opfer der ehemaligen Haftstätte Prenzlauer Allee' p. 16.
140. Christian Sachse, 'Denkzeichen für die Inhaftierten im NKWD-Haftkeller. Ein Bericht', *Zeitschrift des Forschungsverbundes SED-Staat*, 17 (2005), 179–81 (180).
141. 'Denkzeichen für die Opfer der ehemaligen Haftstätte Prenzlauer Allee: Protokoll der Preisgerichtssitzung', 9 December 2004, Kiör-Büro.
142. Thomas Flierl, cited in D. Krampitz, 'Wo jetzt Akten lagern, wurden früher Gefangene gefoltert', *Welt am Sonntag*, 30 October 2005.
143. Knigge, 'Die Umgestaltung der DDR-Gedenkstätten nach 1990', p. 106.
144. See Harold Marcuse, 'Holocaust Memorials: The Emergence of a Genre', *American Historical Review*, 115 (2010) February, 53–89 (66).
145. Doss, *Memorial Mania*, p. 94.

 Chapter 4

17 JUNE 1953 UPRISINGS
Remembering a Failed Revolution

The date 17 June 1953 marks the only major uprising in GDR history prior to 1989, and thus holds a central place in East German history. On this day, approximately a million people – primarily workers – took part in demonstrations, strikes and rallies in over seven hundred towns and communities across the GDR, angered by a 10 per cent increase in work norms.[1] While the initial purpose of the strike was to ensure the retraction of these norms, protesters' demands escalated, calling not only for the reduction of living costs, but also for free elections and the resignation of the government. These demands followed a period of unrest in the GDR, in which the 'building of socialism', announced in the summer of 1952, had brought with it an intensification of the battle against the churches, the increased militarization of society, the collectivization of farmland and private businesses, and greater emphasis on heavy industry. Not only did many farmers and independent tradesmen leave the GDR, but the population at large suffered consumer shortages, higher living costs and the withdrawal of ration cards and other social benefits. While these measures were withdrawn in the 'New Course', announced on 9 June 1953 under pressure from the new Soviet leadership following Stalin's death, the increase in workers' norms remained, triggering the impetus for the events of 17 June. The uprising was, however, quashed by Soviet tanks, with at least fifty-five people losing their lives, a significant number sentenced to death and thousands subsequently imprisoned.[2]

Although the uprisings clearly undermined the legitimacy of the GDR as a 'workers' and peasants' state' and highlighted its dependency on the Soviet Union, the subsequent effect was ironically one of consolidation of SED power in the GDR, alongside the adoption of more subtle and underhand forms of government, in particular the intensification of surveillance activity through the expansion of the Stasi. A large number of citizens continued, however, to leave the GDR over the following years until the Berlin Wall was built in 1961; others withdrew into the private sphere, while many saw little choice but to conform – at least outwardly – with the new system. In the longer term, 17 June also symbolized for the leadership the potentially dangerous power of the masses, and references to 1953 among SED functionaries in the summer and autumn of 1989 indicated that these events continued to prey on their collective consciousness.[3]

The official memory of this event was radically different in East and West Germany. In the East, the strikes and demonstrations were interpreted as the work of fascist agents and saboteurs from West Berlin, who had provoked and misguided Eastern workers. The uprisings received very little coverage in official histories and schoolbooks, and where they did feature, they were overtly instrumentalized to demonstrate the dangers of the imperialist West. While 17 June 1953 could not be erased from official historiography – as in the case of the Soviet special camps – the uprisings remained a taboo area of discussion, and the thesis that they constituted a failed 'fascist putsch' (later a 'counter-revolutionary putsch') dominated until 1989.[4] It is little surprise that the memorial landscape of the GDR remained absent of obvious references to the uprising and its victims; where traces could be found, they were in remembrance of policemen or officials who lost their lives, such as in Magdeburg, where three streets were named in 1954 after policemen Gerhard Händler and Georg Gaidzik and the Stasi employee Hans Waldbach.

In contrast, 17 June rapidly assumed central importance in West Germany, interpreted as an occasion of mass protest in which the East German people rose up against their government, calling not only for freedom, but also for national unity. On 23 June, a funeral service was held outside the West Berlin town hall of Schöneberg, displaying the coffins of those who died in West Berlin hospitals as a result of their injuries. Here, Chancellor Adenauer declared, 'We will not rest and we will not pause – I make this pledge for the whole of the German people – until they also have freedom once again, until the whole of Germany is once again united in peace and freedom'.[5] In the West, 17 June was quickly declared the Day of German Unity, and instated as an official national holiday on 4 August 1953, celebrated as such until 1990. Parallels were drawn between 17 June 1953 and 20 July 1944 – the date of Stauffenberg's plot against Hitler – in an attempt to embed it in a longer tradition of struggle for freedom against a totalitarian regime; references to the revolution of 1848 were also frequent. Adenauer particularly saw the uprisings as an opportunity to promote his policies of Western integration and to highlight the political bankruptcy of the SED regime. Over time, however, and particularly after the building of the Wall, the ever more distant prospect of unity in the 1970s and 1980s meant that for many West Germans this bank holiday lost its relevance, with the slogan 'unity in freedom' (*Einheit in Freiheit*) degenerating rather into 'unity in free-time' (*Einheit in Freizeit*).[6]

Numerous monuments were erected to the victims of 17 June 1953 in West Berlin, the first of which – a simple cross in Zehlendorf – was already in place by 25 June.[7] The use of crosses and gravestone-like monuments was common, with inscriptions commonly emphasizing victims' fight for freedom, not dissimilar to war memorials that dedicate victims' sacrifice to the fatherland. By the time of the second anniversary, a central monument was completed at the West Berlin cemetery on Seestraße for those victims who died in West Berlin. Featuring a sculpture by Karl Wenk, which shows a slave-like figure trying to free itself from chains, the political message was clear; this became the central location for the laying of wreaths, a tradition that continues today. Perhaps the best-known monument to the uprisings, however, is the 'Straße des 17. Juni', the road running from the Brandenburg Gate to today's Ernst Reuter-Platz, which was officially renamed by the Berlin Senate on 22 June 1953. Located in West Berlin, however, neither this street nor the other memorials represented authentic locations of the uprisings, just one of the paradoxes of the divided memorial cultures in East and West. Indeed, as Sabine Bergmann-Pohl, the last and only freely elected president of the East German parliament, highlighted fifty years on, this was a day celebrated by West Germans who had risked nothing, while East Germans who had risked everything had little to celebrate.[8] Perhaps tellingly, the West German bank holiday dedicated to German unity was abolished in the very year that unity was achieved, in favour of the administrative date of 3 October.

The freeing of authentic locations from official GDR narratives and the opening of the GDR archives led to a renewed interest in the memory of this date. In the 1990s, this manifested itself primarily in a number of new historical works on 17 June,[9] and on the fortieth anniversary a plaque was unveiled to the victims of the uprisings on the former 'House of Ministries' (which now houses the Federal Ministry of Finance), the location where Berlin workers presented their demands to ministers.[10] Following a campaign led by eyewitnesses in the working group entitled 'Arbeitskreis 17. Juni', together with the 'Haus am

Checkpoint Charlie' Museum, large-format photos of the demonstrations were also hung on the building between 1994 and 1996 (and again from 2003 to 2005), rendering the history of this location highly visible; a permanent monument was further erected here in 2000 (discussed below). Elsewhere in the 1990s, 17 June was sometimes inscribed into the cityscape in a less formal way. In Halle, for instance, the Monument of the Revolutionary Workers' Movement – a colossal structure dating from 1970 of four clenched fists reaching up to the sky, adorned with significant dates marking the development of the workers' movement – was altered overnight in December 1997 through the addition of four extra dates: 1953, 1961, 1989 and 1990.[11] These were stuck onto the monument in polystyrene (the last of which was painted in black, red and gold), turning it into a counter-monument to the communist ideal, until it was demolished in 2003.

Yet public memory of the date remained sketchy, with a survey in June 2001 revealing that only 43 per cent of all Germans and 19 per cent of eighteen- to twenty-four-year-olds knew what happened on this date.[12] The real memory boom for 17 June came with the fiftieth anniversary in 2003, when a further raft of publications emerged,[13] and the mass media promoted widespread public awareness of the date, alongside the special edition of a postage stamp and a 10 euro commemorative coin.[14] Prior to this anniversary, the Bundesstiftung zur Aufarbeitung der SED-Diktatur also made a public call to encourage localities to name streets or squares after the uprisings and its demonstrators (in 2002 there were only two locations in the east in which this was the case).[15] Consequently, by the fiftieth anniversary, eleven towns had renamed a street or building, with a further twelve stating an intention to do so.[16] Moreover, a number of towns erected plaques to 17 June to mark locations and local personalities who were central to the events; these included, among others, Eisenhüttenstadt, Zittau, Dessau, Bitterfeld and Seyda.[17]

Despite the memory boom of 2003 and a further wave of activity for the sixtieth anniversary in 2013, the complexity of the divided memory of this date inevitably proves problematic for public remembrance and raises significant questions concerning the purpose and form of new commemorative structures. First, what should be remembered: a spontaneous workers' strike, an organized mass revolt, a citizens' rights movement or a campaign for national freedom? There is little doubt that although the demonstrations started as a workers' uprising, the demands moved far beyond the workers' initial concerns; farmers, office workers, students, school pupils as well as some party officials and even a few Soviet soldiers supported the demonstrators' cause. Yet at the same time it was not a coordinated national uprising, for it lacked central leadership, nor was it a clear call for unification. In addition to these complexities, the single date of 17 June represents only the high point of a period of crisis that began in 1952. In many areas, strikes took place days, if not weeks, before 17 June, and unrest continued over the ensuing weeks and months.[18] The focus on 17 June itself often overlooks the broader historical context and the longer-term consequences of the uprisings for those living in the GDR. It is perhaps no surprise that at a symposium prior to the launch of the Berlin monument competition in 1997, a number of speakers expressed their doubts over whether traditional memorial forms could successfully represent these historical ambiguities; some suggested instead a more informative memorial site, while others believed that existing monuments were sufficient, since they also incorporated the divided memory of the uprisings.[19] Perhaps tellingly, the first jury for this competition found the task too demanding and judged none of the entries to be suitable – a pattern that is repeated surprisingly frequently throughout this book, and to which we will return.

The issue of historical accuracy and form is clearly dependent on a second question: what is the purpose of memorializing 17 June afresh today? While any new monument to this date will necessarily commemorate the victims of 1953, to what extent should it also represent a positive monument dedicated to 'national heroes', especially in light of the recent prominence given to the problematic memory of the Holocaust? In other words, to what extent should memory of 17 June signal a move away from united Germany's predominant emphasis on a cathartic dialogue with the past? For supporters of this view, 17 June 1953 can conveniently be slotted into a trajectory of popular uprisings in the name of freedom, from 1848 through to 1918 and most significantly 1989. Of these dates, 17 June arguably holds the most emotional potential, for the earlier dates have never really found a significant place in public consciousness, and 9 November, marking the fall of the Berlin Wall, proves problematic because this date also marks the *Kristallnacht* pogrom of 1938, Hitler's failed Beer Hall Putsch of 1923 and the abdication of the monarchy and proclamation of the republic in 1918. As 17 June 1953 also marks the first of several significant uprisings within the Eastern bloc (Hungary 1956, Czechoslovakia 1968, Poland 1980/81), its relationship to 1989 appears all the more forceful. Within political circles, 17 June is thus often interpreted teleologically as a precursor to the demonstrations of 1989, and its victims as the cornerstone of a reunified German nation. Indeed, despite historical research revealing few clear links between the two movements,[20] this interpretation appears as a leitmotif in political speeches concerning the uprisings. To quote Rita Süssmuth in 1990, for example, 'precisely the events of 1989 make it strikingly clear to us that the victims of the suppressed uprising of 1953 were not in vain'.[21] Other statesmen, such as former president Johannes Rau, have claimed that it is a proud date in the German and European struggle for freedom, with some even comparing it to the storming of the Bastille;[22] Berlin's former mayor Eberhard Diepgen further claimed in 2000 that this was the date that, for Germans, 'saved the concept of the nation'.[23] Regardless of the historical complexities of the post-1953 years in the GDR, this date clearly lends itself to instrumentalization on the part of contemporary politics, a situation that reminds us of its divided legacy. As Peter Steinbach critically states, 'For this reason, 17 June 1953 is also a symbol of our hypocrisy'.[24]

The difficulties in memorializing this date are clearly manifold, but also depend on location. While the national narrative has always been strongly Berlin-focused due to the divided nature of the city and the symbolic importance of the uprisings for the question of unity, it must not be forgotten that events were widespread in the GDR, affecting over seven hundred towns and villages across the country. Drawing on four examples of memorial projects in memory of 17 June 1953 – in Berlin, Hennigsdorf, Leipzig and Magdeburg – this chapter not only explores the ways in which different communities and interest groups have negotiated the concrete remembrance of this date, but also examines the discrepancies between memorial activity in Berlin and in other towns where demonstrations took place. Indeed, as these examples demonstrate, the status of Berlin as Germany's capital, where a new united Germany is symbolically being created, means that mnemonic symbolism often adopts heightened form and is debated more controversially than elsewhere. The less controversial process of monument construction in other towns, and inhabitants' relative acceptance of (if not ambivalence towards) them, is a sobering reminder that we must look beyond Berlin in order to gauge any sense of 'collective' remembrance of the GDR. This chapter also provides continuity with a number of themes in the previous chapter, for the findings once again demonstrate the significance of generation and personal biography in shaping monument projects, as well as the importance of installing commemorative 'software' such as annual ceremonies and activities linked to monuments, in order to keep them alive. In terms of aesthetics, the memorialization of 1953 also appears to favour designs with concrete symbolism, and although the resulting forms are very different to the traditional crosses and stelae witnessed in Chapter 3, they also appear to result from a desire to counter the commemorative silence of GDR years. Once again, past remembrance – or lack of such – proves highly significant.

Conflicting Interpretations in Berlin: Katharina Karrenberg, Wolfgang Rüppel and Beyond

While strikes and demonstrations took place across the GDR, the role of East Berlin was critical; more workers went on strike here than in any other town, the role of Western radio stations such as RIAS played a significant role in disseminating news of the strikes, and the proximity of West Berlin heightened an already tense atmosphere. The subsequent creation of public remembrance sites in West Berlin also meant that after unification there was a strong desire to mark the main historical locations of the uprisings in the eastern part of the city. Moreover, as this case study demonstrates, a strong political will existed in the late 1990s to create a central memorial to 1953, in part to promote symbolically the notion of unity, and in part to create a structure with a potentially positive message that would provide a counterbalance to the much-debated Holocaust memorial. Indeed, the fact that the Berlin Senate pursued a costly project to remember 17 June 1953, despite the city being in debt to the tune of over forty billion DM in 1996, is sufficient to indicate the political importance of this date.[25]

The project originated in March 1994, when the Berlin House of Representatives approved a proposal by the CDU and SPD fractions for a memorial to 17 June; the House subsequently recommended that the Berlin Senate take on the initiative 'for a monument at one of the central locations of the uprising of 17 June 1953, in order to recognize the victims in an appropriate manner'.[26] Later that year, the aforementioned large-format photos of the demonstrations were hung on the Federal Ministry for Finance, raising the profile of the uprisings; the initiators of the photos – the 'Haus am Checkpoint Charlie' Museum and the Arbeitskreis 17. Juni – were also strong advocates of a new memorial. Prior to the launch of a competition in 1997, funded by the Berlin Senate, a symposium was held in September 1996 to discuss the meaning and significance of such a memorial for Berlin, in which historians, artists, art historians, eyewitnesses and civil rights activists from the GDR took part. The wide range of interpretations of 17 June highlighted the complexity of this history and its legacy, with differing views on what such a monument should represent. Would emphasis on the mourning of victims, for instance, preclude positive identification with the demonstrators? Was it, indeed, acceptable to have a central memorial to national heroes now that the plans for Berlin's Holocaust memorial were taking shape? Or should this be a structure dedicated rather to values such as civil disobedience and democratic rights, which would be more suited to a post-national society? Was a traditional memorial even desirable in view of the existing sites of remembrance, which already document the divided remembrance history? As a result of such questions, and in the wake of lengthy discussions concerning the heightened symbolism of the Holocaust memorial, a competition brief was drawn up that was conceived to be as 'open' as possible, urging artists to design a monument that 'commands attention as a thought-provoking stumbling block'.[27] Entries were also required to help the viewer uncover the 'multi-layered historical events', promote the symbiosis of 'the personal memory of the individual, social memory and historical information', and thematize 'the substance of the uprising as democratic, pro civil rights and critical of the leadership'.[28]

Perhaps most importantly, artists were left to choose the location(s) for their designs from three possibilities outlined in the competition brief, although not precluding other locations. The first option was the former Stalinallee (now Karl-Marx-Allee), where building workers of Block 40 were the first to down their tools, thus marking the main starting point of the demonstrations in East Berlin; a memorial located here would emphasize the original demands of the protesters. The second location was the square outside the former House of Ministries (on Leipziger Straße/Wilhelmstraße) representing the high point of the protest, where demonstrators placed their escalating demands to ministers. Third, entrants could choose the adjoining squares of Leipziger Platz and Potsdamer Platz, where the demonstration was brutally quashed, thus symbolizing the totalitarian aspirations of the GDR regime and the site of repression. As with many locations in Berlin, however, the history of some of these sites is multi-layered. Most significantly, the former House of Ministries is a National Socialist construction that originally housed the Reich Air Ministry. Following the war, it was used temporarily by the East German parliament and is thus the building in which the GDR was founded in 1949. After unification, it housed the headquarters of the Treuhandanstalt (the agency tasked with privatizing East German enterprises) until 1994. Now housing the Ministry of Finance, it represents the continuities and ruptures of recent German history, and provides one example of the complex web of associations facing many potential locations for new monuments in the city.

The task given to artists was thus demanding, and entries were wide-ranging, with a number rejecting conventional monumental form. The most radical proposal, by artists p.t.t.red, suggested the institutionalization of an annual five-second power cut in order to provoke memory of the emergency measures of 1953. Others worked with the theme of demonstrations: Horst Hoheisel proposed transporting an obelisk in ritual fashion along the route of demonstrators every year, deliberately disrupting traffic flows, while Kurt Buchwald envisaged an annual demonstration on topical issues, to which protesters would find their way by following street signs marked 'people's uprising'.[29] The complex demands of the competition, however, almost brought it to a standstill, for the jury found none of the fifty-four entries to be suitable, declaring in February 1998: 'As a high-profile event of contemporary history, 17 June 1953 cannot be represented by a self-contained work with a homogenous aesthetic structure and clear-cut semantics and impact'.[30] While this announcement appeared to be as much a comment on the unfeasibility of the competition itself, rather than on the submitted entries, a second jury was subsequently appointed, which completed a two-stage selection process in 1998, drawing on seven entries from the first competition and a number of newly invited competitors. Significantly, the second jury included a representative of the veterans from 1953, Werner Herbig (chair of the Arbeitskreis 17. Juni), a controversial omission from the first. On 23 November 1998, Katharina Karrenberg was announced as the winner.

Karrenberg chose the location of Leipziger Platz, where she proposed installing in the ground the sentence: 'who am I to say: a heroic act' (*wer bin ich, dass ich sagen könnte: eine heroische tat*). Measuring 65 metres long and 2.5 metres wide, this was to be written with 467 circular lamps embedded in the ground, with the road through the square dividing the sentence at the colon; the lamps would contain historical material, either in written or photographic form, through which the viewer could piece together the history of the uprisings. Approximately half of the lamps would be left blank, so that the memorial could evolve with time as new documents were found and history revised. The use of the first person in the illuminated question was intended to provoke observers to examine their own conscience and feel humbled by the courage of those who risked their lives for freedom of speech. As Karrenberg stated in her proposal, 'the tribute lies in negation'.[31] The memorial was also intended to challenge the observer's concept of history, for the division of the sentence would mean that only one half could be read at once. If, for example, 'a heroic act' was read first, the viewer's perception of a heroizing memorial would have to be revised on crossing the road – a process of revision typical of historical research, and of the remembrance history of this date. In this way, the intention was to bring together many of the contradictions evident in monumental constructions: heroization and information, emotional and factual messages, as well as the need to pay tribute and self-reflect; as she stated, 'Today the consolidation of the Federal Republic is far enough advanced for us to no longer need to frame the events in terms of the nation. It can, in fact, dedicate itself to self-scrutiny when dealing with these events'.[32] Karrenberg's design was thus an attempt to escape the construction of a traditional, heroic and static memorial, and to challenge the historical, social and political consciousness of the observer – elements that found favour with most members of the jury.[33]

For many others, however, the complexity of the winning design was problematic. One of the first voices to object was jury member and veteran Werner Herbig. Together with other veterans, he strongly opposed Karrenberg's sentence, claiming that it questioned and trivialized their courageous acts, belittled the terror of that day and vilified the heroes of the uprising.[34] Moreover, Karrenberg's choice of venue represented the location of 'defeat' for the veterans, rather than that of 'victory' outside the House of Ministries, where they had presented their demands to ministers. The outrage within the veterans' group was so great that they called for a boycott of Karrenberg's design, and even threatened legal action.[35] It was not long before the then mayor of Berlin, Eberhard Diepgen, and other CDU representatives backed the veterans' cause.[36] The president of the Federal Building Directorate, Florian Mausbach, also saw the monument to be indicative of the inability not only to mourn, but also to distinguish between good and evil.[37] The press followed suit, fuelling the campaign against Karrenberg's design, which was clearly difficult to swallow for those with a specific agenda, as the rhetorical gesture of leaving a question hanging in the air precluded any kind of ritual or cathartic function, causing some critics to see the design as elitist and 'a piece of intellectual applied art'.[38]

Criticism was often bound up with other ongoing debates of the time. At a public debate about the monument, for instance, one participant questioned where this trend might lead other monument designs, polemically suggesting that the next step would be to remember the Holocaust by asking 'who am I to say: a crime'.[39] While the direct comparison of these two periods in history proved highly controversial, the prevalence of Holocaust remembrance in Berlin at that time had clearly left its mark and the two projects often became intertwined. The fact that plans for the Holocaust memorial were becoming more concrete at this point enabled those in favour of a more heroic monument to make their case more forcefully; until the Holocaust memorial was formally approved by the Bundestag in June 1999, however, there remained concern over any tendency towards positive national memorialization. On the other hand, a new project emerging in 1998 – the proposed monument to German unity (see Chapter 6) – also influenced discussions. It is perhaps little surprise that two of the initiators of this monument project, Florian Mausbach and Günter Nooke, were also outspoken opponents of Karrenberg's design, for it failed to capture the positive sentiment that they hoped to evoke in a monument to unity. It was, indeed, telling that Nooke was critical of the fact that the decision-making process had not been more strongly influenced by politicians rather than artists and civil servants.[40] Interestingly, the debate surrounding Karrenberg's design thus became bound up with the fates of two other monuments still to be constructed, demonstrating the entanglement of monument projects not only with past traditions and aesthetic forms, but also those on the future horizon.

In an effort to make concessions to the veterans' cause, Karrenberg proposed moving the second part of the sentence ('a heroic act') to the former House of Ministries, while retaining the first half on Leipziger Platz. However, the Senate failed to approve her design in early February 1999, voting instead for that of the second prize winner, Wolfgang Rüppel. This caused outrage among artistic circles, as evidenced in an open letter to the mayor of Berlin and the Senate, coordinated by the NGBK and signed by a large number of artists, historians and academics.[41] As they argued, this decision would prevent any true debate over the meaning of 17 June, and contravened the widely accepted democratic process of holding a competition. In contrast to Karrenberg's design, however, Rüppel's found favour with many for its more clear-cut imagery and message. Located in front of the former House of Ministries, his design consists of an enlarged photograph (twenty-five by four metres) of workers marching arm in arm at the front of a procession of demonstrators. It is etched into glass, which is laid in the ground and surrounded by a stone border, somewhat reminiscent of a gravestone entombing the victims. The photograph is designed to contrast with a mural by Max Lingner on the side of the building, which was commissioned by the SED in 1949 and inaugurated in January 1953 (see Figure 4.1). The colourful mural depicts different sectors of GDR society working together to build socialism, and in the background a mass demonstration of support for the regime and Communist Party is depicted – a piece of artwork that was deemed necessary at the time for political and practical reasons, in order to cover a metal relief on the same wall by Arnold Waldschmidt depicting Nazi soldiers and Luftwaffe motifs.[42] The two images are the same size, with Rüppel's memorial aligned so that the viewer may see both at once. The position of the photograph as a commentary on the mural is

Figure 4.1 Memorial to 17 June 1953 (Wolfgang Rüppel, 2000), also showing mural by Max Lingner (1953) on the wall of the Federal Ministry for Finance, Berlin. Photograph by Anna Saunders.

clear, yet the result – the 'fictive' image of socialist realist propaganda versus the supposedly 'objective' photographic image – represents a polarized image of history. Although the contrast with the mural highlights the fact that different regimes promote different heroes, and Rüppel attempts to falsify the photo through repetition, deliberately choosing an 'unheroic image of the masses' depicting 'sceptical-looking individuals',[43] it perpetuates precisely the division between 'heroes' and 'villains' – in this case the demonstrators and the Party – that Karrenberg had sought to evade. Any grey areas of the uprising, and indeed of life in the GDR, are lost between the two images, not to mention the complicated legacy of the post-1953 years and the divided history of remembrance of this date.

As some critics have suggested, this memorial prescribes an 'end to the debate' rather than providing an impulse for further questions, thus failing to fulfil the competition brief.[44] Much of the critical debate was, however, influenced by the broader contours of twentieth-century German history and its commemorative legacy. In defence of Karrenberg's design, for example, Berlin's Professional Association for Fine Artists (BBK) criticized the direct involvement of politicians as a regressive development, stating that 'the experience of National Socialism has sensitized the politics of the Federal Republic not to instrumentalize art and culture for political purposes'.[45] It was not only the National Socialist past that was brought into the debate, but also Germany's divided history; the fact that a western interpretation of events had largely prevailed did not escape those who felt that western cultural hegemony had often ignored East German interests. Art historian Hiltrud Ebert, for example, claims that 'a symbolic reintegration of the "victims of Stalinism" into the political context of unified Berlin was more than opportune for the self-stylization of the autochthonous Western CDU as the moral victor of post-war German history'. Similarly, she suggests that the construction of a memorial to 17 June 1953, rather than to 9 November 1989 or 3 October 1990, fails to respect eastern German sensibilities, and – alongside the destruction of socialist monuments – demonstrates a lack of political sensitivity.[46] This criticism is somewhat undermined, however, by the fact that the memorial does, in fact, remember East Germans as resisters, thus crediting GDR citizens with a sense of democracy and courage. Yet it was clearly bound up with the politics of the time, and as architect Wolfgang Kil claimed, the development of this monument project doubtless demonstrated the vested interests of those in power in Berlin, for whom the city was a 'laboratory of unity', rather than attempting to explain the historical circumstances and political context of 1953.[47] While this memorial is dedicated to one specific event, its message concerning the GDR is thus broader and it tells us more about the concerns of contemporary identities than historical complexities.

This case study also throws intriguing light on the contours of communicative and cultural memory. The fact that Rüppel's design was backed by an alliance of veterans and predominantly CDU politicians demonstrates that the two types of memory need not be contradictory. Indeed, the communicative memory of veterans and the desire of CDU politicians to create a more established form of cultural memory clearly overlapped, as both desired a specific interpretation of events. What bound them together was their reluctance to allow an exploratory and critical examination of history in more contentious artistic form. The personal involvement of veterans, whose lived memories of this period were very strong, is clearly understandable here, and is not dissimilar to the emotional debates that took place at Buchenwald; once again, a desire for clear symbolism related to desire for recognition. It is also interesting that of the monument designs submitted, those that highlighted the ambiguities and historical continuities were largely by female artists. Some critics have suggested that one reason for

Karrenberg's rejection was the fact that her design did not fit with the demands of the male veterans' group and the largely male community of politicians.[48] Interestingly, the attitude of these groups has resurfaced in an unexpected epilogue to events, for elements of Rüppel's memorial have apparently also failed to satisfy these communities of memory. Its horizontal position, for example, making it somewhat hidden to the passer-by, and the deliberate distortion of the photograph through the etching process, are seen by some to be unsatisfactory, as its symbolism is not immediately apparent. Alexandra Hildebrandt, director of the 'Haus am Checkpoint Charlie' Museum, has claimed that it is a monument 'only for those in the know', which 'does not adequately honour its heroes', and that 'a visible, meaningful and proud monument is long overdue'.[49] Moreover, the fact that Lingner's illuminated mural dominates the square at night has also angered this community, causing many comments in largely conservative newspapers that the monument remains 'invisible'.[50]

Such objections were quietened between 2003 and 2005, when the large-format photographs that had hung on the Ministry of Finance building between 1994 and 1996 were reinstated by the 'Haus am Checkpoint Charlie' Museum, thus making this historical site once again more visible. However, the forced removal of the banners in 2005 due to a preservation order on the building – and the fact that Hildebrandt had only obtained permission to hang the pictures for two weeks – caused a high-profile campaign on the part of veterans and members of the CDU, who called for a return of the banners and for extra signage at the site. Sympathizer and right-wing political activist Carl-Wolfgang Holzapfel also staged a hunger strike on the monument – significantly draped in a German flag – in protest against the removal of the photographs.[51] While the photo-banners have not since been reinstalled, four information boards have been erected next to the monument, which explain the history of the building, the uprisings and the monument itself. In honour of the sixtieth anniversary, a temporary outdoor exhibition about 1953 was also mounted on the square, which itself was renamed 'Platz des Aufstandes' (Square of the Uprising), thus raising the profile of this location. In view of Hildebrandt's repeated appeals for the photo-banners to return – alongside observations from opponents that this not only damages Rüppel's concept but represents little more than an attempt to turn the cityscape into a 'dramatic theme park of the Cold War'[52] – it seems that the resulting monument has not presented an 'end to the debate', for two decades after the original proposal for a monument, this past continues to live on.

The contours of this debate contrasted starkly with a smaller project in Berlin dating from 2003, which demonstrates the varying ways in which 17 June may be appropriated. While the debate over Karrenberg and Rüppel was dominated by the political right and centred primarily on questions of centralization, normalization and the interpretation of German unity, this second example shows that memory of 17 June may also be deployed by a broader political spectrum for less nationally-motivated reasons. In order to mark the fiftieth anniversary of 17 June 1953, an initiative was instigated by several trades unions, a local history association (Förderverein Karl-Marx-Allee e.V.) and a civil rights group (Bürgerbüro e.V.), which involved building a so-called *Denk-Stein* (memorial stone) during a commemorative ceremony on Karl-Marx-Allee, outside the former Block 40. The construction of the memorial – a low wall made of bricks recovered from a rubble pit dating back to the post-war period – was led by artist Karla Sachse. The bricks were put in place by former building workers of the time, schoolchildren, politicians and trades union members, with the intention of raising the profile of this history and remembering the courage of those who demonstrated against the SED dictatorship. The inscription on the wall read, 'We want to be free people', and speakers at the event included Berlin's mayor, Klaus Wowereit (SPD), the chair of the Confederation of German Trade Unions, Michael Sommer, civil rights activist Konrad Weiß, as well as the mayor of the Friedrichshain-Kreuzberg district, Cornelia Reinauer (PDS).[53] As indicated by the inscription, the emphasis of the day lay not on the national importance of the uprisings, but rather on the democratic rights for which workers demonstrated in 1953, as well as their contemporary relevance. These values were perhaps most clearly articulated in Weiß's speech: 'Even today, freedom and democracy are endangered. They are endangered by the all-powerful state, by the egotism of parties and through our indifference. And through the removal of social rights. The battle for social justice is also a battle for human dignity and democracy'.[54] Some of those present took this message further, using the opportunity to protest against the government's social cuts, displaying banners with slogans such as 'Needed again: Resistance like 53', thus calling to reactivate the values of 17 June.[55]

While this project was much smaller and less controversial than Rüppel's memorial, it still revealed the difficult legacy of 1953. Many local residents, for example, proved resistant to the project; often long-standing inhabitants of the adjacent building, a number were former GDR functionaries who saw themselves to be the 'losers' of unification. As reported by the project's initiators, they were often unwilling to speak about 17 June or to re-evaluate its history, and largely saw this commemorative symbol to be unnecessary.[56] Some individuals felt so strongly about it that the plaque was vandalized and removed twice by the end of 2004. In strange contrast to Rüppel's monument, on which demonstrations were staged for its relative invisibility, this one was attacked for its very presence, demonstrating the heightened importance of location and local politics. Also revealing are the different messages taken from the events of 1953: while the central Berlin memorial highlights the national importance of the uprising for united Germany, thus appealing largely to the political right, this local example rather draws on more universal issues such as social rights and democratic responsibilities, in order to provide a critique of contemporary German society from a left-wing perspective. Evidently, this history remains open to interpretation, and whatever form its commemoration takes in Berlin, it persists as an active part of the city's self-presentation and understanding.

Remembering Hennigsdorf's Steelworkers

In contrast to developments in the capital, the small Brandenburg town of Hennigsdorf, located north-west of Berlin, witnessed one of the earliest post-*Wende* monuments to 17 June 1953, which has been assimilated into the local community with relatively little debate. The main aim of the project was to remember the workers of Hennigsdorf who played a particular role in the uprisings of 1953: while hundreds demonstrated in the town itself on 17 June, approximately ten thousand local workers – primarily those in the steel and railway industries – marched twenty-seven kilometres into Berlin, in order to support the demonstrators there.[57] As Hennigsdorf bordered West Berlin, this involved forcing their way past GDR border guards and marching through the French sector of West Berlin, where they received applause and encouragement from West Berliners, as well as handouts of food, cigarettes and drink. Although they arrived in Berlin after the Soviet tanks and had to make a swift retreat, their strike continued the following day, and the actions of the Hennigsdorf workers remained firmly entrenched in the communicative memory of the town, despite being a taboo subject during the GDR. While a monument to the Hennigsdorf workers was erected in the West Berlin district of Tegel in 1963 to mark one of the streets through which they marched, this history inevitably remained unmarked in Hennigsdorf during division.[58]

The proposal for a monument came first from the local CDU in October 1991, with a view to holding an unveiling ceremony on the fortieth anniversary in June 1993. The motion put to the town council, however, proposed a monument to both 17 June 1953 and 9 November 1989, with the justification that 'the uprising on 17 June 1953 and the opening of the borders on 9 November 1989 stand for the unbroken will of our citizens for freedom and democratic self-determination'.[59] Approved in May 1992, a competition was subsequently launched for a monument entitled simply '17 June 1953 – Autumn 1989'. While the bringing together of these two dates would initially appear to place this example in an even stronger national tradition than the Berlin monument, the emphasis on freedom and democracy throughout the competition process, and indeed during commemorative events afterwards, appears to have become the main focus of the memorialization process. Perhaps for this reason, there also appears to have been very little party-political wrangling over the suitability of the monument, and the competition was designed primarily with local, rather than national interests at heart: competing artists were to live in the *Land* of Brandenburg, and residents of Hennigsdorf were given the opportunity to attend a public exhibition and vote on their favourite design, with their collective vote counting as one of the seven votes on the jury.[60]

Of the four entries, the vast majority of votes went for the design by Heidi Wagner-Kerkhof, which consists of two main elements reflecting the dual purpose of the monument (see Figure 4.2).[61] The first element, bearing the inscription '17 June 1953', comprises three tall stelae made from Franconian limestone, which loosely resemble human figures due to their head-like tops. The central stele, taller than the others and positioned at an angle indicating forward movement, is intended to represent determination, whereas the two outside stelae stand for the solidarity of the masses. The second sculpture, positioned over thirty metres away with the inscription 'Autumn 1989', consists of a steel wall with openings, through which the visitor may look in the direction of Berlin. While the openings symbolize the autumn of 1989, horizontal iron bars on the wall also represent the confinement and restrictions that were imposed not only by the Wall but also following the uprisings of 1953.[62] The use of steel, the surface of which is rusty, not only evokes the Iron Curtain, but is also intended to be a tribute to the steelworkers of Hennigsdorf. The imagery of the wall is particularly apt for this town, which was cut off from adjacent neighbourhoods in West Berlin by the Berlin Wall. The viewer is encouraged not only to view these two sculptures, but to 'experience them actively', by retracing the steps of the former workers.[63] Two paths thus lead to the first sculpture, representing the coming together of workers in Hennigsdorf; from here, a second path, approximately thirty-six steps long – representing the

Figure 4.2 '17 June 1958 – Autumn 1989' (Heidi Wagner-Kerkhof, 1993), Platz des 17. Juni 1953, Hennigsdorf. Photograph by Anna Saunders.

thirty-six years between the two demonstrations – leads to the second sculpture. The distance between the two is intended to provoke reflection on the length of time that elapsed before a second uprising; while a clear progression from the first event to the second is implied here, the abstract symbolism of the ensemble does not encourage restrictive interpretations of either event. It is notable that this 'active experience' of the monument has become a ritual part of anniversaries of 1953 at the site, at which local politicians lay wreaths at the first monument, before walking the path to the second, in a sense accompanying this history into the present day. This idea was further pursued on the sixtieth anniversary, when a bus trip was organized for locals to retrace the route taken by demonstrators from Hennigsdorf to Berlin. Following the commemorative trip, the square next to the monument was named 'Platz des 17. Juni' in order to embed this date more firmly into the urban landscape.

While the monument has become a ritual site largely for 17 June rather than for the autumn of 1989, it is interesting that it was unveiled on 3 October 1993. As with many such projects, the practical issue of time pressure made 17 June unfeasible, but the decision to use 3 October rather than 9 November symbolizes the decision to place emphasis on values in contemporary united Germany, rather than on a specific historical event. As SPD mayor Andreas Schulz emphasized in his speech, the path from 17 June did not end with the fall of the Wall; instead, it was more important 'to tread the daily path for democracy, human dignity and social justice in unity with all democratic forces'.[64] Only three years after unification, this was still an uncertain time for many, and the monument paid tribute to the Hennigsdorf workers from past and present, as the steel in the monument had come from a Hennigsdorf firm and been worked by a local steelworker. Indeed, for Heidi Wagner-Kerkhof, the monument was a symbol as much for the steelworkers of the 1990s, many of whom had suffered unemployment, as for those of the past.[65] The project also adopted for her the true sense of east-west cooperation as the limestone had been sourced by a west Berlin stonemason.[66] Speeches at the unveiling drew strongly on communicative memory of the GDR, in the attempt to underline the positive values of unity. As council chair Hartmut Nischik (CDU) said to those present, 'Think back to entry into the Pioneer Organization, to the petitioning of registration offices for trips to non-socialist countries, to non-attendance at the 1st May demonstration ... Think back to the GDR, and how it wasn't always dear to everyone'.[67] Interestingly, the emphasis here was not so much on the horrific crushing of the 17 June uprisings, but rather on the thirty-six years that followed in its wake, and which marked the vast majority of those assembled at the unveiling. Unlike the black and white imagery that accompanied much of the Berlin debate surrounding 17 June, the narrative around Hennigsdorf's monument thus focused on a broader, lived experience of life in a dictatorship. While this may result, in part, from the fact that the Hennigsdorf memorial was unveiled only three years after unification, this attitude is also exemplified in later years, for example in a local press interview in 2002 with two of the town's veterans from 1953, who claimed that they did not want to leave the GDR after 17 June, but rather decided to stay and work for change.[68] This provides a clear contrast to the most vocal opponents in the Berlin debate – Werner Herbig, a veteran who later fled to West Berlin, and Carl-Wolfgang Holzapfel, himself a West

Berliner – demonstrating the different motivations of those involved. Free of the need to represent a national narrative, the monument in Hennigsdorf has clearly attracted less controversial attention, but at the same time represents a focus in the community that has come to symbolize a broader engagement with the GDR and its legacy.

Tank Tracks in Leipzig

The uprisings of 17 June clearly affected regions much further from Berlin than Hennigsdorf. The town of Leipzig, for instance, witnessed up to eighty thousand demonstrators, and although statistics vary, sources widely cite twelve deaths and more than ninety-five casualties in the region.[69] The legacy of 1953 plays a particularly important role here, for the town prides itself on being the major starting point for the demonstrations of 1989 (see Chapter 6). Much local literature on 1953 thus draws a specific line between the two events, with frequent claims that, for example, 'the demonstrators of autumn 1989 completed what the insurgents began in 1953'.[70] The heavy commemorative focus on 1989 in Leipzig, however, caused concern among some that the historical detail of 1953 was being forgotten. Not only did surveys in 2003 reveal a serious lack of knowledge about 1953 among young generations,[71] but some critics also feared that the peaceful revolution of 1989 had produced the illusion among young people that civil rights demonstrations were no longer potentially dangerous events that could end in bloodshed. As journalist Andreas Tappert reminded local readers, 'Not only are the victims of the people's uprising in the GDR being forgotten, but also the fact that freedom must be secured through principled attitudes and civil courage'.[72]

The anniversary year of 2003 thus saw much commemorative activity in Leipzig. Eleven information boards were erected around the city in memory of the main locations of the uprisings; a high-profile exhibition was displayed in the town hall on the demonstrations (significantly ending with reference to the events of 1989);[73] weekly tours of the town entitled 'On the Trail of 17 June in Leipzig' took place during the second half of 2003; and the eastern half of Beethovenstraße was renamed 'Straße des 17. Juni'.[74] Many of these activities took place under the Leipzig Tourism and Marketing office's slogan *Leipziger Freiheit* (Leipzig['s] freedom), a campaign that began in 2002 to highlight the historical, cultural and scientific legacy of the city. This was, of course, particularly suited to the events of both 1953 and 1989, yet also incorporated more distant events, such as Leipzig's role in the anti-Napoleonic battles of 1813 and the March revolution of 1848. Writer Erich Loest suggested that this sentiment needed to be taken further, and could be implemented via the introduction of an annual 'day of the bold citizen' on 17 June, in order to continue the strength of courage displayed by former demonstrators. As he claimed, 'It seems to me that we are not only remembering an anniversary, but are also in search of historical identity';[75] for him, as for others, 17 June provided an opportunity to link past and present through the foregrounding of human rights and social responsibility.

It was a desire to develop this sense of historical identity that led a group of young, politically active Leipzig residents to develop plans for a monument to 17 June in the city centre, a project that had not been suggested through official channels in the town. The idea grew out of the Young Social Democrats Forum, a left-leaning independent group, in 2002. The intention for a monument was to express historic pride in demonstrators' courage and desire for freedom, and a number of its members formed the 'Association for a Monument to the People's Uprising of 17 June 1953'. As the association's twenty-nine-year-old chairperson, Tobias David, claimed, 'Through this, we want to demonstrate to future generations the high value of freedom'.[76] Unlike most examples of monuments to 17 June, this proposal did not come from an established political party, and can be seen as a genuine citizens' initiative – albeit from a left-leaning group – that consequently attracted the praise of Leipzig's then mayor, Wolfgang Tiefensee (SPD), and gained the support of the town's administration.[77] The project was financed without funds from local government, and donations from local firms, individuals and all the main political parties – notably including the PDS – ensured that the project went ahead.[78] In this sense, it became a community endeavour that was not primarily driven by party-political concerns.

The association developed the design of the monument, rather than holding a competition or engaging an artist. The concept consists of bronze imprints of tank tracks in the ground, measuring four metres long (the length of a Soviet T-34 tank); between the two tracks, a bronze plaque simply reads '17 June 1953' (see Figure 4.3). The location of the monument on Salzgäßchen, just off the Market Square, was chosen for the fact that one of the few photographs of the demonstrations pictures a tank standing in approximately this position. Also in line with a desire for historical accuracy, the imprints of the tracks were taken from an original T-34 tank, located in Dresden's Museum of Military History. The issue of practicality was also important for the initiators: Christmas markets are annually held on the square, and

Figure 4.3 17 June 1953 Memorial (Young Social Democrats Forum, 2003), Salzgäßchen, Leipzig. Photograph by Anna Saunders.

sometimes the markets spill out onto Salzgäßchen. While this means that the monument is occasionally covered, it is usually traversed by a large number of pedestrians on an annual basis, thus raising its profile.[79] The decision to avoid the Market Square itself not only meant that planning permission would be more straightforward, but it also distanced the project from a proposal by a local action group to place a real T-34 tank on the square in memory of the fiftieth anniversary of June 1953. Having caused heightened controversy in the town and protests from citizens who did not wish to see a symbol of war in their town, the project never went ahead; instead, the less intrusive monument represented a compromise, and responded to memorial discussions in the town.[80]

The bronze plaque was laid on 17 June 2003 in the presence of Mayor Tiefensee, in advance of the monument itself. Perhaps inevitably, the initiators were keen to use the high-profile anniversary to raise public awareness of the monument, although a shortage of funding meant that it could not be completed for that day. The intention was to complete and unveil the monument on 13 August – marking the building of the Wall – but delays meant that it finally took place on 9 November.

While the final choice of date was largely a result of logistics, the shift from 13 August to 9 November placed the emphasis more strongly on a tradition of civil unrest and freedom, which was emphasized in the unveiling speech by Tiefensee. The initiators themselves admit that the line of continuity between the two dates is rather contrived, but see a heightened relevance in bringing them together in Leipzig.[81] What is most notable about this monument is the relative lack of controversy and attention that it has caused in the town, both before and after its installation. As it resulted from a citizens' initiative with relatively modest aims and did not involve any competitive process, it has not provoked the political attention associated with other such projects. Its instigation by a younger generation and the lack of direct involvement on the part of veterans has also meant that engagement in the project has been less personal or emotional than witnessed in Berlin. This relates also to the profile of the monument in later years, for although the association has tended to necessary renovations, it has not attempted to install an annual ceremony at the monument or use it as a location for commemorative or political events. While the monument was used as the location for a minute's silence by the Federation of Victims of Stalinism on the sixtieth anniversary of 1953, and the Tourist Office includes it in some of its walking tours, the fact remains that many Leipzig citizens appear to be unaware of its presence.[82] As a 'stumbling stone' waiting to be discovered by pedestrians, this is perhaps one of its real values, in contrast to the following example, where unwelcome attention has provided for high-profile memorial status.

Tank Tracks in Dresden

Five years after Leipzig, Dresden also saw the erection of a monument to 17 June 1953 based on the concept of tank tracks. While this similarity is striking, the appropriation of the monument by very different groups and the establishment of a seemingly strong and controversial ritual around the monument provide a marked contrast. The monument is located on Dresden's Postplatz, a busy square in the town centre where, on 17 June 1953, approximately ten thousand demonstrators amassed. Here they attempted to storm the telecommunications office, but were prevented by Soviet troops and a T-34 tank. Despite the dispersal of demonstrators that day, 18 June also saw a large demonstration on Postplatz, which was once again quashed by Soviet troops, and resulted in a large number of arrests.[83] The proposal for a monument was submitted by the FDP to the town council in 2007 at the time that the Postplatz was undergoing major renovations. As the party argued, the plaque that was mounted in 1993 at the edge of the square in memory of the demonstrations was not sufficient, as it was tucked away in a corner and barely noticed by Dresden residents. Instead, the FDP proposed that this be supplemented by a 'dignified monument that is appropriate to the meaning of the event', which would be frequented by locals and tourists alike and provide ample space for commemorative ceremonies.[84]

Following the approval of the FDP motion, a competition was launched by the town in 2008, which was won by Dresden artist Heidemarie Dreßel and erected in time for the fifty-fifth anniversary of 17 June 1953 that year. The monument consists of an original, 5.7-metre-long T-34 tank chain made available by Dresden's Museum of Military History. One end is embedded in a sand bed, which is laid into the pavement, while the other end curves up into the air, revealing the more recognizable underside of the tank track (see Figure 4.4). A plaque at the end of the sand bed reads: 'In memory of the people's uprising in the GDR. Here on the Postplatz, on 17 June 1953, thousands of Dresden

Figure 4.4 17 June 1953 Memorial (Heidemarie Dreßel, 2008), Postplatz, Dresden. Photograph by Stephanie Bostock.

citizens demonstrated for democracy and free elections, and against the tyranny of the communist dictatorship. After the violent suppression of the uprising, many of them were convicted and imprisoned'. In spring 2011, an iron barrel was fixed under the chain – on the suggestion of the artist – in place of the smaller, temporary concrete support that had been damaged by frost. Representing resistance to the forward motion of the tank, the addition of the barrel somewhat alters the symbolism of the monument, for it strengthens the imagery of rebellion and civil disobedience.[85]

The monument was unveiled on 17 June 2008 after a ceremony in the town hall, at which speeches were given by town officials and eyewitnesses from 1953.[86] At the monument itself, wreaths were laid and roses placed in the tank chain as a sign of remembrance and freedom. The most notable element of these memorial acts was not the usual reference to the values of democracy, freedom and civil rights, but rather the attempt of the right-wing National Democratic Party of Germany (NPD) to appropriate this date for its own means. Having gained over 9 per cent of the vote in the 2004 local elections, the party held twelve seats in Saxony's Landtag at this time, and was keen to make its political presence known. The commemoration of 17 June provided it with a platform to do so, with six of its Landtag representatives attending the unveiling ceremony in order to lay a wreath. As its spokesman claimed, 'The 17 June is and remains one of the most important days of German history. … The monument on Dresden's Postplatz … is one of few examples of a successful German site of memory'.[87] The NPD's rhetoric unsurprisingly adopted a strong anti-communist stance and highlighted the desire of demonstrators to free themselves from foreign rule and to attain national unity. The party also criticized other political parties for sending small numbers of delegates to the unveiling ceremony, and thus failing to demonstrate an appropriately strong moral duty to this historical event.[88] The NPD subsequently used this location as a platform from which to promote nationalist values on 17 June, and from 2010 staged an annual procession around the town centre, starting at the monument. This date became such an important moment in the calendar of the local NPD that the Regional Office for the Protection of the Constitution drew parallels between the appropriation of this date and 13 February 1945 (marking the bombing of Dresden), also adopted by right-wing groups.[89] In building a tradition around 17 June, however, it is somewhat ironic that the NPD was unwittingly echoing the propaganda of the SED, in which the nationalist motivations of Western 'fascists' and 'provocateurs' were blamed for instigating the uprisings.

As the NPD increasingly appropriated this date, other regional political parties saw it necessary to respond. In 2010, for instance, Mayor Helma Orosz (CDU) explicitly used her speech at the monument on 17 June to stress that democracy is a not a self-evident value, but rather one for which we must all carry responsibility. As she stated in her closing lines, the demonstrators of 1953 'show us how important it is to defend freedom time and again from its enemies. Whoever misuses this memory today in order to preach intolerance, nationalism and racism, has not understood history and is engaging in activities outside of the free democratic constitution. Our resistance towards the misuse of our history in Dresden is not only limited to 13 February, but applies equally to 17 June'.[90] Similarly, a spokesman for the SPD in 2012 called for all Dresden citizens who supported freedom, democracy and tolerance to take part in the central ceremony on 17 June, in order not to allow the NPD to subvert the meaning of this date.[91] However, swelling numbers of NPD representatives and supporters at the annual ceremony meant that the party continued to claim that it was the only one to remember the 'heroes' of 1953 honourably.[92] With the mounting financial crisis in Europe, the party also used the values of national identity and national sovereignty associated with 17 June to argue against European financial politics and for the return of the Deutsche Mark. Since the erection of the monument, remembrance of 1953 had become hotly contested in Dresden.

In response to the activities of the NPD and other right-wing groups, a campaign entitled 'Dresden1706', bringing together left-wing groups, trades unions, youth organizations and civil rights organizations, organized a counter-demonstration in 2012 'against a Nazi march and the distortion of history'.[93] On the one hand, initiators of this campaign called on the town to do more to prevent neo-Nazis from appropriating this date, and berated mainstream politicians for standing side by side with NPD representatives at the official ceremony. On the other hand, they also demonstrated a desire to use the values of 1953 for their own means. As claimed in the 'Dresden1706' appeal, 'we should view the day [17 June] in a tradition of social conflict for justice, co-determination, fair pay and shorter working hours. For in times of ... permanent capitalist crisis, these demands are more topical than ever'.[94] The result in 2012 was a massive police presence on Dresden's Postplatz on 17 June, in order to control what was reported to be between 150 and 250 neo-Nazis and counter-demonstrators numbering between 100 and 400.[95] The sixtieth anniversary in 2013 saw a change in tradition, with the town organizing a ceremony first in the Dreikönigskirche, before embarking on an official tour of the historical locations of 1953, including

Postplatz. The absence of any official ceremony at the monument made it more difficult for the NPD to disrupt activities, but the party still attracted approximately one hundred followers for its own procession, which began with a demonstration at the monument. Interestingly, this tradition had become so entrenched that the counter-demonstration of left-wing groups attracted up to one thousand demonstrators.[96] With the sixtieth anniversary marking the high point of this conflict, the monument continues to attract demonstrators on 17 June, even after the NPD failed to be re-elected to the Landtag in 2014.

In an ironic turn of events, this date has become a battleground for present-day political concerns, in which demonstrators exercise their views on the streets of Dresden. It is difficult not to draw parallels with the events of 1953 themselves, especially considering demonstrators' criticism of mainstream political parties for their remembrance politics, and their evident distrust of official policing policy.[97] What remains notable, however, is the fact that this date continues to be interpreted for different purposes by the most divergent of political groups; there is clearly little agreement on the long-term legacy of 17 June, thus keeping associated political demonstrations – whether desirable or not – alive. These events all began with the unveiling of the monument in 2008, the opening ceremony of which triggered political disagreements. Since its erection, however, the monument has proven both central and peripheral to Dresden's 17 June ceremonies. On the one hand, it has provided a concrete site of memory at which interest groups may symbolically express their political views. On the other hand, the monument itself has never been a serious point of controversy in the town, as in Berlin, and has become the backdrop for political action rather than a truly integral part of it. The contrast with Leipzig, however, demonstrates just how differently two conceptually similar monuments may be appropriated at different locations; whether a monument succeeds in provoking remembrance may, indeed, depend more on the political circumstances of the environment in which it is built than any material or aesthetic conditions. As the Dresden example underlines, a monument may unleash a tradition that is quite unexpected or unwanted by its initiators, demonstrating the dependence of concrete structures on the circumstances of the present.

Conclusion: Diverse Remembrance

In terms of aesthetics, the absence of a memorial tradition in the East relating to 17 June provided a clean slate for memorial designs.

Interestingly, as in the previous chapter, this appears to have led to monument designs that eschew ambiguity. While the traditional symbolism used for special camp memorials is not in evidence here – perhaps because these initiatives have been driven largely by political groups rather than the families of victims – the four central case studies all use concrete imagery to evoke a clear message, and indeed efforts in Berlin to promote a more provocative memorial form were rapidly quashed. It is interesting that debates concerning memorial design were much more controversial in Berlin than elsewhere, partly due to the heightened weight of mnemonic symbolism in the capital, but also given the stronger involvement of veterans there. Outside Berlin, the formal memorial structures provoked little, if any debate, yet none of the designs there were as radical as that of Karrenberg – perhaps, itself, a comment on differing expectations in the capital. Broadly speaking, however, the resulting symbolism across all these case studies is one that underlines the brutality of the regime and promotes a narrative of heroes versus villains, leaving little space for the more difficult exploration of the complexities of this date or its subsequent interpretation. Whether this may be tackled in subsequent generations of 17 June memorials remains to be seen.

In terms of appropriation, however, remembrance of 17 June 1953 has appealed to an unusually broad range of interest groups in unified Germany. While the CDU may prove to be the leading party in terms of initiating monuments to 17 June, often due to its proximity to veterans' organizations, the above case studies demonstrate that this date has been appropriated by the full range of political parties, from the PDS/Die Linke through to the NPD. In many ways, the divided memory culture surrounding this date means that it continues to be interpreted in a variety of ways; parties on the left may choose to use it to appeal to values such as social justice, human rights and democratic freedom, whereas those on the right are more likely to emphasize the national agenda. While all projects were instigated in the same vein as the majority of examples in this book – with the desire to demonstrate the democratic credentials of the present in contrast to the dictatorship of the SED – their subsequent appropriation by sometimes very different groups demonstrates how the meaning of monuments may shift far beyond their intended purpose. In this way, we also see how they may become agents of change, provoking discussions and interaction between divergent groups, and bringing about new reflections on the relationship between past and present. It is interesting, for instance, that it was the very presence of a visible monument in Dresden that provoked more active engagement with this date in the town, whether desirable or not. It is also clear that the building of a tradition around memorial structures is essential in order to maintain active remembrance. In Leipzig, where no annual tradition has developed, the monument often appears to be overlooked. In contrast, tensions in both Berlin and Dresden have kept the memory of 1953 alive. It seems, indeed, that the more unsatisfactory the monument (Berlin) or its associated tradition (Dresden) appear to be, the more likely this past is to be kept alive in perpetual irresolution. In both cases, however, debate is linked to the continuing protests of specific groups: in Berlin, veterans and their supporters, and in Dresden, the NPD and associated right-wing groups. While the former call on communicative memories of 1953, the latter draw more strongly on right-wing cultural memory of the uprisings and their interpretation, yet both are equally fragile: veterans will inevitably pass away with time, and the strength of the NPD is at the hands of the electorate and local supporters. Whether the demise of both groups may lead to new interpretations remains to be seen.

It is above all notable that the West German tradition of linking 1953 to a desire for national unity, and thus to 1989, has influenced all projects. In Berlin, the desire of some influential politicians to celebrate national heroes, especially against the background of the seemingly never-ending discussions over the Holocaust memorial, clearly shaped decisions. It is, however, in the regions that this element has been strongest and embedded in local politics: in Hennigsdorf, the monument is centred on the very idea that 1953 led to 1989, and is linked to the local steel industry; in Leipzig, the town's strong historical relationship with 1989 in many ways prepared the ground for the monument to 1953; and in Dresden, the NPD has emphasized the focus on national unity. Where left-wing demonstrations have taken place as part of commemorative acts – both in Berlin at the unveiling of the *Denk-Stein*, and in Dresden in recent years – there have also been obvious parallels to the demands of 1989, in which citizens' rights, social justice and democratic freedoms have all featured heavily. The linking of these two dates appears, indeed, set to continue. A monument unveiled for the sixtieth anniversary of 1953 in Stralsund, for example, explicitly links 1953 and 1989, with the inscription 'Wir sind das Volk' ('we are the people') set alongside both dates.[98] Contrary to Karrenberg's view that the Federal Republic is 'far enough advanced for us to no longer need to frame events in terms of the nation',[99] it seems that remembrance of 17 June remains firmly tied to the event of German reunification and may, with time, become a cornerstone for a new, more positive – and democratically embedded – national memory culture.

Notes

1. See Bernd Eisenfeld, Ilko-Sascha Kowalczuk and Eberhart Neubert, *Die verdrängte Revolution: Der Platz des 17. Juni 1953 in der deutschen Geschichte* (Bremen: Edition Temmen, 2004), p. 34.
2. For named victims, see 'Die Toten des Volksaufstandes vom 17. Juni 1953', 17 May 2013, http://www.bpb.de/geschichte/deutsche-einheit/der-aufstand-des-17-juni-1953/152604/die-toten-des-volksaufstandes?p=all (accessed 15 September 2016).
3. See Gareth Dale, *Popular Protest in East Germany, 1945–1989* (London; New York: Routledge, 2005), p. 35.
4. See Eisenfeld, Kowalczuk and Neubert, *Die verdrängte Revolution*, pp. 343–45.
5. Cited in Erhard Neubert, 'Intellektuelle Bewältigung in Politik, Wissenschaft und Literatur', in *Volkserhebung gegen den SED-Staat: Eine Bestandsaufnahme zum 17. Juni 1953*, ed. by Roger Engelmann and Ilko-Sascha Kowalczuk (Göttingen: Vandenhoeck & Ruprecht, 2005), pp. 378–413 (382).
6. Edgar Wolfrum, 'Der Umgang mit dem 17. Juni 1953 in der Bundesrepublik Deutschland 1953–1991', in *Symposium zum Denkmal für die Ereignisse des 17. Juni 1953 – Dokumentation* (Berlin: Senatsverwaltung für Bauen, Wohnen und Verkehr, 1996), pp. 41–44 (42).
7. Eberhard Elfert, 'Bestehende Denkmäler für die Ereignisse des 17. Juni in Berlin', in *Symposium zum Denkmal für die Ereignisse des 17. Juni 1953*, pp. 70–80 (70).
8. V. Müller, 'Juni-Erinnerungen von beidseits der Barrikade', *Berliner Zeitung*, 19 June 2003, p. 14.
9. See, for example, Torsten Diedrich, *Der 17. Juni 1953 in der DDR: Bewaffnete Gewalt gegen das Volk* (Berlin: Dietz, 1991); Armin Mitter and Stefan Wolle, *Untergang auf Raten: Unbekannte Kapitel der DDR-Geschichte* (Munich: Bertelsmann, 1993), pp. 27–162; Ilko-Sascha Kowalczuk, Armin Mitter and Stefan Wolle (eds), *Der Tag X – 17. Juni 1953: Die 'innere Staatsgründung' der DDR als Ergebnis der Krise 1952/54* (Berlin: Ch. Links, 1995); Heidi Roth, *Der 17. Juni in Sachsen* (Cologne: Böhlau, 1999).
10. Christoph Hamann, 'Berliner Erinnerungsorte und Denkmäler', in *Der 17. Juni 1953: Eine Handreichung für den Unterricht*, ed. by Elena Demke, Christoph Hamann and Falco Werkentin (Berlin: Berliner Landesbeauftragte für die Unterlagen des Staatssicherheitsdienstes der ehemaligen DDR / Berliner Landesinstitut für Schule und Medien, 2003), pp. 68–76 (73).
11. '"Fäuste" zeigen vier neue Daten aus Styropor', *Mitteldeutsche Zeitung*, 16 December 1997.
12. 'Wissenslücke', *Der Spiegel*, (2001) 25, p. 20.
13. See, for example, Torsten Diedrich, *Waffen gegen das Volk: Der 17. Juni in der DDR* (Munich: Oldenbourg Wissenschaftsverlag, 2003); Thomas Flemming, *Kein Tag der deutschen Einheit – 17. Juni 1953* (Berlin: be.bra, 2003); Karl Wilhelm Fricke and Roger Engelmann, *Der 'Tag X' und die Staatssicherheit: 17. Juni 1953 – Reaktionen und Konsequenzen im*

DDR-Machtapparat (Bremen: Edition Temmen, 2003); Hubertus Knabe, *17. Juni 1953: Ein deutscher Aufstand* (Munich: Propyläen Verlag, 2003); Ilko-Sascha Kowalczuk, *17 Juni 1953. Volksaufstand in der DDR. Ursachen – Abläufe – Folgen* (Bremen: Edition Temmen, 2003); Ulrich Mählert (ed.), *Der 17. Juni 1953: Ein Aufstand für Einheit, Recht und Freiheit* (Bonn: Dietz, 2003); Rolf Steininger, *17. Juni 1953 : Der Anfang vom langen Ende der DDR* (Munich: Olzog, 2003).
14. Eisenfeld, Kowalczuk and Neubert, *Die verdrängte Revolution*, p. 806.
15. 'Aufruf im Jahr 2003: Orte des Erinnerns', http://www.stiftung-aufarbeitung.de/aufruf%3A-orte-der-erinnerung-2708.html (accessed 26 July 2012).
16. 'Auswertung zum Aufruf "Orte des Erinnerns"', http://www.stiftung-aufarbeitung.de/uploads/pdf/auswertungort.pdf (accessed 26 July 2012).
17. Eisenfeld, Kowalczuk and Neubert, *Die verdrängte Revolution*, p. 803.
18. Volker Koop, *Der 17. Juni 1953: Legende und Wirklichkeit* (Berlin: Siedler Verlag, 2003), pp. 106, 175, 226.
19. See *Symposium zum Denkmal für die Ereignisse des 17. Juni 1953*.
20. See Dale, *Popular Protest in East Germany*; Walter Süß, 'Von der Ohnmacht des Volkes zur Resignation der Mächtigen: Ein Vergleich des Aufstands 1953 mit der Revolution von 1989', in *Volkserhebung gegen den SED-Staat*, ed. by Engelmann and Kowalczuk, pp. 426–62; Hermann Wentker, 'Arbeiteraufstand, Revolution / Die Erhebungen von 1953 und 1989/90 in der DDR: ein Vergleich', *Deutschland Archiv*, 34 (2001) 3, 385–97.
21. Rita Süssmuth, in *Gedenkstunde anläßlich des 17. Juni, Schauspielhaus Berlin, 17. Juni 1990*, ed. by Volkskammer der DDR and Deutscher Bundestag (Berlin, 1990), p. 17.
22. See '"Stolz auf diesen Tag"', *Berliner Morgenpost*, 18 June 2003, p. 3; 'Einer der "wenigen positiven Tage"', *Neues Deutschland*, 13 June 2003, p. 15; 'Juni-Erinnerungen von beidseits der Barrikade', *Berliner Zeitung*, 19 June 2003, p. 14.
23. Cited in BM, 'Opfer des 17. Juni gewürdigt, Demo ohne Zwischenfälle', *Berliner Morgenpost*, 18 June 2000, p. 33.
24. Peter Steinbach, 'Statement zum Denkmal des 17. Juni 1953', in *Symposium zum Denkmal für die Ereignisse des 17. Juni 1953*, pp. 54–57 (55).
25. Dietrich Schubert, 'Warum, für wen und zu welchem Ziele nach 44 Jahren ein Denkmal für den 17. Juni 1953', in *Symposium zum Denkmal für die Ereignisse des 17. Juni 1953*, p. 95.
26. Senatsverwaltung für Bauen, Wohnen und Verkehr (ed.), *Kunstwettbewerb Denkmal 17. Juni 1953: Begrenzter zweiphasiger Realisierungswettbewerb – Ausschreibung* (Berlin, 1997), p. 61. Some of the material in this case study is published in Anna Saunders, 'Challenging or Concretising Cold War Narratives? Berlin's Memorial to the Victims of 17 June 1953', in *Memorialization in Germany since 1945*, ed. by Bill Niven and Chloe Paver (Basingstoke: Palgrave Macmillan, 2010), 298–307, reproduced with permission of Palgrave Macmillan.
27. Senatsverwaltung für Bauen, Wohnen und Verkehr (ed.), *Kunstwettbewerb Denkmal 17. Juni 1953*, p. 61.
28. Ibid., p. 62.

29. Hiltrud Ebert, 'Ereignisse und Opfer', in *Verlorene Inhalte, Verordnetes Denkmal: Beiträge zum Wettbewerb '17. Juni 1953'* (Berlin: Neue Gesellschaft für Bildende Kunst, 2000), pp. 33–43.
30. 'Erklärung der 1. Jury vom 26.2.98', in *Verlorene Inhalte, Verordnetes Denkmal*, p. 73.
31. Katharina Karrenberg, 'Entwurf für ein Bodendenkmal zum 17. Juni 1953', in *Verlorene Inhalte, Verordnetes Denkmal*, p. 47.
32. Ibid., p. 48.
33. 'Ergebnisprotokoll', Kiör-Büro.
34. Rainer Stache, '"Verniedlichung des Schreckens"', *Berliner Morgenpost*, 29 November 1998, p. 6; Harald Jähner, 'Wer bin ich, daß ich denke', *Berliner Zeitung*, 3 December 1998, p. 11.
35. Helmut Caspar, *Marmor, Stein und Bronze: Berliner Denkmalgeschichten* (Berlin: Berlin Edition, 2003), p. 126.
36. 'Diepgen kritisiert Entwurf zum 17.-Juni-Denkmal', *Berliner Morgenpost*, 8 December 1998, p. 10; Torsten Harmsen, 'Seelenschmerz statt Gedenken', *Berliner Zeitung*, 7 December 1998, p. 11.
37. Kathrin Hoffmann-Curtius, 'Presserezeption zum 1. Preis der Jury für ein Denkmal zum 17. Juni 1953', in *Verlorene Inhalte, Verordnetes Denkmal*, pp. 53–60 (56).
38. 'Ein Orakel am Leipziger Platz?', *Berliner Morgenpost*, 7 December 1998, p. 4.
39. Hoffmann-Curtius, 'Presserezeption zum 1. Preis der Jury für ein Denkmal zum 17. Juni 1953', p. 57.
40. Torsten Harmsen, 'Seelenschmerz statt Gedenken', *Berliner Zeitung*, 7 December 1998, p. 11.
41. 'Offener Brief an den Regierenden Bürgermeister von Berlin, Eberhard Diepgen, und an den Senat von Berlin', in *Verlorene Inhalte, Verordnetes Denkmal*, pp. 75–76.
42. Bruno Flierl, *Gebaute DDR – Über Stadtplaner, Architekten und die Macht – Kritische Reflexionen 1990–1997* (Berlin: Verlag Bauwesen, 1998), pp. 95–96.
43. Wolfgang Rüppel, 'Kunstwettbewerb "Denkmal 17. Juni 1953"', *kunststadtstadtkunst*, 45 (1999), p. 14.
44. Wolfgang Kil, 'Der 17. Juni – ein Erinnerungsdiktat?', in *Verlorene Inhalte, Verordnetes Denkmal*, pp. 27–32.
45. 'Pressemitteiling', Berufsverband Bildender Künstler Berlins, February 1999, Kiör-Büro.
46. Hiltrud Ebert, 'Ereignisse und Opfer', in *Verlorene Inhalte, Verordnetes Denkmal*, pp. 33–43 (34–35).
47. Kil, 'Der 17. Juni – ein Erinnerungsdiktat?', p. 32.
48. Silke Wenk, 'Statt eines Vorwortes', in *Verlorene Inhalte, Verordnetes Denkmal*, pp. 7–10 (9–10).
49. Alexandra Hildebrandt (ed.), '17. Juni 1953: Ein sichtbares, aussagekräftiges und stolzes Denkmal ist längst überfällig', collection of documentation for 149th press conference of the Arbeitsgemeinschaft 13. August e.V., June 2007, pp. ii, 11 and 17.

50. See, for example, Manfred Wilke, '17. Juni 1953: "Es fehlt ein sichtbares Denkmal"', *Berliner Morgenpost*, 19 June 2005, p. 18; Jochim Stoltenberg, 'Unwürdige Demontage', *Berliner Morgenpost*, 21 June 2005, p. 2.
51. Antje Lang-Lendorff, 'Bis die Fotos wieder hängen', *Berliner Zeitung*, 23 June 2005, p. 26; Alexander Schäfer, 'Tafeln zum Gedenken an den 17. Juni vom Finanzministerium entfernt', *Tagesspiegel*, 21 June 2005, p. 9.
52. Martin Schönfeld, 'Sichtbare Zeichen im öffentlichen Raum', *kunststadtstadtkunst*, 52 (2005), p. 12.
53. 'Ästhetik des Widerstands', *Der Spiegel*, (2003) 25, p. 177.
54. Konrad Weiß, cited in Hans Böckler Stiftung (ed.), *17. Juni, von der ungewöhnlichen Entstehung eines kleinen Denksteins vor dem Rosengarten in der Karl-Marx-Allee, der ehemaligen Stalinallee, 17. Juni 2003* (Berlin-Friedrichshain: Oktoberdruck AG, 2005), p. 22.
55. Bernd Kammer, 'Gedenken endete mit Eklat', *Neues Deutschland*, 18 June 2003, p. 11.
56. Hans Böckler Stiftung, *17. Juni, von der ungewöhnlichen Entstehung*, p. 27; see also Holger Kulick, 'Stein des Anstoßes', *Spiegel Online*, 15 June 2003, http://www.spiegel.de/panorama/denkmal-zum-17-juni-stein-des-anstosses-a-252214.html (accessed 2 August 2012).
57. Martin Klesmann, 'Der lange Marsch', *Berliner Zeitung*, 14 June 2003; Ulrich Bergt, 'Bei denen oben Respekt verschafft', *Märkische Allgemeine Zeitung*, 17 June 2003.
58. Hamann, 'Berliner Erinnerungsorte und Denkmäler', pp. 71–72.
59. 'Beschluß der SVV Hennigsdorf, 23 October 1991', Beschluß-Nr 87/18/91, Stadtarchiv Hennigsdorf.
60. 'Wettbewerbsausschreibung: Gestaltung eines Denkmals in Hennigsdorf', Stadtverwaltung Hennigsdorf, 10 April 1992, Stadtarchiv Hennigsdorf.
61. 'Denkmal 17. Juni/Herbst '89 eingeweiht', *Hennigsdorfer Amtsblatt*, October 1993, p. 4.
62. Heidi Wagner-Kerkhof, 'Denkmal 17. Juni 1953 – Herbst 1989', http://www.bbk-brandenburg.de/kub/site/seiten/werke.asp?kid=32&pid=117 (accessed 4 August 2012).
63. 'Erläuterungsbericht zum Wettbewerb "Gestaltung eines Denkmals zum 17. Juni 1953 / Herbst 1989" in Hennigsdorf', document from private collection of Heidi Wagner-Kerkhof.
64. 'Denkmal 17. Juni/Herbst '89 eingeweiht', p. 4.
65. Conversation with Heidi Wagner-Kerkhof in Halle, 8 November 2010.
66. Ibid.
67. Andrea Linne, 'Geschichte zum Nacherleben in Hennigsdorf', 4 October 1993 (newspaper cutting from private collection of Heidi Wagner-Kerkhof).
68. Dietmar Stork, '"Hier stand der Panzer"', *Oranienburger Generalanzeiger*, 18 June 2002.
69. See Koop, *Der 17. Juni 1953*; 'Brennpunkte des Volksaufstandes: 17. Juni in Leipzig', brochure published by Bürgerkomitee Leipzig e.V. and Stiftung zur Aufarbeitung der SED-Diktatur, 2003.
70. See, for example, 'Brennpunkte des Volksaufstandes: 17. Juni in Leipzig'; www.denkmal-volksaufstand.de (accessed 9 July 2009).

71. 'Hier reden wir – die LVZ-Umfrage am Mittwoch', *Leipziger Volkszeitung*, 18 June 2003, p. 15.
72. Andreas Tappert, 'Wettlauf gegen das Vergessen', *Leipziger Volkszeitung*, 31 May 2003, p. 13.
73. '17. June 1953 in Leipzig', http://www.17-juni-1953-in-leipzig.de/ (accessed 7 August 2012).
74. See Armin Görtz, '50 Jahre danach: Leipzig gedachte des 17. Juni', *Leipziger Volkszeitung*, 18 June 2003, p. 15.
75. Cited in Mathias Orbeck, 'Kränze am Grab, Mahnung bei Festakt', *Leipziger Volkszeitung*, 18 June 2003, p. 15.
76. Andreas Tappert, 'Leipzig erhält Denkmal zum 17. Juni', *Leipziger Volkszeitung*, 31 May 2003, p. 13.
77. Mathias Orbeck, 'Symbol der Gewalt erinnert an den Wert der Freiheit', *Leipziger Volkszeitung*, 10 November 2003, p. 11.
78. Conversation with Christopher Zenker and Falk-Thoralf Günther, Leipzig, 11 March 2011.
79. Ibid.
80. Ibid.; Tappert, 'Wettlauf gegen das Vergessen', p. 13.
81. Conversation with Christopher Zenker and Falk-Thoralf Günther.
82. Observation based on informal discussion with a number of Leipzig residents.
83. Reiner Burger, 'Dresden Eingehegte Panzerkette', *Frankfurter Allgemeine Zeitung*, 17 June 2008, http://www.faz.net/themenarchiv/2.1148/dresden-eingehegte-panzerkette-1548015.html (accessed 8 August 2012); Helma Orosz, 17 June 2010, http://www.dresden.de/media/pdf/oberbuergermeister/aufstand_17_juni.pdf (accessed 1 August 2012).
84. 'Antrag', http://www.fdp-fraktion-dresden.de/initiativen-87.html (accessed 1 August 2012).
85. Christiane Raatz, 'Ist das Kunst oder kann das weg?', *Sächsische Zeitung*, 7 March 2012, http://www.sz-online.de/nachrichten/ist-das-kunst-oder-kann-das-weg-2426768.html (accessed 19 December 2017).
86. 'Erinnerung an den Volksaufstand am 17. Juni 1953', 12 June 2008, http://www.dresden.de/de/02/035/01/2008/06/pm_044.php (accessed 8 August 2012).
87. 'NPD-Fraktionen gedenken der Helden des 17. Juni', http://www.volksfront-medien.org/index.php/menue/61/thema/69/id/8684/anzeigemonat/06/akat/1/anzeigejahr/2008/infotext/21.06.2008_NPD_Fraktionen_gedenken_der_Helden_des_17._Juni/Aktuelles.html (accessed 6 August 2012).
88. Ibid.
89. Thilo Alexe, 'Dresden wehrt sich gegen Rechtsextreme', *Sächsische Zeitung*, 17 June 2010, http://www.sz-online.de/nachrichten/artikel.asp?id=2489910 (accessed 6 August 2012).
90. Helma Orosz, 17 June 2010, http://www.dresden.de/media/pdf/oberbuergermeister/aufstand_17_juni.pdf (accessed 1 August 2012).
91. Richard Kaniewski, '17. Juni ist ein Tag der Demokraten, nicht der Neonazis', www.richard-kaniewski.de/index.php?nr=6651&menu=1 (accessed 6 August 2012).

92. Frank Franz, 'NPD-Fraktion legte Kranz am Denkmal für die Opfer des 17. Juni 1953 nieder', 17 June 2011, http://www.npd-fraktion-sachsen.de/2011/06/17/npd-fraktion-legte-kranz-am-denkmal-fuer-die-opfer-des-17-juni-1953-nieder/ (accessed 20 December 2017); Frank Franz, 'NPD-Fraktion legt Kranz am Denkmal für die Opfer des 17. Juni 1953 nieder', 17 June 2012, http://www.npd-fraktion-sachsen.de/2012/06/17/npd-fraktion-legt-kranz-am-denkmal-fuer-die-opfer-des-17-juni-1953-nieder/ (accessed 20 December 2017).
93. 'Aufruf dresden1706', www.linke-hsg-dresden.de/?cat=7 (accessed 5 August 2012).
94. Ibid.
95. dbr, 'Neonaziaufmarsch in Dresden am 17. Juni: Demos gegen Rechtsextreme', *DNN-Online*, 17 June 2012, http://www.dnn-online.de/dresden/web/regional/politik/detail/-/specific/Neonaziaufmarsch-in-Dresden-am-17-Juni-Wenig-Protest-gegen-Rechtsextreme-3727702733 (accessed 6 August 2012); 'Pressemitteilung', 18 June 2012, http://dresden1706.noblogs.org/ (accessed 6 August 2012).
96. szo, 'Rechte demonstrieren am Postplatz', *Sächsische Zeitung*, 17 June 2013, http://www.sz-online.de/nachrichten/rechte-demonstrieren-am-postplatz-2597607.html (accessed 27 June 2013); dbr/sl/fs/hh, 'Jahrestag 17. Juni: Bis zu 1000 Dresdner protestieren gegen 100 Rechtsextreme', *DNN-Online*, 17 June 2013, http://www.dnn-online.de/dresden/web/regional/kultur/detail/-/specific/Jahrestag-17-Juni-1953-100-Rechtsextreme-versammeln-sich-in-Dresden-1000-Menschen-zeigen-Courage-4161569719 (accessed 27 June 2013).
97. This can clearly be seen on websites produced by both sides, e.g. 'Rückblick auf die vergangenen Naziaufmärsche am 17. Juni', 9 June 2013, http://uradresden.noblogs.org/post/2013/06/09/ruckblick-auf-die-vergangenen-naziaufmarsche-am-17-juni/ (accessed 27 June 2013); Thorsten Thomsen, 'Widerstand gegen die EU-Fremdherrschaft im Geiste des 17. Juni und der Befreiungskriege', 18 June 2013, http://www.npd-dresden.de/ (accessed 27 June 2013) – text now available at https://www.facebook.com/npd.de/posts/10151552055804584 (accessed 20 December 2017).
98. Anne-Dorle Hoffgaard, 'Granit, Stahl und Rosen', 16 June 2013, http://www.kirche-mv.de/MV-erhaelt-sein-erstes-Denkmal-zum-DDR-Volksaufstand-vom-17-Juni-1953.31175.0.html (accessed 27 June 2013).
99. Karrenberg, 'Entwurf für ein Bodendenkmal zum 17. Juni 1953', p. 48.

Chapter 5

THE BERLIN WALL
Historical Document, Tourist Magnet or Urban Eyesore?

The Cold War was symbolized above all by one structure: the Berlin Wall. As the most notorious part of the Iron Curtain, it represented the division of the world into two political spheres, as well as providing a curious – and fragile – sense of stability. After standing for twenty-eight years, its 'fall' on the night of 9 November 1989 became one of the most arresting moments of twentieth-century history, with images of crowds dancing on the Wall and hacking at it with pick-axes appearing across the world. On losing its practical function, however, the Wall's symbolic function strengthened, for not only did it still represent the political repression and systemic weakness of communism, but it suddenly also symbolized the overcoming of this system, becoming an icon of freedom. The Wall as a 'political metaphor' only strengthened.[1] As an 'unintended' monument of the post-communist era, it has thus been aptly described as the 'central monument of 20th century European history'.[2] Yet for much of the 1990s and 2000s, the material Wall was notable for its absence rather than its presence in the cityscape of Berlin, a cause of complaint not only among preservationists, but also among tourists, politicians and victims' associations, each with their own agendas. Indeed, as this chapter demonstrates, the desire to commemorate the Wall in concrete form became bound up in a complex web of interconnected hopes, demands and expectations.

Built on 13 August 1961, the Berlin Wall was erected to prevent an ever-increasing flood of East Germans leaving the GDR through West Berlin, fleeing escalating economic problems, the collectivization of agriculture and hard-line SED policies. Initially consisting of barbed wire and breeze blocks, it ran 43.1 kilometres between the two halves of Berlin and 111.9 kilometres around the outside of West Berlin.[3] Developed into a ferocious border system over the years and aptly named the 'best-maintained edifice in the GDR',[4] 'the Wall' was a misleading term for this construction. Not only did it take the form of bricked-up buildings or riverbanks in places, but it consisted of two walls – an outer wall facing the West and a hinterland wall facing the East – enclosing a death strip, watchtowers and anti-tank devices. By 1989, different generations of wall also existed, as it became increasingly fortified over the years. Several walls thus existed in time and space, causing some to object that the euphemism of 'the Wall' trivialized the brutality of the border,[5] and above all complicating discussions over what to demolish, preserve or reconstruct.

The image of the Berlin Wall also varied depending on one's viewpoint. In the GDR it was presented as a fortification facing the West, in order to protect the socialist state from ideological affronts and intruders from West Berlin, and as a contribution to world peace. In SED parlance, it was thus designated as the 'antifascist protection rampart'. In reality, however, its purpose was rather to keep the GDR population in, leading to Western terms such as the 'wall of shame' or 'death wall'.[6] The visible presence of the Wall on both sides also varied. In West Berlin, it was not long before memorials to victims of the Wall were erected, such as a small symbolic wall in the middle of the Straße des 17. Juni dedicated 'To the Victims of the Red Dictatorship',[7] and a memorial cross that was placed close to where victim Peter Fechter was shot near Checkpoint Charlie in 1962. White crosses were also erected elsewhere to mark the places where victims had died; on the tenth anniversary of the building of the Wall in 1971, these were brought together by the 'Berlin Citizens Association' to create a central memorial site of white crosses near the Reichstag. West Berlin also housed one of the first museums to the Wall, the 'Haus am Checkpoint Charlie' Museum, which was opened in 1963 by Rainer Hildebrandt, a vigorous campaigner against the GDR. The Wall soon became a popular destination for 'dark tourism' in the West, with viewing platforms allowing visitors to look over the Wall to the East; as Leo Schmidt recounts, tourists even posed next to it for photo opportunities.[8] In contrast, the only victims to be commemorated in the East were border guards, in whose memory memorials were erected or streets were named; Egon Schultz, the best known of these, thus became a common-name hero in the GDR. Yet unlike in the West, a restricted area next to the Wall meant that East Germans could not get close to it, nor were they allowed to take photos of it. Whereas the Wall was one of the most common postcard motifs in the West, it never appeared on GDR images, and Eastern maps of the city blanked out

West Berlin as if it did not exist. The discrepancy between Eastern and Western visions of the Wall was no better demonstrated than through graffiti. By the 1980s, the Western side had become a colourful canvas of graffiti, yet on the Eastern side the very same Wall was painted in uniform white or pale green-grey. As Manghani states, there can be no single reading of the Wall; it was 'never simply a concrete edifice, but actually a panoply of symbols, myths and images'.[9] For those who had to live with the Wall, however, it slowly became an accepted part of daily life behind which Easterners and Westerners got on with their lives, strangely omnipresent and invisible at the same time. In light of its complex history, it is little surprise that this Cold War edifice became a new battleground of interests after its notorious 'fall'.

Like the Wall itself, reference to its 'fall' is also a euphemism, widely used to refer to the end of the Cold War. In this sense, it began to crumble on 11 September 1989, when the Hungarian government opened its border to Austria, allowing several thousand East Germans to flee to the West; it perhaps only finished falling in 1991, after the Soviet Union imploded. Yet 9 November 1989 remains the key date associated with the fall of the Berlin Wall, the day on which government spokesman Günter Schabowski announced that GDR citizens would be able to travel to the West, unexpectedly causing crowds to amass at Berlin's border crossings, which in turn brought the border guards finally to open the barriers. But the Wall did not physically 'fall' on that night; its concrete substance and symbolic status represented very different things. Newspapers on 10 November, for instance, reported on the Wall itself in the past tense as if it no longer existed, yet physically it remained standing.[10] Today, in contrast, references to 'the Wall in people's heads' evoke its symbolic legacy rather than its concrete presence. Despite its evocative strength, it was the concrete substance of the Wall that quickly became sought after. Within hours, 'wall-peckers' were at work: East and West Berliners, tourists and entrepreneurs hacked away lumps of it, either to sell or simply to take home as pieces of history. Suddenly this concrete monstrosity became available to everyone and fragments of Wall adopted a special aura as icons of freedom. Some of the pieces on sale were not, however, wholly authentic; as fragments with graffiti sold better than those without (confirming the popular Western image of the Wall), some entrepreneurs first spray-painted Eastern sections of Wall before hacking it away, thus 'forging history, with genuine materials'.[11] Larger sections of the Wall were auctioned off by the GDR government at high prices and sent around the world; in 1999, one Berlin newspaper claimed that there were 'more wall remnants in the rest of the world than in Berlin', tracking down pieces as far as Canberra,

Buenos Aires, Jakarta and Honolulu.[12] By the end of November 1990, soldiers had dismantled the majority of the concrete edifice, over forty thousand segments of which were crushed and reused in the construction industry.[13] According to Frederick Baker, four years after its opening there was less left of the Berlin Wall than of Hadrian's Wall.[14] The Wall thus became commodified precisely because it was disappearing, embodying both national and international values.

The rapid disappearance of the Wall slowly began to trigger concerns over preservation and remembrance, and a number of key questions dominated public debate in the 1990s and 2000s: if the very concept of 'the Wall' is so complex, for example, what should be remembered and to what purpose? Which sections should be preserved; should any be reconstructed? Who is to engage in Wall remembrance; where should it be located; what forms should remembrance take? This chapter discusses such issues through a number of high- and low-profile case studies, all of which raise questions concerning location, form and authenticity. It also traces the central trends in Wall remembrance over time, and in doing so, presents the earlier examples as indicative of debates during the 1990s, when there was little joined-up thinking regarding Wall remembrance in the city. In contrast, the latter examples all address questions of victimhood, which emerged more strongly from the late 1990s when it became increasingly clear that all Wall-related sites were not only strongly interlinked, but also linked to other sites of memory in the capital. Indeed, all the examples discussed in this chapter influenced the Berlin Senate's development of a centralized plan for a 'decentralized' concept of Wall remembrance in the city (entitled the *Gesamtkonzept zur Erinnerung an die Berliner Mauer*), which – as an overarching concept – has led the way since 2006. Not only do more recent developments contrast dramatically with the chaotic situation of the early years, but as this chapter shows, they also represent a more complex understanding of historical events, demonstrating that cultural memory becomes far from simplified or unified with the passage of time.

The Early Post-*Wende* Years: From Commodification to Preservation

The first year after the opening of the Wall witnessed some innovative and creative attempts to mark the disappearing structure and associated memories. For example, the contemporary art project *Die Endlichkeit der Freiheit* (The Finiteness of Freedom; see also Chapter 2), held in September and October 1990, saw a number of artists interact with the notion of the border regime in Berlin. Ilya Kabakov's installation was particularly innovative, and consisted of two narrow wooden corridors on Potsdamer Platz, one marking the course of the outer wall and the other the hinterland wall. Visitors walking along the corridors were confronted with fragments of conversations written on cards hanging at head height, interspersed with pieces of litter found on the ground. The quotations and fragments displayed the prejudices and irrational fears of those who lived on either side of the Wall, thus reminding viewers of the situation only a year previously.[15] One of the more visibly provocative projects was Hans Haacke's installation 'Freedom is now simply sponsored – out of petty cash', in which he restored a watchtower in the former border strip and 'crowned' it with a large Mercedes logo. Not only did this juxtaposition of symbols force the viewer to reconsider each in a new light, but it encouraged a reassessment of East Germany's newfound freedoms. The Mercedes star also proved reminiscent of the Soviet red star that had often adorned monuments in the East, raising questions of continuity as much as rupture.[16]

Two other art projects from this period can still be viewed today. To mark the one-year anniversary of 9 November, artist Ben Wagin created an installation along the death strip across the Spree from the Reichstag, which consisted of a combination of memorial stones, elements from the border, images, texts and newly planted trees; on sections of the Wall he painted the number of victims that the Wall was thought to have claimed each year. Dedicated as the 'Parliament of trees against war and violence', it also contains memorial stones to soldiers who died in the Second World War, thus suggesting a layering of history and memory. Due to the construction of the government quarter in the later 1990s, part of the structure was incorporated into the newly built Bundestag library building; the rest remains, somewhat altered, as a memorial today. In contrast, the most widely known art project of this period reflects the joyful exuberance of this year: the East Side Gallery. In the spring of 1990, 118 artists from twenty-one countries painted 106 large-format images on the eastern side of a 1.3-kilometre length of hinterland Wall, at that point still a virgin white canvas.[17] Although the original intention was to take the exhibition (and thus this section of Wall) around the world, and finally to auction the images, its popularity ensured that it remained in place. The open-air gallery soon became one of the most-visited stretches of Wall, symbolic of both the euphoria of the *Wende* months and the international dimension of the border. Despite being put under protection in November 1991, the future of the East Side Gallery has not always been secure, with high renovation costs and disagreements over development of the area endangering its survival during much of its first fifteen years.[18] As highlighted in the introduction of this book, the removal of a section of the Wall in March 2013 to create access to a building site for a luxury apartment block also caused massive protests, with demonstrators numbering up to six thousand.[19] However, as Ladd points out, this site as a whole provides a 'welter of confusion' for tourists, for not only do the images stem from the post-Wall era, but they are painted on the Eastern side of the Wall.[20] In many ways, this monument is thus representative of battles elsewhere – examples of which feature in this chapter – in which the desire to free the city from decades of physical and mental division have conflicted with a need both to satisfy tourist demand and to document and preserve the past in an authentic manner.

Despite such projects, the popular desire to preserve the Wall remained weak in the first years after 1989. For many Berliners it had become synonymous with the SED dictatorship and was to be toppled in much the same way; the slogan 'The Wall must go!' rang true long after 9 November. Calls for its preservation – led by the (West) German Historical Museum (DHM), the GDR Museum for German History and Pastor Manfred Fischer of the *Versöhnungsgemeinde* (parish of the West Berlin Reconciliation Church) – in spring 1990 were thus highly controversial, and efforts to protect the concrete from both 'wall-peckers' and border troops ordered with its demolition proved difficult. With the GDR government about to leave power, the situation was chaotic, and as Helmut Trotnow recalls, the East Berlin administration put one section of Wall under protection that had already been destroyed.[21] However, on 2 October 1990, one day before unification, the East Berlin administration placed three sections under monumental protection, including the section at Bernauer Straße.[22] As the below discussion of Bernauer Straße demonstrates, however, this did not mean that such sites were protected from disputes over land ownership, and 'wall-peckers' continued their work across the city, with the length of Wall at Niederkirchnerstraße (now at the Topography of Terror) having to be fenced off in 1999 to add extra protection. The same year also witnessed a group of protesters sleeping out at Potsdamer Platz, in order to protect a piece of Wall from demolition by the Berlin Senate.[23] With time, the popular will to protect the Wall did, indeed, increase and on 13 August 2001, the fortieth anniversary of its construction, all remaining sections were placed under preservation order;[24] two years later, archaeologist Leo Schmidt even made the controversial suggestion that the Wall should become a UNESCO heritage site.[25] While this has not, to date, occurred, the very suggestion would have appeared totally absurd a decade previously.

After most traces of the Wall had disappeared, a number of suggestions emerged for ways in which to mark the former course of the border. These ranged from Manfred Butzmann's idea of planting the border strip with lupins, to a set of proposals for ways in which to trace the course of the Wall with various materials. Kreuzberg's Civil Engineering Office, for instance, advocated a double row of cobblestones; architecture critic Gerwin Zohlen proposed a copper strip; and artist Angela Bohnen favoured coloured cement inlays, red for the outer Wall and blue for the hinterland Wall.[26] The Berlin City Parliament allowed both Zohlen and Bohnen's designs to be 'tested' in front of the parliament building in 1994, which caused much debate and led to a 'hearing on marking the course of the Wall' in June 1995.[27] At the hearing, however, neither design was deemed suitable. Some participants objected that the debate was dominated by western attitudes, for it failed to take the Eastern experience of the Wall into consideration and demonstrated the superiority of the Western system. In contrast, others claimed that the proposals attempted to monumentalize the Wall and represented the closure of a highly complex and controversial subject; as Wolfgang Kil stated, 'For us contemporaries, the wound can still be kept open for a little longer'.[28] The decision was thus made for 'as prosaic a marking as possible',[29] which refrained from symbolic or artistic interpretation: a double row of cobblestones. This was widely regarded to be the best compromise, and as Berlin's Green Party spokesman stated, the cobblestones represented 'a very suitable material for Berlin … We don't need any precious metal in order to be reminded [of this past]'.[30] As the report of the hearing stated, this solution was to be understood by the public 'as part of a broad process of remembrance and discussion',[31] and at this stage there was evidently still a reluctance to mark the recent past in any monumental way; the past was not yet fully history.

Initially a red line marked the border strip from 1997,[32] due to the cost of installing the double cobblestones – itself a contentious issue among some Berliners, who believed the money could be better spent elsewhere; as one reader of the *Berliner Zeitung* complained, 'Is this expense supposed to help integration [of east and west]?'[33] However, by the end of 1999 – ten years after the fall of the Wall – the majority of its 7.5-kilometre course through central Berlin was cobbled, along with intermittent metal plates that read 'Berlin Wall 1961–1989'.[34] Placed along the outer Wall facing the former West, however, and with the plates only legible from the western side, this solution represented, in Thomas Flierl's words, a 'typical Western perspective' of the Wall.[35] Moreover, in the longer term this solution clearly lacked sufficient engagement with its complex history, and in the eyes of many historians it was 'hardly suited to remind us of the real character of the Wall'.[36] The following two projects, both initiated relatively early in the commemoration process, provided contrasting solutions to these issues.

Übergänge: Remembering Border Crossings and Transitions

The initiative entitled *Übergänge* – meaning both 'crossings' and 'transitions' – is one that rarely appears in today's guides to Berlin or accounts of Wall remembrance, due to its deliberate emphasis on the transitory nature of change during the early 1990s; as such, its prime audience was resident Berliners rather than tourists. The Berlin Senate commissioned the project in 1996, with the intention of harnessing public art to mark the city's former border crossings, located at seven different sites. As outlined in an early development report from 1991, the dual meaning of *Übergänge* provided the conceptual heart of the project:

> We find ourselves in the midst of a process of 'transition' – of the growing together of East and West. ... the actual border crossings are gradually disappearing due to the hectic construction of new buildings, where for a brief period the Wall and the death strip could still be experienced. Structurally and spatially the city is growing together again. But there is still today an endlessly deep cleft between the people and both communities.[37]

The competition thus aimed to stimulate communication between residents and encourage reflection on the deep-rooted changes of the previous years, while at the same time drawing attention towards the physical location of the former crossings. The initial intention was to hold a relatively quick competition at limited financial cost, in order to reflect the sentiment of the time. However, despite plans to launch a competition in 1992, this did not happen until 1996 – once a suitable method of marking the former course of the Wall had been agreed upon – when thirty-five local artists from Berlin were invited to participate. Despite the shifting timeframe, very little time had passed for any deep reflection on the immediate past, as recognized in the original report, and organizers were concerned to allow for exploratory designs that responded to the notion of transition, rather than necessarily aspiring to permanence or conveying fixed messages. Contrary to many press reports, this was intended to be much more than a project that simply marked the fast-disappearing border between East and West.[38]

A closer analysis of the competition brief uncovers the political motivations of the project. Indeed, through harnessing public art, competition organizers intended to challenge – and ultimately counteract – persisting cultural, social and political divides by promoting a sense of common identity. Most significantly, the following question was posed in the rubrics: 'Is there a view of the most recent historical events and their pre-history which can be shared without reservation by the inhabitants of both halves of the city?'[39] Clearly this was a contentious question, and given the difficulties of the unification process, the document recognized that there was an 'overwhelming need for imagination in order to overcome the exceptional challenges'.[40] At a time when the 'wall in people's heads' was arguably at its height, artists were thus challenged to promote future visions of unity by evoking common memories of a divided past, and in doing so, bolster the reunification process: '*Übergang* signalizes movement, process, a pathway. If the Wall is thematized solely as a border, reflections will be directed predominantly towards the past'.[41] This was evidently a memory project directed by future concerns, yet the overt politicization of art caused one critic to accuse the Senate of employing 'art for the purpose of legitimizing the state', an accusation that unavoidably evokes memories of public art in the GDR.[42]

Despite criticisms of instrumentalization, the competition differed from other Wall remembrance projects in explicitly attempting not to represent the overriding western view of the Wall. Although the choice of border crossings, used infrequently by most East Germans, represented a largely western experience, the competition rubrics highlighted the problematic nature of unification for easterners: 'For them [East Berliners], the border was an existential experience that was to do with constriction, limiting life or even destroying a biography, [representing] an end of the personal horizon that could never be imagined away'.[43] In criticism of the commodification of the Wall, it also stated: 'The sale of colourful wall fragments as souvenirs is a western invention. East Germans don't need such "souvenirs"; the wall exists inside them as the background colour of their biography'.[44] Most significantly, it claimed that the history of division and unification was the history of all Berliners, and that its interpretation 'must not lead to the dominance of one historiography over the other'.[45] Although this was a competition as much about the future as the past, it was clearly one in which present sentiments about the past remained highly sensitive.

From a total of thirty-two entrants, one winner was announced for each location in September 1996, and all seven designs were publicly exhibited.[46] In connection with the exhibition, the State Secretary for Planning and Housing admitted that, 'Perhaps, with German thoroughness, we have now removed too many traces of division',[47] marking somewhat of a turning point in public perceptions regarding the Wall. Although the cost of the project was relatively low, a spending freeze in Berlin meant that not all the designs were completed until 1999, for the tenth anniversary of 9 November. While the majority are still in evidence at the time of writing, the competition did not intend for them to be enduring structures, and some are inevitably showing signs of age or have been engulfed by extensive city centre construction. Urban change has been particularly prominent given that all but one installation – located at Checkpoint Charlie – are situated in predominantly residential areas; indeed, one of the main aims of the competition was to interact with Berlin residents, and to engage with individual memories of the divided city as well as personal experiences of unity. The following three examples serve to illustrate the variety and potential of the different designs.

The first project to be realized in 1997 was designed by Thorsten Goldberg and consists of two neon circles, one installed on either side of Oberbaumbrücke, a bridge crossing the Spree. Barely noticeable during daytime, the circles light up at night, each displaying at regular intervals the outline of a hand in one of three positions: a fist, an open palm or with two fingers extending forwards (see Figure 5.1).[48] The

Figure 5.1 'Stone, paper, scissors' (Thorsten Goldberg, 1997), Oberbaumbrücke, Berlin (*Übergänge* competition). Photograph by Anna Saunders.

illuminated circles thus play the children's game of 'stone, paper, scissors' against each other – one on the eastern side of the bridge, the other on the western side. It is up to chance which side wins, and inevitably sometimes the two sides draw. Clearly there is no attempt to take political sides, and the installation highlights the apparently arbitrary nature of political decision-making during division – at least in the eyes of the Berlin citizen – and calls into question the assumed superiority of western capitalism over the socialist system. The artist also states that this is a symbol of two people standing opposite each other trying to come to a decision, and of the first uncontrolled encounters between Easterners and Westerners in 1989.[49] The contact between individuals rather than power elites is particularly important at this location, where from 1972 foot passengers could cross the border. It is thus fitting that pedestrians observing the light display in united Berlin may meet on the bridge and those who watch it for a few minutes will, from time to time, see the constellation of two open palms reaching out towards each other – a gesture that was familiar in late 1989, and one that, in line with the competition aims, provides hope for the future.[50]

Frank Thiel's installation was the second to be completed in 1998, and given its location at the former Checkpoint Charlie, it is the most visible and centrally located of all seven designs. Although it is now viewed in conjunction with the replica of an American control hut, this was not part of Thiel's design, and was installed first in August 2000 by the 'Haus am Checkpoint Charlie' Museum, much to the dismay of art critics who regard it as belittling Thiel's message.[51] The installation consists of a huge illuminated picture frame standing on a post five metres high, each side of which bears the picture of an American and a Russian soldier looking towards their former sectors of Berlin (see Figure 5.2). Both photos originate from a series taken by the artist in 1994, shortly before the withdrawal of Allied troops from Berlin. The height and size of the photos present the soldiers as symbols of authority and of the Allied military presence in Berlin, rather than as individuals. Yet a closer examination proves somewhat unnerving: their uniforms are surprisingly similar (apart from the symbols on their medals and decorations), and the faces of both soldiers appear to be too young to have experienced the realities of war – which, due to the nature of the Cold War conflict, they did not. Our gaze thus moves from the uniform to the person, or from the political to the private, and we realize that they are standing back to back, no longer facing each other as enemies, where Soviet and American tanks once faced each other. In this way, the installation encourages viewers to consider not only the international impact of division, but also the curiously parallel experiences of some

Figure 5.2 'Illuminated box' (Frank Thiel, 1998), former Checkpoint Charlie, Berlin (*Übergänge* competition). Photograph by Anna Saunders.

individuals on both sides of the Wall. The installation's resemblance to an advertising stand is no coincidence, for the artist effectively uses his pictures to advertise the overcoming of the border – ironically, perhaps, uncovering the whole competition as little more than an advertising stunt.

The most controversial installation was that by Karla Sachse, around the site of the former crossing point on Chausseestraße. Here she embedded the silhouettes of 120 bronze rabbits into the pavement and road. She justified her choice of the rabbit as a 'symbol of the peaceful infiltration of the border strip, as a peaceful inhabitant of no-man's-land, and as an object of projection from both sides of the Wall'.[52] Able to burrow beneath the political boundaries, rabbits had become a symbol of hope that Berliners in East and West could recognize and experience. Pedestrians who stumble across the randomly distributed rabbits are thus challenged to recall the history of this area and to recollect their own memories of division. Those who pass regularly are also forced to reflect on the changes that have taken place in more recent years, not least because by 2008 a third of the rabbits had disappeared under new constructions, a fact that led one resident to set up the website www.kaninchenfeld.de in order to help 'protect' the remaining rabbits. In this way, the installation itself interacts with the unification process, and adopts multiple meanings and interpretations akin to the very nature of Wall remembrance. The apparently apolitical nature of the design also challenges the expectations of memorial art; although Sachse's proposal caused much controversy among the jury, it stated in its final assessment that 'the work convincingly maintains its autonomy in the face of the unreasonable demands of political didactics'.[53]

As unobtrusive additions to the cityscape, all seven *Übergänge* installations confront Berliners in their daily lives, challenging them to reflect on their memories of a divided past, as well as the tumultuous changes that took place in the wake of 1989. Indeed, only through the careful contemplation of passers-by can they be invested with meaning, and thus the installations seek neither to impose a fixed message nor to categorize East and West; instead they rely on communicative memory, and are kept alive through interaction and active remembrance. As a result, diverse memories are encouraged, and the fact that some installations have been altered by time reflects the fluidity of memory and the constant reinterpretation to which it is subjected. In terms of form, each visually interrupts the daily environment of Berliners, bringing past and present into direct conversation with each other. They are all subversive in some way, inverting the expected norms of monumental form: Goldberg's can only be seen at night; Thiel draws on advertising techniques; and Sachse inters her rabbits in the ground. Situated in authentic locations, these installations use the power of art to draw on the experience of division, rather than highlight the image of division. It is thus inevitable that they are largely unknown to tourists and even to some locals, yet they demonstrate that physical markers may, indeed, promote a nuanced way of remembering the past. Like many instances of modern art, however, they may also be accused of fleeing reality, and in this case, of failing to engage with the pressing questions of what to do with material remnants of the Wall or how to ensure that this history is made accessible to those who did not live through it. While they provide an innovative and intentionally transitory way of dealing with the past, this approach must also be combined with longer-term strategies of remembrance. It is perhaps for this reason that Feversham and Schmidt describe the artworks only as 'essentially a nod in the direction of commemoration' and as 'lightweight gestures, neither bold nor beautiful'.[54] Moreover, tourist interests cannot be ignored in a capital city, and as Schlör claims, 'memory of "the wall" – a building, a political fact, a symbol – does indeed need some piece of concrete wall, be it "real" or "false", in order to visualize and symbolize this memory'.[55] These are all issues pertinent to the next case study.

Bernauer Straße Wall Memorial (Part I): Peripheral Remembrance?

Parallel to discussions over the *Übergänge* competition, a highly controversial debate took hold regarding the stretch of Wall at Bernauer Straße, a site located slightly out of the city centre, but one at which some of the most dramatic images of 1961 were taken: those of GDR citizens letting themselves down from windows on ropes or jumping into the safety nets of the West Berlin fire service, as well as that of soldier Conrad Schumann jumping over the barbed wire fence and fleeing to the West. The best-known and most successful tunnels were also dug here, and the demolition of the Versöhnungskirche (Reconciliation Church) in 1985, which was located in the death strip, underlined the highly destructive nature of SED policy. In short, Bernauer Straße had become a 'crystallization point of German-German history'.[56] With this section of border strip placed under preservation in October 1990, the question soon arose as to what should be done with it. Initial debate was dominated by two viewpoints. First, a number of historians – led by Helmut Trotnow, then working for the DHM – proposed maintaining a section of the border in its entirety, as a memorial site that would enable visitors to see exactly what 'the Wall' used to look like. As many elements of the border were destroyed in 1990, however, such a memorial site would involve a degree of reconstruction. In Trotnow's eyes, this would have been little different to repairs made to the Brandenburg Gate after 1945, thus an essential part of historical preservation. As he stated, 'The "historical" monument as memorial site is the best solution, not some artistically interpreted or even created products'.[57] In contrast, preservationists such as Gabi Dolff-Bonekämper from Berlin's Office for Historical Monuments strongly opposed historical reconstruction, arguing that a memorial site should focus on the preservation of what remains. In her eyes, the brutality of the border regime could not be represented by material substance alone: 'The "authentic horror" belongs to those who experienced it; it cannot be accessed via re-enactment. It's over'.[58] Instead, it was argued that the traces and remains of the border system should be used to explain where the border was, to display its development since 1961 – as well as debates since 1989 – and to encourage genuine engagement with this history. A one-to-one reconstruction would also limit the memorial site to a specific section of border in time and space, leading to the widespread criticism of 'Disneyfication'.[59] Arguments for and against reconstruction, preservation and artistic intervention continued even twenty years on,[60] but the example of Bernauer Straße demonstrates that the fate of a site is often strongly influenced by more practical, financial and social concerns on the ground.

The idea of a Wall memorial is one that was suggested by the West Berlin 'History Workshop' even before its fall,[61] but most prominently by Willy Brandt in his speech of 10 November 1989 in West Berlin, where he suggested retaining a section of Wall as 'a historical monstrosity'.[62] In 1990, this idea was further suggested at the round table in Berlin-Mitte, but above all by the DHM and the Protestant *Versöhnungsgemeinde*, led by Pastor Fischer.[63] A year later, to mark the thirtieth anniversary of the building of the Wall on 13 August 1991, the Berlin Senate agreed on the construction of a Wall memorial at Bernauer Straße. This decision took place, however, against a background of considerable protest among conflicting interest groups. First, the *Sophiengemeinde* (the East German Protestant parish of St Sophia), which had been forced to give up some of its cemetery to the GDR government for the building of the Wall, proved resistant. Having received the land back after unification, the parish priest, Pastor Hildebrandt, argued that the site housed the mass graves of victims of Second World War bombing, and was thus unsuitable for a Wall memorial site. In his words, 'a memorial site that is built on the desecration of another memorial site disqualifies itself'.[64]

Second, the West German Lazarus Nursing Home, formerly a hospital where injured escapees were treated, and subsequently an old people's home, argued for the Wall's demolition. Its matron, Sister Heckel, stated in 1990 that the home's residents 'experienced the terror of this Wall being built, had to live with it for twenty-nine years and are now suffering psychologically from still seeing it outside their window long after the border has opened'.[65] As a church-owned institution, it also wanted direct access to graves that had previously been located in no-man's land. Both religious communities found considerable support from neighbouring districts and politicians keen to see the Wall removed.[66] A third group consisted of city planners who wished to reclaim the land in order to create a multi-lane inner ring road, the space for which would be severely restricted if the Wall were to continue standing. As Dolff-Bonekämper stated of this period, 'It was no longer global powers that stood opposite each other on Bernauer Straße, but citizens, politicians and clergymen from [the districts of] Wedding and Mitte'.[67]

The ensuing years involved complex negotiations and the development of a concept approved by the Senate in 1993, which divided the 212-metre section of border into three sections, for use as a cemetery, a monument and for a border reconstruction. The continuing resistance of the *Sophiengemeinde*, however, led to a further agreement with the parish in 1994 that a full reconstruction of the Wall would be abandoned and that the monument should be dedicated 'to the memory of the victims of the Second World War and the victims of German division'.[68] On the basis of this agreement, the federal government launched a competition in April 1994 for the design of a memorial site, in which seventy metres of border strip were to be retained as they were, sixty metres would be dedicated to a monument and the remaining seventy metres would be returned to the *Sophiengemeinde* for its cemetery.[69] The competition brief demanded that entrants 'expose and raise awareness of the historical layers',[70] yet the requirement to take into consideration the Second World War graves, the victims of the Wall and the remaining traces of the border was considered by critics to be contradictory. In Christoph Stölzl's eyes, this constituted 'historical misrepresentation'[71] and Green Party representative Alice Ströver feared that the site would become a 'memorial hotchpotch of recent German history'.[72] At the same time, it was to be 'a place of quiet remembrance, conceptualized in a restrained manner', thus making the demands on artists highly complex.[73] Moreover, so soon after the fall of the Wall there had been little time for reflection, and as Dolff-Bonekämper stated, the lack of historical distance from events 'hindered artists' power of imagination, rather than inspiring them'.[74]

Of the 259 entries, the jury announced three second prize winners in October 1994, failing to be convinced by any single design, yet also stating that the complex demands on artists had failed to ignite clear designs.[75] Interestingly, one of the prize winners (a design by Markus-Antonius Bühren and Markus Maria Schulz) thematized this concern, and suggested conserving the site exactly as it stood, stating that five years was too short a time after the fall of the Wall to make such a decision.[76] Eventually, however, the contract went to Stuttgart architects Kohlhoff & Kohlhoff, who proposed enclosing a seventy-metre stretch of border strip between two high steel walls, the polished inside surfaces of which would reflect a never-ending length of wall, with the rusted outer surfaces recalling the Iron Curtain (see Figure 5.3). Some jury members saw this attempt to 'save' a small section of border through artistic means to be a clever representation of the ambivalent relationship with the Wall throughout this period.[77] In contrast, others claimed that the small section threatened to reduce the Wall to little more than a 'town square', and its inaccessibility limited the perspective from which it could be experienced. However, the Kohlhoff & Kohlhoff design was widely regarded to represent the path of least resistance, for it claimed the shortest section of Wall for the monument, thus meeting with the agreement of the *Sophiengemeinde* and politicians. The chair of the jury denounced this unsatisfactory outcome as

Figure 5.3 Berlin Wall Memorial (Kohlhoff & Kohlhoff, 1998), Bernauer Straße, Berlin. Photograph by Anna Saunders.

a sign of 'the helplessness and anxiety in dealing with memory of the Berlin Wall'.[78] Stölzl had objected to such a policy of appeasement the previous year, polemically stating that, 'For the sake of peace, the CDU and SPD in Berlin are smothering conflicts concerning the assessment of the past. There is an atmosphere like after 1945, life carries on – repression'.[79] Unlike the *Übergänge* installations, which were largely unintrusive and worked with the very notion of transition, efforts here were considerably more politically and socially charged.

Aside from conflict on the ground, financial difficulties also meant that funding was not approved until April 1997. Most controversial during this period, however, was the decision of Pastor Hildebrandt of the *Sophiengemeinde* to remove thirty-two segments of the Wall in April 1997 in two places, first to make space for the reconstruction of a brick gateway, in order to show that the Wall was constructed on a cemetery, and second to create a gap of over twenty metres, in order to allow the nuns a clear view of the cemetery.[80] In Hildebrandt's eyes, the continued existence of the Wall on top of mass graves was unacceptable, and with this action he hoped to 'force the Senate to the negotiation table'.[81] However, as an expert investigation found the following month, there was no evidence of mass graves in this area, most probably removed by the GDR regime before it built the Wall.[82] As a result, the requirement to dedicate the monument to victims of both the war and the Wall was removed, yet the gaping hole reinvigorated the long-standing debate over reconstruction versus preservation – one that was only concluded in 2009, when it was decided that the gap should be marked by steel poles.[83] On the other hand, Hildebrandt's actions highlighted the fragile status of the Wall and inadvertently raised public awareness of the need to protect it. It is little coincidence that shortly afterwards, in August 1997, the Senate agreed to a documentation centre and the reconstruction of the border strip at Bernauer Straße, in addition to the Kohlhoff & Kohlhoff monument.[84] The monument continued, however, to be viewed by critics as an unsatisfactory compromise, with Green and PDS representatives claiming that the temptation of federal money and the pressure to meet anniversary deadlines had led to poor judgement.[85]

The construction of the monument began symbolically on 9 November 1997, and was officially dedicated on 13 August 1998, in the presence of Berlin's Mayor Eberhard Diepgen (CDU) and the then Environment Minister Angela Merkel (CDU). As Diepgen claimed in his speech, 'The memorial site should not wear itself out with remembrance and admonishment, but must rather be a mental stumbling block',[86] echoing the views of preservationists that no memorial or reconstruction can, fortunately, reproduce the brutality or horror of the border system today. Public response to the monument, however, focused largely on this element, with newspaper reports reflecting views that 'history is being sweetened [*verschönt*]',[87] and that 'the Wall is being trivialized through too much artistic interpretation'.[88] Objections to the high steel walls were rife, not only because their height appeared to dwarf the Wall itself, but also because they prevented entry into the death strip – a somewhat curious objection, considering that the death strip was strictly out of bounds during division. There has also been abundant criticism of its 'sterile' form,[89] which some have described as 'over-aestheticizing'[90] and removing remembrance 'out of everyday life'.[91] Objections on the part of victims and their families were particularly strong, and resulted in part from the inscription on the monument, which initially read: 'Berlin Wall Memorial Site. In memory of the division of the town from 13 August 1961 to 9 November 1989 and in commemoration of the victims'. Following objections that this failed to name the perpetrators, the inscription was altered to end 'in commemoration of the victims of communist tyranny'.[92] As Patrick Major notes, this change 'echo[ed] the monuments to Nazi terror around the city and provid[ed] a more explicit totalitarian equation'.[93] The monument also failed to offer victims and their relatives any direct emotional relationship to the past, for it neither documented the individual names or fates of victims, nor did it attempt to portray the pain or distress they suffered.[94] The monument evidently failed to live up to the expectations of many, yet as Gabriele Camphausen, chair of the Berlin Wall Association, highlighted, the monument cannot correct the mistakes that were made after 1989 concerning the handling of the Wall, but can, instead, attract attention or act as a stumbling stone in the everyday environment.[95] Less than a decade after the fall of the Wall, it seems, indeed, that much of the dissatisfaction concerning the monument revolved around unrealistic expectations of what a physical structure alone can achieve. While some critics drew parallels with commemorative structures to victims of Nazism, it was often forgotten that the timeframes involved were very different, and that very little time had passed for any considered reflection of the memorialization process.

In view of widespread criticism, the years immediately following the completion of the structure witnessed the development of other forms of remembrance at the site. On 9 November 1999, a document centre was opened opposite the monument, containing exhibitions and information about the Wall. In 2003, it was expanded to include a viewing platform, which enabled visitors to view the monument from above – a development that provided a welcome overview of the whole border strip, yet which also provided a western perspective on the Wall.[96] Exactly a year after the opening of the documentation centre, the 'Chapel of Reconciliation' was dedicated in the border strip, a small wooden and loam structure that was built in commemoration of the Versöhnungskirche, destroyed in 1985. The trio of monument, documentation centre and chapel – nicknamed 'Kohlhoff Plus' – together formed the broader memorial site which, according to its website, 'enables one to approach the history and consequences of the Berlin Wall in different ways and in different forms: through artistic, documentary and spiritual means'.[97] The site as a whole, however, suffered from a severe lack of funding, as the running costs were to be taken on by the *Land* of Berlin, which was experiencing massive financial strain.[98] Relying heavily on the work of volunteers, further conceptual development of the site proved extremely difficult, and its location just outside the historical centre of Berlin meant that it struggled to attract as many visitors as other more tourist-centred 'Wall' remembrance sites, such as the 'Haus am Checkpoint Charlie' Museum.

The suitability of the site for the commemoration of victimhood became an increasingly hot topic over the following years, causing notable political conflict between victims' groups and their representatives on the one hand and those considered to represent or protect the interests of the former GDR elite on the other. Tensions became increasingly visible in the late 1990s, with wreaths laid at the monument by PDS politicians regularly being removed or destroyed by victims and their families.[99] The mounting tensions exploded in 2001, a year that marked the fortieth anniversary of the building of the Wall, but also the height of a wave of *Ostalgie* and crucially the possibility of a red-red coalition in Berlin. On arriving at the Bernauer Straße monument on 13 August 2001, Berlin's new SPD mayor, Klaus Wowereit, and Chancellor Schröder were both booed and verbally abused for their involvement with the PDS; wreaths laid by the PDS were destroyed to much media attention, and victims' groups and GDR dissidents – largely supported by the CDU – used this platform to voice their discontent at the possible future coalition and to renew their demands for a more visible and appropriate memorial site.[100] While the pressure mounted for the PDS to apologize to victims for the building of the Wall and the brutality of the SED dictatorship, accusations of other parties' involvement with the GDR regime also abounded, resulting in a general atmosphere of political back-stabbing. Despite the fact that the red-red coalition did go ahead, and indeed went on to develop the *Gesamtkonzept* under Thomas Flierl (PDS), this moment can also be identified as a turning point. As Sebastian Richter argues, 2001 acted like the needle of a compass that 'pointed towards the crime *of the Wall* and the will ... of all parties to develop public commemoration accordingly'.[101] Indeed, not only did Wall remembrance become increasingly sanctioned in the political sphere from this point, but the desire to raise the visibility of the Wall's victims also began to change the memorial landscape – a trend that further shaped the role of the Bernauer Straße monument a decade later (see the later section in this chapter on the extension of the site).

The change was, in part, also caused by victims' groups' continuing objection that existing attempts to mark the Wall – such as the cobbled strip, the *Übergänge* project and above all the Bernauer Straße monument – lacked emotional engagement with the experience of victimhood.[102] While some critics argued that remembrance of the Wall – itself an inhuman construction – would only be 'watered down through emotionalization',[103] the late 1990s and early 2000s saw a growth of private projects in memory of victims. The best known of these include the installation of a stele at the Peter Fechter commemorative site in 1999, a stele in memory of Chris Gueffroy in 2003, and the opening of the Günter Litfin memorial site in 2003, located in a former watchtower. Such private projects were all dedicated to individuals yet, in wanting to put a face to victims, contributed to more widespread changes in Berlin. As the following three examples demonstrate, however, the commemoration of Wall victims did not follow any particular formula, and although such structures attempted to provide more emotional symbolism than early commemorative structures, questions of form, location and local politics all provoked very different outcomes.

Victimhood and Visibility I: Remembering Child Victims in Treptow

The creation of monuments to multiple victims of the Wall has rarely been straightforward. The matter of agreeing on the total number of victims alone was much debated in the 2000s, and varied according to the institution collating the figures. It was only after a research project from 2006 to 2009 that the fates of at least 140 victims were documented.[104] Efforts to remember victims of the GDR border regime thus often emerged in the later 1990s because the painstaking examination of files and records was first necessary in order to establish who the victims were. Moreover, in some cases the enforced silence of relatives – or the 'repressive erasure' of their experiences – meant that the past was slow, and often too painful, to be rediscovered. Both cases were true in the eastern district of Treptow, where at least fifteen people lost their lives attempting to cross the border, among whom were two children, Jörg Hartmann (aged ten) and Lothar Schleusener (aged thirteen). On 14 March 1966, the two friends were shot at the Wall, Hartmann being killed on the spot and Schleusener dying later that night in a police hospital.[105] Why they had attempted to breach the border is unclear, but it is thought that Schleusener may have been trying to reach his father in the West, and that they had attempted to climb through a pipe under the barbed wire fencing.[106] Like other young victims of the border, their motives were unlikely to have been politically motivated, but were rather driven by normal pubescent turmoil and family conflict.[107] However, their deaths were an embarrassment to the GDR authorities, who could not allow themselves to be made responsible for the deaths of innocent children. Consequently, Hartmann's family was informed two weeks later that he had drowned in a lake and been caught by a ship's propeller; the body had been burned due to the danger of pestilence.[108] Schleusener's mother was told that her son had been electrocuted in an accident near Leipzig; similarly, the body had been burned to hide all evidence. For fear of the possible consequences, the families were forced to remain quiet, despite having heard a western report on RIAS (Broadcasting Service in the American Sector) that two children had been shot at the Wall. Similarly, Hartmann's teacher, Ursula Mörs, who tried to investigate his fate immediately after his disappearance, was told not to question the official version; her conscience led her to flee the GDR with her son that summer.[109] Those who may have seen or heard the incident were unlikely to have reported it, considering that citizens living in the immediate vicinity next to the border had to be considered loyal to the cause of the SED.

The boys' deaths came to light thirty-one years later, when the case was taken up by the Central Investigation Office for Government and Unification Criminality. Consequently, one of the two border guards responsible was put on trial for two counts of manslaughter in November 1997, the other having already passed away. In court, the fates of the children were exposed and those present heard how forty-two bullets were fired at the children; in his defence, the former border guard claimed that he did not know they were children, as he only saw a shadow.[110] Following the trial, the district parliament of Treptow decided to erect a memorial plaque at the place of the boys' death, and to document their fates through a public exhibition.[111] The motion, proposed by the SPD, was notably carried with no dissenting votes and little debate, despite the fact that the PDS was the strongest fraction. The initiative came from the district rather than relatives, who wished not to be heavily involved; the project was thus intended to be a gesture to rectify some of the injustices of the past, rather than to be primarily a site of mourning. Research carried out by Barbara Zibler, director of the then Heimat Museum Treptow, was central to the process, as was the exhibition 'Divided Neighbourhood', which opened on 13 August 1999 and documented the boys' fates, as well as life during division in Treptow and the bordering western neighbourhood Neukölln. Hartmann's former teacher, Ursula Mörs, also became a key figure in reworking this history, in the desire to make their fates public.

Although the district authorities initially planned a plaque to remember the two children, this became a larger project once the deaths of thirteen other people on the Treptow border had been established, and it was decided to erect a monument in their memory. A competition was thus launched on 30 June 1999, to which entries from five artists (or partnerships) were invited. The competition outline demonstrated very clearly the change in atmosphere over the last decade, claiming that in the euphoria of 1989, nobody spared much thought for the victims of the Wall.[112] This project was thus a sign of the times, and became one of the earliest of a new wave of memorials to victims. On the one hand, its aims were clear: 'The injustices of the totalitarian system of the GDR should be remembered through the commemoration of the victims of the Wall'.[113] On the other hand, however, the rubrics stated that 'the artistic object should create free space for commemoration',[114] in recognition of the fact that it would represent different memories for different people. Most notable was the tight timeframe: designs were to be submitted by 6 September 1999, a winner announced on 17 September, and the winning design unveiled on 9 November the same year, in time for the tenth anniversary – almost unthinkable in today's competition terms. However, the broad political and local support for the monument meant that there was little delay, and generous donations – as well as the winning artists' decision to forgo some of their fees – ensured there were no financial delays. In contrast to the majority of larger, national projects, we see once again how locally-led projects often evolve with relatively little resistance.

It is inevitable that the depiction of walls was a common theme among the five entries. The winning design by Jan Skuin and Rüdiger Roehl consists of two steel walls, one representing a life-size section of the Berlin Wall, alongside a jagged section of wall featuring a cut-out figure surrounded by bullet holes (see Figure 5.4). An inscription reads: 'In Treptow fifteen people died at the Berlin Wall. Among the victims were two children. Jörg Hartmann, 10 years old and Lothar Schleusener, 13 years old, shot on 14.3.1966'. Interestingly, this was the

Figure 5.4 Memorial to Treptow's Wall victims (Jan Skuin and Rüdiger Roehl, 1999), Kiefholzstraße, Berlin-Treptow. Photograph by Anna Saunders.

only design to be noted in the jury's preliminary report as evoking an emotional response, stating that the design guarantees 'an immediate and intuitive experience' and 'should satisfy emotions such as sorrow and sympathy in the longer term'.[115] The combination of the cut-out figure and the bullet holes indeed portrays the brutality of the Wall yet also evokes an element of pathos in the viewer – aspects that victims' groups claimed the initial Bernauer Straße memorial lacked. However, there is more to the construction of the monument than meets the eye.

As the artists had wanted real bullet holes in their monument, they had taken it to a Bundeswehr training centre, where the commanding general allowed his soldiers to use it for shooting practice, ensuring that forty-two shots were fired – the same number that were fired at the boys.[116] The most important part of this process for the artists was that it added an extra layer of meaning to the monument; in learning about the deaths of the boys at the Wall, future soldiers were forced to reflect on their own responsibilities and duties. In this way, the monument brought together past and future in an unusual way, making the construction process itself part of the remembering process.

Treptow's monument to its Wall victims is modest in comparison with more central monuments. However, despite its difficult subject matter, it is notable for its widespread local acceptance and the speed with which it was erected. Standing in a peripheral location, away from tourist areas, its aim was clearly different to monuments in central Berlin, yet it carries no less meaning for those who were involved in its creation and in the uncovering of the boys' fates. As a site visited by local school groups and a meeting point for those who wish to remember victims on 13 August or 9 November,[117] it serves a continued commemorative function in the local area, and demonstrates the way in which a monument may provoke the process of *Aufarbeitung* before, during and after its construction.

Victimhood and Visibility II: White Crosses in Duplicate

In contrast to the Treptow monument, a long-standing memorial site in central Berlin dedicated to the victims of the Wall has been highly politicized and caused ongoing controversy in recent years. In the 1960s, a number of white crosses were installed by the Berlin Citizens Association in various locations on the Western side of the Wall, in memory of its victims. These were later brought together in two locations to ensure they were better maintained: on Bernauer Straße and on the north-eastern side of the Reichstag building. Those near the Reichstag, erected for the tenth anniversary in 1971, have remained a memorial site until today – albeit in slightly different form and location. However, due to the complex demands of victims' groups, politicians and town planners, two sites of memory have existed since 2003, causing a curious doubling effect.

Attached to a fence on the Western side of the Wall next to the Spree, the 1971 memorial was dedicated to all victims of the Wall, and by the end of the GDR it named thirteen individuals (eleven of whom were killed in the 1960s), with two further crosses in memory of 13 August 1961 and the unknown victims of the Wall. It remained in situ until building work for the new government quarter along the Spree began, necessitating the crosses to be moved in 1995 to the southern side of the Reichstag building, and located at the edge of the Tiergarten on Ebertstraße. This was done in agreement with the Berlin Citizens Association and on the understanding that when the building work was finished, they would be returned to their original location.[118] In 1999, discussions began concerning their second relocation, with the Senate's Arts Advisory Board recommending that they be moved back 'to their original location in as documentary and authentic a fashion as possible'.[119] After negotiations between the Citizens Association, the Senate and federal representatives, a location next to the Spree was allocated, which was close to the original location, yet deemed more suitable for memorial purposes.[120] The landscape architects Cornelia Müller and Jan Wehberg were given the task of integrating a new memorial site into the redevelopment of the area, and according to Bundestag president Wolfgang Thierse at its opening in 2003, their concept was also approved by the Citizens Association.[121] The design consists of seven crosses with names inscribed on both sides, meaning that six names and a cross to 'The "unknown" victims of the Wall' are visible from Ebertplatz, and seven names are visible from the Spree (see Figure 5.5). The fact that a large number of victims died in the Spree was significant in the decision for this location, and the inscriptions on both sides of the crosses represent the fact that during division they could only be seen from the western side; now, after unification, they can also be seen and read from the eastern side.[122] The absence of a cross in the middle of the row also reminds the visitor of the unnamed victims, and of victims whose fates may yet be uncovered.

As in Treptow, the naming of victims at this site personalizes the remembrance of victims in a way that the (pre-expansion) Bernauer Straße monument did not. However, as highlighted in Thierse's opening speech, its geographical location lends the memorial a much broader political function. This is apparent even from the choice of day for its dedication: 17 June 2003, the fiftieth anniversary of the GDR uprisings. This provided an opportunity to link the building of the Wall with 17 June, allowing Thierse to speak not only about GDR oppression, but also about the importance of social engagement and human rights, stating: 'If this day [17 June] had not ended in defeat, we would have been spared the Wall and all the victims that we are remembering today'.[123] He praised the work of the Citizens Association in relentlessly maintaining the memory of the victims as 'civil engagement at

Figure 5.5 White crosses (Cornelia Müller and Jan Wehberg, 2003), Spreeufer, Berlin. Photograph by Anna Saunders.

its best', and expressed his hope that all those who work at the 'heart of our democracy' will regularly visit the crosses. In stating that 'the "white crosses" call for a commitment to freedom', he concluded that there should be no future for 'mechanisms for repression that lead to memorial sites such as this'. This speech clearly placed the memory of the Wall within the broader context of present-day democracy, and justified its location at the centre of the government district.

However, neither the Citizens Association nor victims' families and representatives were satisfied with the new location or design. Not only did the reduced number of crosses minimize the size and impact of the site, but the fact that half the names could only be read from the water reduced their visibility. In contrast, the site on Ebertstraße often features biographies of individual victims (albeit hung on makeshift boards next to the crosses), providing for a more personal engagement with victims' individual fates (see Figure 5.6). Many further objected that the new location was set back from the main tourist trail and argued for keeping the more centrally located old crosses.[124] Members of the Citizens Association also expressed emotional attachment to the original crosses; in the words of Karl-Georg Welker, chair of the association, 'We put the crosses up in 1971 on the tenth anniversary of

Figure 5.6 White crosses (in this location since 1995), Ebert-/Scheidemannstraße, Berlin (showing wreaths laid on 13 August 2011). Photograph by Anna Saunders.

the building of the Wall, we moved with them to Ebertstraße and have cared for them until today. The crosses belong to us, not to anyone else. They will not be removed!'[125] In many ways, the memory of the crosses themselves, as well as the practical and emotional investment in them, had become as important as what they stood for; the act of remembrance thus became strongly objectified. In stark contrast to Thierse's speech, Welker complained 'that instead of the will of citizens, there is only party will left', and as a sign of their engagement for the crosses, the Citizens Association – later replaced by the 'Federation of Central Germans' – continued to look after the old site on Ebertstraße, only a few hundred metres from the new site. In 2005, when the district authorities of Mitte, responsible for this area, decided to clear the site, there was vigorous protest involving a petition against the district's policies.[126] In the end, the local authorities felt unable to remove the crosses, precisely because a temporary Freedom Memorial (discussed below), also consisting of crosses, had already been removed that year;[127] the red-red government could clearly not be seen to be responsible for two such actions in one year, however justified they felt their reasons may have been. In this way, we see how the fate of a site of memory may not only be linked to, but dependent on associated synchronous debates and conflicts.

The site has, however, also become the battleground of one particular individual: former political prisoner Gustav Rust, who spent nine years in numerous GDR prisons before being bought free by the West. As a militant campaigner against the GDR, he sees it as his 'mission in life' to protect this site,[128] and has used it as a means not only to draw tourists' attention to the brutality of the GDR, but also to protest against the memory politics of the red-red government. However, his right-wing views and actions have been highly controversial, and not only has he been charged with assault, but many find his comparisons of victims of the Holocaust and those of the Wall offensive.[129] Moreover, some of the flyers that he has distributed at the memorial have been particularly contentious, with references, for example, to Angela Merkel as an 'FDJ activist' or the PDS as a 'gang of murderers'.[130] Although the 'Association of Central Germans' renounced any association with Rust, and the authorities have attempted to remove him from the site,[131] his presence remains constant. The very fact that he himself suffered under the GDR means that any direct action against him – and the site itself – is extremely difficult, and would indeed appear perverse.[132] While his views may not be representative of the masses, this provides a further example of a single individual influencing the very existence of a site of memory.

At the time of writing, there is still a situation of stalemate over this duplicate site of memory; while the new site appears in official government documentation and is included in the *Gesamtkonzept*, it seems only a matter of time before the 'old' site will disappear, especially considering that those responsible for it are struggling to maintain it.[133] In the meantime, however, the privately run site has adopted the air of a slightly makeshift memorial, adorned with home-made placards and signs (largely due to Rust), yet it became a particularly important location of political interest for those opposed to Berlin's red-red government from 2002 to 2011. The CDU, for instance, promoted the cause of the original crosses, stating that the memory of victims warranted more dignified remembrance in a central location: 'The crosses at the Reichstag are especially well suited for this [memory of the victims], because they belong to the few existing authentic documents [*Zeugnisse*] that remember the dead of the border regime. Their current neglected condition is unacceptable. The crosses must be presented and explained in an appropriate manner'.[134] While the question of authenticity is not insignificant – the crosses have, after all, become complex symbols of meaning in much the same way as the extended memorial site at Bernauer Straße (see below), reflecting far-reaching changes since 1989 – the accusation that the physical state of this site 'is evidence of [official] disinterest in working through GDR history' is questionable, given the existence of a central and orderly site of memory dedicated to the crosses.[135] It is little surprise that the 13 August Association, located on the right of the political spectrum, has also strongly fought for the retention of the original crosses, holding vigils at the site as a sign of protest. As one of its committee members stated, 'The obstruction and littering [of the memorial] disgusts us as a GDR victims' association. It is undignified and impious'.[136] The original white crosses clearly became caught up in a battle of political wills, in which the past was used to justify present actions. Indeed, arguments such as that of CDU representative Kai Wegner that the removal of the crosses would represent a 'further step towards ousting Wall remembrance from the cityscape',[137] or that the symbol of the cross must be kept alive in the face of abstract memorial art,[138] held little water, precisely because a second site already existed nearby. Such arguments did, however, provide ammunition for those unhappy with the fact that the PDS/Die Linke had been in power in Berlin for nine years. On the fiftieth anniversary of 13 August, for example, the site was adorned with wreaths, notably from a particular group of organizations: the CDU/CSU, as well as the 'Haus am Checkpoint Charlie' Museum, the Association of Central Germans, the 13 August Association and the German Conservative Party, all clearly on the right of the political spectrum. In many ways, this was as much a political statement as a sign of mourning, and the site had become one of protest against present-day memory politics.

While the 'old' site has been used to protest against left-wing memory politics, an interesting postscript to the 'new' site saw memory of Wall victims being used for a very different political purpose. On 3 November 2014, just a few days before the twenty-fifth anniversary of the fall of the Wall, the action group Centre for Political Beauty secretly removed the crosses next to the Spree and transported them (or replicas) to the borders of the EU in order to protest at the thousands of migrants who had lost their lives attempting to cross the border. The crosses were photographed at various points on the border, and with a number of refugees living in woodland in Morocco, next to the 'death strip' of Melilla. According to the organization, 'In an act of solidarity, the victims [white crosses] fled to their brothers and sisters across the European Union's external borders, more precisely, to the future victims of the Wall'.[139] This action ensured high-profile press coverage, especially given the timing of the event, and brought the German past into uncomfortable proximity with the plight of contemporary refugees. Through crowd funding, the organization coordinated two buses to take one hundred 'peaceful revolutionaries' to Bulgaria's outer borders, armed with bolt cutters and electric angle grinders, to bring about the 'first fall of the European Wall'. As stated on their website, 'While Berlin's politicians sent balloons up into the air listening to nostalgic and sedating speeches in an Oktoberfest-like ceremony [for the twenty-fifth anniversary], German citizens tried to tear down the EU's illegal external borders in an act of political beauty and take a piece of the fence back home with them'.[140] Although the white crosses were finally returned on 9 November, their absence caused uproar in political circles and forced dialogue between the politics of past and present – and above all drew attention to the dangers of allowing remembrance to become little more than ritual lip service to the past.

Victimhood and Visibility III: The Freedom Memorial, Checkpoint Charlie

Political unease also became the hallmark of the final case study in this chapter: the Freedom Memorial (*Freiheitsmahnmal*), which stood near the site of the former Checkpoint Charlie from October 2004 to July 2005. Registered as a temporary 'art campaign' and thus bearing initial similarity to the *Übergänge* project, it was also perceived as transitory in concept; conceived a decade later, however, it strove to install a more culturally ingrained form of memory into the landscape, and sought to portray a specific perspective on the Wall and the GDR, rather than to promote individual reflection. As a privately funded initiative located next to the 'Haus am Checkpoint Charlie' Museum, and instigated by its director, Alexandra Hildebrandt (widow of its founder, Rainer Hildebrandt), the project also began from a very different premise. Indeed, its history must be understood within the context of the museum itself, which displays photos, documents and exhibits relating to successful escapes across the border, but also focuses on documenting political protest against the GDR regime, as well as non-violent resistance to other repressive regimes worldwide. Its aim has remained highly political since its opening in 1963, and in many ways it has become a document to the Cold War itself, yet it continues to attract thousands of tourists, and in the 2000s was consistently the second most visited Berlin museum after the Pergamon Museum.[141] It is, however, criticized by many historians and preservationists as a 'shrill amusement park for tourists',[142] not least due to the reconstruction of an American control hut outside the museum in 2000, together with a copy of the sign reading 'You are now leaving the American Sector', at which students dressed as Allied soldiers pose with tourists and stamp their passports. As Schmidt points out, the reconstruction of the 1961 control hut, complete with sandbags, reflects tourists' expectations shaped by historical footage of 1961, rather than representing the reality of the border crossing in 1989.[143] Relations between the museum and the Berlin Senate had become difficult from the mid 1990s onwards, regarding not only the professionalization of museum work but also the question of coordinated remembrance activities in the city, and 'latent competition' with the memorial site at Bernauer Straße.[144] Tensions came to a head over the use of a vacant plot of land adjacent to the museum – left empty due to the eventual bankruptcy of the Central European Development Corporation, which had bought this land – which became the cause of much haggling between the museum, corporate developers and city authorities.

This background forms an important backdrop for the installation of Hildebrandt's Freedom Memorial in October 2004, which was carefully timed to coincide with the fifteenth anniversary of the fall of the Wall. The memorial was positioned on both sides of Friedrichstraße, on the empty plot for which Hildebrandt had attained a lease agreement, and consisted of 1,065 black wooden crosses placed in front of a whitewashed wall, made out of 120 original Wall segments, together creating a stretch of approximately two hundred metres. Each cross represented a victim of the GDR border regime, bearing the name, dates and in some cases the photo of an individual who had died, as well as the place and cause of death. Given the Berlin Senate's failure to dedicate a central site to Wall victims by this point, the location and the unequivocal symbolism were welcomed above all by their families, but also by tourists eager to witness the few tangible traces of this past. Hildebrandt made little secret of the fact that she aimed to provoke public debate through heightened melodrama in the installation.[145] An explanatory text printed on an information board in four languages made this clear, criticizing the Senate for selling 'this most important square of the free world' to private investors, who in turn had failed to honour their commitment to marking the historical importance of the site. The installation was thus presented as an embodiment of popular opinion: 'As citizens, we do not want to declare ourselves in agreement with this reality fifteen years after the fall of the Wall'.[146] Although the memorial was initially given permission to stand only until the end of the year, Hildebrandt fought for it to become a permanent fixture and refused to move it. The memorial was subsequently forcibly removed by the police in July 2005, after the lease on the plot of land ran out, unleashing angry protests among former GDR prisoners, four of whom chained themselves to crosses, while others carried placards reading 'Remember! Don't forget'.[147] Needless to say, the media had a field day, with images of the 'fall of the Wall' and headlines such as 'The wall is gone' filling newspapers for a second time in sixteen years.[148]

The memorial's success in gaining widespread political and media attention resulted largely from its conventional symbolism. Both the simplicity and the religious overtones of the installation were intended to resonate emotionally with viewers, as did efforts to embed a sense of ritual engagement with the crosses; at the opening, for instance, a wreath was laid at the foot of every cross, and before their demolition each was consecrated by a Catholic priest. The memorial was thus staged to evoke pathos, and despite its short-lived existence, became a site of highly ritualized memory. The photos and names on the crosses – notable for the fact that those bearing photos were all placed at the front of the memorial – provided for a highly personalized form of memory, particularly for victims' families, and as one journalist commented, 'It is satisfying a demand';[149] the site was, indeed, well visited and provoked spontaneous emotional responses from visitors in a way that the Bernauer Straße monument rarely had.[150] In contrast to both sites of white crosses – the older of which does sometimes display personal information on victims – the sheer number of crosses here, as well as the size of the memorial, created a more dramatic and immediate effect. As Hildebrandt herself claimed, 'The world of politics shouldn't be afraid of emotionally charged monuments, for it is precisely because they affect people and even provoke tears that they ease tensions'.[151] Its simplistic message, however, presented a polarized view of GDR society as one divided between victims and perpetrators – far from the more nuanced findings of contemporary historical research that recognized a more complex and fluid relationship between the party and the masses. In line with Hildebrandt's museum, the memorial thus drew on a Western Cold War tradition of remembrance, leaving little space for Eastern or more differentiated interpretations. Indeed, victims were presented as martyrs for the greater cause of freedom; as the information board at the monument stated, 'We commemorate the thus-far identified deaths … to whom we owe today's freedom in unity'.[152] Ironically, the clear political message and interpretation, together with strong symbolism and heightened emotionality, placed this monument in a tradition not far removed from that of former GDR monuments, albeit from a different political perspective.

Hildebrandt's desire to see this location become Berlin's principal site of remembrance for Wall victims was motivated less by historical authenticity – there were few deaths in the immediate vicinity of Checkpoint Charlie – than by political and commercial interests. Indeed, her claim that the history of division was nowhere more visible than at Checkpoint Charlie not only aimed to legitimize the monument,[153] but also foregrounded the symbolic potency of the museum and its marketability in the present. A pamphlet promoting the monument, for instance, ultimately provided little more than a history of the Checkpoint, the Wall and the museum itself.[154] The installation also conformed to tourist expectations, as it provided an easily digestible slice of history in a busy city centre location, representing, in the words of one sightseer, 'exactly what we tourists want to see, and what we are looking for'.[155] Needless to say, the controversial removal of the memorial only highlighted its role as a tourist magnet, with a representative of Berlin Tourism Marketing claiming: 'These are unpleasant pictures that are being sent from Berlin to the outside [world]. They are not conducive to the image-building of our city'.[156] Clearly, the monument did little to counter existing preconceptions about Cold War or GDR history, and provided a 'fast food' version of the Wall, ensuring, according to Schmidt, 'a quick satisfaction of their [tourists'] desires and a picturesque backdrop for their souvenir photographs'.[157] While the area around the former Checkpoint Charlie clearly enjoyed a heightened status, the desire for straightforward aesthetics and a clear-cut message often dominated any real attempt to engage with the complexities of this past.

Beyond tourism, the Freedom Memorial highlighted the fraught memory politics surrounding the GDR border regime and enabled Hildebrandt, who was largely backed by the CDU, to accuse the SPD-PDS coalition in the Berlin Senate of failing to address adequately the public need to remember this past. Although she was legally obliged to remove the installation once her lease ran out, she argued that 'the memorial ... was brutally demolished by Berlin's Social Democrat/reformed Communist coalition city government'.[158] Alongside CDU representatives, such as the mayor of Berlin's Mitte district, Joachim Zeller, and the CDU General Secretary, Frank Henkel, a number of high-profile public figures backed Hildebrandt's cause, such as former activist Bärbel Bohley, who accused the government of wanting to repress 'experienced injustices'.[159] Hubertus Knabe, director of the Hohenschönhausen Memorial Site, also claimed, 'So far, that is the best we have in terms of Wall remembrance', labelling the Bernauer Straße monument 'failed' and 'misleading'.[160] Perhaps inevitably, the mass media attention and controversial nature of the memorial drew a large number of visitors, and as one newspaper reported, 'the installation

[is] less a site of memory than a site at which to provide opinion'.[161] Politically, the monument must also be understood within the frame of other GDR memorial debates at the time. On the one hand, this highly visible monument was a clear response to Wolfgang Rüppel's monument to 17 June 1953 (see Chapter 4), which had received much criticism from both the 13 August Working Group and the 'Haus am Checkpoint Charlie' Museum as being 'invisible' and ill-suited to remember the SED's victims.[162] The fact that the photo banners of 1953 (erected on the Ministry of Finance behind the monument) had been removed in June 2005 against Hildebrandt's will also added grist to her mill in protest against the government's policies. Interestingly, others, such as CDU General Secretary Frank Henkel, portrayed the authorities' plans to erect a monument to Rosa Luxemburg in central Berlin as evidence that the Senate lacked sensitivity in remembering the victims of the GDR regime.[163] Finally, Hildebrandt's insistence on the unique character of the site proved influential in some quarters, and was illustrated by the actions of the CDU which, despite supporting the Wall reconstruction at Checkpoint Charlie, controversially approved a demolition order for an original section of ninety metres close to Bernauer Straße, in order to clear space for new sports facilities.[164] Clearly, the physical landscape had become highly politicized, and the site at Checkpoint Charlie demonstrated the complex nature of its entanglement with other sites of memory.

In many ways, the Freedom Memorial filled a deficit left by the Bernauer Straße monument before it was expanded (see below) in terms of the emotional, geographical and symbolic expectations of victims' associations, tourists and some political groups. However, the segments of Wall were neither reconstructed in the correct location, nor did they originate from this site. Moreover, the fates of some of the victims were historically contested; many were not victims of the Wall itself, but rather of the broader border regime. As a result, the installation proved problematic for historians and heritage professionals, as well as the SPD and PDS, all of whom raised concerns about authenticity and accused Hildebrandt variously of creating a 'Disney' version of the Cold War, promoting historical inaccuracy and encouraging a 'carnival' environment.[165] Indeed, Manfred Kühne, head of the Historic Monuments Protection Authority, claimed that the installation 'only contributes to the confusion [*Verunklärung*] of ill-informed visitors',[166] and others pointed towards the danger of dehistoricizing history by presenting an inaccurate view of the GDR and its border.[167] Senator Thomas Flierl called it a 'phoney monument in the wrong place',[168] and an article in *Neues Deutschland* dubbed it 'a lie that creates false emotions'.[169] Whereas its emphasis on emotional engagement was seen as positive by many, it was viewed negatively by those wishing to impart an educational experience. Observations that 'it appeals only to the emotions and not to the mind'[170] were thus backed by prominent historians of the GDR, who called for a 'more professionally satisfactory form for the commemoration of victims'.[171] Indeed, the Freedom Memorial had no scholarly committee behind it, nor did it provide evidence for the deaths of the 1,065 victims that were commemorated. It was not only the lack of scholarly backing, but also a deficit of democratic decision-making that was problematic for critics, for Hildebrandt had acted alone, with only the mandate of her own museum and the 13 August Working Group (based at the museum), and much press coverage presented it as a one-woman show. Her insistence that the public was united behind her cause, together with the aspiration to install a singular and ritualized narrative of victimhood in central Berlin, demonstrated a claim to sole representation and thus an attempt to monopolize this memory. While Anna Kaminsky, director of the Bundesstiftung zur Aufarbeitung der SED-Diktatur, called it 'guerrilla commemoration',[172] art critic Martin Schönfeld placed it in clear opposition to the monuments and memory markers that had been created in the 1990s on the basis of public art competitions.[173] Much of this criticism was bound up with suspicions that Hildebrandt's main aim was to lure more paying visitors into her museum; Flierl, for example, objected to the economic exploitation of the memorial as well as the 'unbearable privatization of commemoration, which should really be a public matter'.[174] He was not the only one to accuse the museum of attempting to create its own 'house altar',[175] with others viewing it as representing a kind of 'shrine'.[176] Hildebrandt's argument that the removal of the memorial would mean a 'second death for Wall victims' only strengthened such imagery.[177]

The location also triggered much resistance. Although Hildebrandt claimed that 'Checkpoint Charlie is a place of freedom for everyone and a place where world history manifests itself',[178] its role as a crossing point for members of the Allied forces and foreigners meant that it held less symbolism as a specifically German site of memory, and neither was it primarily associated with victims of the Wall. As Sybille Frank points out, this site was not one with which Berliners self-identified, but was rather regarded as a 'foreign' site;[179] even after unification it was sold to investors with international aspirations rather than local concerns, and today the tourist trade ensures a greater international dimension than elsewhere in the city. It is, thus, interesting that a representative survey among Berlin citizens in November 2004 found that 76 per cent rejected the need for a further site of Wall remembrance in the city, only strengthening its primary image as a tourist site.[180] The central location and the timing of the monument, however, also brought forth its association with the nearby Holocaust memorial, under construction at that time, and opened in May 2005.[181] Not only were comparisons between Hildebrandt and Lea Rosh, a key initiator of the Holocaust memorial, widespread as memory activists,[182] but the field of crosses was also seen to mirror the field of stelae at the Holocaust memorial. Described by Senator for Urban Development Ingeborg Junge-Reyer (SPD) as 'overstepping the boundaries of good taste',[183] it was accused of placing victims of the Wall alongside those of the Holocaust, thus equating National Socialism with the SED dictatorship. In Schönfeld's words, 'The accusation of historical revisionism was in the air'.[184] Moreover, unlike contemporary monuments to the Holocaust which had built on several decades of careful deliberations over how best to remember its victims in both content and form, remembrance of the GDR's victims was still in its early stages, and the direct 'borrowing' of aesthetics from Holocaust remembrance was, for many, one step too far, and one that had, for instance, been consciously rejected at Buchenwald (see Chapter 3).

The Freedom Memorial may have conveyed little to visitors about the history of the site, yet it spoke volumes about the state of Wall remembrance in Berlin over the previous fifteen years. Only two years later, the Senate admitted that various 'deficits in Berlin's remembrance politics' had become clear by the autumn of 2004.[185] As a result, the months and years following Hildebrandt's installation were marked by considerable activity in this area. By November 2004, the CDU and Green representatives of the Berlin Parliament had already presented motions demanding that the Senate develop a concept linking together Berlin's memorial and documentary sites, particularly those that remembered the Berlin Wall and the GDR dictatorship.[186] Two months later, an initiative of more than one hundred Bundestag members, led by representatives of the SPD, CDU, FDP and Greens, was put to the Bundestag, which once again called for an overarching concept, as well as a reassessment of the site at Bernauer Straße and the creation of a site of information and Wall remembrance at the Brandenburg Gate.[187] This was passed in June 2005 and an information centre was later created in the new underground station at the Brandenburg Gate. As discussed below, an overarching concept was passed by the Senate in 2006, and at roughly the same time the Senate opened an open-air gallery along Friedrichstraße, flanking the area on which the Freedom Memorial had once stood. Measuring almost three hundred metres long, the gallery presented texts and images in German and English, depicting the history of the Wall and the importance of Checkpoint Charlie, as well as information on other Wall remembrance sites in Berlin. This location was thus deployed in order to present the history of the site, as well as to point visitors towards other sites of 'authentic' memory. While a Cold War museum is being planned on the site in the longer term, a temporary art installation showing a 'wall panorama' by artist Yadegar Asisi was opened in September 2012, alongside a 'black box', housing an exhibition about the Cold War. How exactly this tourist hot-spot will develop in future remains to be seen, but for the moment it continues to draw international crowds in search of an easily digestible history of the Wall. Moreover, Hildebrandt appears unwilling to let memory of the Freedom Memorial disappear; for the fiftieth anniversary of the building of the Wall in 2011, she reinstated fifty of the wooden crosses on Friedrichstraße as a reminder of this project.[188] As one of the most politically and historically rich sites in central Berlin, it appears set to remain a site of complex and entangled narratives of remembrance.

Towards Decentralized Remembrance: The *Gesamtkonzept* and Bernauer Straße (Part II)

The *Gesamtkonzept* was passed by the Berlin Senate in June 2006 at the cost of approximately 40 million euros, and provided an overarching plan for Wall remembrance in the city until the fiftieth anniversary of the Wall in August 2011. It unequivocally set the tone for the years 2006–2011 and beyond, and established remembrance of the Wall and its victims as 'a public, national task'.[189] It provided a solution to the increasingly disparate and fragmented landscape of memory in Berlin, bringing together more than one hundred different sites and traces of Wall remembrance under one umbrella, yet firmly stating that there should be no competition between sites, and that the 'decentralized structure of the remembrance landscape … must be respected'.[190] A number of passages such as this clearly resulted from the conflict over the Freedom Memorial, as did the emphasis on maintaining authentic remains of the Wall. Historians Jarausch, Sabrow and Hertle are even quoted in the document as stating that 'a Hollywood-style reconstruction of the Wall as a trivialized "theme park" would indeed be an appalling idea'.[191] It is also interesting that the first page of the *Gesamtkonzept* pictures an image of the first memorial to victims of the Wall in 1961, and the concept as a whole is dedicated to victims of the GDR dictatorship; the conflicts and debates of previous years had clearly played a key role here. The development of the *Gesamtkonzept* was, however, also driven by the pending fiftieth anniversary of the building of the Wall in August 2011, and its rapid realization was deemed by Rainer Klemke, Berlin's chief advisor on memorial sites and museums, as one that 'has few parallels in the rich history of German remembrance culture since 1945'.[192] The concept is above all politically significant, as it was not only created under the red-red Berlin government, but headed by PDS/Die Linke representative Thomas Flierl, then Senator for Science, Research and Culture. Despite widespread fears that the involvement of the PDS/Die Linke would result in downplaying the brutality of the SED dictatorship, as well as calls from the CDU to intensify the concept and to meet a deadline of 2009 rather than 2011,[193] dissenting voices lessened in subsequent years. Early animosity was largely stoked by the conflict over Hildebrandt's installation, and as Klemke states, many of the accusations against the Senate's memory politics in 2005–2006 were 'in reality nothing more than taking sides for [or against] the hotly debated crosses for Wall victims'.[194] Rather than becoming ostracized through its memory politics, Richter even claims that 'through its active involvement in Wall remembrance, the PDS has become more strongly integrated into the all-German reality'.[195] As with its role in marking 'Haus 3' on Prenzlauer Allee (see Chapter 3), the opportunity to take a leading role in memory politics in the capital enabled the party to demonstrate a responsibility to the present through remembrance of the past.

The very title of the concept (*gesamt* meaning 'overall' or 'complete') indicates the nature of the project, for not only does it feature the main sites of Wall remembrance, including remaining watchtowers and former 'ghost stations', but it also features the development of information columns around Berlin, the marking of footpaths and cycle paths following the former course of the Wall, as well as audiovisual guides, maps, flyers, tours and an extensive internet portal.[196] In this way, it attempts to be as all-encompassing as possible, incorporating a whole range of sites from across Berlin. Despite the decentralized approach and insistence that no single site should monopolize memory of the Wall, the *Gesamtkonzept* does invest significantly in the site at Bernauer Straße, stating that 'the commemoration of victims of the Berlin Wall finds its central location' here.[197] Somewhat ironically, perhaps, this resulted in a site that was originally deemed too far from the centre and too intellectually demanding of visitors becoming the centrepiece of Wall remembrance in Berlin, a decision that appears to have found broad consensus during much of the consultation process and doubtless benefitted from criticism of Hildebrandt's installation.

Following the recommendations of the *Gesamtkonzept*, a massive extension of the site at Bernauer Straße began after a competition in 2007, which was won by the landscape architects 'sinai. Faust. Schroll. Schwarz', the architects 'Mola Winkelmüller' and 'ON architektur'.[198] Funded by Berlin, the federal government and Lotto money, it includes an open-air exhibition, and traces the course of the border from the Nordbahnhof to the Mauerpark, creating one of the largest memorial sites in Germany. While this extension is not the main focus of the present discussion, the role of the Kohlhoff & Kohlhoff monument within the extended project is worth brief exploration. Despite widespread criticism in 1998 of its abstract and emotionally void aesthetics, this monument has, in Pastor Fischer's words, proved to be a 'wolf in sheep's clothing'.[199] Not only did it constitute the first step towards securing the long-term future of this section of border, but its very concept provided much of the impetus for 'Kohlhoff Plus' as well as this later expansion. Above all, the emphasis on preservation rather than reconstruction has remained central. The sections of Wall removed by Pastor Hildebrandt in 1997, for instance, have not been reinserted, but remain stacked up on the grounds of the cemetery, serving as a reminder of the disputes and difficulties of Wall remembrance in the first decade of unification. In this way, the site recounts not only the story of the division of Germany or Berlin, but also the history of the political and geographical disputes over the Wall after its fall.[200] It is also significant that the material of the Kohlhoff design – Corten steel, providing a rusty-looking effect – has been adopted in the winning design of the extended memorial site, used to mark the traces of former border elements, such as a watchtower, part of the patrol route, or the missing Wall segments. In this way, visitors are encouraged to read the site as a palimpsest, with attention being drawn to the different layers of history without material reconstruction. Despite the initial reservations and criticism from some quarters that the site failed to replicate the ferocity of the border (itself a highly problematic notion), the emphasis on authenticity has clearly won out, as demonstrated by growing visitor numbers and a reportedly greater sense of historical sensitivity among visitors.[201] As Axel Klausmeier, director of the Berlin Wall Foundation, states, 'With the guiding principle of "no reconstruction", the visitor's trust in the authenticity of the site is not broken'.[202]

While the emphasis on historical accuracy and documentation remained central, the extended memorial site at Bernauer Straße appears to have met with widespread approval not least because it responded to criticism that it failed to offer a suitable site of mourning for victims and their families. Remembrance of victims was thus strongly personalized here during the second decade of unification through various means, notably the introduction of short midday services (daily, Tuesday to Friday) from 2005 in the Chapel of Reconciliation, at which the biography of a victim is read, and the creation of a 'Window of Commemoration' as part of the expanded site in 2010, as well as the erection of information boards where victims were killed. The 'Window of Commemoration', constructed out of the site's trademark Corten steel, contains 162 windows, 130 of which feature the name, dates and photograph of each identified victim of the Wall (see Figure 5.7). As Hope Harrison claims, this represents 'the new heart of the Berlin Wall Memorial', and is significant as a place of both private and public mourning.[203] While the extension of the site has resulted in an 'experiential landscape',[204] its premise resists that of the 'passive visitor'. As stated in the competition rubrics for the extended site, 'The visitor should not be presented with an easily consumable "ready meal" or seductive "Wall-Disneyland"'. Instead, visitors should be encouraged to interact with the multiple layers of the site and to 'play an active role in terms of deciphering and interpreting' what they see.[205] The opening of the first new section in May 2010 found the approval of the chair of the union of victims' associations (UOKG), Rainer Wagner,[206] and the opening of the main site in August 2011 took place to considerable acclaim in the press.[207] The contrast with press

Figure 5.7 Window of Commemoration (2010), Berlin Wall Memorial Site, Bernauer Straße, Berlin. Photograph by Anna Saunders.

reports from 1998 following the opening of the Kohlhoff & Kohlhoff design could hardly have been more stark, yet the extension of the site was founded largely on the aesthetics and principles of this initial design. Within little more than a decade, public and political expectations had shifted dramatically.

The remembrance of victims and the emphasis on documentation has also resulted in a more inclusive approach to commemoration, for in 2010 a steel column was unveiled in memory of eight border guards who lost their lives at the border. While this was highly controversial and carefully separated from the 'Window of Commemoration', it demonstrates once again how the passing of time can clearly influence remembrance politics, and – as was the case concerning memorialization at Soviet special camps – complicate previously clear-cut notions of 'victims' and 'perpetrators'. Indeed, this provided heightened contrast to the situation in the early post-*Wende* years, when memorials to dead border guards were removed, as recommended by the commission for political monuments in east Berlin in 1993 (see Chapter 2), which objected to their heroization in the GDR.[208] Such changes can be seen elsewhere. In the case of Egon Schultz, for instance, plaques were removed and schools and streets were renamed after the *Wende*. However, in the light of changing attitudes, in 2004 an initiative of former escape helpers, escapees and friends of Egon Schultz erected a new plaque in his memory, in order to both remember his death and correct GDR propaganda that he was shot by Western agents (he was, in fact, killed by a stray bullet from a fellow border guard).[209] Yet once again, we see here the ambiguity of the term 'victim', for Schultz was as much a victim of memory politics before and after 1989 as of the border itself. It seems, indeed, that memory politics has turned full circle since the early 1990s, and more controversial events are finding space in the memory landscape, increasingly highlighting the grey areas of history. This is further illustrated by a project led by the Berlin Wall Foundation in 2011, in which twenty-nine 'remembrance stelae' were erected along the Berlin-Brandenburg border for fifty victims of the border regime who died there. These include one in the Potsdam district of Sacrow to the victim Lothar Hennig, an IM killed in error by a border guard during a 'fugitive alert'.[210] Perhaps inevitably, the stele caused much controversy in the locality, with some residents reluctant to remember a Stasi informant in such a public way, yet as the Foundation's director claimed, the project was about communication and attaining acceptance on the ground, rather than pushing through top-down decisions and policies.[211] Indeed, as Maria Nooke, head of the project, stated, 'We don't undertake a moral evaluation of the victims, we don't divide them into good and evil'.[212] This memory marker thus demonstrates the complexities and multi-layered nature of remembering the victims of the Wall, which would have been very unlikely to find acceptance in the early years of unification.

Sensitivities clearly changed over the first two decades of unification, and the Kohlhoff & Kohlhoff monument demonstrates just how quickly a structure doomed to failure may, within a short period of time, invest new meaning into a broader site of remembrance. Now the centrepiece of Germany's principal Wall memorial site, it has moved from the periphery of Wall remembrance to its heart, and from a structure widely deemed too 'intellectual' and 'sterile' to one that draws high acclaim from victims, politicians, historians and tourists alike. Contrary to Schmidt and Feversham's observation in 1999 that – save for two remaining kilometres – the Berlin Wall inhabited the realm of 'shadow architecture', in which it was often visible only in unexpected ways (such as through the small yellow flower that grew in the former border strip),[213] its memorial presence has made a comeback in today's cityscape. Indeed, some have expressed concern that the booming memory of the Wall is now dominating the memory landscape of Berlin. As Thomas Loy observed in *Der Tagesspiegel*, this is the only event of twentieth-century history to warrant a 'history mile': 'The border is secured for posterity. But what came afterwards? And above all before? Why is there no "Second World War History Mile", no "GDR Memorial Site Concept"? And where is the First World War remembered?'[214] Similarly, Kaminsky has observed that memory of the Wall and its consequences has increasingly become the 'dominant memory of the second German dictatorship', overshadowing other traumatic experiences of dictatorship in the GDR, such as 17 June 1953.[215] To what extent this will continue to be the case remains to be seen.

Conclusion: Shifting Remembrance

The question of what should be remembered of the Berlin Wall clearly extends far beyond the question of what should be preserved, for its symbolism adopts contrasting meanings, depending on who is engaging in remembrance. The tourist industry, for instance, seeks to satisfy the popular demand for tangible remains of the Wall and the border regime in city centre locations. In contrast, interest groups representing victims and their families favour sites where they can mourn and remember the individuals who were killed, as well as those that underline the brutal nature of the SED regime and its abuse of human rights.

Politically, memory of the Wall is commonly evoked to highlight the moral bankruptcy and dubious legitimacy of the GDR, and to denounce communism more broadly as a system, while bolstering a sense of commitment to present-day democracy. Although parties on the right are more likely to engage in and actively promote Wall remembrance than those on the left, this has clearly become a widely accepted duty within political circles; the political diversity of the wreaths that are laid annually at the Bernauer Straße memorial serves as a prime example of this. Likewise, the official recognition – and cultivation – of this memory by local and national government proves fundamental to the process of German unification and to contemporary understandings of a 'normalized' national identity based on modern democratic ideals. For residents of the capital who had previously grown used to the 'normality' of division, however, such official narratives of the Wall often fail to acknowledge their own lived experiences, which often point towards the more complex and ambiguous characteristics of life in the divided city. Indeed, to quote Mühlberg's observation of east Germans in 2002, 'for the most part, their memory and "need to remember" have little to do with the official representation of their past'.[216]

What binds all interest groups is the increased need to remember as we move temporally further from 1989. It is, perhaps, no surprise that early attempts to engage with Wall remembrance were either designed to be transitory in nature or proved highly contentious, for there had been little time for reflection. Round anniversaries of 9 November 1989 or 13 August 1961, however, often provided the widespread impetus for memorial projects to develop. The growing need to create physical signs of remembrance has, however, come into increasing conflict with a city wanting to move forward and develop prime urban sites where the Wall once stood. As a result, larger projects intended for city centre sites have regularly become stages for political protests with much broader objectives than the specific memory in question. On the one hand, this has led to the need to seek compromises and adopt pragmatic solutions, as seen in decisions over the design for the Bernauer Straße memorial, which was chosen primarily for representing the path of least resistance. Over time, however, this initial compromise has influenced the development of the whole area, shaping the expansion of the site both conceptually and physically, particularly through its use of Corten steel. On the other hand, the politicization of city centre sites has meant that decisions regarding one site inevitably influence others, thus linking numerous sites in a complex web of remembrance. This is particularly evident regarding memory of the Berlin Wall, in which the fates of the Bernauer Straße memorial, the Freedom Memorial and the white crosses are not only interdependent, but also influenced by nearby monuments to the Holocaust and 17 June 1953. The development of the *Gesamtkonzept* indeed underlined the political need to coordinate memory of the Wall at a time when its remembrance was burgeoning.

The influence of other sites of memory is particularly evident concerning the aesthetics of remembering victimhood. Perhaps inevitably, victims' groups and memorial sites are likely to learn from tried and tested methods of commemoration in the capital; as Knischewski and Spittler state, 'this branch of German commemorative culture has the advantage over GDR remembrance of some twenty years in fund-raising and professionalization. Organizers of GDR commemorative events thus have a vested interest in benefiting from such experience'.[217] It is significant, for instance, that all the central sites discussed here name and often give a face to victims of the Wall, be it through the 'Window of Commemoration' at Bernauer Straße and the reading of victims' biographies at the Chapel of Reconciliation, or the naming of individuals at the Freedom Memorial, the white crosses and in Treptow. There are clear parallels here to numerous Holocaust memorial projects, such as the *Stolpersteine* or the 'Room of Names' at the Holocaust memorial (where, much like at the Chapel of Reconciliation, short biographies of Jewish victims are read out and projected onto the wall). While these examples of Holocaust remembrance emerged over fifty years after the event, the memorialization of Wall victims has been much faster to develop; not only has it benefitted from tried and tested structures, but it fits within the established (western) mode of cathartic remembrance. The very existence of a documentation or information centre to accompany a monument similarly reflects a long-standing tradition at concentration camp memorial sites and indeed the rise of the 'memorial museum'.[218] It is perhaps also little coincidence that the greater visibility of German victimhood since the millennium has coincided with a stronger voice for victims of the Wall. However, in contrast to contemporary Holocaust memorials often influenced by the notion of the countermonument, the majority of Wall memorials tend towards a more straightforward and emotional commemoration of victimhood. As with memorials to victims of the special camps and 1953, it seems that the immediacy of this past still demands more traditional and easily decipherable symbolism; the extensive use of crosses, for instance, bears parallels to monuments in Buchenwald and Fünfeichen. Once again, the use of Christian symbolism also serves to remember victims in a way that distances them from the atheistic GDR, yet in doing so, it proves reminiscent of Western modes of remembrance, particularly for victims of the Wall in the 1960s. Conversely, the presence of counter-memorial projects remains rare, and while the *Übergänge* installations touched on this mode of remembrance, they did not attempt to deal with the concept of victimhood, but rather the everyday experience of the Wall. Whereas temporal distance from the Holocaust appears to have provoked innovative memorial form, the relative proximity of this past, and associated memories, has tended to lead to easily decipherable symbolism.

Although the emphasis on traditional symbolism would seem to reconfirm fixed boundaries between victims and perpetrators, the passage of time has allowed for an increasingly complex understanding of these categories. Indeed, the erection of a stele to IM Lothar Hennig and the remembrance of border guards killed at Bernauer Straße indicate growing attempts to highlight the fuzzy boundaries between these two categories. Only more recently, however, have such memory markers been possible; shortly after unification they would doubtless have been too controversial to contemplate. Indeed, it is only with time and the gradual disappearance of the Wall that the very concept of Wall remembrance has become accepted. One of the most notable changes over time is the way in which the memorial site at Bernauer Straße has shifted in the public perception. Once considered too peripheral and emotionally void as a memorial site, it is now widely regarded as Berlin's central site for Wall remembrance. While the site is now much more comprehensive than it used to be, the emphasis on authenticity and documentation remains, and sets it apart from other more emotionally laden sites. With time, memory of the Wall is clearly being presented in more complex terms, rather than being fixed in increasingly simplified forms, as Assmann's shift from communicative to cultural memory would suggest. It is notable that communicative memory is still at work here, and often drives the will to produce more lasting forms of memory, whether led by a broad spectrum of memory activists (such as Pastor Fischer, Alexandra Hildebrandt or Gustav Rust) or interest groups (such as victims' organizations, political parties or preservationists). Once again, we see a clear overlap and two-way dialogue between these forms of memory: controversy surrounding the Freedom Memorial, for instance, provoked vociferous debate not only among historians and politicians, but also among ordinary Berliners, many of whom were forced to reflect on what life had been like in the shadow of the Wall. Above all, it seems that many of these monuments provoked a learning experience for those involved, thus seeing the development of communities of memory. As Gabi Dolff-Bonekämper commented of her involvement in the Bernauer Straße site: 'Together with the other participants I remember everything that has taken place ... we are forming a new, extended memory collective, a community of memory which has emerged through struggling and battling over how to deal with the Berlin Wall as a historical monument, not through solemn commemoration ceremonies'.[219] In the effort to create a more enduring cultural symbol, a community of memory emerged that was fed not only by communicative memories of the Wall, but also by memories of the battle to save it after 1989. Under different circumstances, the production of the monument in Treptow also brought about a learning experience for those involved, particularly the young soldiers who helped in its creation. In other instances, the bid to create lasting memory has caused more formal instances of *Aufarbeitung*; as a key player in the coordination of the *Gesamtkonzept*, for instance, the PDS/Die Linke was forced to reassess its relationship to this past, and in doing so demonstrate its responsibility to the present. The very existence of a *Gesamtkonzept* only seventeen years after the fall of the Wall perhaps best illustrates the rapidity with which Berlin began to negotiate this memory and sought ways of enabling a productive conjunction of communicative and cultural forms of memory. While there has been criticism of the 'totalizing' nature of this concept[220] – perhaps denoting a worrying desire to 'complete' remembrance in this sphere – the actions of the Centre for Political Beauty in 2014 demonstrated that Wall remembrance is likely to remain fundamental to the capital's self-understanding for at least the immediate future.

Notes

1. Marion Detjen, 'Die Mauer als politische Metapher', in *Die Mauer: Errichtung, Überwindung, Erinnerung*, ed. by Klaus-Dietmar Henke (Munich: dtv, 2011), pp. 426–39.
2. Frederick Baker, 'The Berlin Wall: Production, Preservation and Consumption of a 20th-Century Monument', *Antiquity*, 67 (1993), 709–33 (709).
3. 'Gesamtkonzept zur Erinnerung an die Berliner Mauer: Dokumentation, Information und Gedenken' (Berlin: Senatsverwaltung für Wissenschaft, Forschung und Kultur, 12 June 2006), p. 4, http://www.berliner-mauer-gedenkstaette.de/de/uploads/allgemeine_dokumente/gesamtkonzept_berliner_mauer.pdf (accessed 15 December 2017).
4. Polly Feversham and Leo Schmidt, *Die Berliner Mauer heute: The Berlin Wall Today* (Berlin: Verlag Bauwesen, 1999), p. 96.
5. Helmut Trotnow, 'Sag mir, wo die Spuren sind... Berlin und der Umgang mit der Geschichte der Berliner Mauer', in '*Asymmetrisch verflochtene*

Parallelgeschichte?' Die Geschichte der Bundesrepublik und der DDR in Ausstellungen, Museen und Gedenkstätten, ed. by Bernd Faulenbach and Franz-Josef Jelich (Essen: Klartext Verlag, 2005), pp. 157–67 (159).
6. Michael Diers, 'Die Mauer: Notizen zur Kunst- und Kulturgeschichte eines deutschen Symbol(l)Werks', *kritische berichte*, 20 (1992) 3, 58–74 (61).
7. Verheyen, *United City, Divided Memories?* p. 213.
8. Leo Schmidt, 'Vom Symbol der Unterdrückung zur Ikone der Befreiung – Auseinandersetzung, Verdrängung, Memorialisierung', in *Die Berliner Mauer: Vom Sperrwall zum Denkmal* (Bonn: Deutsches Nationalkomitee für Denkmalschutz, 2009), pp. 169–86 (171).
9. Sunil Manghani, *Image Critique and the Fall of the Berlin Wall* (Bristol: intellect, 2008), p. 36.
10. Baker, 'The Berlin Wall', p. 719.
11. Ibid., p. 720.
12. P. Schubert, 'Mehr Mauerreste in aller Welt als in Berlin', *Berliner Morgenpost*, 6 November 1999, p. 30.
13. Konrad H. Jarausch, Martin Sabrow and Hans-Hermann Hertle, 'Die Berliner Mauer – Erinnerung ohne Ort? Memorandum zur Bewahrung der Berliner Mauer als Erinnerungsort' (Potsdam: Zentrum für Zeithistorische Forschung, 2005), www.hsozkult.geschichte.hu-berlin.de/daten/.../2005_mauer_memorandum.doc *(accessed* 26 July 2011).
14. Baker, 'The Berlin Wall', p. 709.
15. Saskia Pütz, 'Die Endlichkeit der Freiheit, 1990', in *Kunst in der Stadt: Skulpturen in Berlin 1980–2000*, ed. by Hans Dickel and Uwe Fleckner (Berlin: Nicolaische Verlagsbuchhandlung, 2003), p. 193.
16. Eugen Blume, 'Hans Haacke', in *Die Endlichkeit der Freiheit. Berlin 1990: Ein Ausstellungsprojekt in Ost und West*, ed. by Wulf Herzogenrath, Joachim Sartorius and Christoph Tannert (Berlin: Hentrich, 1990), pp. 102–4.
17. Schmidt, 'Vom Symbol der Unterdrückung zur Ikone der Befreiung', p. 179.
18. Verheyen, *United City, Divided Memories?* pp. 249–50.
19. Jörn Hasselmann and Nele Pasch, 'Tausende wollen die Mauer retten', *Der Tagesspiegel*, 3 March 2013, http://www.tagesspiegel.de/berlin/tausende-wollen-die-mauer-retten/7869978.html (accessed 28 June 2013); Torben Waleczek, Maria Fiedler and Sidney Gennies, 'East Side Gallery: Teilstück in der Nacht überraschend abgerissen', *Der Tagesspiegel*, 27 March 2013, http://www.tagesspiegel.de/berlin/investor-schafft-fakten-east-side-gallery-teilstueck-in-der-nacht-ueberraschend-abgerissen/7990472.html (accessed 28 June 2013).
20. Ladd, *The Ghosts of Berlin*, p. 36.
21. Richard Schneider, Johannes Hildebrandt, Helmut Trotnow and Gabi Dolff-Bonekämper, 'Grenzanlage Bernauer Straße – Friedhof, Museum, Denkmal', in *Verfallen und vergessen oder aufgehoben und geschützt? Architektur und Städtebau der DDR – Geschichte, Bedeutung, Umgang, Erhaltung* (Bonn: Deutsches Nationalkomitee für Denkmalschutz, 1997), pp. 93–99 (97).

22. Gabi Dolff-Bonekämper, 'Denkmalschutz – Denkmalsetzung – Grenzmarkierung: Erinnerungsarbeit an der Berliner Mauer', in *Markierung des Mauerverlaufs. Hearing am 14. Juni 1995. Dokumentation* (Berlin: Senatsverwaltung für Bau- und Wohnungswesen, 1995), pp. 39–40 (39).
23. Ulrich Paul, 'Abriß-Stopp für Mauerreste aufgehoben', *Berliner Zeitung*, 22 April 1999.
24. Schmidt, 'Vom Symbol der Unterdrückung zur Ikone der Befreiung', p. 181.
25. Katja Füchsel, 'Weltkulturerbe Mauer heftig umstritten: Der Vorschlag erhält in Berlin mehr Ablehnung als Begeisterung', *Der Tagesspiegel*, 8 August 2003.
26. 'Gesamtkonzept zur Erinnerung an die Berliner Mauer', pp. 10–11.
27. *Markierung des Mauerverlaufs*, p. 7.
28. Ibid., p. 46.
29. '"Schwer emotional besetzt"', *Der Spiegel* (1995) 45, 80–85 (81).
30. Ibid.
31. *Markierung des Mauerverlaufs*, p. 8.
32. Christine Dankbar, 'Ein roter Strich soll den Verlauf der Mauer markieren', *Berliner Zeitung*, 21 February 1997.
33. H.-D. Döpmann, 'Erinnerung an die Mauer', *Berliner Zeitung*, 19 December 1997.
34. Ulrich Paul, 'Steine als Markiereung', *Berliner Zeitung*, 22 April 1999.
35. Dankbar, 'Ein roter Strich soll den Verlauf der Mauer markieren'.
36. Jarausch, Sabrow and Hertle, 'Die Berliner Mauer – Erinnerung ohne Ort?', p. 4.
37. 'Stellungnahme zum beabsichtigten Kunstwettbewerb Übergänge', Berlin, 2 September 1991 (Kiör-Büro).
38. gus, 'Denkmale erinnern an die Teilung Berlins', *Berliner Zeitung*, 11 September 1996, p. 26; Rainer Stache, 'Was 60 Kaninchen im Pflaster suchen', *Berliner Morgenpost*, 11 September 1996.
39. *Übergänge. Ausschreibung* (Berlin: Senatsverwaltung für Bauen, Wohnen und Verkehr, 1996), p. 89.
40. Ibid.
41. Ibid., p. 90.
42. M. Koltan, 'Hauptstadtkunst statt freier Kunst', *kunststadt. stadtkunst*, 40 (1996) Autumn, 10–17 (10).
43. *Übergänge. Ausschreibung*, p. 89.
44. Ibid.
45. Ibid., p. 90.
46. The prize winners were: Susanne Ahner (Heinrich-Heine-Straße), Gabriele Bausch (Invalidenstraße), (e.) Twin Gabriel (Bornholmer Straße), Thorsten Goldberg (Oberbaumbrücke), Heike Ponwitz (Sonnenallee), Karla Sachse (Chausseestraße) and Frank Thiel (Friedrichstraße/Checkpoint Charlie).
47. Stache, 'Was 60 Kaninchen im Pflaster suchen'.
48. This and one further paragraph have previously been published in Anna Saunders, 'Remembering Cold War Division: Wall Remnants and Border

Monuments in Berlin', *Journal of Contemporary European Studies*, 17 (2009) 1, 9–19, reprinted by permission of Taylor & Francis Ltd.
49. Uwe Aulich, 'Zwei Hände und ein Kinderspiel, wo einst der Staat endete', *Berliner Zeitung*, 3 December 1997.
50. Frédéric Bußmann, 'Leuchtkästen', 'Kaninchenzeichen' and 'Stein-Papier-Schere', in *Kunst in der Stadt*, ed. by Dickel and Fleckner, pp. 51–53, 100–101, 127–28 (128).
51. Schönfeld, 'Kritisches Denkzeichen und restauratives Denkmal', pp. 141–74 (158).
52. T. Pannen, 'Kaninchen an der Grenze der Erinnerung', *die tageszeitung*, 11 September 1996.
53. 'Übergänge: Protokoll der Preisgerichtssitzungen am 4. und 5. September 1996', Berlin, p. 16 (Kiör-Büro).
54. Feversham and Schmidt, *Die Berliner Mauer heute*, pp. 159–60.
55. Joachim Schlör, '"It Has to Go Away, but at the Same Time It Has to be Kept": The Berlin Wall and the Making of an Urban Icon', *Urban History*, 33 (2006) 1, 85–105 (88).
56. Gabriele Camphausen, 'Das Denkmal "Gedenkstätte Berliner Mauer"', in *Berliner Mauer: Gedenkstätte, Dokumentationszentrum und Versöhnungskapelle in der Bernauer Straße*, ed. by Verein 'Berliner Mauer – Gedenkstätte und Dokumentationszentrum' (Berlin: Jaron, 1999), pp. 18–22 (18).
57. Schneider et al., 'Grenzanlage Bernauer Straße – Friedhof, Museum, Denkmal', p. 97.
58. Gabi Dolff-Bonekämper, 'Grenz-Fall: Die Berliner Mauer als Denkmalthema', 1997, Deutsches Nationalkomitee für Denkmalschutz website, http://www.dnk.de/Im_Fokus/n2372?node_id=2372&from_node=2402&beitrag_id=374 (accessed 1 August 2011).
59. Trotnow, 'Sag mir, wo die Spuren sind…', p. 161; Ulrike Plewnia, 'Berliner Geschichtsverlust', *Focus* (1994) 38, http://www.focus.de/politik/deutschland/zeitgeschichte-berliner-geschichtsverlust_aid_148776.html (accessed 1 August 2011).
60. Werner van Bebber, 'Diepgen will Teile der Mauer neu aufstellen lassen', *Der Tagesspiegel*, 19 June 2011, p. 10.
61. Gabriele Camphausen and Manfred Fischer, 'Die Bürgerschaftliche Durchsetzung der Gedenkstätte an der Bernauer Straße', in *Die Mauer: Errichtung, Überwindung, Erinnerung*, ed. by Henke, pp. 355–76 (355).
62. Willy Brandt, 'Rede am 10. November 1989 vor dem Rathaus Schöneberg', www.bwbs.de/Beitraege/78.html (accessed 1 August 2011).
63. André Schmitz, '20 Jahre Mauerfall', in *Jahrbuch für Kulturpolitik 2009. Thema: Erinnerungskulturen und Geschichtspolitik*, ed. by Bernd Wagner (Essen: Klartext Verlag, 2009), pp. 117–22 (119).
64. Schneider et al., 'Grenzanlage Bernauer Straße – Friedhof, Museum, Denkmal', p. 98.
65. Baker, 'The Berlin Wall', p. 728.
66. Dolff-Bonekämper, 'Grenz-Fall'.
67. Gabi Dolff-Bonekämper, 'Im Niemandsland', *Frankfurter Allgemeine Zeitung*, 25 May 1994, p. 39.

68. Camphausen, 'Das Denkmal "Gedenkstätte Berliner Mauer"', p. 20.
69. 'Architektonisch-künstlerischer Ideenwettbewerb. Gedenkstätte Berliner Mauer in der Bernauer Straße. Ausschreibung', Deutsches Historisches Museum (Berlin, April 1994), kindly made available by Günter Schlusche, Planungs- und Baukoordination, Gedenkstätte Berliner Mauer.
70. Ibid., p. 3.
71. Plewnia, 'Berliner Geschichtsverlust'.
72. Renate Oschlies, 'Ein Museum und die Sorgen der Maueropfer', *Berliner Zeitung*, 13 May 1998.
73. 'Architektonisch-künstlerischer Ideenwettbewerb', p. 20.
74. Dolff-Bonekämper, 'Grenz-Fall'.
75. 'Architektonisch-künstlerischer Ideenwettbewerb', p. 23.
76. Ibid., p. 243.
77. Ibid., pp. 12 and 19.
78. Hilde Léon, 'Mauerseligkeit', *Der Tagesspiegel*, 31 August 1995.
79. Ulrike Plewnia, '"Bedeutung verkannt"', *Focus* (1994) 38, http://www.focus.de/politik/deutschland/deutschland-bedeutung-verkannt_aid_148777.html (accessed 1 August 2011).
80. Mechthild Küpper, 'Immer Ärger um die Mauer', *Frankfurter Allgemeine Zeitung*, 21 February 2009, p. 8.
81. ua/cri, 'Neuer Mauerabriß: Pfarrer stellt den Senat bloß', *Berliner Zeitung*, 23 April 1997; U. Paul, 'Der frühere Grenzstreifen wird mit System zerlöchert', *Berliner Zeitung*, 28 April 1997.
82. Uwe Aulich, 'Massengräber – alles nu rein Schwindel?', *Berliner Zeitung*, 24 May 1997.
83. Brigitte Schmiemann, '20 Jahre Mauerfall', *Die Welt*, 10 February 2009.
84. Camphausen, 'Das Denkmal "Gedenkstätte Berliner Mauer"', p. 21.
85. Uwe Aulich, 'Senat ebnet Weg für Mauergedenkstätte', *Berliner Zeitung*, 6 August 1997.
86. Christine Richter, 'Diepgen: Mauergedenkstätte muß "mentaler Stolperstein" sein', *Berliner Zeitung*, 14 August 1998.
87. Thomas Eisenkrätzer, '"Ich vermisse alles: Hier wird die Geschichte verschönt"', *Berliner Zeitung*, 15 August 1998.
88. Christine Richter, 'Debatte über Mahnmale', *Berliner Zeitung*, 15 August 1998.
89. Jan Thomsen, 'Historiker plädieren für zentralen Ort des Mauer-Gedenkens', *Berliner Zeitung*, 15 November 2004.
90. Thomas Rogalla, 'Mensch, wo stand den die Mauer?', *Berliner Zeitung*, 5 November 2004.
91. Bernhard Schulz, 'Das Kreuz mit der Erinnerung', *Der Tagesspiegel*, 9 November 2004.
92. Christine Richter, 'Architekten lehnen neue Inschrift an der Mauer-Gedenkstätte ab', *Berliner Zeitung*, 12 August 1998.
93. Patrick Major, *Behind the Berlin Wall: East Germany and the Frontiers of Power* (Oxford: Oxford University Press, 2010), p. 280.
94. Oschlies, 'Ein Museum und die Sorgen der Maueropfer'.
95. Camphausen, 'Das Denkmal "Gedenkstätte Berliner Mauer"', p. 22.

96. Gerd Knischewski and Ulla Spittler, 'Remembering the Berlin Wall: The Wall Memorial Ensemble Bernauer Straße', *German Life and Letters*, 59 (2006) 2, 280–93 (285).
97. http://www.berliner-mauer-gedenkstaette.de/de/entstehungsgeschichte-211.html (accessed 2 August 2011).
98. Knischewski and Spittler, 'Remembering the Berlin Wall', p. 286.
99. Sebastian Richter, 'Die Mauer in der deutschen Erinnerungskultur', in *Die Mauer*, ed. by Henke, pp. 252–66 (263).
100. Philipp Gessler, 'Eine Mauer aus Kränzen', *die tageszeitung*, 14 August 2001, p. 19.
101. Richter, 'Die Mauer in der deutschen Erinnerungskultur', p. 265. Emphasis in original.
102. Sabine Gundlach, 'Zeitreise zu den Maueropfern', *Die Welt*, 25 July 2005.
103. Martin Schönfeld, 'Sichtbare Zeichen im öffentlichen Raum', *kunststadt, stadtkunst*, 52 (2005), 12.
104. For the most recent review of the project, see Hans-Hermann Hertle and Maria Nooke, 'Die Todesopfer an der Berliner Mauer 1961–1989', Potsdam/Berlin, July 2011 (updated August 2017), http://www.chronik-der-mauer.de/system/files/dokument_pdf/2017_08_08_Hertle_Nooke_Berliner_Mauer_140_Todesopfer_FINAL.pdf (accessed 20 December 2017). See also Hans-Hermann Hertle and Maria Nooke (eds), *Die Todesopfer an der Berliner Mauer 1961–1989: Ein Biographisches Handbuch* (Berlin: Ch. Links, 2009).
105. Christine Brecht, 'Jörg Hartmann' and 'Lothar Schleusener', in *Die Todesopfer an der Berliner Mauer*, ed. by Hertle and Nooke, pp. 224–28 (228).
106. Stefan Jacobs, 'Das Leben geht nicht weiter', *Der Tagesspiegel*, 14 March 2006, p. 10.
107. '"Einfach umgemäht"', *Der Spiegel* (1995) 37, 90–91.
108. Barbara Zibler, 'Kinder als Opfer der Mauer', in *Thomas Brussig. Am kürzeren Ende der Sonnenallee. Lehrerheft*, ed. by Günther Gutknecht and Brigitte Rapp (Biberach: Krapp & Gutknecht, 2001), pp. 71–77 (75).
109. Claudia Fuchs, 'Die Suche nach der Wahrheit', *Berliner Zeitung*, 6/7 November 1999, p. 29.
110. Sigrid Averesch, 'Ex-DDR-Grenzsoldat weist Totschlagvorwurf zurück', *Berliner Zeitung*, 13 November 1997.
111. BVV Treptow, Beschluß Nr. III/1121, 26 November 1997. My thanks go to Barbara Zibler (Museum Treptow-Köpenick) for making these documents available.
112. Bezirksamt Treptow, 'Kunst-am-Bau Wettbewerbsausschreibung: Gedenktafel für Maueropfer', Berlin, 30 June 1999.
113. Ibid., p. 1.
114. Ibid., p. 2.
115. Bezirksamt Treptow, 'Künstlerischer Wettbewerb "Maueropfer": Bericht der Vorprüfung', Berlin, 13 September 1999, p. 6.
116. Conversation with artists Jan Skuin and Rüdiger Roehl, 28 October 2010.
117. Conversation with Barbara Zibler (Museum Treptow-Köpenick), 28 October 2010.

118. Abgeordnetenhaus von Berlin, 'Plenarprotokoll 12/87', 22 June 1995, p. 7,486.
119. Uwe Aulich, '16 Mauerkreuze sollen zum Reichstag zurückkehren', *Berliner Zeitung*, 2 November 1995.
120. Senatsverwaltung für Stadtentwicklung, 'Feierliche Übergabe des Erinnerungsortes "Mauerkreuze"', Berlin, 17 June 2003, http://www.stadtentwicklung.berlin.de/aktuell/pressebox/includes/archiv/arch_0306/nachricht1292.html (accessed 24 December 2010).
121. Wolfgang Thierse, 'Deutscher Bundestag. Pressemitteilung', Webarchiv des Deutschen Bundestages, 17 June 2003, http://webarchiv.bundestag.de/archive/2006/0807/aktuell/presse/2003/pz_0306173.html (accessed 3 August 2011).
122. Lothar Heinke, 'Die Rückseite des Gedenkens', *Der Tagesspiegel*, 22 June 2003, p. 10.
123. Thierse, 'Deutscher Bundestag. Pressemitteilung'.
124. E.g. ToKi, 'Bloß nicht erinnern…', *BZ*, 6 October 2005; Katleen Fietz, 'Die Nervensäge mit Deutschlandtick', *die tageszeitung*, 25 April 2008.
125. Heinke, 'Die Rückseite des Gedenkens'.
126. ToKi, 'Bloß nicht erinnern…'; xskh, 'Mauerkreuze am Reichstag bleiben stehen', *Berliner Zeitung*, 7 October 2003.
127. xskh, 'Mauerkreuze am Reichstag bleiben stehen'.
128. Tomas Kittan, 'Pate der Kreuze', *BZ*, 14 July 2010.
129. Fietz, 'Die Nervensäge mit Deutschlandtick'.
130. Stefan Berg and John Goetz, 'Der Mann, der Berlin blamiert', *Spiegel Online*, 31 March 2008, http://www.spiegel.de/politik/deutschland/protest-am-reichstag-der-mann-der-berlin-blamiert-a-543460.html (accessed 29 September 2016).
131. Fietz, 'Die Nervensäge mit Deutschlandtick'.
132. Conversation with Rainer Klemke, Museums- und Gedenkstättenreferent, Senatskanzlei Berlin, 27 October 2010.
133. Kittan, 'Pate der Kreuze'.
134. Abgeordnetenhaus von Berlin, 'Antrag der Fraktion der CDU', Drucksache 16/0236, 2007.
135. CDU/CSU-Bundestagsfraktion, 'Gedenken an die Opfer der Berliner Mauer: Positionspapier des Vorstands der CDU-CSU-Bundestagsfraktion', 10 September 2007, http://www.cducsu.de/Titel__text_interview_gedenken_an_die_opfer_der_berliner_mauer/TabID__6/SubTabID__9/InhaltTypID__3/InhaltID__5943/Inhalte.aspx (accessed 30 July 2011).
136. Kittan, 'Pate der Kreuze'.
137. '48. Jahrestag des Mauerbaus', 2009, Kai Wegner (CDU) webpage, http://www.kai-wegner.de/index.php?option=com_content&view=article&id=103&Itemid=99 (accessed 2 August 2011).
138. Gustav Rust, 2010. Protest flyer available at original white crosses memorial.
139. 'The Victims at the EU's Borders', http://www.politicalbeauty.com/wall.html (accessed 3 October 2016).
140. Ibid.

141. '2009 weiter steigende Besucherzahlen in zeitgeschichtlichen Museen und Gedenkstätten', Press Release, Berlin, 9 December 2010, http://www.berlin.de/sen/kultur/presse/archiv/20101209.1200.322353.html (accessed 8 August 2011).
142. Trotnow, 'Sag mir, wo die Spuren sind...', p. 162.
143. Schmidt, 'Vom Symbol der Unterdrückung zur Ikone der Befreiung', p. 182.
144. 'Gesamtkonzept zur Erinnerung an die Berliner Mauer', p. 8.
145. Carsten Volkery, 'Mehr Disneyland wagen', *Spiegel Online*, 29 October 2004, http://www.spiegel.de/politik/deutschland/0,1518,325446,00.html (accessed 18 September 2008).
146. Cited in Sybille Frank, *Der Mauer um die Wette gedenken* (Frankfurt am Main: Campus, 2009), p. 202.
147. Susanne Kailitz, 'Zwist am Checkpoint Charlie', *Das Parlament*, 11 July 2005.
148. Stefan Schulz, 'Die Mauer ist weg', *Berliner Morgenpost*, 6 July 2005, p. 11.
149. Dirk Westphal, 'Mauergedenkstätte Checkpoint Charlie?', *Welt am Sonntag*, 14 November 2004.
150. Thomas Loy, 'Botschaft mit Kreuzen', *Der Tagesspiegel*, 2 November 2004.
151. Alexandra Hildebrandt, *Die Freiheit verpflichtet: Das Freiheitsmahnmal am Platz Checkpoint Charlie*. Sozialwissenschaften 34 (Berlin: Technische Universität, 2005), p. 27.
152. In Frank, *Der Mauer um die Wette gedenken*, p. 202.
153. This claim was made on one of the information boards at the open-air exhibition about the Wall, erected on Friedrichstraße in 2006.
154. Hildebrandt, *Die Freiheit verpflichtet*.
155. Anna Reimann, 'Mauer-Mahnmal im Touristenrummel', *Spiegel Online*, 31 October 2004, http://www.spiegel.de/politik/deutschland/0,1518,3258 79,00.html (accessed 18 September 2008).
156. kh/schoe/wick, 'Flierl plant Museum des Kalten Krieges', *Berliner Morgenpost*, 6 July 2005, p. 12.
157. Leo Schmidt, 'The Berlin Wall: A Landscape of Memory', in *On Both Sides of the Wall: Preserving Monuments and Sites of the Cold War Era*, ed. by Leo Schmidt and Henriette von Preuschen (Berlin: Westkreuz, 2005), pp. 11–17 (16).
158. As stated on one of the information boards at the open-air exhibition about the Wall, erected on Friedrichstraße in 2006.
159. Konrad Jahr-Weidauer, 'Kreuze weg – Bürgerrechtler empört', *Berliner Morgenpost*, 7 July 2005, p. 16.
160. In Loy, 'Botschaft mit Kreuzen'.
161. Petra Ahne, 'Getünchtes zum Erinnern', *Berliner Zeitung*, 9 November 2004.
162. Schönfeld, 'Kritisches Denkzeichen und restauratives Denkmal', pp. 161–62.
163. Claudia Fuchs, 'Ein Pater soll die Kreuze segnen', *Berliner Zeitung*, 4 July 2005, p. 19. For further information on the Rosa Luxemburg memorial, see

Anna Saunders, 'The Luxemburg Legacy: Concretising the Remembrance of a Controversial Heroine?', *German History*, 29 (2011) 1, 36–56.
164. Uwe Aulich, 'Mauergedenken à la CDU', *Berliner Zeitung*, 7 July 2005, p. 21.
165. Schmidt, 'The Berlin Wall'; 'Zitate zum Mauer-Mahnmal', *Berliner Morgenpost*, 4 July 2005, p. 12.
166. In Andrea Puppe, '"Hier wird Geschichte verfälscht"', *Die Welt*, 12 December 2004.
167. Tobias Miller, 'Deutsche Lösung', *Berliner Zeitung*, 5 June 2004, p. 23.
168. In Michael Sontheimer, 'Zweiter Tod', *Der Spiegel* (2005) 27, 50.
169. 'Bagger gegen Lügen', *Neues Deutschland*, 5 July 2005.
170. Nikolaus Bernau, 'Kreuze und Stelen', *Berliner Zeitung*, 13 January 2005.
171. Jarausch, Sabrow and Hertle, 'Die Berliner Mauer – Erinnerung ohne Ort?'.
172. Anna Kaminsky, '"…es gibt gute Gründe, den 13. August nicht aus dem Auge zu verlieren"', *Deutschland Archiv* (2011) 7, http://www.bpb.de/geschichte/zeitgeschichte/deutschlandarchiv/53543/erinnerung-an-die-berliner-mauer?p=all (accessed 29 September 2016).
173. Schönfeld, 'Kritisches Denkzeichen und restauratives Denkmal', pp. 141–74.
174. Tobias Miller and Thomas Rogalla, 'Das Geschäft mit der Mauer: Senatoren kritisieren Kunstaktion', *Berliner Zeitung*, 11 October 2004.
175. In Marc Neller, '"Die Spuren der Teilung fehlen uns heute"', *Der Tagesspiegel*, 6 November 2004.
176. Schönfeld, 'Kritisches Denkzeichen und restauratives Denkmal', p. 160.
177. In Sontheimer, 'Zweiter Tod'. It should be noted that private monuments do not always provoke controversy, especially if they are recognized as a private concern. The erection in 2009 of a 'Mauer-Denkmal' by sculptor Stephan Balkenhol outside the Axel-Springer-Haus and financed by *BILD* (in memory of both the twentieth anniversary of the fall of the Wall and the fiftieth anniversary of the laying of the foundation stone of his publishing house in Berlin) caused no unusual political or public discussion.
178. Hildebrandt, *Die Freiheit verpflichtet*, p. 5.
179. Frank, *Der Mauer um die Wette gedenken*, p. 202.
180. Christine Richter, 'Berliner wollen keine weitere Mauer-Gedenkstätte', *Berliner Zeitung*, 20 November 2004.
181. Indeed, Hildebrandt proclaimed at the opening of her memorial that 'we are bringing a counterpart to the Holocaust Memorial', cited in Hope M. Harrison, 'The Berlin Wall and Its Reconstruction as a Site of Memory', *German Politics and Society*, 29 (2011) 2, 78–106 (86).
182. Bernau, 'Kreuze und Stelen'; Sontheimer, 'Zweiter Tod'.
183. 'Das Kreuz mit der Mauer', *Frankfurter Allgemeine Sonntagszeitung*, 7 November 2004.
184. Schönfeld, 'Kritisches Denkzeichen und restauratives Denkmal', p, 160.
185. 'Gesamtkonzept zur Erinnerung an die Berliner Mauer', p. 12.
186. Deutscher Bundestag, Drucksache 15/3378 and 15/3379.
187. Deutscher Bundestag, Drucksache 15/4795.

188. '"Das ist sehr berührend"', *Der Tagesspiegel*, 14 August 2011, p. 9.
189. 'Gesamtkonzept zur Erinnerung an die Berliner Mauer', p. 3.
190. Ibid., p. 17.
191. Ibid., p. 15.
192. Rainer Klemke, 'Das Gesamtkonzept Berliner Mauer', in *Die Mauer*, ed. by Henke, pp. 377–93 (377).
193. Deutscher Bundestag, Drucksache 16/0236.
194. Klemke, 'Das Gesamtkonzept Berliner Mauer', p. 387.
195. Richter, 'Die Mauer in der deutschen Erinnerungskultur', p. 265.
196. www.berlin.de/mauer.
197. 'Gesamtkonzept zur Erinnerung an die Berliner Mauer', p. 17.
198. For more detail on this second competition, see Harrison, 'The Berlin Wall and Its Resurrection as a Site of Memory'.
199. Conversation with Pastor Manfred Fischer, 27 October 2010.
200. Gabi Dolff-Bonekämper, 'Denkmalschutz für die Mauer', *Die Denkmalpflege* (2000) 1, 33–40.
201. Schmidt, 'Vom Symbol der Unterdrückung zur Ikone der Befreiung', p. 184; Axel Klausmeier, 'Die Gedenkstätte Berliner Mauer an der Bernauer Straße', in *Die Mauer*, ed. by Henke, pp. 394–406 (405).
202. Klausmeier, 'Die Gedenkstätte Berliner Mauer an der Bernauer Straße', p. 399. The only exception to the policy of authenticity was the addition of a watchtower to the monument in 2009. Although this was part of the original design, the original watchtower could no longer be returned to this position; on the discovery of an identical tower from a different part of the wall, however, it was installed in its stead. Information from e-mail correspondence with Günter Schlusche, Stiftung Berliner Mauer, 12 August 2011.
203. Harrison, 'The Berlin Wall and Its Resurrection as a Site of Memory'.
204. Sybille Frank, 'Der Mauer um die Wette gedenken', *Aus Politik und Zeitgeschichte*, 61 (2011) 31–34, 47-54 (54).
205. Schmidt, 'Vom Symbol der Unterdrückung zur Ikone der Befreiung', p. 186.
206. Klemke, 'Das Gesamtkonzept Berliner Mauer', p. 393.
207. See, for example, Alexander Cammann, 'Stadtlandschaft mit Todesstreifen', *Die Zeit*, 11 August 2011, p. 15; Marijke Engel, Thomas Rogalla and Thorkit Treichel, 'Ein Ort zum Nachdenken', *Berliner Zeitung*, 15 August 2011, p. 17.
208. Kommission zum Umgang mit den politischen Denkmälern der Nachkriegszeit im ehemaligen Ost-Berlin, 'Bericht' (Berlin, 15 February 1993), p. 75.
209. Kaminsky, *Orte des Erinnerns*, p. 94.
210. Hertle and Nooke (eds), *Die Todesopfer an der Berliner Mauer*, pp. 371–74.
211. Thorsten Metzner, 'Schwieriges Erinnern – besonders in Potsdam', *Potsdamer Neueste Nachrichten*, 8 August 2011, www.pnn.de/potsdam/557967/ (accessed 23 August 2012).
212. Ibid.
213. Feversham and Schmidt, *Die Berliner Mauer heute*, p. 132.

214. Thomas Loy, 'Lücken der Erinnerung', *Der Tagesspiegel*, 23 May 2010.
215. Kaminsky, '"…es gibt gute Gründe, den 13. August nicht aus dem Auge zu verlieren"'.
216. Dietrich Mühlberg, 'Vom langsamen Wandel der Erinnerung an die DDR', in *Verletztes Gedächtnis: Erinnerungskultur und Zeitgeschichte im Konflikt*, ed. by Konrad H. Jarausch and Martin Sabrow (Frankfurt am Main: Campus, 2002), pp. 217–51 (217).
217. Knischewski and Spittler, 'Remembering the Berlin Wall', p. 291.
218. Paul Williams, *Memorial Museums: The Global Rush to Commemorate Atrocities* (Oxford; New York: Berg, 2007).
219. Gabi Dolff-Bonekämper, 'Conservation as Found – Erhalten wie vorgefunden?', in *Denkmalpflege für die Berliner Mauer: Die Konservierung eines unbequemen Bauwerks*, ed. by Axel Klausmeier and Günter Schlusche (Berlin: Ch. Links Verlag, 2011), pp. 82–92 (91).
220. Jonathan Bach, 'The Berlin Wall after the Berlin Wall: Site into Sight', *Memory Studies*, 9 (2016) 1, 48–62 (58).

Chapter 6

Remembering the 'Peaceful Revolution' and German Unity

The East German demonstrations of autumn 1989 and the unification of Germany on 3 October 1990 mark one of the major watersheds in contemporary German history, dividing the past into a clear 'before' and 'after'. Even amidst the uncertainties of 1989, this period was lived as a historically significant moment; the organizers of the mass demonstration in Berlin on 4 November, for example, collected together the banners and posters brought to the demonstration and later delivered them to the Museum of German History.[1] The demonstrations, the fall of the Wall, the elections of March 1990 and the arrival of the DM are all moments that are indelibly inscribed on the memories of east Germans who lived through events. While 1989/90 thus marked the end of the GDR, it also heralded the beginning of a new era, one commonly dubbed the 'Berlin Republic'. The notion of beginnings is particularly important to the concept of memorialization, for as social scientists have found, the most significant part of a society's past is its beginning.[2] Founding myths are, thus, typically marked in memorial and ritual ways, and as Eviatar Zerubavel states, beginnings hold a 'special mnemonic status' marked by 'disproportionately high representation': of the 191 national calendars he examined, 176 officially celebrated one or more national holidays that commemorated their spiritual 'origins'.[3] It is, thus, perhaps little surprise that from 1990 onwards, Germany's new national holiday became 3 October, the 'Day of German Unity'. The fact that the more emotionally charged day of 9 November continues to be widely celebrated, especially on round anniversaries, also marks the popular importance of this memory. As this chapter demonstrates, however, the commemoration of Germany's most recent caesura has proved far from straightforward, for it is marked as much by continuity as by change; the concept of a *Stunde Null* (zero hour), as in 1945, is clearly not appropriate, for although lives were turned upside down in eastern Germany, many western citizens experienced little direct change, as the constitution and institutional structures of the West were largely transferred to the East. This raises many questions for the memory landscape: should commemoration and memorialization of 1989/90 mark both continuity and change? Should the so-called 'peaceful revolution' be understood as a national and an eastern occasion? Should 1989 and 1990 be remembered together?

On the surface, the so-called 'super memory year' of 2009 displayed few mnemonic tensions, with the celebrations on the twentieth anniversary of the fall of the Berlin Wall appearing self-confident and jubilant. This anniversary year also saw numerous weighty publications on the demonstrations of 1989,[4] a large open-air exhibition on Alexanderplatz, a wide range of exhibitions documenting the demonstrations, the mounting of information pillars at notable sites of the revolution in Berlin, as well as numerous regional events and a whole host of associated websites.[5] Celebrations in 2014 for the twenty-fifth anniversary were equally self-confident, with events and exhibitions taking place throughout the year.[6] The attempt, however, to erect a representative, national monument to the events of 1989/90 in Berlin by 2009 – or indeed 2014 – failed. The debate concerning a central Freedom and Unity Monument (discussed below) demonstrated that memory of this period was far from homogeneous, and that 1989/90 was clearly still, in Jarausch's words, an 'emergent site of memory'.[7] Unlike memory of the Wall, which is fixed in specific locations and tied to two central dates, memory of 1989/90 is much more heterogeneous, with a whole host of associated dates, locations, values, actors and interpretations; as Kowalczuk states, 'The revolution of 1989 cannot be narrated or explained mono-causally'.[8]

The defining dates and locations of the revolution of 1989 are clearly linked, yet the fact that many events formed part of a causal chain means there is no single, overriding memory. While media representations of autumn 1989 invariably fall back on images of the fall of the Wall, which were both plentiful and dramatic, numerous earlier events prepared the ground for this breakthrough: widespread regional demonstrations, protests on the fortieth anniversary of the GDR, the foundation of citizens' rights groups such as 'Neues Forum', the opening of Hungary's border, and the uncovering of GDR election fraud in May 1989. Longer-term influences, such as Gorbachev's policies of glasnost and perestroika, or the economic bankruptcy and environmental devastation of the GDR, also bear considerable weight. Later events, such as the formation of national and regional round tables, the storming of the Stasi headquarters in January 1990, the elections of 18 March, the 'two-plus-four' negotiations, currency union in July, and finally unification on 3 October, all add a further layer of complexity. While November 1989 is widely regarded as the key period, the lack of a single location or date means, inevitably, that attempts to commemorate this past in concrete form cannot easily represent this past in its complexity. Jarausch saw these multiple events to impede the development of a stable memory culture: 'The formation of memory is paradoxically hindered by the diversity of potential connecting factors, each of which additionally refers to different symbols'.[9]

Questions concerning the iconic locations and dates of 1989 are perhaps less important than the question of which values from 1989 commemorative activities seek to promote. The slogan 'We are the people', chanted by demonstrators in October and early November, represents the first central value of this period: the fight for freedom and democracy. Civil rights activists who initiated the demonstrations had made the active decision to stay in the GDR to effectuate change, in contrast to the thousands who were fleeing the country. As some banners at the time read (quoting Christa Wolf's speech on Alexanderplatz on 4 November), 'Imagine it is socialism, and no-one is running away';[10] for these demonstrators, the notion of a reformed socialism was still a real and positive alternative, and unification was not on the agenda. As Dorothee Wierling states, 'It was only in retrospect that we identified 9 November with the end of the GDR. On the day itself, that was by no means clear'.[11] By 20 November, however, the new slogan 'We are *one* people' began to emerge, and the masses began to demand unification, the buying power of the DM and with it the end of socialism.[12] The fall of the Wall thus brought about a *'Wende* within the *Wende'*, in which the values of the original movement were overtaken by the will of the masses, leading to disappointment and disillusionment among some activists. What, then, should be remembered: the initial battle for freedom and democracy or the popular desire for unification? Or should both be remembered together? The latter was clearly only possible after the former, yet the two sets of values did not always exist in harmony with each other.

The different demands associated with 1989 inevitably also raise the question as to who should be remembered and who should partake in remembrance. Unlike elsewhere, no obvious national hero figure emerged from this period, such as Lech Wałęsa in Poland or Mikhail Gorbachev in the Soviet Union; instead, one of the lasting images of this period is that of a floundering Günter Schabowski at the news conference on 9 November 1989, juxtaposed with images of jubilant crowds later that night. While Sabrow puts this down to a 'post-heroic remembrance culture',[13] the very fact that the original reform movement was overtaken by the popular desire for unification meant that those activists who stuck to the ideal of a 'third way' no longer represented the popular will. Although Helmut Kohl was viewed in heroic terms by some, and dominated this period in many ways, his role as 'Chancellor of Unity' came only after the fall of the Wall, and his status as a Westerner prevented true identification in the East. It is thus little surprise that a suggestion in 2010 by the CDU to erect a monument to Kohl in Dresden was rejected as unsuitable, largely because Kohl himself vetoed the suggestion.[14] The different groups of historical actors – civil rights activists, mass demonstrators, fugitives, as well as SED reformers – means that there were not only numerous historical subjects, but that different mnemonic communities exist today. Who, then, has the right to remember this period officially? Whose memories bear more weight? Official government celebrations have often seen a dominance of Western speakers at such events; the Bundestag's plans to remember the tenth anniversary of 9 November, for instance, received widespread criticism because not a single civil rights activist was on the original list of speakers,[15] and in Leipzig, where from 2001 an annual 'democracy speech' was initiated on 9 October, the majority of speakers have been west German politicians, who lecture an east German audience on their achievements.[16] It is perhaps for this reason that, as Jarausch claimed in 2009, 'the memory of these dramatic events among the German population appears to be weak'.[17] Indeed, experiences of high unemployment and a shrinking population in the eastern *Länder* led to disillusionment among many, not only among former activists, and contributed to election successes of the PDS/Die Linke in the east. It is perhaps no surprise that the tradition of the 'Monday demonstration' was subsequently adopted as a form of protest against numerous other social issues, such as *Hartz IV*, education cuts, the expansion of Schönefeld airport and, more recently, immigration; as Ralph Jessen finds, this tradition of exercising the right to free speech is perhaps the most effective monument to the demonstrations of 1989, rather than any fixed, material symbol.[18]

A final difficulty for the commemoration of 1989/90 lies in the fact that it does not easily fit into a clear national narrative. There are three interrelated issues here. First, 9 November is a difficult historical date, representing not only the fall of the Wall, but also the proclamation of the republic on 9 November 1918, Hitler's failed putsch on 9 November 1923, and most significantly the pogrom against the Jews on 9 November 1938.[19] This confluence of events on 9 November highlights a second problem: attempts to integrate 1989/90 into a more positive history of freedom and democracy, marked by the revolutions of 1848 and even 1918, are largely overshadowed by the darker history of twentieth-century Germany, in which the commemoration of victimhood is highly prevalent. As Sabrow observes, 'the joy over 1989/90 cannot offset the pain over 1933/45';[20] similarly, theologian Richard Schröder notes 'the inability of Germans to rejoice'.[21] Third, attempts to concretize this memory follow an aesthetic tradition that developed as a direct result of efforts to commemorate the victims of the Holocaust, seen most prominently in countermonuments and ephemeral *Denkzeichen*. Celebratory monuments to 1989/90 must thus find a new acceptable form, which treads carefully between the dominant aesthetics of Holocaust memorials and the jubilatory propaganda of GDR monuments.

There is little doubt that difficulties in remembering 1989/90 also exist today because the events themselves are still so recent. As David Lowenthal somewhat traditionally states, 'the memorial act implies termination. We seldom erect monuments to ongoing events or to people still alive. Hence our queasiness when *we* are commemorated'.[22] While some monuments clearly are erected to living figures today, and the countermonument questions the notion of termination, the contemporary nature of events often leads to heightened emotions and diverse understandings, and it is little surprise that the early 1990s witnessed very few attempts to memorialize the events of 1989. Interpretations of 1989/90 have far from reached a consensus, as demonstrated by debates over whether the term *Wende* or 'peaceful revolution' should most appropriately denote the autumn of 1989.[23] It is notable, however, that with time, attempts to concretize the past have increased. While the tenth anniversary of 1999 witnessed widespread celebrations and events, there were few attempts to instil central concrete symbols; the most visible marker in Berlin, for example, was the massive banner that hung on the Haus des Lehrers building on Alexanderplatz, reading 'We were the people', an attempt to provoke Berliners to think about the relationship between their actions in 1989 and ten years later.[24] It has largely only been in more recent years that permanent structures have been proposed and indeed constructed, and although a number of older, West German monuments to unification still exist, such as Berlin's 'Reunification' by Hildegard Leest, these inevitably stand on former western territory only.[25] As the case studies below demonstrate, it is significant that regional monuments have largely been erected earlier than in central Berlin, where the demands of national symbolism have once again proven to be restricting. This chapter thus begins by outlining the Berlin project for a Freedom and Unity Monument before examining earlier, regional examples. As the case studies demonstrate, the interaction between the centre and the periphery proves particularly important here, often providing a catalyst for regional projects. While these examples highlight on the one hand the diversity of such memorials, together they illustrate a number of emergent trends, most notably the growing importance of 1989/90 in the memory culture of contemporary Germany and the development of a self-confident and more positive tradition of remembrance. At the same time, this remains rooted in a clear emphasis on democratic values, and can only be understood as an integral part of the complex memory dynamics of unified Germany.

Building National Memory? Berlin's Freedom and Unity Monument

The history of Berlin's plans for a Freedom and Unity Monument dates back to May 1998, when the newly formed 'Initiative for a Monument to German Unity' published an open letter calling for an international design competition for a monument to the demonstrations of 1989 and German unity.[26] The main impetus was the forthcoming tenth anniversary of the fall of the Berlin Wall in 1999. While the letter was supported by a number of politicians, intellectuals and public personalities, the initiative was driven by four individuals: Florian Mausbach (then president of the Federal Office for Building and Regional Planning), Lothar de Maizière (first and only democratically elected prime minister of the GDR), Günter Nooke (co-founder of Democratic Awakening, later CDU politician) and Jürgen Engert (journalist). Although they viewed their project as a 'citizens' initiative',[27] it came primarily from a group of high-profile figures, the first three of whom were members of the CDU. Despite this political allegiance, they succeeded in proposing a motion to the Bundestag in April 2000, which was signed by 177 members of the Bundestag from four different parties (CDU/CSU, SPD, FDP and Green Party). On 9 November 2001, however, after lengthy debating in sub-committees and in the Bundestag, the proposal for a monument failed to gain a majority, largely due to opposition votes in the SPD and PDS. In 2005, the project was adopted by the 'German Society' (a civic association founded in 1990 to promote political and cultural projects in Germany and Europe), which organized three public hearings on the proposed monument in 2006 and 2007. Subsequently, the proposal was accepted by the Bundestag on 9 November 2007, under Angela Merkel's chancellorship. A public design competition for a Freedom and Unity Monument was finally launched in December 2008, with a view to announcing a winner on 9 November 2009. However, the competition was halted in April 2009 when the jury failed to select any of the 533 entries for a second round. A revised, two-stage competition was subsequently launched, in which thirty-three designs were chosen to compete from a larger pool of applicants in March 2010; on 3 October 2010, three first prize winners were announced, and after minor modifications, the design by the Stuttgart communication agency 'Milla und Partner' and Berlin choreographer Sasha Waltz (who withdrew from the project in 2012) was announced in April 2011. This consisted of a huge golden, shallow bowl-like construction, which was to tilt under the weight of pedestrians, and on which the slogans 'We are the people. We are one people' could be read in large lettering; on the undersurface of the bowl, visitors would see images and slogans from 1989/90.[28] After numerous deadlines passed and complications arose due to bats in the vaults of the historic pedestal and the uncovering of historical mosaics on the site[29] – not to speak of the logistical and safety challenges of the design – the project was halted in April 2016, allegedly due to its ever-increasing cost (projected to be at least 15 million euros).[30] However, in November that year, the same Federal Budget Committee that put a stop to the project unexpectedly made available 18.5 million euros to fund the reconstruction of the imperial colonnades that had flanked the original Kaiser Wilhelm memorial, the pedestal of which was to support the new structure (see below). This decision perhaps inevitably ignited the debate afresh, and following further discussions and calls from high-profile political figures, the Bundestag voted with a clear majority in June 2017 to go ahead with construction once again, with a view to completion for the thirtieth anniversary in 2019. As many commentators have noted, the planned seesaw-like structure provides an apt symbol of the vacillating decision-making process, and while it seems at the time of writing (July 2017) that the project will go ahead, there is currently little certainty of its future.

This chronology reveals two interesting points relating to the timings of decisions. First, the project was driven by anniversaries of the peaceful revolution and in particular the fall of the Berlin Wall on 9 November 1989. Initially, the project was to be completed by the twentieth anniversary on 9 November 2009, then – as the process stumbled – this date was to mark the laying of the foundation stone, and subsequently the announcement of the winner. Whether or not it will be completed for the thirtieth anniversary in 2019 remains to be seen. The initial Bundestag decisions were also symbolically made on 9 November, and although the competition failed to meet any of the 9 November targets, the three winners were finally announced on 3 October 2010 – yet another significant milestone: the twentieth anniversary of unification. The continual efforts on the part of politicians and competition organizers to appropriate specific dates clearly demonstrates the intention to create a renewable tradition of remembrance centred on the importance of Berlin, the fall of the Wall and the popular desire for unity. By aspiring to create a ritual tradition even before the monument was built, initiators thus hoped to ensure a secure and lasting future tradition of remembrance that would extend beyond the memories of those who experienced 1989 first-hand. While the centrally funded project failed to meet the initial target of 9 November 2009, it is interesting that this triggered private initiatives; the *BILD* newspaper, for instance, took pride in the fact that it erected a monument outside its headquarters at the Axel-Springer-Haus in time for this deadline, claiming: 'The federal government's planned Unity Monument cannot be expected any time soon – BILD is quicker'.[31]

The time-span of decisions made in the Bundestag also reveals an interesting pattern, for the discussions in 2000 and 2001 saw objections on the part of SPD and PDS members that it was too soon for a memorial and that the proposal required more reflection. Some also expressed reservations about the suitability of the monument for the present day, given that unification was not yet complete, while others questioned the central motive of its advocates – many of whom had been active in the demonstrations of 1989 – as little more than an act of self-celebration.[32] Interestingly, communicative memory of this period thus provided arguments both for and against the creation of a monument, demonstrating that it was not simply first-hand experience of the demonstrations that influenced opinions, but rather the nature and extent of individuals' participation. By 2007, however, objections had become less vociferous – although criticism of the tight timeframe around 2009 persisted – and it was not only a different political configuration in the Bundestag that secured success the second time round, but also the passing of time; by 2017, Die Linke was the only party in the Bundestag to oppose the monument's construction. While this history had still been experienced first-hand by many involved, it was no longer felt to be quite so close, thus making its mediation into a fixed form of political memory somewhat less contentious. Genuine widespread enthusiasm for the project has not, however, taken root; not only was there a notable absence of public outrage when its termination was announced in 2016, but only a week before the project was officially reinstated in June 2017, one public opinion poll found only 16 per cent of Germans and 18 per cent of Berliners to favour the design by Milla und Partner.[33]

On first impressions, the project appeared to be rooted in the apparently straightforward desire to remember the demonstrations of 1989 and the subsequent event of German unity. The decision to place 'freedom' in the title before 'unity' was thus to indicate that freedom came before – and was a precondition for – unity.[34] The monument was also intended to reflect the future aspirations of Germany as a nation, and to highlight the historical importance of the 'peaceful revolution' to Germany's young generation. However, a more detailed examination of the initial competition outline and the hopes of initiators show that this project became inextricably linked to Germany's past cultures of remembrance and to periods of history much older than the GDR. Above all, the monument proposal was marked by the desire for three key elements: democratic credentials, national symbolism and positive historical connotations, each of which responded directly to the existing memorial landscape, and proposed a new direction from old traditions. The first of these – the desire for a monument that celebrated democracy in both content and form – not only reflects the political order of unified Germany, but also aims to provide distance from the remembrance cultures of previous regimes, in which party colours dictated the shape of the memorial landscape, most evident in former socialist monuments (see Chapter 2), as well as numerous Prussian equestrian statues, whose origins were often far from democratic. In response to such historic structures, it is little surprise that abstract and unheroic monumental forms were expected by the monument's advocates. As Werner Schulz (Green Party) typically claimed, 'It is ... a new trend in monument culture that we no longer place people on pedestals. The era of bronze sculptures that weigh several tonnes has probably passed'.[35] Regarding process rather than form, Mausbach was similarly at pains to emphasize that their project came 'from the midst of society', and was not to be seen as 'a representative state monument ... but rather a citizens' memorial'.[36] Markus Meckel (SPD) also claimed that 'it should not be a heroic monument',[37] and Nooke even called for it to become a 'Mecca for democrats'.[38] The monument as a symbolic vehicle for the democratic transmission of memories thus became an integral part of the project from its inception, paving the way for an open, public competition. Although the competition process proved problematic, it is notable that entries to both competitions were publicly exhibited in Berlin, and together with numerous associated public discussions, websites and documentations, these exhibitions were testament to the desire for a democratic project, themselves becoming an important part of the process.[39] Indeed, many politicians voiced the opinion that while the failed competition of 2009 was regrettable, the fact that time was being taken to seek further opinion underlined the concern to uphold as democratic a process as possible.[40]

Alongside marking democratic credentials, the monument is also intended to be a 'national symbol in the centre of the German capital', displaying positive historical connotations.[41] It is thus to mark another break with past commemorative traditions: that of a nation which had struggled for years with the concept of 'negative nationalism' and the widespread construction of cautionary monuments (*Mahnmale*), represented above all by Berlin's Holocaust memorial, but also by the increasing focus on repression and victimhood during the GDR. Ever conscious of this tradition, advocates have consistently tried to turn the tide, regularly dubbing the proposed monument a *Freudenmal* ('mark of joy'); Wolfgang Thierse (SPD) even attempted to link the cautionary tradition with a celebratory one, claiming: 'We should erect a *Mahnmal* to our historical happiness, so that we do not forget how precious and vulnerable freedom and unity are, nor the values to which our national fortune commits us'.[42] Similarly, yet in a more direct tone, Nooke claimed: 'Let us intone a new key for our national memory, in the major not in the minor'.[43] In light of such comments, it became difficult to disentangle the proposed Freedom and Unity Monument from the Holocaust memorial, as a new, positive monument was inevitably viewed as a counterweight or 'antimonument' to the Holocaust memorial. Although Nooke explicitly denied this intention, he also claimed: 'we will not let ourselves be defined as a nation by twelve frightful years of Nazi dictatorship'.[44] It is thus little surprise that many cynics have viewed this monument proposal as an antidote to the Holocaust memorial, with some even suggesting that the initial plan to include an information centre was intended as a direct parallel to that of the Holocaust memorial.[45] The tone of parliamentary debates also indicated that monuments to the victims of the Holocaust were widely regarded as a prerequisite for such a *Freudenmal*; as the SPD stated, 'We can allow ourselves such a monument because we do not suppress the dark side of our past'.[46] Significantly, of course, the Freedom and Unity Monument was not approved before the Holocaust memorial was completed. The proposed monument thus attempts to break with the tradition of 'negative nationalism' by enabling the celebration of a national tradition of freedom and unity much in the same way that other European nations have done for years (demonstrated by the French slogan *liberté, égalité, fraternité*); to quote Thierse, 'Let us finally be a normal, an average, an ordinary European people'.[47] As a 'national' project, the monument also aims to create a focal point for east and west Germans alike, and by focusing on an element of eastern heritage, it responds to other memory debates in which western narratives had frequently dominated (as seen in the destruction of the Palast der Republik, the dismantling of socialist realist monuments and the renaming of streets). Nooke actually suggested that the monument could aid the national project of unification:

> I even believe that such a monument would rather speed up the process of so-called inner unity. This is especially important from the viewpoint of eastern Germans, because in past years they have sometimes had the feeling that their own primary contribution towards German unity, namely the peaceful revolution, has taken somewhat of a back seat in terms of public interest.[48]

Preliminary debates did, indeed, invest great faith in the potential symbolic power of a new monument for the nation, and the willingness of the German state to invest 10 million euros in such a project at a time of economic downturn highlighted its political importance.[49]

The initial hopes and desires placed in this project represented somewhat of a dichotomy. On the one hand, the construction was to represent a new start, a break with numerous traditions of remembrance and the end of the so-called 'short twentieth century'. On the other hand, however, the choice of location and the associated political rhetoric indicated the desire to demonstrate continuity with two longer-standing German traditions: freedom and unity. While the first of these concerns one of the central values for which demonstrators campaigned in 1989, it is interesting that the attempt to draw on a broader tradition of freedom has often steered the debate away from the GDR. Advocates of the monument project, for example, have looked back to the nineteenth century and proposed that the monument should demonstrate the 'overcoming of a martial nationalism and the completion of the democratic revolution of 1848',[50] as well as highlight the importance of other movements for freedom over previous centuries.[51] Others have been keen for the monument to represent Germany's debt to neighbouring Eastern European countries, whose reform movements proved significant in giving courage to GDR citizens.[52] In the aftermath of September 2011, Cornelia Pieper (FDP) even promoted the proposed monument as a '*Mahnmal* against war and terrorism', thus linking it with much broader global trends.[53] The battle for freedom from various regimes and at various historical junctures was, thus, to be incorporated in equal measure with the East German demonstrators' fight for freedom from SED control. The initial timeframe for the monument was critical in this respect, for not only did 2009 mark twenty years since the fall of the Wall, but also 160 years of the Paulskirche in Frankfurt, ninety years of the Weimar constitution and sixty years of the Federal Republic. Through wishing to highlight a longer tradition of freedom, the initiators thus attempted to 'organize' political memory in a systematic way, with the aim of creating a stable tradition in the present that would retain the emotional pull of past traditions.

Alongside freedom, the notion of unity is also intended to promote a longer tradition, largely due to the proposed location: a platform measuring approximately eighty by forty metres that was built to support a colossal monument to Kaiser Wilhelm I, completed in 1897 for the hundredth anniversary of his birth.[54] Although the monument itself was dismantled by the GDR regime in 1949/50, the platform has remained, providing a sizable area of derelict land in the heart of Berlin, next to the site of the (now destroyed) Palast der Republik. The fact that the platform did not mark the location of the 1989 demonstrations – other than being on the route of demonstrators on 4 November – was problematic for those who valued a sense of authenticity,[55] and indeed many advocated Leipzig as a preferable location, where the demonstrations first gathered major momentum (see below). Historically, however, this choice of location highlights continuity with the past, for the imperial monument was also designed as a national monument for the German people, in celebration of the unification of Germany in 1871. Thus, by drawing a line between 1871 and 1989/90, the proposed project would highlight a longer historical tradition, once again demonstrating the concern to construct a stable national identity rather than necessarily reflect the historical complexities of 1989. This was particularly problematic for those on the left who feared that it highlighted 'a national-conservative continuity, which has nothing to do with the freedom movement in the GDR'.[56] In this case, the choice of location clearly reflects the needs of contemporary political identities, yet as this example shows more broadly, the geographical fixity of monuments often provokes a confrontation with other political memories that different representative forms may be less likely to encounter; in short, there can never be a clean slate on which to build a monument.

In light of the numerous hopes and desires that were placed in this project, it is little surprise that the first competition ran aground. As journalist Andreas Kilb quipped, so much was promised in the monument that it had become the 'symbolic all-in-one solution [*eierlegende Wollmilchsau*] for the Berlin Republic'.[57] Perhaps unsurprisingly, the desire to embed the 'peaceful revolution' in the cultural memory of the Berlin Republic proved too ambitious in terms of both procedure and expectations of form, forcing State Minister for Culture Bernd Neumann to admit that the concept was 'overloaded and too complex'.[58] The attempt to promote a genuinely democratic competition demonstrates some of the problems. The open competition attracted so many entries, for instance, that jury members had at most one minute to pass judgement on each design – clearly not enough time to draw well-considered conclusions.[59] Moreover, the broad spectrum of entries provided for a wide range of quality, and while a number were original and thought-provoking, a large proportion were questionable. Critics commented on the 'deficient inspiration' of artists,[60] as well as the 'symbolic harmlessness' and 'irrelevance' of many designs, some of which were described as 'naive' and 'embarrassing'.[61] The media inevitably highlighted the more absurd entries, such as those including a large yellow banana, a twenty-five-metre-high giraffe, or a group of demonstrating smurfs.[62] As one of the jury members, writer Thomas Brussig claimed: 'The lesson learned from the whole exercise: an open competition, in which the weight of artistic merit holds sway – through fully democratic means – is an illusion. Word has got out that democracy favours mediocrity'.[63] As the process indicated, a true 'citizens' monument' is, perhaps, an unattainable quest. The problem of quality, however, largely resulted from the complex demands placed on entrants, for not only did the competition brief call for designs to incorporate German and European traditions of freedom and unity from 1848 onwards, but three further requirements were included. First, proposals were to refer to other towns and cities, especially Leipzig, where demonstrations had taken place; second, they were to point the public towards associated nearby sites of memory; and third, they were to include plans for an information centre.[64] In overloading the symbolic meaning of the monument, it seems that organizers were in danger of promoting amnesia rather than remembrance of 1989. Additionally, the looming date of 9 November 2009 had pushed the competition out of its comfort zone – for not only had it become highly complex, but there appeared to be little time to allow for considered reflection.

These facts were all recognized by the Federal Committee for Culture and Media, which in July 2009 set recommendations for a revised competition that was launched in early 2010. A number of changes were made: the requirement to link Berlin to other locations of protest in 1989 was removed (as Leipzig was to receive its own monument), the inclusion of an information centre was withdrawn (as the nearby DHM would house such information), and the requirement to link the monument to other relevant sites of memory was dropped. Most significantly, however, the call to draw on historical continuities was also removed, and the committee stressed that 'the memory of the peaceful revolution in the autumn of 1989 and the act of regaining German unity should be the artistic focus of the Freedom and Unity Monument'.[65] Finally, the new competition was to invite entrants from a pool of applications, thus ensuring a much smaller number of professional entries. The decision to back down on a significant number of the initial requirements demonstrates an important element of politically driven remembrance, namely that – in being imposed 'from above', rather than growing organically 'from below' – it is always likely to be subject to simplification, particularly when dealing with symbolic forms such as monuments. With this in mind, a journalist from Die Zeit polemically commented that 'perhaps a national monument can only function under the conditions of propaganda'.[66] The process did, however, highlight the nature of the national community as both 'imagined' and as one in which myth-building is intrinsic.

After three finalists were announced by the jury in October 2010, the eventual winner of the second competition was decided by the Federal Representative for Culture and Media, together with the Federal Ministry of Transport, Building and Urban Development, and announced in April 2011. The winners, 'Milla und Partner', together with Sasha Waltz, viewed their design, entitled 'citizens in motion', to be a 'social sculpture' after Joseph Beuys, intending visitors 'to become part of the monument themselves',[67] as they would mount the monument and use their collective mass – the weight of democracy – to tilt the giant bowl-like structure. While the design met the competition aims to produce a 'democratic' monument in form, it was precisely this element that attracted the ridicule of the media, which dubbed it not only a 'federal seesaw', 'salad bowl of unity' or 'halfpipe', but also a 'fun monument' and 'monumental toy', in which the 'fun factor' dominated over historical remembrance.[68] Critics widely considered the design to be a new visitor attraction in Berlin, typical of the 'memory-idle fun society' of contemporary times, rather than a serious attempt to engage with the ambitions of 1989 and 1990.[69] Interestingly, public perception of the competition process thus swung from one that initially viewed the aims to be too overloaded with history, to one that was considered too 'history-light'.

This perception can partly be explained by the dominance of the political class in driving the project. Despite claims on the part of its initiators that the monument was to be a citizens' initiative, it was commonly perceived as being led by the ruling elite, standing in a tradition that, in Martin Schönfeld's words, understood 'the monument to be an image of official state pedagogy'.[70] Jury member Matthias Flügge, for instance, who disagreed with the choice of the winning design, claimed that it had appealed to the politicians on the jury, as 'all critical, all rebellious elements of the unification process have, so to speak, been polished away under gold leaf'.[71] The chair of the jury, Meinhard von Gerkan, reportedly left the meeting in disagreement with the decision-making process, and a number of jury members also questioned the structure's monumental proportions (sixty by twenty-five metres).[72] With this in mind, critic Jens Bisky thus envisaged that the monument would 'illustrate empty phrases of political rhetoric, instead of providing an image of unity'.[73] A number of – largely CDU – politicians were, indeed, closely identified with the project, in particular Minister for Culture Neumann, after whom it was dubbed the 'Neumann-swing' in some press reports.[74] However, the central criticism relating to the instrumentalization of the GDR past for contemporary politics lay, without doubt, in the consistent pairing of freedom and unity throughout both competitions. Die Linke, for example, repeatedly argued against remembering the demonstrations of 1989 together with the event of unity,[75] for in bringing these events together, such a monument would suggest – at least to future generations – that the desire for unity was one of the principal aims of the demonstrators in 1989, thus rewriting history. A further criticism on the part of left-wing critics has been that the peace groups of the early 1980s, as well as the 'swords into ploughshares' movement and the critical role of the churches, would be downplayed, if not forgotten, in such a monolithic reading of history.[76] However, if such detail were to be taken into account, the monument would fail to act as a 'national' symbol; as Egon Bahr warned, such a monument could result in estranging west Germans from such a symbol.[77] There is, indeed, a danger that historical detail may be brushed aside in the interests of future aspirations, and in light of persisting differences between east and west, one could argue that the proposal failed to correspond to contemporary realities; as one critic insisted in 2009, 'Germany needs the unity of the country not on a pedestal, but rather in everyday life'.[78]

To date, genuine public interest in the monument has been notably lower than in other recent national projects, such as the *Neue Wache*, the Holocaust memorial or the rebuilding of the City Palace. While initial discussions over the location of the monument – whether Berlin or Leipzig – generated impassioned debate in Leipzig (see below), response in Berlin remained lukewarm.[79] The exhibition of the winning designs in 2010 attracted relatively small numbers of visitors,[80] and the media response to both competitions consistently adopted a derisory tone, resisting engagement in a more meaningful debate.[81] According to Nooke, even many parliamentarians showed little genuine passion for the debate.[82] Outside Berlin, concern was raised that the monument project would divert funds and attention from regional efforts to remember the GDR,[83] and interest in the discussions organized in the regions was, on the whole, underwhelming.[84] Within Berlin, then governed by a left-left coalition, the Senate also showed little open enthusiasm for the federally funded project, which was driven largely by the CDU, with mayor Klaus Wowereit (SPD) publicly expressing his dislike of the three final winners in October 2010.[85] In contrast to debates concerning victims of the GDR border regime (see Chapter 5), discussions regarding the Freedom and Unity Monument were clearly less emotionally driven in the competition stages, largely because there were few competing organizations with obviously vested interests, other than those politicians who led the project, together with the German Society.

The second reason that this project has been considered 'history-light' results from its comparison with other significant monument projects of previous decades, most prominently the Holocaust memorial. While the proposed Freedom and Unity Monument has frequently been criticized as a projected 'antimonument' to the Holocaust memorial, critics have used much of the discourse around the Holocaust memorial to belittle the project. Journalist Harry Nutt, for instance, described the winning design as 'a place that one should enjoy going to', immediately recalling Chancellor Schröder's much-criticized comment regarding the Holocaust memorial.[86] Similarly, the common conclusion from the Holocaust memorial that 'the debate is the monument' has been used by critics to question the weight of the Freedom and Unity Monument, in light of the apparent lack of public interest and debate.[87] Alternatively, comparisons were drawn between the 'participatory' element of the Holocaust memorial (i.e. the fact that it must be explored by pedestrians) and the winning design, claiming that the latter sought inspiration from the former.[88] Despite the fact that the central aims of the two monuments are radically different, it seems that the dominance of the Holocaust memorial in Berlin is likely to colour perceptions of further national memorial projects for the foreseeable future. Other national monuments have, however, also influenced opinion, with the Brandenburg Gate frequently being cited as the best monument to freedom and unity, thus annulling the need for a new monument in the capital.[89] Most notable, however, is the former Kaiser Wilhelm National Memorial, the direct association with which proves highly questionable for art critics, who see the use of its 'pedestal' – now an outmoded notion in monumental art – together with the celebration of the nation and freedom, to constitute little more than a 'restoration of the traditional concept of the monument'.[90] Moreover, the decision in 2016 to make funds available for the reconstruction of the former monument's imperial colonnades demonstrated a desire to privilege older historical continuities, unsurprisingly causing outrage among advocates of the modern construction. Thierse, for instance, claimed that it was a 'surprise coup', which not only glorified the empire but demonstrated 'contempt for the peaceful revolution'.[91] Indeed, this decision reignited debate on the monument's role, setting in motion a series of heated debates and discussions, which had been all but absent in recent years. The Freedom and Unity Monument, if it is built, will clearly be shaped by its relationship to other national structures.

The process of embedding this project in the physical, symbolic and anniversary landscapes of Berlin has doubtless proven difficult, not least because there is little agreement over its historical trajectory. The broader relevance of 9 November is also problematic, for the pogrom of 1938 serves as a constant reminder of Germany's darker past on this date, and any attempts to incorporate 1918 into a longer historical trajectory potentially demonstrate continuities with the left-wing revolutionary traditions and GDR commemoration. The debates of 2016–17 appeared, however, to reveal the strengthening of a political desire to instil the monument within a clear national trajectory. Quite apart from the fact that the planned structure has gained the popular nickname of the *Einheitswippe* (unity seesaw), official statements issued by its advocates after the Bundestag's decision of June 2016 clearly underlined national continuities. The press statement issued by the German Society, for instance, stresses the importance of the monument's location next to the reconstructed Berlin Palace, claiming that demonstrations in the name of democracy took place on the palace square in 1848, 1918 and 1989. While this narrative stresses a revolutionary trajectory, the location – representing unity and national symbolism – remains the prime focus, and the statement even cites the first line of the national anthem by stating 'Unity and justice and freedom have prevailed'.[92] The CDU/CSU press statement also underlines the importance of a positive national history, and significantly stresses that the high point of Europe's history of freedom was the 'overcoming of communist dictatorships in the GDR and Eastern Europe'.[93] It is perhaps little surprise that the CDU places the monument in a national-conservative tradition, but the anticommunist nature of this message clearly refashions the complexities of demonstrators' demands in the autumn of 1989 to fit a nationally oriented agenda. Whether or not the construction of the Freedom and Unity Monument will, indeed, bolster this agenda may depend on popular consent. If democratic narratives are to be upheld in this project, success is unlikely if it fails to resonate with the population; accusations that decisions were made in 'closed' committee meetings in 2016 and 2017 show how far the project had moved from its early years, which were driven by concerns over participation and transparency. On the other hand, the growth of nationalist movements in Germany, such as Pegida, may prove to be the undoing of the monument. It has not gone unnoticed that the intended inscription of 'We are the people. We are one people' bears similarity to the anti-immigration slogans of mass demonstrations from 2014 onwards. While the German term *Volk*, used here for 'people', is clearly a historically loaded term, recent political developments have shed an increasingly critical light on this inscription, regardless of the intended historical reference to 1989. As many other examples in this book demonstrate, memorials can adopt new and often unexpected meanings, in this case before they have even been built.

Remembering the Leipzig Demonstrations: The Nikolaikirchhof and Beyond

Discussions over the Freedom and Unity Monument spread to Leipzig after the failure of the first Berlin competition in 2009, when it was decided that the Saxon town should receive its own monument. The focus on Leipzig pays tribute to the significant role that its citizens played in the demonstrations of 1989, the concrete legacy of which has become increasingly prominent in recent years. The first efforts to commemorate the events of 1989 centred on the square next to Leipzig's Nikolaikirche (St Nicholas Church), which has become one of the central sites of memory of 1989. It was here that, from the early 1980s, peace and environmental groups began to meet regularly for Monday evening peace prayers at 5 p.m. The church offered such groups space for critical discussion, and from 1988 it attracted growing numbers, particularly exit-visa applicants and citizens wanting to change the status quo in the GDR. The first demonstration took place on 4 September 1989, when a small group of people protested for freedom to travel and for internal change; week by week these slowly grew. However, it was not until after the GDR's fortieth anniversary on 7 October, when a number of protests and violent clashes with police took place, that the scale of the demonstrations grew. On 9 October, with significantly more protestors expected, large numbers of armed forces and security personnel were put on standby, and tensions mounted, particularly in light of the Politbüro's show of solidarity with the Chinese 'solution' on Tiananmen Square only a few months earlier. The demonstration, however, was allowed to take place peacefully; after the peace prayers, seventy thousand protestors gathered on Augustusplatz and walked around the ring road to the Runde Ecke (the district headquarters of the Stasi), where the protest peacefully disbanded. The slogans 'We are the people' and 'No violence' could be heard among the demonstrators.[94] The date of 9 October has widely been considered the 'deciding day',[95] as it was followed by ever-growing Monday demonstrations both here and in numerous other towns, and Leipzig was subsequently dubbed the 'GDR's city of heroes' after Christoph Hein's ironic suggestion at the 4 November demonstration in Berlin.[96] Regardless of whether this title is fitting, there is little doubt that without the events of 9 October, later demonstrations are unlikely to have gathered such mass support.

In recent years, Leipzig has become increasingly celebrated – and marketed – as the birthplace of the 'peaceful revolution'. In 1998, the town authorities and the tourist office announced the intention to raise the profile of Leipzig specifically as the 'town of the *Wende*', with the aim of attracting more tourists in the tenth anniversary year.[97] Consequently, October 1999 witnessed a wide range of events, concerts, exhibitions and a 'festival for Leipzig', as well as the opening of the Forum for Contemporary History (Zeitgeschichtliches Forum Leipzig), the unveiling of a plaque outside the Runde Ecke and the dedication of the town's first monument to the revolution next to the Nikolaikirche. Ten years later, however, celebrations took place on a much larger scale, with a 'Festival of Lights' – now an annual tradition – attracting more than 100,000 people.[98] The year 2009 also witnessed a wide range of exhibitions, concerts and discussions, as well as the unveiling of another monument, the 'Democracy Bell' on Augustusplatz. While these and other projects indicate an apparently growing desire in Leipzig to lay claim to its role in recent history and to move away from a 'remembrance tradition fixed on the capital' that is dominated by the fall of the Wall,[99] the following examples reveal an interesting dialogue between earlier and later mnemonic projects, suggesting that a growth in material markers need not always result in the intensification of memory.

The earliest project to commemorate 9 October was led by the Leipzig Cultural Foundation, an organization established in January 1990 to protect and promote the cultural heritage of the town. In 1992, in cooperation with the town authorities, it announced an international competition to redevelop the Nikolaikirchhof (the square next to the church), which then functioned simply as a through road. The aim of the competition was to develop an 'individual, communicative and urban space' that would reflect the events of autumn 1989 through artistic form and generate 'a dynamism between age-old cultural history and current events and processes'.[100] Four finalists were announced from fifty-four entries, and in early 1994 Leipzig artist Andreas Stötzner was announced as winner.[101] His concept was relatively simple and involved placing on the square a replica of one of the eight central pillars in the church. The effect, however, is particularly striking due to the unusual design of the interior pillars, the result of Johann Friedrich Carl Dauthe's classical renovation of the gothic church in the late eighteenth century, inspired by French enlightenment style.[102] The resulting monument, a tall white pillar with light green palm leaves extending upwards to the sky, stands as an eye-catching structure in the square, both familiar and strange at the same time (see Figure 6.1). While Stötzner's idea of a column harks back to traditional monumental form, as seen in the concept of the 'victory column', it refrains from all sense of heroism, instead drawing together the cultural history of the town with more recent political history. In bringing the column out of the church, Stötzner thus reflects the movement of oppositional ideas in 1989 from inside the church onto its streets; the palm leaves further stand as a symbol of peace, and the green shoots growing from stone represent hope for the future. However, the question of whether the pillar was to be constructed from marble, as Stötzner originally intended, or concrete caused some discussion. As the then director of the Cultural Foundation, Birgit Damrau, stated, 'Many of us believe that concrete is more appropriate for the event ... Because it was ultimately ordinary Leipzig citizens who left the church and processed around the *Ring* [Leipzig's ring road] in the autumn of 1989'.[103] Discussions regarding the fabric thus concerned the very meaning of 1989, and the resulting choice of concrete reflected mass participation in the demonstrations.

Although the competition was launched in 1992, the pillar itself was not unveiled until 1999, as the cost of 260,000 DM had to be met largely through fundraising. While the town of Leipzig and the federal government gave substantial donations, two-thirds of the money was donated by citizens, businesses and organizations;[104] the fundraising effort was also backed by a number of significant figures from 1989, such as conductor Kurt Masur and Pastor Christian Führer. Numerous articles in the *Leipziger Volkszeitung* advertised for donations, and Führer was even quoted as saying that 'each Leipzig citizen who demonstrated on the *Ring* back then should participate with a personal donation'.[105] The campaign drummed up considerable support from across the town, and

Figure 6.1 St Nicholas Column in memory of the demonstrations of 9 October 1989 (Andreas Stötzner, 1999), Nikolaikirchhof, Leipzig. Photograph by Anna Saunders.

the names of all those who donated money were inserted into a copper tube inside the monument.[106] Once funds were secured, the replica, created by sculptor Markus Gläser, was unveiled on 9 October 1999 in front of over a thousand people and in the presence of Chancellor Gerhard

Schröder, Saxony's Minister President Kurt Biedenkopf and Leipzig's Mayor Wolfgang Tiefensee.[107] Significantly, the unveiling took place after a 5 p.m. service in the Nikolaikirche, thus at the same time that the demonstration began ten years earlier; in this way, remembrance took place through repetition, adding weight to the symbolism of the pillar and thus building ritual memory. A plaque reading '9 October 1989' was laid in the ground near the pillar, and at a later date – in response to public requests – an information board was erected nearby, explaining the history of the pillar.[108] The monument has since become an iconic symbol of the city, and has attracted remarkably little criticism; indeed, as the *Leipziger Volkszeitung* reported six months after its inauguration, 'it has long since become a landmark' of the town.[109] Not only does it appear on postcards and tourist brochures, but from 2001 a media prize awarded by the Leipzig Sparkasse's Media Foundation presents winners with a miniature golden copy of the column.[110] As a prize awarded to journalists active in fighting for the freedom of the press, the miniatures symbolically transport GDR protestors' calls for free speech into a wider sphere. Since 9 October 2009, the monument is also illuminated at night, and it is significant that the recent debate over a Freedom and Unity Monument in Leipzig prompted several public figures, such as author Erich Loest and cabarettist Bernd-Lutz Lange, to declare their preference for the column and its authentic location over any new project.[111] Numerous comments in online fora and readers' pages of the *Leipziger Volkszeitung* have echoed such sentiments, declaring the column to be the most appropriate icon for this history, and 'the ultimate monument'.[112]

While the St Nicholas column was relatively uncontroversial, the competition triggered a more divisive debate concerning the installation of a fountain on the square. As pictures of the square in the seventeenth century depicted a fountain here, Stötzner had included one in his design, the idea of which had appealed to the jury. Although his specific fountain design was rejected, the idea led to a separate competition for a fountain in 1997/98. The winner of this competition, the architecture firm 'Weis und Volkmann', together with an artist group 'solitaire FACTORY', envisaged a long stream of water on the square, starting at the monument and ending in a round basin, thus reflecting the vertical of the pillar on the horizontal of the square. Controversially, however, a low wall was projected to accompany the flow of water across the square, provoking the criticism – particularly from Stötzner – that the unity of the square would be destroyed and the symbolism of the column lost.[113] Many locals agreed with Stötzner, and protest grew against the design, with claims that 'the construction of a wall' on this of all squares was inappropriate.[114] Despite a public discussion on the design, as well as efforts to draw an outline of the fountain on the square in sand, protest persisted. With a projected bill of 240,000 DM for the fountain, and in the face of public objections and indecision even among initiators, the town decided in early 1999 that the project should be put on hold. As Mayor Wolfgang Tiefensee claimed, the symbolism of the Nikolaikirchhof was so great that 'broader approval would be desirable'.[115]

The Cultural Foundation retained interest in the idea, however, and launched a further fountain competition in 2002, together with a competition for a 'light installation', both of which were intended to complete the landscaping of the square. The projected cost of 460,000 DM for both was to be met by the Hamburg Foundation 'Lebendige Stadt' and the city of Leipzig. As Wolfgang Hocquél of the Cultural Foundation stated, the aim was to make the history of the Nikolaikirche and the associated square 'permanently tangible' as the 'point of departure for the deep-seated social changes'.[116] The winning fountain design by London architect David Chipperfield proved highly symbolic, for it represented in physical form the German expression 'der Tropfen, der das Fass zum Überlaufen bringt' (literally 'the drop that causes the barrel to overflow', or more idiomatically 'the straw that breaks the camel's back'). Consisting of a simple low cylindrical basin made from Lausitz granite, water brims to the top, seemingly about to overflow, metaphorically representing the political situation in 1989. More self-contained than the previous proposal, and having gained the approval of Stötzner, this design triggered relatively little discussion, and has been well integrated into the square. The parallel competition for a light installation to highlight the 'interaction between church, square and column' was intended to draw attention to the history of the square at night.[117] The winning design by Leipzig artists Tilo Schulz and Kim Wortelkamp consists of 146 square lamps set among the cobblestones on the square. Between 8 p.m. and 11 p.m., they become illuminated one by one, at a rate of roughly one per minute, across the whole square, representing the gradual amassing of people on the square and at the entrance to the church. At 11 p.m. they disappear, only to return the next evening; the lamps are coloured blue, green and pink, in order to represent 'the diversity of the participants'.[118] In the artists' words, the design does not aspire to be a traditional monument, but rather 'to reflect the process, the situational flare-up'.[119] The designs from both competitions were displayed publicly in March 2003 and unveiled later the same year, on 9 October, once again highlighting the symbolism of this date for Leipzig.[120] Together with Stötzner's column, they work together to form a 'multi-part memorial for the political *Wende* of 1989',[121] highlighting an authentic location in an unheroic fashion. As a gradual process of development in which each layer responded to the other, this ensemble also reflects the organism of the 1989 demonstrations, which grew gradually from their activist roots in the early 1980s.

The ensemble around the Nikolaikirche exists in marked contrast to other more recent monuments relating to 1989. While the aim here is not to examine these in depth, a brief overview illustrates some interesting differences. The first example is the so-called 'Democracy Bell', located on Augustusplatz and unveiled on the twentieth anniversary of 9 October in 2009. The project was initiated by a network of east German foundries in 2007, who wanted to cast a bell and donate it to Leipzig as a symbol of gratitude for the city's role in 1989.[122] Subsequently, the Cultural Foundation launched a competition for a monument to incorporate such a bell, with the intention that the resulting structure would become one of several future pieces of artwork placed around Leipzig's ring road, envisaged by Mayor Jung to be a 'path of remembrance' for the peaceful revolution.[123] Of the six invited entries, Via Lewandowsky's bronze egg, in which the bell was to be housed, was announced as winner in late 2008 and unveiled ten months later. The swift nature of the competition resulted in part from the fact that public fundraising was not necessary: half of the 80,000 euros was donated by the east German foundries, and the other half was organized by the Cultural Foundation, consisting largely of donations from local companies and organizations. Yet it was this very swiftness and lack of local consultation that proved to be a point of contention among many locals, as demonstrated by a large number of readers' letters written to the *Leipziger Volkszeitung*.[124] Siegfried Neumann, for example, lamented that those who had been active in 1989 had not been consulted on the matter, and Ralph Grüneberger complained that the inscription around the base of the egg, by author Durs Grünbein, should have been written by one of Leipzig's own authors.[125] A large number also objected to the form of an egg, which for many did little to conjure up images of 1989. Although it was to represent the concept of new beginnings and new life that emerged from 1989, as well as an aesthetically harmonic whole, this symbolism was lost on many, who preferred to poke fun at the structure by dubbing it an 'Easter egg'.[126] The bell itself rings every Monday at 6.35 p.m., the time at which the demonstration began on 9 October 1989, and once every hour between 8 a.m. and 8 p.m. at a randomly generated time, representing the fact that a mass movement may start at any moment of the day. Unlike the ensemble on the Nikolaikirchhof, its symbolism proved too abstract and the lack of formal public input caused considerable objection – a somewhat ironic outcome, considering that the project initially emerged as a genuine sign of public engagement on the part of the eastern foundries. It seems, however, that public identification, if not acceptance, requires a sense of involvement, especially if the resulting symbolism is not immediately evident.

The run-up to the twentieth anniversary of 1989 saw the discussion of several other plans for concrete memory markers in Leipzig. One of the more controversial was American artist Miley Tucker-Frost's design for a monument, which she intended to give to Leipzig in memory of the twentieth anniversary of 9 October. Through a figurative design of protesters assembled around candles (later reworked into a smaller group standing arm in arm), the artist hoped to evoke an emotional response among viewers. Critics, however, such as the director of Leipzig's Gallery for Contemporary Art, Barbara Steiner, claimed that it was out of tune with contemporary discussions in the field of art; others dismissed it as 'kitsch'.[127] Criticism was also directed at Mayor Burkhard Jung (SPD) for initially accepting the small-scale model without the proposal having been discussed in appropriate circles. Once again, popular criticism focused on the lack of consultation and democratic decision-making, and as a result of lacking enthusiasm for the design, only a model of the revised design was given to the town on 9 October 2009; the realization of a full-scale monument remains uncertain.[128]

Similar issues have also been prevalent in the project for a Freedom and Unity Monument in Leipzig. As with the previous two examples, funding for the project was not a problem, with 5 million euros of federal funds and 1.5 million euros of regional funds having been made available. After the town council passed a resolution to initiate a monument competition (symbolically on 17 June 2009), the project engendered much media debate and involved local personalities, with the town organizing youth and expert workshops on the theme, as well as a citizens' forum. Above all, discussions prior to the competition launch on 9 October 2011 concerned the location of such a monument, and the final decision for Wilhelm-Leuschner-Platz – not a former location of the demonstrations – was related as much to the needs of town planning as to other considerations.[129] This location was also advocated by some, as it would form the end point of a central axis through the city which begins at the *Völkerschlachtdenkmal* (Monument to the Battle of the Nations, in remembrance of the Battle of Leipzig in 1813); in Mayor Burkhard Jung's eyes, this would build a bridge between the ideas of 'freedom, unity and above all reconciliation'.[130] However, like the

Berlin project, there was little outspoken public support for the project prior to the competition launch, and while a town council survey in 2011 found approximately half of the 1,002 respondents to be in favour, surveys carried out at various intervals by the *Leipziger Volkszeitung* revealed much lower levels of enthusiasm.[131] In view of this response, the town encouraged public discussion via an online forum after three prize winners were announced in July 2012 (following a two-stage competition involving 325 initial entries and thirty-nine resubmitted designs). Despite such efforts, public reaction to the designs of the three finalists was far from enthusiastic, with that of the first prize winners, M+M / ANNABAU, attracting much negative attention in the online forum. The CDU and Die Linke also argued that the decision should be put to a popular vote, a scenario not envisaged in the competition regulations.[132] Interestingly, much public criticism of the designs was similar to that of the Berlin monument, in which the colourful and playful nature of many proposals was not seen to be appropriate for portraying an event of such historical weight. In contrast, the final designs in Leipzig were less burdened by the demands of national symbolism, and all three attempted not only to reflect the different understandings of 1989, but also to link its remembrance to contemporary concerns. The design by M+M / ANNABAU, for instance, entitled 'Seventy thousand', envisaged a square of seventy thousand coloured floor slabs, as well as the same number of coloured pedestals, in order to represent the approximate number of people who demonstrated on 9 October 1989. While some of the pedestals would be taken home by Leipzig citizens, others would remain in situ and act as platforms for debate, thus turning the area into a space for the exchange of opinion and political debate, and acting as a bridge between the achievements of 1989 and their future potential.[133] In 2013, however, after the three designs were reworked and the comments of hundreds of citizens were taken into account, the jury announced the final ranking of the three designs, which reversed their initial order, apparently to accommodate popular opinion. Perhaps unsurprisingly, the lack of transparency in this process caused the original winners to instigate legal proceedings, and in 2014 the city announced the decision to terminate the competition, while still expressing a desire to mark publicly the peaceful revolution in the longer term.[134] Inevitably, the revival of the Berlin project for a Freedom and Unity Monument has since triggered fresh debate in Leipzig, with renewed calls for a Leipzig equivalent.[135]

The lack of public enthusiasm – if not widespread scepticism – towards the Freedom and Unity Monument, as well as Tucker-Frost's proposal and the Democracy Bell, reflects the reticence observed in Berlin, in part because – in contrast to the column on the Nikolaikirchhof – they did not grow from within the community. Despite the fact that none of them demanded local funds, the feeling that they had been imposed upon the community without adequate consultation was a common trait. Although the authorities undertook numerous activities to include the population in discussions concerning the Freedom and Unity Monument, and to connect 1989 with contemporary concerns, turnout at such events was low and, as in Berlin, many continued to see it as a project led from above, in which democratic decision-making processes played very little part.[136] The perception that communicative memory was being driven from above thus provoked resistance to the project, which – together with the perceived lack of democracy, the abundance of existing memory markers and a strong annual ritual – suggests that attempts to revive the project face numerous challenges.[137]

Schwerin's Controversial Remembrance of the Round Table

Although Leipzig's St Nicholas column may have been the first well-known concrete symbol of 1989, it was far from the first to exist. The town of Schwerin provides a very early example with its 'Round Table' monument, created in the summer of 1990, before unification had even taken place. Created by sculptor Guillermo Steinbrüggen at the second 'Symposium of Metal Designers' in Schwerin, which for the first time had involved participants from East and West Germany, it was one of two works from the symposium to be bought by the town from a specific public art fund left from the GDR. Although the theme of the symposium was 'Water-Marks',[138] Steinbrüggen deliberately chose a more provocative and timely theme for his creation: that of the socio-political upheaval of 1989 and 1990. As a resident of the relatively nearby West German town of Lübeck, he had observed these changes with great interest and found the round tables that met throughout the GDR between December 1989 and March 1990 to be a fitting subject for his work.[139] Schwerin itself hosted two sets of round table talks, one for the town and one for the district, at which representatives of the GDR's block parties and mass organizations met together with those of the newly formed parties and civil rights organizations. Issues such as the control of local administration, the use of state property and the dissolution of the Stasi, as well as changes to the education system, the economy and other local matters, were all discussed here. The wide variety of backgrounds, political opinions and viewpoints at the round tables were represented by Steinbrüggen through a variety of abstract

Figure 6.2 Round Table (Guillermo Steinbrüggen, 1990), Großer Moor/Puschkinstraße, Schwerin. Photograph by Anna Saunders.

characters sitting around a table (see Figure 6.2). In the artist's words, the sculpture depicts 'the provocateur and the revolutionary, as well as the courageous citizen, but also the political turncoats [*Wendehälse*]'.[140] The sculptures resulting from the symposium were exhibited around Schwerin in the late summer and early autumn of 1990. Steinbrüggen's structure was erected on the Market Square, a seemingly appropriate location because of its proximity to the town hall (where the round table had met) and the cathedral (where the demonstrations had begun), and for its symbolic qualities as a space that facilitates communication.

After the town purchased the sculpture, it remained on the Market Square until 1995. During this period, however, it provoked largely negative responses from the local population. On the one hand, its modern aesthetics were deemed inappropriate for the old Market Square, which was the historic centre of the town. On the other hand, and more significantly, Steinbrüggen's choice of steel, which quickly went rusty, proved to be a bone of contention among residents. The local newspapers regularly featured articles and readers' letters that dubbed it variously as 'the eyesore of Schwerin', a 'scrap heap', 'tasteless' and even 'dangerous' for children playing on the square.[141] Others were willing to donate money in order to have it removed, and one anonymous resident placed their own scrap metal next to it, with a notice reading 'Because scrap metal likes to associate with scrap metal, I've put this thing here'.[142] These objections can partly be explained by the atmosphere of the early 1990s, in which many GDR citizens found themselves finally able to throw out antiquated East German household items and replace them with new western goods. Rust, a sign of decay, was seen to be synonymous with the grey and decrepit image of the GDR city, in contrast to the colourful and newly renovated houses that were beginning to emerge on the Market Square. As such, the monument was interpreted as a damning sign of the past, rather than as a hopeful symbol of the future. It should also be noted that this relatively abstract work was far removed from the style of public art that adorned most East German cities, and as the head of the press office claimed, the authorities were perhaps too reticent to 'direct' public opinion: 'Earlier it was the case here that many explanatory guides were provided in order to show how a work should be interpreted. And I think that out of reticence to prescribe too much, possibly too little is [now] in evidence'.[143] As the work of a west German artist, Steinbrüggen's interpretation of the round table was also open to criticism as that of an outsider. Although critical voices barely focused on this element in the press, the artist noted considerable antipathy towards himself when he carried out work on the monument in October 1992; the fact that this coincided with a period of growing disappointment about unification and high unemployment is not insignificant.

The monument gained only a small number of advocates while it remained on the Market Square. Some found it to be thought-provoking, seeing it to represent the 'rusting' of the ideals and values of 1989, or providing the opportunity for a democratic exchange of opinions.[144] Others used it for their own purposes: one group attached gas masks, protective clothing and blood-stained bandages to the steel figures in 1991 in protest against the Gulf War, while another dressed the figures for an anti-racism initiative in 1993.[145] For as long as it stood on the Market Square, however, it remained an undemocratic symbol of the fact that the town authorities were not listening to public opinion. Plans to move it to another location had, in fact, already been discussed by the town council, and motions had been passed in 1991 and 1993,[146] but indecision over a new location prolonged its removal until 1995, when it was relocated to the junction of two smaller streets, only a few hundred metres from the Market Square. This location was significant for two reasons: first, the monument stood in the place of an older GDR monument, the so-called Ceramic Column, on which an ideologically coloured version of Schwerin's local history had been depicted; and second, it stood opposite the former SED district headquarters, which subsequently became the 'House of Democracy' during the transition period, in which part of the building was made available for the newly formed parties and groups. Despite the fact that a lexicon of buildings and urban structures in Schwerin listed the sculpture in its old location as a 'dubious "monument"',[147] it caused little unrest in its new surroundings. One element that aided its integration was the fact that it was renovated by Steinbrüggen before being reassembled, and the figures were given different pigmented coatings. Not only is the rust less prevalent, but the colours are suggestive of different parties sitting together round a table, or – as the artist himself sees it – of the different character traits of those partaking in discussions.[148] Since 1995, the local newspapers have rarely featured the monument, and it seems that it has become a symbol of compromise and tolerance, representing much the same values that were discussed at the round tables of 1989/90.

Steinbrüggen's Round Table can only, however, be fully understood within the context of two other monuments: the Ceramic Column, in whose place it now stands, and the so-called 'Lion Monument', which has replaced it on the Market Square. The first of these was a column made up of twenty-seven large ceramic reliefs mounted on a steel frame, by Dresden artist Anni Jung.[149] The reliefs depicted the history of Schwerin from its beginnings in 1255 to GDR times, and after being erected in 1986 it became a popular site for tour guides to recount the history of the town. Although some of the reliefs depicted clear socialist ideology, the monument was taken down not for ideological reasons, but because it was partially damaged by a lorry during building work on the street in 1993. Since its removal, the museum in which it is housed (although not displayed) has received repeated calls for its repair and reinstatement, as an important part of the town's history;[150] the PDS also called for it to be re-erected in 2003.[151] In contrast to the more abstract Round Table, it appears to have attracted widespread favourable opinion (especially after its removal), due to its visual storytelling and depiction of a longer town history, and evoked feelings of nostalgia for a more conventional – and familiar – notion of public art.[152] In contrast, the Lion Monument by Peter Lenk was erected on the Market Square in August 1995, shortly after the Round Table was removed, in memory of the eight hundredth anniversary of the death of Schwerin's founder, 'Henry the Lion'. Much more traditional in appearance (a white pillar supporting a lion), it has proven popular in the town partly due to its aesthetics, but also because the four reliefs on the sides of the pillar provide a satirical commentary on Henry's history, which – although presenting him as a brutal despot – are humorous and easily decipherable, once again presenting an element of storytelling. The relative popularity of both the Ceramic Column and the Lion Monument in contrast to the Round Table is significant in terms of form and memory; it seems that Steinbrüggen's monument could not compete with them for two reasons. First, the material of rusting steel was deemed inappropriate and unsightly, in contrast to the more sophisticated ceramic tiles or the clean, white surface of the pillar. Particularly in the immediate post-*Wende* years, there was little appetite for a structure that might tarnish the image of a fast-changing town. Second, the histories portrayed by Jung's and Lenk's monuments were those that reached back over centuries, consolidating a sense of historical identity among its citizens. In contrast, Steinbrüggen's structure was never taken seriously as the depiction of a defining, historical event, in part because it was too soon after the event for considered reflection, and represented a past about which many, especially in the early 1990s, still had very mixed emotions. Even by the time of the twentieth anniversary celebrations of 1989, the town did not attempt to draw the monument into its celebrations or educational events;[153] its early history, it seems, continued to prove problematic. Aesthetics aside, this monument also suffered from the same issue as some of the later Leipzig projects: the fact that it was funded and 'imposed' on the population from above, and lacked popular grassroots support. Once again, perceptions of deficient 'democratic' engagement with the local population proved to be particularly influential.

Swords into Ploughshares: Dessau's Peace Bell

Like in Schwerin, Dessau's monument to 1989 also finds its roots in the period before unification, and relates to a specific aspect of the democratization process of 1989/90. In contrast to the Round Table, however, it reflects a historical event that is singular to the town of Dessau, and has become rather more accepted within the town. Mass participation in the demonstrations of 1989 took place relatively late in Dessau, with the first small demonstration on 20 October, yet it is estimated that at least half (some claim two-thirds) of the town's 100,000 inhabitants turned out on 3 November, demonstrating widespread solidarity with the reform movement.[154] This was taken further by workers in the town's major magnetic tape factory, for despite subsequent changes in the party leadership, many felt that their daily routine had remained essentially the same. A group of workers thus proposed a democratic vote in the factory on three issues: the prohibition of party political work during working hours (except for trades unions); the dissolution of paramilitary brigades (*Kampfgruppen*) in the factory, together with the destruction of their weapons; and the removal of the Stasi office within the factory. The organizers took care to create voting booths and transparent ballot boxes, and with almost 69 per cent of workers voting on 6 December 1989, each issue was approved with over 97 per cent in favour.[155] It was the second of these issues that became the most contentious and ultimately resulted in a memorial. Paramilitary units were voluntary organizations based in large factories, state organizations and universities across the GDR, in which members undertook training, including the handling of weapons, to provide support to the army in times of need. As a large plant, Dessau's magnetic tape factory housed a significant armoury, and although the weapons were subsequently taken to the police headquarters for safekeeping, there was considerable concern among workers that these could be used in the event of an attempted putsch, or that they may be sold onto other conflict areas in order to gain much-needed income for the GDR.[156]

In January 1990, a group of factory workers formed the '6 December Initiative', which began to lobby first for an inventory of the weapons and second for their destruction, addressing crowds on the Market Square at a mass demonstration and bringing the issue to the town's round table on 30 January 1990. Here it was decided that the weapons should be destroyed the following day, when – following lengthy discussions in the police headquarters and after the arrival of representatives from both Modrow's government and the central round table – the action was finally sanctioned.[157] In the late afternoon on 31 January, 1,250 machine pistols, 208 machine guns, 174 pistols and 87 bazookas were crushed by military tanks and hydraulic presses.[158] While a small number of the destroyed weapons were sent to the DHM in Berlin and to the Museum for Town History in Dessau, thus acknowledging that this was a historic event, it was unclear what should be done with the remainder. Although a West German firm offered to take the remnants in exchange for medical equipment for the town, its intention to market the misshapen weapons as 'souvenirs' did not find favour with the Initiative, which claimed: 'Even if the projected Western money is much needed, we believe that no-one should sacrifice morals for money'.[159] Although the Initiative initially considered constructing a monument from the metal parts, concern that they might fall into the wrong hands meant that the metal was melted down on 15 March 1990, resulting in a block of steel weighing over four tonnes. This action called forth the much-cited slogan of the peace movement of the 1980s – 'swords into ploughshares' – yet the steel block subsequently sat in a churchyard until the late 1990s, as there was little money and the town's priorities lay elsewhere. On 31 January 1997, however, exactly eight years after the destruction of the weapons, Lothar Ehm, one of the initiators of the vote in the factory and speaker of the '6 December Initiative', met with former colleagues to discuss the future of the steel. They decided that a bell should be cast from the metal, an idea that dated back to 1990, and which presented an interesting reversal of the fate of many church bells in the First and Second World Wars, which were melted down for weapons.[160] The group thus formed an official 'Peace Bell' Board of Trustees, with Ehm as its chairperson; as an active member of the CDU, he was familiar with local politics and had served for a short period on the town council. The group began by raising public awareness of the project and reminding Dessau's residents of the history of the steel in order to raise enough money to cast a bell. Discussions also focused on where the bell should be located and what it should look like, and it was initially decided that the monument should stand on the Market Square in front of the town hall, where the demonstrations had been held in 1989.

A competition was subsequently launched in 1998, in which students from the local higher education college were invited to submit designs for a structure to house a bell. Of five entries, architecture student Julia Bucher's design won first prize: a sixteen-metre-high, white concrete tower in parabola form, with the open side facing the town hall. The idea was that when the bell rang, its sound would be audible in the town hall, but not be a nuisance to nearby residents.[161] The design provoked criticism, largely on the part of the town's SPD mayor, Hans-Georg Otto, who not only feared that it would attract beer-drinking delinquents to shelter in the structure, but that it was architecturally unsuitable for the square because of its height, a concern shared by others.[162] Eventually the design had to be dropped, making the completion date of 3 October 1999 unfeasible. In 2000, however, a motion was passed in the town council in favour of a monument, with the town agreeing to finance the bell frame if the Board of Trustees funded the casting of the bell.[163] A second competition was subsequently launched among local architects, but once again the winning design (by Leo Kottke) was not realized. As a frame consisting of two curved arms joining at the top to hold the bell, one made symbolically from rusty steel and the other from stainless steel, it proved too expensive due to the rapidly rising price of steel. Moreover, the competition caused outrage among some architects, who claimed that they were not adequately represented on the jury, and that the Board of Trustees was interested only in the bell, not the architecture.[164]

In the meantime, the bell had been cast on 29 September 2000 at a forgery in Dessau.[165] Its symbolism as a peace bell was highlighted through text on the bell itself: large letters spelling 'Keine Gewalt' in the centre of the bell, and smaller lettering around the bottom which made the link to 1989: 'I ring for peace and freedom + Without freedom no peace + Without peace no freedom'. It was still unclear, however, what would happen to the bell and where it would stand. In October 2001, the Board provisionally placed the bell on a simple platform on the Market Square (close to the originally proposed location), with the aim of provoking public debate during a three-month period. Here it also adopted wider symbolism; it was the venue for 'peace prayers' on 3 October, thus harking back to 1989, and soon became the location of regular peace vigils, especially in the aftermath of 9/11.[166] For some, however, it became little more than a hindrance for the Christmas Market on the square, and for others its proportions (over two metres high) were 'monstrous'.[167] The result of the exercise was that the bell became a concrete concept in residents' minds, yet it also came to represent a tortuous history of delays, conflicts and compromises. Indeed, the final decision represented a compromise, for rather than initiate a third competition, the design of second prize winner Dieter Bankert was realized: a simple frame that holds the bell eleven metres above the ground (see Figure 6.3). The final location – between a busy shopping centre and the town hall – maintains proximity to the latter, but does not allow the bell such a central position as originally intended. Inaugurated at an open-air service on 9 November 2002, once again highlighting the role of the church in 1989, it rang thirteen times, once for each year that had passed since the fall of the Wall.[168] It now sounds at 6 p.m. on Fridays, when the demonstrations used to begin, and on other special occasions relevant to its function as a peace bell, such as anniversaries of the bombing of Dessau in 1945. On 3 October 2010, in honour of the twentieth anniversary of unification, the area around the bell was named Square of German Unity.[169]

Controversies concerning the location, the finances and the form of the bell did little to promote it in a positive sense, and discontent continued even after its erection, with the frame gaining nicknames such as the 'Dessau gallows' or the 'guillotine'.[170] However, the large amount of public time, effort and money invested in the project had raised awareness of its history, achieving one of the main aims of its initiators, and there were few outspoken voices against the idea of a peace bell per se. Indeed, its final form represented a compromise

Figure 6.3 Peace Bell (frame designed by Dieter Bankert, 2002), Platz der Deutschen Einheit, Dessau. Photograph by Anna Saunders.

for all concerned, even the Board, reflecting the democratic decision-making processes that had resulted in the destruction of the weapons in the first place. Similarly evocative of 1989, it became a popular meeting place of demonstrators for peace, civil rights and often anti-government groups. In 2003, for example, protests against the Iraq War witnessed banners reading not only 'vigil for peace' but also 'Dessau citizens for peace' and 'against war, the breaching of international law and nationalism', thus reflecting the values for which Ehm and his colleagues fought in 1989/90.[171] Having become a central point for demonstrations, however, it has more recently also been used by right-wing and 'Gida' demonstrations – as well as numerous counter-demonstrations. In many ways, this once much-criticized site has thus become the 'spiritual centre' of the town that its architect had hoped for, and one at which citizens – of all political colours – are exercising their democratic right to demonstrate.[172] Memory activist Ehm was not, however, content to conclude the history of the peace bell there. On 9 November 2009, the Board launched a further fundraising campaign, with the aim of creating stelae around the site on which images and texts would explain the history of the demonstrations in Dessau, the specific history of the factory and the bell, as well as the relevance of the term 'swords into ploughshares'.[173] Ehm is, indeed, highly conscious that this history is gradually slipping from collective memory, and while social activity at the bell may renew its central values, he is keen for its specific history not to be forgotten. For this reason, he also gives talks in schools and aspires to link information around the site to scannable QR codes in order to enable visitors to access further information, film clips and documents online.[174] In this way, the ongoing development of the bell has provided the impetus for a much wider sphere of documentary and community activity, fusing cultural and communicative forms of remembrance together in order to strengthen local engagement in this past.

Transforming the Fortunes of Magdeburg? The Development of a Citizens' Monument

In contrast to Dessau, the roots of Magdeburg's monument to 1989 lie in the post-*Wende* period, yet it bears a number of similarities to the former, especially in debates over form and location, as well as the involvement of a group of engaged citizens in intensive fundraising efforts. This group, officially the 'Board of Trustees for the Magdeburg Citizens' Monument', was formed in March 1999 and chaired by Rudolf

Evers, equally as deserving of the title 'memory activist' as Ehm. Despite chairing a non-party group, it is significant that Evers was also a member of the CDU (the party that provided the most financial backing for the monument) and an active participant in the demonstrations of 1989. Alongside his student memories of and participation in the uprising of 1953, it is this period that he considers to have significantly influenced his political attitudes. As in Leipzig, the most important turning point of 1989 in Magdeburg had been 9 October, a tense date on which 4,500 attended the Monday evening peace prayers at the cathedral, despite approximately two thousand members of the security forces being on standby outside.[175] After the *Wende*, however, disillusionment over the political changes was quick to set in, and by the mid 1990s Evers became increasingly concerned by growing discontent among the Magdeburg population, as seen in the high unemployment rate, serious economic problems, rising levels of right-wing extremism, and widespread disappointment resulting from 1989. He thus founded the Board with a view to remind people of what they had achieved in 1989 and to encourage a new pride in the past as well as social engagement in the present. Evers even suggested that the monument should help to counteract the growing wave of *Ostalgie* by reminding people of the repression and infringement of human rights that took place in the GDR.[176] He considered the monument to be an *Erinnerungsmal* (sign of remembrance), a structure that would provoke active memories of a past period and encourage reflection on the present. In this way, its designation as a 'Citizens' Monument' was key to its existence, and as Evers claimed, 'For me it is important that as many [people] as possible are able to say: that is my monument'.[177] The constitution of the Board thus incorporated in its aims the promotion of local history and the care of local heritage, and saw the future monument to constitute a 'contribution to the present and future of [the community] living together'.[178]

The Magdeburg town council approved the monument project in July 1999 with no dissenting votes and two abstentions.[179] Significantly, the motion was put forward by all political parties except the PDS, and explicitly highlighted the need for such a project ten years after 1989.[180] The tenth anniversary of 9 October 1989 was thus marked by the laying of a sandstone plaque near the cathedral, stating the intention to build a monument: 'WE ARE THE PEOPLE. The Magdeburg Citizens' Monument will be built here, funded by donations from the people of Saxony-Anhalt'. Significantly, however, its final location had not been agreed upon, echoing heated controversies over location seen in other case studies. Suggestions including locations in front of the *Land* parliament building, which would have reminded politicians of their duty to the people, or on the cathedral square, where the demonstrations took place, were both deemed inappropriate due to questions of logistics, finances and preservation orders.[181] The region's Head of Conservation also harboured concerns that a central location for a traditional, upright monument would lead to an unwelcome and old-fashioned 'heroization' of 1989.[182] Consequently, three further locations close to the cathedral were considered, with the decision finally falling in favour of a small square to the west of its main entrance, which symbolically marked the starting point of the demonstrations. Evers countered the criticism that monuments should not be built to living people by reiterating its symbolism as a structure to highlight the values of 1989, such as civil courage, freedom and democracy, rather than specific people.[183] This attitude was demonstrated in the design competition of 1999, which asked artists to consider four elements in their entries, all of which reflected the wider values of 1989: 'the protection of the church for all', 'the spirit of civil courage', 'non-violence' and 'will'.[184]

In January 2000, three prize winners were announced, each of whom was asked to refine their design. In April, the first prize went to Magdeburg artist Andreas Kaiser, who proposed to embed 2,500 footprints into the ground, in memory of protesters' demonstrations through the town. These would be accompanied by hundreds of small, ground-level lights, which would be illuminated on Monday evenings in memory of the candles carried by demonstrators. Kaiser hoped to involve local citizens by asking them to bring their own shoes, in order to make individual footprints on the concrete.[185] Despite being a truly participatory monument that involved the local population, this design was never realized as the long-term costs were deemed too high, the technicalities of the under-floor electricity over a large area were seen to be too risky and the longevity of the design proved questionable. Indeed, it was estimated that it would last for a maximum of thirty years, given that the area was used by pedestrians and subject to cold winter temperatures. As a structure that was 'primarily intended for posterity', and which initiators hoped would still stand in 250 years, this proved problematic.[186] Traditional understandings of monumental form thus resonated, despite the fact that a heroic monument was not desired. Instead, the design of second prize winner Norbert Zagel was realized. This took the form of a truncated cone, sliced down the middle, with one half placed upside down (see Figure 6.4). Together the two parts resemble a torch, especially at night, when lights in its base shine out of the structure. Thematizing the two halves of Germany and the idea of light emerging from darkness, the structure evokes memories

Figure 6.4 Citizens' Monument (Norbert Zagel, 2003), west of cathedral entrance, Magdeburg. Photograph by Anna Saunders.

of candles. The four words 'peace, freedom, democracy, unity' are also inscribed around the base, highlighting the central values of 1989.

The initial completion date of 9 October 2001 could not be met, due to a lack of finances. For the Board, the raising of funds for a people's monument uniquely through public donations was crucial; as Evers explicitly stated, 'We don't want any state subsidy'.[187] The funding consequently became an integral part of the monument, and donors' names were to be made visible around the monument. To this end, 'citizen stones' were sold from 2002 to individuals, social organizations and businesses for the symbolic amounts of 89, 189 and 1,989 euros respectively. Each stone was engraved with the name of the donor, and by the time of the monument's erection, 470 stones were engraved and laid in the ground around the monument.[188] Stones were bought by numerous Magdeburg residents, firms, political parties (predominantly the CDU), schools and youth groups, as well as some of Magdeburg's partner towns (e.g. Braunschweig and Nashville, USA). Some donations came from other towns in Saxony-Anhalt, although despite initiators' intentions for the monument to represent the whole region, local loyalties meant that support from beyond Magdeburg's boundaries remained relatively weak.[189] Critical anniversaries were also used to raise the profile of the monument; a press conference was arranged on 12 August 2002, for instance, deliberately timed to ensure press reports on 13 August, the anniversary of the building of the Berlin Wall. In this way, the brutality of the SED regime could be highlighted, underlining the nature of the monument's message.[190]

Alongside Lotto money and donations in kind from local firms, the total sum was secured by June 2003, when a foundation stone was laid on the site of the monument. The unveiling then took place on 3 October 2003, the occasion on which Magdeburg hosted the national 'day of unity' celebrations in the presence of Chancellor Schröder and President Rau. The ceremony was symbolically rich, not least because it took place after a service in the cathedral, thus seeing crowds come out of the building onto the square as they would have done in 1989. The actual unveiling was carried out by two representative individuals, a thirteen-year-old schoolgirl, Paula Grünheid, who was born in the autumn of 1989 and had requested a 'citizen stone' for her birthday, and the writer Elisabeth Graul, who had spent numerous years in prison in the GDR.[191] Both represented the essence of the monument: the desire to spread the message of 1989 to future generations, while at the same reminding those present of the repressive nature of the GDR. A metal cylinder was also built into the base of the monument, containing a copy of the *Magdeburger Volksstimme* newspaper, a list of the sponsors and a set of euro coins, thus situating it in a specific time for future generations. Local newspaper reports highlighted not only 1989 as a moment of pride, but also the achievement of locals in erecting this monument so swiftly, as a 'bottom-up' enterprise. As Wolfgang Böhmer, Minister President of Saxony-Anhalt, claimed, the monument demonstrated what could be achieved 'if they [the people] take their own fate into their hands',[192] and Evers hoped that it would represent 'the true spirit of the town';[193] once again, the values of 1989 came to the fore in discourse surrounding the monument. Interestingly, requests have continued to arrive from citizens who wish to purchase stones, demonstrating the eagerness of some to have their names associated with this historical event in retrospect, and the building of a local tradition around the monument that may continue to grow for a number of years to come.[194]

A Truly Democratic Project? Plauen's *Wende* Monument

The final case study demonstrates many traits typical of the above regional monuments to the peaceful revolution in terms of its initiators and its local standing. Above all, however, it illustrates the importance attached to the notion of democracy and the significance of regional pride. The latter was particularly significant in Plauen, a small town at the southern tip of the GDR near the Czech and former German-German borders, which played a key role in 1989 that has often been forgotten. Here, on 7 October 1989 – significantly the GDR's fortieth anniversary – the first mass peaceful demonstration took place in the GDR, in which up to a quarter of the town's population of seventy thousand took to the streets. In historian Ilko-Sascha Kowalczuk's words, 'the real earthquake on this day didn't take place in East Berlin, Leipzig or Dresden, but in Plauen'.[195] The town had registered strong opposition to the SED during the previous year, and even official statistics from the 7 May elections showed Plauen to have had the highest number of 'no' votes (3.82 per cent).[196] Moreover, on 5 October, when trains taking GDR refugees from Prague (where they had camped out in the grounds of the West German embassy) to the Federal Republic drove through Plauen, several hundred people gathered at the station and a number were arrested. Two days later, crowds amassed in response to the circulation of individually written flyers and to word of mouth. While the police attempted to scatter demonstrators with water cannons, this resulted only in greater resolve among protesters to stay. Superintendent Thomas Küttler, head of Saxony's protestant church, played a significant role in calming the crowd and negotiating with the party and police to withdraw armed forces, thus ensuring a peaceful outcome and resulting in this being the first mass demonstration to see the SED capitulate.

Plauen's role in 1989 has often been forgotten, primarily because images of the demonstration were few and far between, and the absence of Western cameras – in contrast to East Berlin on the same day – meant that the news was not quickly disseminated and was soon overtaken by the larger demonstration in Leipzig two days later. Indeed, as Wolfgang Sachs, one of the initiators of the monument claimed, 'Within German memory, Plauen citizens are simply forgotten'.[197] It was for this reason, alongside the fact that large-scale monument proposals were simultaneously taking root in both Berlin and Leipzig, that in March 2008 Sachs presented a proposal for a monument to the local Lions Club, a society that engaged in promoting civil, cultural and social activities. The forthcoming twentieth anniversary provided the ideal opportunity to promote such a cause, and three other societal organizations, the Rotary, Kiwanis and Soroptimists, joined the Lions Club with the aim of gaining political backing for a monument and raising public awareness. The town council passed a motion for the monument in an uncontroversial vote – despite objections from Die Linke – and Saxony's Minister President Stanislaw Tillich became the project's patron.[198] Although the town council had previously considered it too early to erect a monument, the fact that the proposal came from within the population gave it the necessary mandate.[199] Indeed, Sachs, himself a demonstrator in 1989, was at pains to stress that this was not to be a monument 'from above', but rather one that came from the people themselves;[200] as in Magdeburg, the initiators undertook to organize and finance the project without the direct involvement of the town council, inevitably leading to complex discussions over finances. The issue of location was, however, decided reasonably early. Although one obvious location was outside the theatre, where the demonstration began, this was not logistically possible, as the space was already occupied by a sculpture. Instead, it was agreed that it would be built on the 'Tunnel', a pedestrian area within view of the town hall and on which demonstrators protested in 1989; the authenticity of location was considered one of the most important criteria. While the town provided money for landscaping, the monument itself was to be funded through public donations, which were encouraged through a variety of activities such as auctions, public collection boxes and sponsorships from local businesses. By the time the monument was built, 90 per cent of the funds had come from donations, with the town covering the shortfall.[201]

It was not until the design competition was in full swing that the project provoked controversial debate. Nine artists were invited to submit designs in April 2009, with the jury choosing two finalists in June, who were to revise their designs. From the end of June, all fourteen designs (some artists had submitted more than one) were displayed anonymously in the town hall. After the opening of the exhibition, however, critical voices emerged, with a number of residents objecting that they had had little say in the competition, especially considering that many had donated considerable funds to the project. The local newspaper printed numerous readers' letters that claimed the process was undemocratic, and many adopted slogans from 1989 to defend their interests, stating, for instance, 'We are still the people' or 'We are the people – not the jury'.[202] A smaller number objected that any kind of monument was inappropriate given the ongoing economic problems, and one reader suggested instead a monument to the 'nameless unemployed'.[203] State Secretary Rolf Schwanitz (SPD), chronicler of the peaceful revolution in Plauen, further objected to the depiction of walls in many designs, for although the demonstration on 7 October may have helped pave the way for the fall of the Berlin Wall, this was not one of its primary aims.[204] In the first instance, the competition organizer defended decisions, stating that 'art is not democratic' and 'we don't want a decision like at the [Eurovision] Song Contest'.[205] Relatively quickly, however, the message changed, with initiators claiming they had always believed that public opinion should hold weight in the discussion, and that the process should be as transparent as possible.[206] Within two weeks, it was announced that the designs would be exhibited in the town's indoor shopping centre, in order to reach a greater proportion of people.[207] The public was also encouraged to vote for their favourite design, either using a voting slip (copies of which were also printed in the local newspaper) or online. The exhibition was opened with a citizens' forum in the shopping centre, at which the mayor, initiators of the monument and activists from 1989 raised the profile of the project and the history of 1989. Identification with the project grew during August, as more people became involved and the exhibition was extended from its two-week period, due to significant levels of interest.[208] Although the vote was initially to be taken into account simply alongside the jury's final decision, the popular vote was given increasing weight. On 17 September 2009, the result was announced: of the 2,849 votes, the design by Peter Luban won 34.7 per cent, winning head and shoulders above over designs (second place gaining 14.4 per cent).[209] On the admission of Sachs, this was a huge relief, for a close vote or an unclear winner would have caused further problems and

Figure 6.5 *Wende* Monument (Peter Luban, 2010), Melanchthonstraße ('Tunnel'), Plauen. Photograph by Anna Saunders.

potentially delayed the project.[210] Furthermore, as a demonstrator in Plauen himself, Luban's mandate was seen to be particularly appropriate. The timely decision allowed the foundation stone to be laid on 7 October 2009 – the twentieth anniversary – in the presence of Federal President Horst Köhler. As in Magdeburg, a capsule was symbolically laid in the foundations, into which numerous eyewitness accounts of 7 October 1989 were placed;[211] once again, the hope for a long-standing monument was clear.

Luban's design consists of three bronze sections, joined together in cylindrical form, in the centre of which stands an illuminated acrylic stele, giving the ensemble the appearance of a candle (see Figure 6.5). Around the edge of the site stand five slim stelae, each of which carries one of the following dates: 1953, 1961, 1968, 1989 or 1990. Marking the most notable dates of social change in the GDR, they represent a story of repression, hope and freedom. This narrative is also represented on the three bronze sections, on which a complex of reliefs depicts themes such as observation and repression, as well as symbols of hope and revolution. While some sections are abstract, with the intention of encouraging the viewer's own interpretation, other sections depict specific elements: a horse, symbolic of Orwell's *Animal Farm*, stands as a warning figure and a reminder that history can repeat itself; depictions of the Markuskirche and the Malzhaus (a social and cultural centre) in Plauen, places of resistance in 1989, remind locals of their specific history; and numerous candles stand as symbols of hope and peace.[212] The text, which is integrated into the monument design, reads: 'On 7 October 1989, the first mass demonstration against the GDR regime took place in Plauen, to which the state power was forced to surrender'. Whatever opinion one may have of the monument's aesthetics – one journalist controversially stated that 'the taste of the masses says little about the quality of art'[213] – it is a design that has provoked very little resistance among residents. Indeed, after the vote was announced, newspapers and readers' pages remained relatively free of criticism, and the democratic decision-making process appeared to have quelled opposition. Participant observation of the monument also revealed relatively high interest from passers-by, with locals often making an extra effort to explain the monument to visitors, thus demonstrating their awareness of its symbolic value and local importance.

The monument was unveiled on 7 October 2010 after a discussion in the Malzhaus organized by the Konrad Adenauer Foundation and followed by a celebratory evening concert in the St Johanniskirche. Two and a half thousand people were present at the unveiling ceremony, at which a huge German flag was lifted off the monument, the national anthem was played and some of the few existing images of the demonstration of 1989 were projected onto a giant screen.[214] The date of 7 October appears to be a particularly logical one, yet it was interestingly the second choice of initiators, who had initially preferred 3 October 2010, the twentieth anniversary of unification. Due to central celebrations on this date, however, it was rejected given the unavailability of political leaders and musicians to attend the event.[215] Here we see the importance of memory politics and publicity; while a significant date must be chosen, the pragmatics of marketing and logistics often win over. The choice of 7 October also allowed a greater emphasis on regional – rather than national – events, which remained at the heart of the project throughout. Indeed, local patriotism was evident in many speeches on the day, with Plauen's leading role being highlighted both in 1989 and in the present; after all, the town had 'beaten' both Leipzig and Berlin to it. As Minister President Tillich claimed in his speech, 'With this monument, Plauen is once again the trailblazer', and in contrast to its previously 'forgotten' history, 'Plauen has won itself a place in the history books'.[216] There was much praise of the courage of demonstrators on 7 October 1989, and of the fact that this day had paved the way for the peaceful revolution as a whole.[217] Former Superintendent Thomas Küttler further claimed that 'the fanfare of freedom was first played in Plauen', and Mayor Ralf Oberdorfer (FDP) expressed his pride, stating that both the actions of 1989 and the monument had helped the reputation of the town.[218] The concept of democracy was clearly one of the winning motifs of the day, with Tillich reiterating the view of an activist from 1989 that 'the revolution continues', not on the streets, but in people's hearts and minds.[219] Interestingly, some used this emphasis to highlight concerns in the present, and a number of employees of Philips and Manroland who appeared at the ceremony with banners protesting against forthcoming redundancy measures were greeted with the applause of those present, and verbally welcomed by Tillich.[220] As in other case studies, this monument came to represent many of the broader values of 1989, symbolized not only by the strong emphasis on democracy, but also through resistance towards dominant state structures. Similarly, much of the history of the demonstrations, the monument and its role in Plauen can be found on a comprehensive website, which provides a documentary counterpart to the concrete monument, once again showing a concern with maintaining this tradition for future generations.[221]

Conclusion: The Concrete Legacy of the Peaceful Revolution

Despite claims that the peaceful revolution lacks a stable tradition of memory in contemporary Germany, there is doubtless a growing memorial presence regarding this period of history. While the first decade witnessed very few monuments, the period from 1999 saw an increase in proposed projects, first in the regions, and then in Berlin. It seems that very early projects, such as the Round Table in Schwerin, encountered difficulties precisely because the turmoil of 1989/90 was still prevalent, preventing a more considered reflection of events. Although they were no less controversial, later projects increasingly emerged as memory of this period began to settle and round anniversaries triggered commemorative events. Most significant in this development is the fact that the majority of monuments were driven by a specific social group: former demonstrators, usually male and in their forties in 1989, whose desire to find a more durable, cultural form of memory for the events of 1989 arose precisely out of the need to communicate this memory while it was still living. Archival or documentary elements of many monuments, such as the capsules inserted into the foundations at Magdeburg and Plauen, plans for information stelae at Dessau, or even the inscriptions of images from 1989 onto Berlin's proposed Freedom and Unity Monument, demonstrate a strong desire to create long-lived structures that will document this history for future generations. Not only has the inclusion of significant anniversary dates into most monument traditions aimed to create a regular point of reference, but the activities of local activists such as Ehm and Sachs in engaging local schools and the community also demonstrate a strong desire to embed this memory in the fabric of society. Once again, we see here a deliberate attempt to bring together communicative and cultural memory, demonstrating the concomitant nature of these forms.

Not only has the number of monuments to this period increased, but an identifiable tradition appears to be emerging. This has been shaped above all by the mnemonic communities that have initiated such monuments, for not only have these been dominated by male activists of a similar generation, but they have largely also been CDU supporters, and thus broadly speaking the 'winners' of unification. It is little surprise that any emerging tradition is largely self-confident and supports the present-day status quo, rather than allowing for reflection on some of the difficulties that emerged in the wake of the *Wende*. What is interesting, however, is that the element that unites most of these monuments is that of process rather than form. The desire to reflect the values of 1989 through mass participation and overtly democratic decision-making processes is evident in the majority of cases, whether through public donations, popular votes, exhibitions, symposia or school projects. In many ways, this element has become more important than the resulting structure, for monuments that have found little public support are precisely those that have failed to engage public discussion; the lukewarm response of Leipzig citizens to both Tucker-Frost's design and the Democracy Bell, as well as initial widespread animosity to the Round Table in Schwerin, appear to result in part from lacking public consultation. In the case of the two proposed Freedom and Unity Monuments in Berlin and Leipzig, both of which sought – and have hitherto largely failed – to gain public backing, the fact that they had been proposed by political actors and funded by the state, rather than emerging from grassroots campaigns, appears to have been a major stumbling block. In a somewhat ironic state of affairs, those projects that were funded without public contributions provoked mass scepticism; as in 1989, public engagement and a sense of democratic entitlement have come to the fore. In contrast, a number of others deliberately profiled their donors, either in the concept itself (as in Magdeburg) or through lists of donors (inserted into the foundations of the column in Leipzig or available online for Plauen's monument). While monuments financed by donation are not a new idea,[222] and donations from the CDU and its supporters were generally higher than from elsewhere, it could be argued that the level of engagement in these examples has been unusually broad, ranging from community groups and schoolchildren to shoppers and online bloggers. As in 1989, the aspiration for mass participation appears to have become one of the central hallmarks of these monuments.

While the importance of democratic processes appears to have found impetus in the event to be remembered, monuments to 1989/90 also appear to have been significantly shaped through their interplay with other monument projects. While this can be seen at the localized level, for example in the relationship between Berlin's proposed Freedom and Unity Monument and the older imperial monument on whose pedestal it is to stand, or between Leipzig's equivalent project and the town's extant monuments to the same period, such interplay is prevalent on a national level in connection with two areas: Holocaust remembrance and GDR monuments. The influence of the former is particularly evident in Berlin, where plans for a Freedom and Unity Monument were frequently seen as a counterweight to the Holocaust memorial, and only formally approved after the Holocaust memorial was completed. More broadly speaking, however, monuments to the peaceful revolution have had to find a suitable formal language that sets them apart from the dominant aesthetics of Holocaust remembrance and countermonumental form. While such aesthetics have now infiltrated mainstream culture to such an extent that 'counter' concepts, such as those emphasizing the transitory and the ephemeral, have become the norm, it is notable not only that a significant number of monuments to 1989/90 are designed to stand firm for generations, but that they draw on traditional concepts: a bell tower, a pillar, a figurative depiction, and two further pillar-like structures, perhaps even reminiscent of the time-honoured obelisk. Interestingly, a number of prize-winning structures also echo West German monuments to unification from the 1960s, in which two halves join together to make a – sometimes incomplete – whole.[223] Although it is notable that many of the designs constructed were not first prize winners, their eventual construction was a reflection of public involvement, and often intervention, as well as financial concern. In this way, principles at the heart of the democratic monument project – that it should be funded by and resonate among the masses – appear to shape its more conservative form. Clearly, the commemoration of 1989 as a largely positive, albeit complex date in history also removes the imperative need to engage with the concepts of absence and fragility that are so central to countermonuments engaging in Holocaust remembrance. While designs for the two proposed Freedom and Unity Monuments may not have been traditional in form, criticism that they were 'history-light' demonstrated the extent to which they ruptured past traditions. In this sense, subject matter, mass involvement and aesthetics go very much hand in hand.

In contrast, it seems that the eastern heritage of socialist realist monuments has also influenced the resulting aesthetics of monuments to the peaceful revolution. It is notable, for instance, that initiators have been keen to distance themselves from traditional heroic structures, not only in their democratic emphasis, but also in their attempt to allow for plural interpretations. Although the resulting structures have relied largely on traditional, rather than countermemorial forms, they have notably veered away from common tropes in the GDR, such as figurative forms, realism and structures of monumental proportions. Of particular note is the absence of structures that depict the masses (except for Tucker-Frost's design in Leipzig, which received negative press), a trope that could have been an obvious choice for such structures, yet which was common in GDR aesthetics. Instead, the presence of symbols such as candles (in Magdeburg and Plauen, as well as in numerous submitted designs) and concepts such as 'swords into ploughshares' depict the values and mass participation of 1989.[224] In contrast, where contemporary monument proposals have displayed a tendency towards the aesthetics of GDR monuments, objections have invariably been raised. The monumental proportions of Berlin's Freedom and Unity Monument, for example, proved to be one of its major points of contention, as was the high cost of the project at a time of economic crisis, a situation not dissimilar to the circumstances in which many GDR projects were constructed.

While monuments to the peaceful revolution thus respond to previous traditions of remembrance, they also respond to each other. This is seen above all in peripheral responses to centralized projects and narratives. Efforts in Plauen, for instance, to raise the profile of the town's legacy resulted very much in response to plans for Freedom and Unity Monuments in Berlin and Leipzig. Plans for the Leipzig monument also triggered a renewed wave of support for existing symbols of remembrance in the town, such as the St Nicholas column. Elsewhere, the problematic evolution of Berlin's national project caused an element of regional pride in local structures, which were created through local commitment and public engagement. It seems, indeed, that the regional case studies reveal a rather different situation regarding remembrance of 1989 to that in Berlin, and increasingly Leipzig. Although regional projects may not necessarily have set out to counter national narratives, their existence demands a reassessment of dominant images of this period, which feature above all Leipzig on 9 October, and Berlin on 4 and 9 November. While the importance of these dates cannot be denied, the fact remains that, as Friedrich Schorlemmer put it, 'The music of the revolution first sounded in the provinces'.[225] As such, 1989 is finding a permanent place in the memorial landscapes of regional towns, representing a democratization of remembrance and promoting a multiplicity of narratives. On the other hand, it should not be forgotten that these monuments convey the experiences and political outlook of a particular generation and mnemonic community. Their message thus presents a specific interpretation of the GDR, and represents one written by the 'winners' of unification, or indeed the 'victors' of history.

The growing memorial presence of 1989 doubtless denotes a move away from the cautionary tradition of the *Mahnmal* and a break from the 'negative nationalism' of recent decades. As the examples in this chapter show, however, the resulting memorials are hardly celebratory or heroic in nature. Indeed, their entanglement with past and present memorial trends appears to have guarded against such an approach, with many memory activists and organizations proving to be all too aware of the pitfalls of previous remembrance cultures, whether imperialist, national socialist or socialist. Fundamental concerns over democratic processes, as well as the desire to portray regional variation, also promote a diverse memorial landscape that resists a primarily national message. With this in mind, it is noteworthy that the majority of projects have chosen to emphasize the protests of 1989 rather than the resulting unification of Germany, once again avoiding clear national symbolism. If Berlin's Freedom and Unity Monument is finally built, its national focus may somewhat modify this picture, but it remains significant that both Berlin's and Leipzig's plans for national memorials have failed to ignite widespread enthusiasm, provoking instead satire and scepticism. While the events of 1989 and 1990 changed the course of German history, their memorialization so far appears to be modifying, rather than revolutionizing, the development of German memorial culture.

Notes

1. Anna Kaminsky, 'Gedenkstätten für die Opfer des Stalinismus', p. 99.
2. See Schwartz, 'The Social Context of Commemoration', *Social Forces*, pp. 375–76.
3. Zerubavel, *Time Maps*, p. 101.
4. To name but a few: Ehrhart Neubert, *Unsere Revolution: Die Geschichte der Jahre 1989/90* (Munich: Piper, 2008); Ilko-Sascha Kowalczuk, *Endspiel: Die Revolution von 1989 in der DDR* (Munich: Beck, 2009); Klaus-Dietmar Henke, *Revolution und Vereinigung 1989/90: Als in Deutschland die Realität die Phantasie überholte* (Munich: dtv, 2009); Michael Richter, *Die Friedliche*

Revolution: Aufbruch zur Demokratie in Sachsen 1989/90 (Göttingen: Vandenhoeck & Ruprecht, 2009); Andreas Rödder, Deutschland einig Vaterland: Die Geschichte der Wiedervereinigung (Munich: C.H. Beck, 2009).
5. For example: www.friedlicherevolution.de; www.zeitzeugenportal8990. de; www.chronikderwende.de; www.revolution89.de; www.meinherbst-89.de; www.freiheit-und-einheit.de; http://www.deinegeschichte. de.
6. See the anniversary website at www.berlin.de/mauerfall2014.
7. Jarausch, 'Der Umbruch 1989/90', p. 527.
8. Ilko-Sascha Kowalczuk, 'Die Vorgeschichte und die Revolution 1989 in der DDR', in Zwanzig Jahre friedliche Revolution, ed. by Martin Hermann (Jena: IKS Garamond, 2010), pp. 37–48 (38).
9. Jarausch, 'Der Umbruch 1989/90', p. 528.
10. A. Mielke, '"Glasnost ist keine Banane"', Berliner Morgenpost, 9 October 1999, p. 29.
11. Dorothee Wierling, 'Das Ende der DDR erinnern', in Bewältigte Diktaturvergangenheit? 20 Jahre DDR-Aufarbeitung, Helmstedter Colloquien Heft 12, ed. by Martin Sabrow (Leipzig: Akademische Verlagsanstalt, 2010), pp. 37–57.
12. Martin Sabrow, '"Wende" oder "Revolution"? Der Herbstumbruch 1989 und die Geschichtswissenschaft', paper presented at Forum Neuer Markt, 2 April 2009, p. 5, www.politische-bildung-brandenburg.de/links/wende_oder_revolution_sabrow.pdf (accessed 31 January 2011).
13. Ibid.
14. Ralf Geissler, 'Erinnern – aber richtig', Die Zeit, 5 January 2011, p. 10; Mahung, 'Ein Helmut-Kohl-Denkmal in Dresden!', Der Freitag, 6 February 2011, http://www.freitag.de/autoren/mahung/ein-helmut-kohl-denkmal-in-dresden (accessed 28 August 2012).
15. Ulrich Deupmann and Renate Oschlies, 'Thierse verteidigt Liste der Redner für den 9. November', Berliner Zeitung, 4 November 1999, p. 1.
16. Ralph Jessen, 'Die Montagsdemonstrationen', in Erinnerungsorte der DDR, ed. by Sabrow, pp. 466–80 (474–75).
17. Jarausch, 'Der Umbruch 1989/90', p. 526.
18. Jessen, 'Die Montagsdemonstrationen'.
19. On the memory of these dates, see Peter Steinbach, 'Der 9. November in der Erinnerung der Bundesrepublik', Deutschland Archiv, 41 (2008) 5, 877–82.
20. Sabrow, '"Wende" oder "Revolution"?'.
21. Richard Schröder, 'Plädoyer für den 3. Oktober', Die Politische Meinung (2007) 447, 6–7.
22. David Lowenthal, The Past is a Foreign Country (Cambridge: Cambridge University Press, 1985), p. 323. Emphasis in original.
23. While the term Wende is seen critically by some, as it was first introduced by Egon Krenz in October 1989, not by the people, the designation 'peaceful revolution' has yet to be adopted widely by the population, and in light of unification, its 'revolutionary' qualities are questioned by some. Numerous other terms have also been suggested, such as

'refolution', 'Zusammenbruch', 'Untergang', 'gewaltfreie Revolution' and 'democratic revolution'. See Michael Richter, 'Die Wende: Plädoyer für eine umgangssprachliche Benutzung des Begriffs', *Deutschland Archiv*, 40 (2007) 5, 861–68; Rainer Eckert, 'Gegen die Wende-Demagogie – für den Revolutionsbegriff', *Deutschland Archiv*, 40 (2007) 6, 1,084–86; Michael Richter, 'Ebenfalls gegen die Wende-Demagogie und für den Revolutionsbegriff', *Deutschland Archiv*, 40 (2007) 6, 1,086–87.

24. Flierl, *Berlin: Perspektiven durch Kultur*, pp. 177–78.
25. Gerhard Marcks' 'The Caller', erected on the Straße des 17. Juni in May 1989, provides another example; while representing peace, its symbolism has gained an extra layer following the demonstrations of 1989.
26. Some of the material in this section appears in Anna Saunders, 'The Politics of Memory in Berlin's *Freiheits- und Einheitsdenkmal*', in *Remembering and Rethinking the GDR: Multiple Perspectives and Plural Authenticities*, ed. by Anna Saunders and Debbie Pinfold (Basingstoke: Palgrave Macmillan, 2013), pp. 164–78, reproduced with permission of Palgrave Macmillan.
27. See, for example, Florian Mausbach, *Über Sinn und Ort eines nationalen Freiheits- und Einheitsdenkmals* (Berlin: Bundesamt für Bauwesen und Raumordnung, 2008), p. 3.
28. The other two winners in 2010 were Stephan Balkenhol, with a monumental kneeling man, and Andreas Meck, with a gazebo-like structure, the roof of which spelled out the words and slogans of demonstrators. Balkenhol withdrew from the competition – when all three were asked to make revisions – before the final decision was made.
29. Stefan Berg and Steffen Winter, 'Fledermäuse im Bauch', *Der Spiegel* (2014) 10, pp. 34–36.
30. Ralf Schönball, 'Einheitswippe wird nicht errichtet', *Der Tagesspiegel*, 12 April 2016, http://www.tagesspiegel.de/berlin/denkmal-in-berlin-einheitswippe-wird-nicht-errichtet/13438360.html (accessed 4 October 2016).
31. 'Ein Mauer-Denkmal von BILD für Berlin', *BILD*, 20 May 2009, http://www.bild.de/regional/berlin/berlin/fuer-berlin-8392040.bild.html (accessed 10 August 2011).
32. Deutscher Bundestag, 'Plenarprotokoll, 14/99', 13 April 2000, p. 9,328(C).
33. Rainer Haubrich, 'Denk mal, eine Wippe', *Die Welt*, 29 May 2017, https://www.welt.de/print/welt_kompakt/debatte/article165021466/Denk-mal-eine-Wippe.html (accessed 6 June 2017).
34. See Deutscher Bundestag, 'Plenarprotokoll, 14/99', p. 9,331(A).
35. Ibid., p. 9,331(C).
36. Mausbach, *Über Sinn und Ort eines nationalen Freiheits- und Einheitsdenkmals*, pp. 3 and 6.
37. Deutscher Bundestag, 'Plenarprotokoll 14/99', p. 9,328(C).
38. Ibid., p. 9,327(D).
39. Designs from the first competition were exhibited in the Kronprinzenpalais in May 2009, and from the second competition in the Martin-Gropius-Bau in October 2010. Documentations include: *Gestaltungswettbewerb für ein Freiheits- und Einheitsdenkmal in Berlin: Dokumentation des offenen Wettbewerbs 2009* (Berlin: Bundesamt für Bauwesen und Raumordnung,

2009) and Andreas Apelt (ed.), *Der Weg zum Denkmal für Freiheit und Einheit* (Schwalbach: Wochenschau, 2009). The main website is managed by the Deutsche Gesellschaft e.V.: http://www.freiheits-und-einheitsdenkmal. de/.

40. See, for example, Bernd Neumann, cited in Susanne Beyer, '"Monument des Glücks"', *Der Spiegel* (2009) 19, p. 148.
41. *Gestaltungswettbewerb für ein Freiheits- und Einheitsdenkmal Berlin: Auslobungstext – 1. Stufe* (Berlin: Bundesamt für Bauwesen und Raumordnung, 2008), p. 4.
42. Deutscher Bundestag, 'Plenarprotokoll 16/124', 9 November 2007, p. 12,965(B).
43. Günter Nooke, 'Ein Denkmal für die Einheit in Freiheit? Formen der Auseinandersetzung mit der DDR', in *Woran erinnern? Der Kommunismus in der deutschen Erinnerungskultur*, ed. by Peter März and Hans-Joachim Veen (Cologne: Böhlau, 2006), pp. 111–22 (122).
44. Deutscher Bundestag, 'Plenarprotokoll 14/99', pp. 9,327(D)–9,328(A).
45. Godehard Janzing, 'Ein neuer Boom der Memorialkultur', *die tageszeitung*, 8/9 April 2000, p. 25. See also Schönfeld, 'Kritisches Denkzeichen und restauratives Denkmal'.
46. 'Freiheitsdenkmal soll beim ehemaligen Berliner Stadtschloss entstehen', hib-Meldung, 13 March 2008, http://www.bundestag.de/aktuell/ hib/2008/2008_078/01 (accessed 12 August 2008).
47. Deutscher Bundestag, 'Plenarprotokoll 16/124', p. 12,965(C).
48. Deutscher Bundestag, 'Plenarprotokoll 14/199', 9 November 2001, p. 19,507(A).
49. Ten million euros were to go to the Berlin monument, and five million to a monument in Leipzig.
50. 'Gruppenantrag im Deutschen Bundestag, 2000', cited in Nooke, 'Ein Denkmal für die Einheit in Freiheit?', p. 112.
51. Deutscher Bundestag, 'Drucksache 16/6974', 7 November 2007, p. 4.
52. Wolfgang Tiefensee, in 'Plenarprotokoll 16/124', p. 12,950.
53. Deutscher Bundestag, 'Plenarprotokoll 14/199', p. 19,507(D).
54. Interestingly, the competition for the monument to Wilhelm I was anything but democratic. See Jürgen Tietz, *Berliner Verwandlungen: Hauptstadt / Architektur / Denkmal* (Berlin: Verlag Bauwesen, 2000), pp. 78–80.
55. See, for example, Petra Pau (PDS), in Deutscher Bundestag, 'Plenarprotokoll 14/99', p. 9,332(A).
56. Lukrezia Jochimsen, cited in 'Einheitsdenkmal soll auf den Berliner Schlossplatz', *Süddeutsche Zeitung*, 13 March 2008.
57. Andreas Kilb, 'Ei der Nation', *Frankfurter Allgemeine Zeitung*, 30 April 2009, http://www.faz.net/aktuell/feuilleton/einheitsdenkmal-ei-der-nat ion-1790200.html (accessed 28 August 2012).
58. Presse- und Informationsamt der Bundesregierung, 'Neues Wettbewerbsverfahren zu Berliner Freiheits- und Einheitsdenkmal beschlossen', Press Release No. 293, 2009, https://www.firmenpresse.de/ pressinfo99811/neues-wettbewerbsverfahren-zu-berliner-freiheits-und-einheitsdenkmal-beschlossen.html (accessed 20 December 2017).

59. This fact caused outrage among participating artists and architects, over 180 of whom signed an online petition. See http://freiheitsdenkmal-berlin.de/.
60. A. Mania, 'Ausstellung zum Wettbewerb für ein Freiheits- und Einheitsdenkmal, Berlin', artnet, 29 May 2009, http://www.artnet.de/magazine/kommentar/mania/mania05-29-09.asp (accessed 8 September 2009).
61. '"Kompletter Schrott" Wettbewerb für Einheitsdenkmal', *Welt Online*, 28 April 2009, http://www.welt.de/kultur/article3641729/Wettbewerb-fuer-Einheitsdenkmal.html (accessed 8 September 2009).
62. See, for example, Andreas Kilb, 'Einheitsdenkmal: Freiheit für die Schlümpfe', FAZ.NET, 5 May 2009, http://www.faz.net/aktuell/feuilleton/debatten/einheitsdenkmal-freiheit-fuer-die-schluempfe-1801909.html (accessed 20 December 2017).
63. Thomas Brussig, 'Brussig: "Nicht die Künstler, wir haben versagt"', *Der Tagesspiegel*, 8 May 2009, http://www.tagesspiegel.de/kultur/Einheitsdenkmal-Thomas-Brussig-Mitte;art772,2792018 (accessed 8 September 2009).
64. *Gestaltungswettbewerb für ein Freiheits- und Einheitsdenkmal Berlin. Auslobungstext – 1. Stufe*, p. 33.
65. Presse- und Informationsamt der Bundesregierung, 'Neues Wettbewerbsverfahren zu Berliner Freiheits- und Einheitsdenkmal beschlossen'.
66. Evelyn Finger, 'Mehr Revolution wagen!', *Die Zeit*, 9 July 2009, p. 48.
67. Johannes Milla, cited in Amber Sayah, 'Nicht nur ein Denkmal, sondern ein Mach-mal', *Stuttgarter Zeitung*, 7 October 2010, p. 33.
68. Michael Bienert, 'Rauf auf die Bundeswippe!', *Stuttgarter Zeitung*, 5 October 2010, p. 26; H. Nutt, 'Auf der Deutschland-Wippe', *Berliner Zeitung*, 14 April 2011, p. 23; Jens Bisky, 'Salatschüssel der Einheit, Spielort für bewegte Bürger', *Süddeutsche Zeitung*, 14 April 2011, p. 11; Andreas Kilb, 'Unter diesem Dach können wir in Ruhe von Deutschland träumen', *FAZ*, 5 October 2010, p. 31; Harald Jähner, 'Der Bürger in der Waagschale', *Berliner Zeitung*, 13 April 2011, p. 4; Ralf Schönball, 'Bewegt vom Bürgerwillen', *Der Tagesspiegel*, 15 April 2011, p. 9.
69. Hanno Rauterberg, 'Das ist das Denkmal!', *Die Zeit*, 21 April 2011, pp. 41–42.
70. Schönfeld, 'Kritisches Denkzeichen und restauratives Denkmal', p. 166.
71. Matthias Flügge, interviewed by Joachim Scholl on *Deutschlandradio Kultur*, 14 April 2011, http://www.dradio.de/dkultur/sendungen/thema/1435816/ (accessed 8 September 2011).
72. *Gestaltungswettbewerb für ein Freiheits- und Einheitsdenkmal in Berlin – 2010: Protokoll der Preisgerichtssitzung* (Berlin: Bundesamt für Bauwesen und Raumordnung, 2010), p. 18.
73. Bisky, 'Salatschüssel der Einheit'.
74. See, for example, Andreas Kilb, 'Bewegte Bürger, umstellt von Zäunen und Wachen', *FAZ*, 15 April 2011, p. 33.

75. For example, 'Plenarprotokoll 16/124', p. 12,963(A); Jochimsen, 'Die linke Gegenstimme zu'.
76. For example, Deutscher Bundestag, 'Plenarprotokoll 14/199', p. 19,509(A).
77. Egon Bahr at second 'Hearing', 14 June 2007, cited in *Der Weg zum Denkmal für Freiheit und Einheit*, ed. by Apelt, p. 105.
78. Wolfgang Hübner, 'Einheit ohne Sockel', *Neues Deutschland*, 7 July 2009, p. 6.
79. See Jähner, 'Der Bürger in der Waagschale'; Harry Nutt, 'Einheit', *Frankfurter Rundschau*, 19 June 2008, http://www.fr.de/kultur/times-mager-einheit-a-1184147 (accessed 20 December 2017).
80. Information from museum attendant on 28 October 2010, who estimated approximately one hundred visitors per day.
81. The *Berliner Zeitung*, for instance, presented the choice between the three finalists as one between 'the plague, cholera or typhus', in Sebastian Preuss, 'Verschaukelt', *Berliner Zeitung*, 13 April 2011, p. 25.
82. Günter Nooke at second 'Hearing', 14 June 2007, cited in *Der Weg zum Denkmal für Freiheit und Einheit*, ed. by Apelt, p. 95.
83. See, for example, Fabian Klaus, 'Grenzmuseen brauchen mehr Unterstützung', *Thüringische Landeszeitung*, 16 September 2010.
84. Nutt, 'Auf der Deutschland-Wippe'.
85. 'Einheitsdenkmal-Entwürfe gefallen Wowereit nicht', Deutsche Presse-Agentur, 7 October 2010. Also confirmed in discussion with Rainer Klemke.
86. Harry Nutt, 'Schaukeln für Deutschland', *Berliner Zeitung*, 4 October 2010, p. 29.
87. See, for example, Christiane Peitz, 'Mehr Demokratie wiegen', *Potsdamer Neueste Nachrichten*, 13 April 2011, http://www.pnn.de/kultur/391889/ (accessed 20 December 2017); Jähner, 'Der Bürger in der Waagschale'.
88. See, for example, Jähner, 'Der Bürger in der Waagschale'.
89. See, for example, Rauterberg, 'Das ist das Denkmal!'; André Schmitz, cited in Rudiger Schaper, 'Diven und Denkmäler', *Tagesspiegel*, 13 May 2009, p. 23. Most prominently, this argument was made by the Minister of Culture, Monika Grütters, after the project was ended. See 'Brandenburger Tor ist Symbol für Einheit, Freiheit und Frieden', *Deutschlandfunk*, 7 September 2016, http://www.deutschlandfunk.de/monika-gruetters-zum-einheits-denkmal-brandenburger-tor-ist.691.de.html?dram:article_id=365238 (accessed 6 October 2016).
90. Schönfeld, 'Kritisches Denkzeichen und restauratives Denkmal', p. 172.
91. Peter Wensierski, 'Streit um Einheitsdenkmal – Es lebe der Kaiser', *Spiegel Online*, 26 November 2016, http://www.spiegel.de/kultur/gesellschaft/berlin-streit-um-einheitsdenkmal-die-kaiserzeit-lebt-a-1123153.html (accessed 7 July 2017).
92. 'Unity and justice and freedom' is the first line of the German national anthem. 'Pressemitteilung Deutsche Gesellschaft e.V.', 2 June 2017, http://www.freiheits-und-einheitsdenkmal.de/images/pdf/02062017pressemitt ilungdg.pdf (accessed 7 July 2017).

93. 'Freiheits- und Einheitsdenkmal beschlossene Sache', 1 June 2017, http://www.freiheits-und-einheitsdenkmal.de/images/pdf/01062017pressemitteilung-_CDU_CSU-Fraktion.pdf (accessed 7 July 2017).
94. For historical details, see Reiner Tetzner, *Leipziger Ring. Aufzeichnungen eines Montagsdemonstranten. Oktober 1989 bis 1. Mai 1990* (Frankfurt am Main: Luchterhand Literaturverlag, 1990); Ekkehard Kuhn, *'Wir sind das Volk!' Die friedliche Revolution in Leipzig, 9. Oktober 1989* (Berlin: Ullstein, 1999); Martin Jankowski, *Der Tag, der Deutschland veränderte. 9. Oktober 1989* (Leipzig: Evangelische Verlagsanstalt, 2007); Doris Mundus, *Leipzig 1989: Eine Chronik* (Leipzig: Lehmstedt Verlag, 2009).
95. See, for example, Ekkehard Kuhn, *Der Tag der Entscheidung: Leipzig, 9. Oktober 1989* (Berlin: Ullstein, 1992).
96. Ironic, as it followed the Soviet example of declaring towns as such for their heroism during the Second World War. See excerpt of Hein's speech on 4 November 1989 at http://www.mdr.de/damals/avobjekt1650.html (accessed 10 September 2011).
97. Mathias Orbeck, 'Von Leipzig ging 1989 die Friedliche Revolution aus – das Jubiläum soll 1999 Touristen anziehen', *Leipziger Volkszeitung*, 1 October 1998, p. 16.
98. Stadt Leipzig, 'Lichtfest Aufbruch Leipzig', 2009, http://www.leipzig.de/de/buerger/politik/herbst89/2009/lichtfest/ (accessed 10 September 2011). See also Alexandra Kaiser, '"We Were Heroes." Local Memories of Autumn 1989: Revising the Past', in *Remembering and Rethinking the GDR*, ed. by Saunders and Pinfold, pp. 179–94.
99. Evelyn Finger, 'Welche war die Heldenstadt?', *Die Zeit*, 17 September 2010.
100. 'Nikolaikirchhof Leipzig: Ausschreibung', 1992, document in files of Kulturstiftung Leipzig. I am particularly grateful to Dr Wolfgang Hocquél for his help in viewing these files.
101. Kulturstiftung Leipzig, 'Der neue Nikolaikirchhof', brochure (no date), p. 4.
102. Markus Cottin, Karl-Heinz Kretzschmar, Dieter Kürschner and Ilona Petzold, *Leipziger Denkmale*, vol. 2 (Beucha: Sax-Verlag, 2009), p. 49.
103. Andreas Tappert, 'Heiße Phase bei Neugestaltung des Nikolaikirchhofes beginnt', *Leipziger Volkszeitung*, 6 January 1998, p. 11.
104. Kulturstiftung Leipzig, web archive, http://kulturstiftung-leipzig.de/projekte/archiv/ (accessed 10 September 2011).
105. 'Spender für '89-Kunstwerk gesucht', *Leipziger Volkszeitung*, 10 September 1997, p. 11.
106. Kulturstiftung Leipzig, 'Die Säule auf dem Nikolaikirchhof', *Sonderdruck Leipziger Blätter*, Nr. 35/1999.
107. Andrea Richter, 'Denkmal neben dem Gotteshaus enthüllt', *Leipziger Volkszeitung*, 11 November 1999, p. 13.
108. Andrea Richter, 'Schutz für Nikolaisäule', *Leipziger Volkszeitung*, 10 November 1999, p. 15.
109. *Leipziger Volkszeitung*, 15 April 2000, p. 9.

110. Andreas Tappert, 'Stiftung überreicht Preise an engagierte Journalisten', *Leipziger Volkszeitung*, 5 May 2001, p. 8.
111. Erich Loest, 'Nie waren Genies so wertvoll', *Nordwest-Zeitung, Oldenburger Nachrichten*, 15 January 2010, p. 14; Thomas Mayer, '"Wir sind das Volk"', *Leipziger Volkszeitung*, 22 December 2010, p. 19.
112. Christiane Lösch, 'Jury favorisiert Würfel-Entwurf als Leipziger Einheitsdenkmal – Leser für "Herbstgarten"', *LVZ online*, 7 July 2011; 'Einheitsdenkmal bewegt die Leser', *Leipziger Volkszeitung*, 15–16 January 2011, p. 19.
113. Christine Hochstein, 'Anhörung im Rathaus: Gestaltung des Nikolaikirchhofes erhitzt die Gemüter', *Leipziger Volkszeitung*, 21 July 1998, p. 6; Andrea Richter, '"Brunnen macht den Platz kaput"', *Leipziger Volkszeitung*, 19 June 1998, p. 16.
114. See, for example, readers' letters in *Leipziger Volkszeitung*, 24 June 1998, p. 21; Hochstein, 'Anhörung im Rathaus'.
115. Andrea Richter, 'OBM legt Brunnen für Nikolaikirchhof auf Eis', *Leipziger Volkszeitung*, 8 February 1998, p. 11.
116. Ingolf Rosendahl, 'Dritter Anlauf für Brunnen an St. Nikolai', *Leipziger Volkszeitung*, 1 March 2003, p. 15.
117. 'Künstlerische Lichtinstallation – Nikolaikirchhof Leipzig. Ausschreibung', 2002, document in files of Kulturstiftung Leipzig.
118. 'Protokoll der Jury zum Gutachterverfahren Lichtinstallation auf dem Nikolaikirchhof am 27.02.2003', document in files of Kulturstiftung Leipzig.
119. Tilo Schulz and Kim Wortelkamp, 'public light_öffentliches licht', competition entry in files of Kulturstiftung Leipzig.
120. dahl, 'Schau zeigt Ideen für Nikolaikirchhof', *Leipziger Volkszeitung*, 13 March 2003, p. 16.
121. Cottin et al., *Leipziger Denkmale*, p. 50.
122. Werner Klötzer, 'Info- und Diskussionsmaterial für die Beratung am 13.12.2007', Leipzig, 30 November 2007, document in files of Kulturstiftung Leipzig.
123. 'Gutachterverfahren. Künstlerische Installation – Demokratieglocke Herbst 89. Ausschreibung', Leipzig, 5 June 2008; Klötzer, 'Info- und Diskussionsmaterial für die Beratung am 13.12.2007'.
124. See, for example, *Leipziger Volkszeitung* in 2009, on 5 January, p. 18; 14 January, p. 16; 17 January, p. 18; 7 April, p. 16.
125. Readers' letters in *Leipziger Volkszeitung*, 5 January 2009, p. 18.
126. While the Easter egg clearly also symbolizes new life, this nickname was evidently intended to undermine the serious intentions of its patrons.
127. Robert Schimke, 'Kulturkompetenz', *Kreuzer*, 1 July 2008; Robert Schimke, 'Erinnerung polieren', *Die Tageszeitung*, 16 June 2008, p. 13.
128. The design is in the hands of the museum in the Runde Ecke, outside of which the monument was initially to be built.
129. As this square was being totally redeveloped, a new monument at its heart would have provided it with a suitable focus. The other popular location, Augustusplatz, considered more historically 'authentic', was

already overburdened with monuments and fountains. At the time of writing, Leuschnerplatz has partially been renamed, now carrying the rather cumbersome official name of 'Wilhelm-Leuschner-Platz/Platz der Friedlichen Revolution'. The long-term name of the square seems uncertain, given the failure of the monument competition.

130. Mathias Orbeck, 'Die Welt nach Leipzig einladen', *Leipziger Volkszeitung*, 27 April 2010, p. 18.
131. Stadt Leipzig, 'Medieninformation', Leipzig, 14 February 2011, 141/mmb (document available at the 'citizens' forum', 8 March 2011); Peter Krutsch, 'Wir brauchen kein Denkmal', *Leipziger Volkszeitung*, 7 February 2009; Mathias Orbeck, 'Anrufer lehnen Denkmal ab', *Leipziger Volkszeitung*, 13 January 2011, p. 19; 'Einheitsdenkmal bewegt die Leser', *Leipziger Volkszeitung*, 15–16 January 2011, p. 19.
132. See http://www.denkmaldialog-leipzig.de/ (accessed 31 August 2012); mi/bm, 'Freiheits- und Einheitsdenkmal: Leipziger CDU will Bürger über Entwürfe entscheiden lassen', *LVZ online*, 17 August 2012, http://www.lvz-online.de/leipzig/citynews/freiheits-und-einheitsdenkmal-leipziger-cdu-will-buerger-ueber-entwuerfe-entscheiden-lassen/r-citynews-a-151509.html (accessed 31 August 12).
133. M+M / ANNABAU, 'Erläuterungstext', http://www.leipzig.de/fileadmin/mediendatenbank/leipzig-de/Stadt/02.4_Dez4_Kultur/41_Kulturamt/LFED/ueberarbeitete_Entwuerfe/LFED_P1_Text.pdf (accessed 10 July 2017).
134. Evelyn ter Vehn, 'Aus für das Freiheits- und Einheitsdenkmal: Leipziger Stadtrat stoppt Verfahren', *LVZ online*, 16 July 2014, http://www.lvz-online.de/leipzig/citynews/aus-fuer-das-freiheits-und-einheitsdenkmal-leipziger-stadtrat-stoppt-verfahren/r-citynews-a-246993.html (accessed 5 August 2014).
135. See, for example, Stiftung Friedliche Revolution, 'Presseerklärung', 15 February 2017, http://www.freiheits-und-einheitsdenkmal.de/images/pdf/15022017pressemitteilungsfr.pdf (accessed 10 June 2017); Clemens Haug, 'SPD-Bundestagskandidat Katzek will Freiheitsstatue für Leipzig', *Leipziger Volkszeitung*, 30 March 2017, http://www.lvz.de/Leipzig/Lokales/SPD-Bundestagskandidat-Katzek-will-Freiheitsstatue-fuer-Leipzig (accessed 10 July 2017).
136. As suggested at the 'citizens' forum' in Leipzig on 8 March 2011, at which approximately one hundred people were present, considerably lower than expected. See also readers' letters in 'Einheitsdenkmal bewegt die Leser', *Leipziger Volkszeitung*, 15–16 January 2011, p. 19, and http://www.denkmaldialog-leipzig.de/ (accessed 31 August 2012).
137. Other memory markers include the Nikolaikirche itself, twenty information pillars erected in 2010 and 2011 at sites of the peaceful revolution (see 'Stelenausstellung', http://www.runde-ecke-leipzig.de/index.php?id=500, accessed 31 August 2012), as well as a huge wall painting in memory of the peaceful revolution by artist Michael Fischer-Art.
138. See Rüdiger Wiese and Klaus Joachim Albert (eds), *2. Bildhauer-Symposium Metall, Schwerin 1990* (Lübeck: Kaiser & Mietzner, 1990). I am very grateful

to Barbara Wils from the Kulturbüro der Landeshaputstadt Schwerin, who kindly gave me this and other materials relating to the symposium and the monument.
139. As revealed in conversation with Guillermo Steinbrüggen, 19 January 2011.
140. 'Verbannt von der Mitte ins Zentrum', Stadtarchiv Schwerin: D 16 Nr. 1: Kunst im öffentlichen Raum (Manuskript 1990er Jahre).
141. Timo Weber, 'Der Runde Tisch wieder neu', *Schweriner Volkszeitung*, 2 October 1992; Heiner Kläbsch, 'Warum kommt der Tisch nicht weg?', *Schweriner Volkszeitung*, 2 July 1993; mw, 'Was ist das?', *Schweriner Blitz am Sonntag*, 29 September 1991. Conversations with numerous residents also confirmed this viewpoint.
142. Walter Garrandt, 'Spenden für Runden Tisch', *Schweriner Volkszeitung*, 3 July 1993; Christa Dittmann, 'Runder Tisch vermehrt sich', *Schweriner Volkszeitung*, 18 June 1993.
143. Cited in Gudrun Reinke, 'Runter Tisch aus Stahl und Stein – bizarre und provokativ', *Schweriner Volkszeitung*, 6 April 1994.
144. See, for example, Karin Müller, 'Runder Tisch rostet wie die Hoffnungen', *Schweriner Volkszeitung*, 10 July 1993.
145. 'Die Uhr am Schweriner Rathaus ist fünf nach zwölf', *Norddeutsche Zeitung*, 22 January 1991; 'Künstler verkleiden den Runden Tisch', *Schweriner Volkszeitung*, 5 April 1993.
146. 'Protokoll der 121. Sitzung des Magistrats am Mittwoch, dem 27.01.93', Stadtarchiv Schwerin, Büro des Magistrats.
147. Klaus-Ulrich Keubke, *Schwerin: Kontinuität im Wandel* (Schwerin: APH, 1992), p. 109.
148. Guillermo Steinbrüggen, 'Runder Tisch – Bunter Tisch', 9 August 1995, document from Kulturbüro Schwerin.
149. See Günter Wittiber and Irma Emmrich, *Die keramische Säule*, Schweriner Reihe (Rat der Stadt Schwerin, Abteilung Kultur, 1986).
150. As revealed in conversation with Norbert Credé, Mecklenburgisches Volkskundemuseum, 21 January 2011.
151. 'Protokoll über die 80. Sitzung des Ausschusses für Bauen, Verkehr und Stadtentwicklung', 19 June 2003 (Stadtgeschichtliche Sammlungen Schwerin. Akte: Keramische Säule).
152. For an outspoken comparison of the two monuments, see Keubke, *Schwerin: Kontinuität im Wandel*, p. 110; see also 'Runder Tisch wird versetzt', *Schweriner Blick*, 30 July 1995.
153. As Martin Klähn from the organization 'Politische Memoriale e.V.' told me in conversation (21 January 2011), a suggestion made to the mayor that the monument could be used for an event in 2009 concerning the history of 1989 was not taken up.
154. See 'Wende '89, Ordner B. Helbig', in Stadtarchiv Dessau.
155. 'MBF – Belegschaftsabstimmung 6.12.1989' in FII/53ci, Vernichtung der Waffen, Stadtarchiv Dessau. I am also extremely grateful to Lothar Ehm, in our meeting of 3 March 2011, for providing me with much detail on the events at the MBF (Magnetic Tape Factory).

156. Ulrich Meisel, 'Waffen zu Schrott: Schwerter zu Pflugscharen. Eine Bürgerinitiative aus Dessau', in FII/53ci, Vernichtung der Waffen, Stadtarchiv Dessau.
157. Alfred W. Radeloff, *Der Runde Tisch der Stadt Dessau, 1989/90* (unpublished manuscript), Stadtarchiv Dessau; Frank Kreißler (ed.), *Runder Tisch Dessau: Beratungsprotokolle, Anträge und Vorlagen* (Dessau: Stadtarchiv, 2000), pp. 15–17.
158. Steffen Brachert, 'Glocke läutet für Freiheit und Frieden', *Mitteldeutsche Zeitung*, 30 September 2000, p. 9.
159. 'Erklärung der Initiativgruppe "6. Dezember"', Dessau, 12 February 1990, in FII/53, Vernichtung der Waffen, Stadtarchiv Dessau.
160. Indeed, there were numerous 'bell graveyards', at which bells were collected for such use, the largest of which was at Hamburg-Veddel. A peace bell also exists at Friedland, on the former border between East and West Germany in Niedersachsen, where a refugee camp existed, initially for returning POWs and expellees from former parts of Germany, but later also for refugees from the GDR as well as a range of other countries.
161. B. Müller, 'Die Jury entschied im Studentenwettbewerb', *Mitteldeutsche Zeitung (Dessau)*, 19 September 1998, p. 8.
162. Thomas Steinberg, 'Eine Friedensglocke aus Waffenstahl', *Zeit online*, 15 April 1999, www.zeit.de/1999/16/Eine_Friedensglocke_aus_Waffenstahl (accessed 10 March 2011) and information from Lothar Ehm, 3 March 2011.
163. 'Beschlussvorlage-Nr 13 für die OB-Beratung am 31. Mai 2000', Amt 01-590 bis 594, Stadtarchiv Dessau.
164. See, for instance, letters written to both the local newspaper and the town council: 'Leserbriefe', *Mitteldeutsche Zeitung*, 6 December 2000.
165. Brachert, 'Glocke läutet für Freiheit und Frieden'.
166. Carla Hanus, 'Angebote künftig koordiniert', *Mitteldeutsche Zeitung*, 17 October 2001, p. 9.
167. J. Günther, 'Springbrunnen auf dem Marktplatz gewünscht', *Mitteldeutsche Zeitung*, 28 December 2001, p. 13; Thomas Steinberg, 'Tonnenschweres Erinnerungsstück', *Mitteldeutsche Zeitung*, 2 October 2001, p. 9; 'Leserbriefe', *Mitteldeutsche Zeitung*, 10 January 2002, p. 5.
168. Thomas Steinberg, 'Große Töne für Frieden und Freiheit', *Mitteldeutsche Zeitung*, 11 November 2002, p. 7.
169. 'Platz an der Friedensglocke bekommt einen Namen', *Mitteldeutsche Zeitung*, 30 September 2010, http://www.mz-web.de/servlet/ContentServer?pagename=ksta/page&atype=ksArtikel&aid=1277474090753 (accessed 28 March 2011).
170. 'Meinungen am Gestell', *Mitteldeutsche Zeitung*, 6 November 2002, p. 9.
171. See photos in FII/53ci, Stadtarchiv Dessau.
172. Steinberg, 'Große Töne für Frieden und Freiheit'.
173. At the time of writing, these plans still remain to be realized, in part due to difficulties getting plans passed by the necessary committees.
174. 'Große Pläne für die Friedensglocke', *Mitteldeutsche Zeitung*, 11 February 2016, http://www.mz-web.de/dessau-rosslau/stadtgeschic

hte-dessau-grosse-plaene-fuer-die-friedensglocke-23540612 (accessed 6 October 2016).
175. Michael Münchow, *Die friedliche Revolution 1989/1990 in Magdeburg: Eine Analyse der Ereignisse* (Kremkau: Block Verlag, 2007), p. 72.
176. Peter Ließmann, 'Stein des Anstoßes gegen Ostalgie-Welle', *Magdeburger Volksstimme*, 2 October 2003.
177. 'Der Grundstein kündigt das Bürgerdenkmal an', *Magdeburger Volksstimme*, 11 October 1999.
178. 'Kuratorium "Magdeburger Bürgerdenkmal e.v.": Satzung', filed in 'Norbert G. Zagel, Bürgerdenkmal, 1999–2006', Kulturbüro der Landeshauptstadt Magdeburg. I am very grateful to Frau Bahr for allowing me to view this material.
179. K. Bote, 'Denkmal soll an die friedliche Revolution von 1989 erinnern', *Magdeburger Volksstimme*, 1 November 2001.
180. 'Antrag, 21.06.1999, Nr. A0167/99', in 'Norbert G. Zagel, Bürgerdenkmal, 1999–2006', Kulturbüro der Landeshauptstadt Magdeburg.
181. 'Protokoll der Vorstandssitzung (Kuratorium), 25. Mai 1999', in 'Norbert G. Zagel, Bürgerdenkmal, 1999–2006', Kulturbüro der Landeshauptstadt Magdeburg; also discussion with Rudolf Evers, 11 November 2010.
182. Letter from Landesamt für Denkmalpflege to Rudolf Evers, 19 April 1999, in 'Norbert G. Zagel, Bürgerdenkmal, 1999–2006', Kulturbüro der Landeshauptstadt Magdeburg.
183. Letters from Evers to Stadtplanungsamt and Landesamt für Denkmalpfege, dated 5 May 1999, in 'Norbert G. Zagel, Bürgerdenkmal, 1999–2006', Kulturbüro der Landeshauptstadt Magdeburg.
184. Dirk Rösler, 'Schuhabdrücke, Kegelstumpf oder ein Eiserner Vorhang', *Magdeburger Volksstimme*, 10 January 2000.
185. Karl-Heinz Kaiser, 'Vorentscheidung für Bürgerdenkmal', *Magdeburger Volksstimme*, 17 April 2000.
186. 'Protokoll der erweiterten Vorstandsitzung, 26 April 2000', in 'Norbert G. Zagel, Bürgerdenkmal, 1999–2006', p. 2, Kulturbüro der Landeshauptstadt Magdeburg; Peter Ließmann, 'Kollektives Gedächtnis', *Magdeburger Volksstimme*, 4 June 2003.
187. Peter Ließmann, 'Stein für Stein wächst das Bürgerdenkmal zusammen', *Magdeburger Volksstimme*, 13 February 2002.
188. Matthias Fricke and Peter Ließmann, 'Bürger-Denkmal: Stele hat endgültig ihren Platz gefunden', *Magdeburger Volksstimme*, 19 September 2003.
189. Information from Rudolf Evers, 11 November 2010.
190. Ließmann, 'Stein für Stein wächst das Bürgerdenkmal zusammen'.
191. Peter Ließmann, 'Paula nahm die Politprominenz gelassen', *Magdeburger Volksstimme*, 4 October 2003.
192. Peter Ließmann, 'Denkmal erinnert an die Montags-Demos', *Magdeburger Volksstimme*, 4 October 2003.
193. Ließmann, 'Stein des Anstoßes gegen Ostalgie-Welle'.
194. For example, letters sent to Kulturbüro, and information from Rudolf Evers.
195. Kowalczuk, *Endspiel*, p. 395.

196. Thomas Küttler and J. Curt Röder, *Die Wende in Plauen: Eine Dokumentation* (Plauen: Vogtländischer Heimatverlag Neupert, 1991), p. 24.
197. Markus Geiler, 'Die Geschichte der friedlichen Revolution im Herbst 1989', *Die Welt*, 7 October 2009.
198. 'Vergessene Helden', *Sächsische Zeitung*, 14 September 2009.
199. Information from Friedrich Riechel, director of Kulturbetrieb der Stadt Plauen, in discussion on 17 March 2011.
200. See, for example, Tino Beyer, 'Plauen setzt sich ein Denkmal', *Freie Presse*, 5 October 2010.
201. mar, 'Ansturm aufs Wende-Denkmal', *Vogtland Anzeiger*, 9 October 2010.
202. 'Leserpost', *Freie Presse*, 2 July 2009, p. 15; 'Leserpost', *Freie Presse*, 22 July 2009, p. 13.
203. Tino Beyer, 'Unbekannte Diebe klauen Spendenbox furs Wende-Denkmal', *Freie Presse*, 21 August 2009, p. 13.
204. Uwe Selbmann, 'Schwanitz: Favoriten voreilig präsentiert', *Freie Presse*, 8 July 2009, p. 11.
205. Tino Beyer and Ellen Liebner, 'Präsentation läutet finale Abstimmung ein', *Freie Presse*, 30 June 2009, p. 11; Tino Beyer, '"Wir wollen keine Entscheidung wie beim Song-Contest"', *Freie Presse*, 1 July 2009, p. 13.
206. Tino Beyer, '"Wir sind das Volk": Votum der Bürger über das der Jury', *Freie Presse*, 9 July 2009, p. 11.
207. Tino Beyer, 'Denkmal: Diskussion ist gewollt', *Freie Presse*, 10 July 2009, p. 11.
208. Beyer, 'Unbekannte Diebe klauen Spendenbox'.
209. 'Plauen hat gewählt: Kerze wird zum Denkmal', *Freie Presse*, 18 September 2009, p. 13.
210. As revealed in conversation with Wolfgang Sachs, 18 March 2011.
211. Martin Reißmann, 'Das neue Wahrzeichen von Plauen', *Vogtland Anzeiger*, 7 October 2010, p. 3.
212. Interpretation provided by Peter Luban, 18 March 2011.
213. Johannes Fischer, 'Die kleine Heldenstadt setzt sich ihr eigenes Denkmal', *Freie Presse*, 29 August 2009, p. 5.
214. mar, 'Ein Denkmal gegen das Vergessen', *Vogtland Anzeiger*, 8 October 2010, p. 1.
215. As revealed in conversation with Wolfgang Sachs, 18 March 2011.
216. 'Festrede des sächsischen Ministerpräsidenten Stanislaw Tillich zur Einweihung des Denkmals für die Friedliche Revolution in Plauen am 7. Oktober 2010', http://www.wendedenkmal.de/wende/dokumente/upload/41d87_2010-10-07_Festrede_Stanislaw-Tillich.pdf (accessed 20 December 2017).
217. mar, 'Ein Denkmal gegen das Vergessen'.
218. Tino Beyer, 'Plauen erlebt Zeremonie mit Gänsehautgefühl', *Freie Presse*, 9 October 2010, p. 9.
219. 'Festrede des sächsischen Ministerpräsidenten Stanislaw Tillich'.
220. Beyer, 'Plauen erlebt Zeremonie mit Gänsehautgefühl'.
221. See www.wendedenkmal.de (accessed 10 November 2016).

222. The Burschenschaft monuments of the late nineteenth century provide an older example, while both the 'Flintstein' and light installation initiatives relating to Berlin's Holocaust Monument illustrate contemporary attempts to encourage public donations. See Caroline Pearce, *Contemporary Germany and the Nazi Legacy: Remembrance, Politics and the Dialectic of Normality* (Basingstoke: Palgrave Macmillan, 2008), p. 140.
223. The *Bürgerdenkmal* in Magdeburg provides such an example, alongside a large number of entries to several competitions. See Godehard Janzing, 'National Division as a Formal Problem in West German Public Sculpture: Memorials to German Unity in Münster and Berlin', in *Figuration / Abstraction: Strategies for Public Sculpture in Europe 1945–1968*, ed. by Charlotte Benton (Aldershot: Ashgate, 2004), pp. 127–46.
224. Dresden saw the unveiling of a 'Schwerter zu Pflugscharen' monument in front of the Kreuzkirche on 8 October 2010, by sculptor Lothar Beck. See 'Der Friedensbewegung ein Denkmal gesetzt', http://www2.evangelisch.de/themen/mitteldeutschland/der-friedensbewegung-ein-denkmal-gesetzt24218 (accessed 14 August 2013).
225. 'Schorlemmer widerspricht Leipzigs Ex-Nikolaipfarrer Führer: Name Bundesrepublik soll bleiben', *Leipziger Volkszeitung*, 20 April 2009, http://www.presseportal.de/pm/6351/1390134 (accessed 7 October 2016).

~§ Conclusion

BEYOND THE PALIMPSEST

The memorial landscape of eastern Germany has witnessed rapid change since the demise of the GDR. While the early years were more typically marked by the destruction of socialist structures, and the majority of new memorials were constructed ten or more years after the fall of the Berlin Wall, patterns of remembrance remain complex. Although many remaining socialist monuments have become accepted as historical documents, for instance, others continue to provoke heated debate. In contrast, structures dedicated to the peaceful revolution of 1989 have adorned some towns since the late 1990s, whereas the two most recent national projects to this history have been mired in difficulty and stalled numerous times. The construction of – and ongoing activity around – memorial projects is thus often less to do with the subject of commemoration itself, than with the way in which monuments relate to their surroundings politically, aesthetically, historically and geographically. In focusing primarily on these relationships, this book demonstrates not only the complex web of associations at play in the commemorative landscape, but also the role of monuments in aiding communities to work through difficult pasts and facilitate communication between different social and political groups. The case studies also testify to a number of overarching trends in the memorialization of the GDR, which will be outlined in this concluding chapter. These concern first the persistence of memorial structures and power relations from GDR times, and second the emergence of particular themes in the memorialization of the GDR since 1989. Third and most crucially, the interrelationship between the case studies in this book, as well as their entanglement with other memorial traditions, demonstrates a memorial dynamism that takes us beyond the notion of the monument as a palimpsest of memory and points towards the importance of dialogism in both diachronic and synchronic perspectives.

What Remains?

While the post-unification era has seen numerous changes in memorial practices, it is worth reflecting on the continuities between socialist and post-socialist monument projects, some of which are indicative of the broader parameters of memorial construction, and some of which demonstrate the continuation of GDR trends. The most apparently mundane of these is perhaps also the most influential, and one that is often overlooked in studies of memory construction: the pragmatic considerations of remembrance projects. As in the GDR, the confines of urban space and planning, financial considerations, the availability or durability of materials, and even matters of health and safety have all been significant in determining the outcome of projects. Even the most lauded of artistic ventures may fail to be realized if resources are short or the intended location becomes unavailable. While such negotiations were ever-present in the GDR, they were largely shielded from public view; since unification, they have been more openly played out, making us increasingly aware of the complex demands associated with memorial spaces.

The role of individuals or specific interest groups also proves central to the initiation and development of monument projects. While in the GDR it was invariably the SED and its leading figures that publicly instigated projects and organized ritual events around memorial constructions, individuals and parties of all political colours may choose to back memorial projects today. Despite this difference, there remains a role for 'memory activists' – individuals or groups who steer a project from its inception through to its construction and beyond, in much the same way that the SED took on the patronage of socialist projects and ensured the building of a socialist tradition around them. Such individuals include Lothar Ehm, Rudolf Evers and Wolfgang Sachs, all instigators of various *Wende* monuments, as well as Rita Lüdtke (Fünfeichen) and Alexandra Hildebrandt (Freedom Memorial, Berlin), to name but a few. In contrast to Jennifer Jordan's reference to the 'memorial entrepreneur',[1] the term 'memory activist' implies a focus beyond the physical structure itself, and a concern rather with maintaining a broader tradition of remembrance. What all these individuals thus share is a desire to keep memory alive through ongoing activity and publicity concerning the memorial site in question, whether this be through the installation of new memorial elements at sites, the promotion of discussions in schools and youth groups, or the organization of high-profile events to draw public attention to such sites. This desire can perhaps be explained by the fact that the majority of such activists are largely – but not exclusively – of the same generation, having lived a significant proportion of their lives under socialism and demonstrated for its overthrow in 1989. It is no coincidence that the majority of those at the helm of the SED leadership responsible for the erection of iconic socialist monuments played a similarly active role in opposing the Nazi dictatorship, and thus saw it as their mission to maintain a ritual remembrance of antifascism in the GDR. Clearly, then, individual biographies prove to be a significant driving force behind the building of a collective remembrance tradition, particularly after regime change.

Considering the biographies of many post-unification memory activists, it is little surprise that the monuments examined in this book are all designed to demonstrate resistance to the SED dictatorship. Given the political system of present-day Germany, this may seem an obvious point to make. What is interesting, however, is the way in which this mirrors memorial activity in the GDR, where monuments to antifascism were erected in large numbers. Clearly, both in the GDR and in contemporary Germany, the desire to show resistance to the previous political regime has constituted an important step in terms of moving on from the past and legitimizing the present. In this way, we see how monuments are still instrumentalized for contemporary political needs and remain symbols of power, regardless of the growing emphasis on democratic forms, narratives and processes (discussed below). With this in mind, it is unsurprising that the CDU – as the main 'winner' of unification – has often been at the helm of memorial activity during post-*Wende* years, whether this be in the destruction of socialist icons, the memorialization of the GDR's victims or the celebration of the peaceful revolution. However, this has not always been the case, and memorial sites have been deployed by diverse political parties for their own needs, as demonstrated especially by monuments to 17 June 1953. Even the PDS/Die Linke has used a number of projects, most prominently the *Gesamtkonzept* for remembrance of the Berlin Wall, but also the former *Haftstätte* on Prenzlauer Allee, to display a sense of responsibility towards the past, and to distance itself from its SED origins. Regardless of political loyalties, the past is thus used in all cases to demonstrate resistance towards the socialist past and to legitimize the actions of the present.

The involvement of memory activists and politicians, as well as a range of other participants, such as town planners, artists and historians, shows one last element of structural continuity with the GDR: that of a predominantly male community of actors. While there are undoubtedly more women in the political sphere today, it is significant that the large majority of politicians, and an even greater proportion of the artists discussed in this book, are male. Those projects designed by female artists, such as Karla Sachse and Katharina Karrenberg, often choose to distance themselves from an overtly political stance and question instead the human and moral dimensions of memory from a more exploratory standpoint, frequently drawing attention to the grey areas of memory. It is significant, however, that these do not always fit with the political framework of the time (Karrenberg's design, for instance, was considered too controversial to be built), showing that despite the evident changes in memorial culture, such structures may represent societal 'power' in more subtle ways than sometimes assumed.

Dominant Narratives

While the structures of remembrance demonstrate a number of continuities from socialist times, the events and narratives to be memorialized have clearly changed. What, then, does the contemporary eastern German memorial landscape tell us about the GDR? To what extent is a 'canon' of remembrance emerging? Although this book is clearly not an exhaustive study of all extant monuments, a number of trends nevertheless emerge that cut across national and regional examples, as well as across remembrance themes. Most prominently, the ritual calendar surrounding memorial constructions largely appears to be limited to a number of key dates: 17 June, 13 August and 9 November (or 9 October in Leipzig). These are often exchanged as symbolic dates of repression and freedom, regardless of the specific history in question. Monument projects in remembrance of the autumn of 1989, for instance, have variously harnessed the dates of 17 June and 13 August to make important announcements; in contrast, dedication ceremonies for monuments in memory of the 17 June uprisings (Leipzig) and victims of the Berlin Wall (white crosses) have taken place on 9 November and 17 June respectively. While the choice of date is sometimes the product of logistical limitations, it is notable how often these dates are used interchangeably, with the anniversaries of 1953, 1961 and 1989 providing significant impetus for memorial milestones, thus helping to build rituals around physical structures that aim to maintain an active memory tradition. However, as is typically the case with anniversarial memory, the high recurrence of these selected dates appears – at least initially – to reduce the GDR to a somewhat monolithic period in which the themes of repression from above and popular revolt from below dominate to the detriment of more nuanced understandings and interpretations.

Despite this apparent homogenization of memory, a focus beyond anniversary dates reveals a more complex picture and a widespread effort to broaden memory narratives of the GDR. This stems above all from the increasingly important role played by the peaceful revolution in the memorialization of the GDR, despite suggestions from some historians that memory of this period is unstable. Indeed, as examples in all chapters of this book have shown, the mass demonstrations of 1989 and the demands for freedom, democracy and human rights have become an underlying leitmotif in the construction – and destruction – of monuments.[2] While this may not necessarily be visible in the material construct of all monuments, the narratives and values associated with 1989 have invariably played a central role in the discussions and debates surrounding memorial processes. The repeated use of slogans and imagery from 1989 was witnessed, for example, in the movements both for and against the destruction of socialist monuments, whereas speeches at unveiling ceremonies for new monuments have regularly included rhetoric and themes from 1989. Similarly, the teleological reshaping of June 1953 to appear as a precursor to 1989, the inevitable linking of 1961 to the fall of the Wall, or constant references to the fight for democratic values and freedom have all ensured that the leitmotif of 1989 modulates through different keys as it resurfaces in contrasting memorial debates. Perhaps unsurprisingly, the values associated with the peaceful revolution resonate strongly with the moral and political dimensions of the present, in contrast to the socialist dictatorship of the past, and to use Bartlett's term, such remembering fits the cultural schemata of contemporary society.[3] Similar patterns of interpretation are thus seen in other contemporary democracies; as Eleanor Bavidge, for instance, notes of the message visitors are encouraged to take from a contemporary memorial in the Tower of London, 'We are not a society that tortures or kills; we are a society that erects memorials'.[4] The past is thus constructed to fit the needs of the remembering community, in this case one that is eager not only to demonstrate its democratic credentials, but also to celebrate its self-liberation from dictatorship. In this way, we see a memorial tradition developing alongside Germany's predominantly cathartic dialogue with the past, which recognizes also the more positive values associated with recent German history.

While the SED's antifascist monuments attempted to achieve the same narrative of self-liberation after 1945, there is a clear difference in the way that this was achieved. Indeed, the leitmotif of 1989 and the emphasis on democratic values today have influenced the very process of memorialization, with case studies demonstrating a deliberate desire on the part of memory activists and politicians to engage in widespread consultation, negotiation and public engagement. The aspiration for mass participation and publicly funded projects has been unsurprisingly strongest in those designed to commemorate 1989, yet this element has influenced numerous other projects, with initiators keen to distance themselves from the heavily top-down process of memorialization evident under the SED. As such, a significant number of projects have originated at grassroots level, initiated and led by citizens who are keen to preserve a part of their local heritage. Whether evident at the Wall memorial at Treptow, the tank tracks in Leipzig or the *Wende* monument in Plauen, these projects have grown from below, demonstrating a desire to reinstate local narratives. In several instances, the memorial process has also involved a public vote, online surveys or campaigns in local newspapers to encourage participation among as many residents as possible. As a result of greater democratization, multiple narratives are thus emerging alongside each other, showing both the varied experiences of particular events (such as the numerous regional experiences of 1989) and the murky areas between the polar extremes of victims and perpetrators (seen, for example, in the remembrance of victims of the special camp at Buchenwald and border guards at Bernauer Straße). With time, it seems that the memorialization process is becoming increasingly complex and diverse, perhaps best symbolized by the decentralized *Gesamtkonzept* for remembrance of the Berlin Wall. As a result, multiple memorial sites are beginning to promote a more differentiated understanding of the GDR, in which commonly accepted narratives are increasingly being challenged.

Interestingly, the emphasis on democratic processes has also influenced the formal elements of some monuments. Perhaps most obviously, this has impacted on the choice of material for a number of structures: Leipzig's St Nicholas column, for example, was constructed out of the 'everyday' material of concrete rather than the initially intended marble; the choice of cobblestones to mark the course of the Berlin Wall was similarly considered more appropriate than costly metal, and the steel for Dessau's bell was integral to the very history of 1989. Conversely, criticism of Berlin's proposed Freedom and Unity

Monument commonly focused on the inappropriately ostentatious appearance of its golden exterior. While such trends cannot be seen in all examples, many of these considerations relate directly to the mass involvement in 1989, and clearly counter the top-down approach to monument construction in the GDR, in which grandeur often won out. Although the large majority of such structures cannot be considered countermemorials in formal terms (see below), they clearly embody a desire to resist established socialist memorial conventions. It is significant that a number of monuments have also had capsules inserted into their foundations, in which artefacts from the time of construction can be found, such as coins, local newspapers or lists of donors; alternatively, in other structures, donors' names have become a visible element of the monument itself. Once again, such examples convey a sense of 'everyday' plurality and the construction of a bottom-up narrative in the present, which becomes an integral part of the structure. Where the substance of monuments themselves does not reflect this approach, associated documentary or archival elements may instead reflect a desire to record the various stages of the memorial process, thereby making it as transparent as possible. In the case of former socialist monuments, this has resulted in a strong documentary tradition, in which the fates of monuments have been recorded and contextualized as part of the democratization process. As a result, many now stand as recognized symbols of compromise or tolerance. Similarly, new or proposed monuments have seen accompanying websites, information boards and exhibitions become common features of an expanded memorial landscape, in order to record the plural process of construction. This trend brings to mind both Paul Williams' notion of the 'memorial museum' (in which museums embrace memorial features) and Bill Niven's concept of the 'combimemorial' (in which memorials adopt aspects associated with the museum, such as archival or exhibition elements), and is doubtless indicative of a new breed of commemorative structure.[5] While, like both these concepts, the strong documentary feature attempts to engage viewers to a greater extent in active remembrance, this appears to arise out of a specific need to demonstrate contemporary qualities, such as plurality, mass engagement and transparency. This desire has, however, proven to be problematic for several projects, particularly those with a national focus. In the case of the two proposed Freedom and Unity Monuments, for instance, both projects encountered difficulties not only because of a lack of popular support, but also because the supposedly democratic nature of the competitions became unsustainable. In Berlin, the sheer number of submissions in the first, open competition was unworkable;

in Leipzig, the belated decision to allow popular opinion to influence the outcome ultimately resulted in a lack of transparency. As several other projects have also highlighted, mass participation (at either the design or selection stages) may result in more conservative forms, as they are dependent on the wider 'cultural repertoire of the public'.[6] In short, art can never be truly democratic, but it is the desire to make it appear as such that has recently dominated processes and forms.

Most importantly for this discussion, monument projects that embrace the notion of democracy should be seen as part of – rather than simply the result of – the process of *Aufarbeitung*. Often seen as objects that may be susceptible to change, monuments are rarely also recognized as potentially powerful agents of change. Indeed, many of the projects discussed in this book have provoked discussions between diverse interest groups and triggered a process of historical research and learning on the part of those involved. This often takes place prior to or during construction, as seen variously in the PDS's involvement in the *Haftstätte* on Prenzlauer Allee, the negotiations between conflicting victims' groups at Buchenwald, the wrangling over land at Bernauer Straße, or the involvement of Bundeswehr soldiers in the creation of the Treptow memorial. It may, of course, also take place years after construction, as demonstrated by discussions over former socialist icons. Process appears to be more important than the resulting form in many of these cases, but it is also evident that the more 'unsatisfactory' a monument design is considered to be, the more likely this process is to continue. Discussions over Karrenberg's design for Berlin's 17 June memorial, Alexandra Hildebrandt's Freedom Memorial, or Leipzig's Freedom and Unity Monument all, in their own ways, provoked significant and widespread engagement with the memories of each period of history, precisely because they failed to find widespread acceptance. Clearly then, memorials constitute more than simply their material outcomes, as demonstrated by Dolff-Bonekämper's emphasis on their *Streitwert* or Young's assertion that the debate itself constitutes the monument. Yet the findings of this book suggest that it is more than simply the debate that we should focus on, but rather the relationships that are set in flow (rather than in stone) throughout the process of memorialization, and which may extend long beyond the dedication of a monument. The majority of memorial projects discussed in this book could thus be considered unfinished projects to an unfinished history; constructed at the junction between communicative and cultural memory, they are bound up with the active – and ongoing – negotiation of the recent, lived past.

Dialogic Remembrance and Entangled Memories

The confluence of communicative and cultural memories in the memorial constructions examined in this book proves to be particularly revealing, for it exposes existing understandings of memory and memorialization to be too restrictive. Contrary to the unidirectional flow of influence suggested by Assmann, for example, the dialogical relationship between communicative and cultural forms of memory has provided for a highly dynamic and creative process, which has brought about a unique period of memorialization following the demise of the GDR. Throughout this period, it has become clear that cultural forms of memory may be as unstable, or subject to as much change, as communicative forms; as Berlin's Lenin monument demonstrated, commemorative structures may be erased in much less than a lifetime, or – as seen in Chemnitz – fast reinterpreted to suit contemporary concerns. Similarly, one single monument may be interpreted by different groups for their own interests (e.g. Dresden's tank tracks), and as we have seen repeatedly throughout this book, the meaning invested in physical sites of remembrance may be numerous, both at one single point in time, and over the course of history. Yet the negotiations and relationships between these different interpretations are central to a monument's future development, and may cause shifting understandings of the past among memory activists, interest groups or political parties. For this reason, the concept of the palimpsest, used increasingly for physical sites of memory, proves somewhat restricting, for it draws our attention to the physical material of the monument, rather than the dialogue implicit in its construction history; put differently, it highlights the layers of history at a site, rather than the gaps between them. Moreover, the tendency of this model to focus on the multiple layers of memory at a single site also misses two important dynamics relating to the diachronic and synchronic dimensions of remembrance. First, the palimpsest implies erasure – at least temporarily – of one text by another, which may only be uncovered in a backwards archaeological process; there is little room in this model for the notion that the first text may influence that which replaces it, both of which may influence a third, and so on. Second, in uncovering layers of memory on the same site, the concept of the palimpsest fails to take the wider synchronic context into consideration. As highlighted throughout this study, memory never exists in a vacuum, and it is above all its dialogic quality that makes it so dynamic.

Questions of aesthetics and memorial form demonstrate clearly this dialogism, and this book highlights how the symbolic language of collective remembrance emerges in conversation with past traditions and present politics. Most obvious in this context is the relationship between the aesthetic norms of SED remembrance and contemporary memorial forms. Here it is little surprise that contemporary projects have attempted to distance themselves from the massive dimensions and heroic nature of public art produced under socialism, and designs of monumental proportions have rarely been proposed since 1989, nor have figurative monuments of individual historical figures. Dresden's proposed monument to Helmut Kohl was, for example, vetoed before it could gain any real impetus, and the few monuments that have been constructed in remembrance of historical actors, such as Karl Liebknecht or Rosa Luxemburg, have rejected both figurative and heroic forms. In contrast, the winning design for Berlin's Freedom and Unity Monument was criticized for its monumental proportions, even though its attempt to capture tangibly the sense of democracy set it apart from its monumental predecessors. Contemporary monuments also resist the socialist realist trend of depicting the working classes and the collective; instead, the focus on democracy and the widespread emphasis on mass participation – particularly in monuments to 1989 – is conveyed through symbols such as candles, bells or local icons (such as the St Nicholas column), and could best be described as a post-heroic celebration of the community. In each case, decisions and debates surrounding aesthetics have involved the negotiation of new, acceptable forms that are sufficiently distinct from the norms of GDR memorialization.

Many case studies in this book not only respond to GDR commemorative traditions, but also to Holocaust remembrance, on both synchronic and diachronic levels. Given the influx of new memorials to the Holocaust after 1989, where the display of 'negative nationalism' became prominent, the very notion of celebratory monuments in memory of the demonstrations of 1989, for example, became a difficult one to grapple with. Indeed, the proposal for, and consequent construction of, Berlin's central Holocaust memorial has influenced the evolution of monuments to the GDR particularly strongly. Discussions concerning the potential celebration of 'national heroes' at Berlin's central memorial to 17 June 1953, for example, became entangled with the nearby site of the Holocaust memorial, where any sense of heroization was clearly inappropriate. Alternatively, plans for the capital's Freedom and Unity Monument were only approved once the Holocaust memorial was completed – a kind of unspoken condition for the construction of a more positive national monument. The temporary Freedom Memorial on Friedrichstraße was also associated with the Holocaust memorial, in part due to its timing, but also in its desire to commemorate victimhood in a central location and through apparent aesthetic similarities: a field of crosses instead of a field of stelae. Indeed, criticism of the Freedom Memorial was heightened precisely because of this association, with critics accusing Hildebrandt of attempting to place victims of the Wall alongside those of the Holocaust; aesthetic considerations thus brought these pasts into direct dialogue with one another. In contrast, other sites have benefitted from the 'borrowing' of techniques developed through Holocaust remembrance. The profiling of Wall victims' biographies at services in the Chapel of Reconciliation on Bernauer Straße, for instance, is reminiscent of those at the information centre underneath the Holocaust memorial. Beyond Berlin, we have also seen how the aesthetics and norms of Holocaust remembrance have influenced post-socialist memorials. In Buchenwald, for instance, elements of the memorial design for victims of the Soviet special camp were erased because they evoked the symbolism of Holocaust memorials, both on the same site and elsewhere. More broadly, it is notable that the established countermemorial trends of recent years, such as ground planes, voids or more ephemeral monuments, many of which have developed out of an established tradition of Holocaust remembrance, have rarely been employed in the examples featured in this book. On the one hand, the need to engage with the notions of absence and fragility that shaped countermemorial aesthetics is not always so prevalent, especially in the case of memorials to 1989; on the other hand, these forms have sometimes become so entangled with Holocaust remembrance that they have become symbolically replete.

Indeed, in contrast to suggestions that Holocaust remembrance has provided a language for the articulation of other traumatic memories,[7] this appears less to be the case regarding remembrance of the GDR, at least in its immediate aftermath. Indeed, on the occasions where countermemorial forms have been proposed, they have either been rejected (e.g. Karrenberg's design) or created very much in recognition of the 'unfinished' nature of the history in question (e.g. *Übergänge* designs; *Haftstätte* Prenzlauer Allee). There are several reasons for this. First, it seems that the aforementioned emphasis on democratic processes takes precedence over aesthetic innovation; while many countermemorials demand the active involvement of the viewer in their meaning-making, few have been constructed on the basis of widespread public endorsement or community funding. Second, where the remembrance of victims is concerned, countermemorial form appears to have been rejected in favour of more traditional memorial structures, such as crosses, stelae and bells, as well as the frequent use of religious services and blessings. While recourse to religious symbolism is doubtless partly a response to the GDR's anti-church policies and atheist symbolism, as well as recognition of the church's leading role in overthrowing the regime in 1989, it seems that it is also a clear call for visibility. Such symbolism has regularly been employed to remember the victims of communism, particularly at Buchenwald and Fünfeichen, as well as at Wall remembrance sites. In all such instances, especially on the sites of special camps, the heavy involvement of victims' families created a desire for sites of mourning and closure. Given the lack of any commemorative tradition for such groups in the GDR, the desire to create visible – and sometimes audible – sites with emotionally immediate symbolism can be understood as a response to the previous silence that surrounded these pasts. Interestingly, this reflects early commemorative trends after 1945, in which the first generation of memorials to victims of the war and Nazism were aesthetically unadventurous and largely consisted of simple stones, plaques and stelae.[8] It seems, indeed, that the involvement of victims is central here, for the comparison with monuments to 17 June 1953, which were largely instigated by political – rather than victims' – groups, is noteworthy: in recognition of their initiators' motives, these structures demonstrate less overtly emotional symbolism, but rather symbols of SED brutality. Whether a second generation of such memorials will develop in either case remains to be seen, but once again we see here the entanglement of past remembrance traditions with post-unification desires.

The memorial politics of the past are also important in shaping contemporary debates beyond questions of form, and their influence can be seen across all chapters and often in the most diverse ways. The fate of the Karl Marx Relief in Leipzig, for instance, became closely bound up with the SED's demolition of the Paulinerkirche in 1968, and the location of Berlin's monument to the 1953 uprisings was as much a result of the artist's interaction with Max Lingner's mural (itself a response to a Nazi mural) as with the history of the uprisings themselves. Similarly, the high-profile post-*Wende* discussions concerning memorialization at Buchenwald arose precisely because of the heightened symbolism of the site during the GDR. In all such cases, the relationship between past and present attitudes to heritage has provoked not only engagement with the SED's management of the past, but also a more considered reflection on current practices. The traditions of other past regimes have, however, also come into play, and it is notable how often Prussian monuments have been drawn into debates. The most obvious example is, of course, the interplay between Berlin's Freedom and Unity Monument and the former Kaiser Wilhelm Memorial, which once stood on the same site; other examples include the linking of the Brandenburg Gate to this same debate, the evocation of parallels with the Victory Column in the campaign to keep Berlin's Lenin monument, and the use of the Battle of the Nations Monument in Leipzig to justify the proposed location of the town's Freedom and Unity Monument. Similarly, the SED's demolition of Prussian structures (most notably the City Palace and the Kaiser Wilhelm Memorial) was frequently brought into debates about socialist monuments after 1989, with those opposing their destruction arguing that history should not be repeated. The diachronic interplay between monument projects from different eras is thus constant, and they become entangled in such a way that the influence can work in a forwards direction (e.g. Lingner's mural shaping Berlin's 17 June memorial) but also in a backwards direction (e.g. the termination of the Freedom and Unity Monument has caused many to propose the Brandenburg Gate as a suitable alternative).[9] Memorial discussions may, thus, invest new meaning into the existing memorial landscape, even if they do not result in a concrete structure, and older symbols may resurface in unexpected ways.

On a synchronic level, the entangled nature of memory narratives is especially clear in Berlin, where the debates around the capital's central memorials to the GDR became strongly interlinked. The development of memorial projects to 17 June 1953, the Berlin Wall and the peaceful revolution cannot be understood in isolation, quite apart from their interplay with the Holocaust memorial. It is interesting, however, that the relationship between Berlin and the regions – or more precisely, memorial centres (including, for instance, Leipzig's growing role in the memory of 1989) and more peripheral locations (including the periphery of Berlin) – has proven to be particularly entangled in recent years. Peripheral responses to the centre, for instance, have seen the construction of monuments in Plauen and Magdeburg, both of which were driven by regional self-assertion and the desire to redress the national narrative of the peaceful revolution and to reassert a sense of regional pride. Elsewhere, such as in Chemnitz, challenges from the outside (notably the former West) provoked the desire to protect its regional heritage, previously considered ideologically and aesthetically suspect. Interestingly, projects beyond the centre, particularly Berlin, have often developed more organically, being driven by citizens' initiatives and grassroots organizations. As a result, they tend not to provoke such heightened controversy, as they are less bound up with the demands and desires of national symbolism. In contrast, Berlin's role as the laboratory of unity means that symbolism is invariably required to adopt representative qualities, with politicians often making unrealistic aesthetic and political demands. While this may lead to more innovative forms in the capital, it inevitably also results in longer, more protracted and increasingly entangled processes. Given these difficulties, it is interesting to note that the regions have often paved the way in terms of memorializing the GDR, with monuments to 1989 and 1953 being erected far in advance of those in Berlin. Similarly, debates concerning former socialist structures have often witnessed more community-led initiatives (e.g. Chemnitz) and creative solutions (e.g. Halle) than those in Berlin. In highlighting the diversity of memorial developments beyond – yet in relation to – Berlin, this book thus demonstrates that the common fascination with the capital often misses an important dynamic in the process of working through the East German past.

Despite the high-profile debates that have been witnessed in recent years, the first quarter of a decade following reunification has seen a slow shift in attitudes and the beginnings of a more 'normalized' way of dealing with the GDR past. Playful interactions with GDR monuments, for example, appear to have become more accepted, and attitudes towards the GDR's concrete legacy have doubtless softened; remaining monuments are now likely to stay, widely regarded as historical documents rather than socialist heroes or villains. Elsewhere, recognition of the hazy divide between victims and perpetrators has grown, with the memory of GDR border guards and prisoners of Soviet special camps having lost some of the political brisance of the early years. Regional memories of events such as the peaceful revolution and the 1953 uprisings have become rooted in the memorial landscape, and while discussions may continue over the gap in the East Side Gallery, Berlin appears to have reached a workable and widely accepted solution to the legacy of the Wall in its decentralized *Gesamtkonzept*. Finally, more positive memories are also making a mark on the memorial landscape, with references to the peaceful revolution of 1989 marking a shift away from notions of shame or victimhood, as well as a move towards more global narratives of freedom, democracy and human rights. These shifts denote a gradual departure from national terms of reference towards a more decentralized network of remembrance, in which the interaction between local and global narratives takes precedence. Despite their clear entanglement with Holocaust remembrance, it seems that trends relating to the immediate East German past are also indicative of new directions in memorial culture, and contrary to Young's view that the monument in Germany is still bound up with its fascist past,[10] this book demonstrates the need to look beyond the established norms of western German standards, towards a different set of memorial negotiations in the former East.

What remains clear is that despite the demise of the GDR, its symbolic presence is likely to remain a visible part of the memorial landscape for years to come. Indeed, on the twenty-fifth anniversary of the fall of the Wall, when Berlin's Freedom and Unity Monument was still provoking controversial discussion, an appeal was made for a new, central memorial to the victims of communism. Whether this will be built, and what shape this will take, remains to be seen, but the growing emphasis on the democratic credentials of monuments means that long, protracted memorial debates are likely to be in store. These will doubtless emerge in dialogue with past traditions and memorial structures and, following the examples in this book, become entangled in future memory projects for years and decades to come.

Notes

1. Jordan, *Structures of Memory*, p. 11.
2. This contrasts with Leonie Beiersdorf's finding that, twenty years after the fall of the Wall, the demonstrations of autumn 1989 found only 'a relatively minor place in the cultural memory' of eastern Germany. While this may be true in terms of the total number of monuments found in the area, a more detailed examination of the narratives embedded in monuments suggests otherwise. See Beiersdorf, *Die doppelte Krise*, p. 204.
3. Frederic Bartlett, *Remembering: A Study in Experimental and Social Psychology* (Cambridge: Cambridge University Press, 1932).
4. Eleanor Bavidge, 'The "When" of Memory: Contemporary Memorials to Distant and Violent Pasts', *International Journal of Cultural Studies*, 16 (2012) 4, 319–34 (331).
5. Williams, *Memorial Museums*; Niven, 'From Countermonument to Combimemorial'.
6. Schittenhelm, *Zeichen, die Anstoß erregen*, p. 206.
7. Aleida Assmann, 'Europe: A Community of Memory?' Twentieth Annual Lecture of the GHI, 16 November 2006, *GHI Bulletin* 40 (2007) Spring, 11–25 (14); see also Young, 'The Memorial's Arc'.
8. See Marcuse, 'Holocaust Memorials', p. 66; Niven, 'From Countermonument to Combimemorial', p. 79.
9. Most prominently Monika Grütters, State Secretary for Culture. See 'Brandenburger Tor ist Symbol für Einheit, Freiheit und Frieden', *Deutschlandfunk*, 7 September 2016, http://www.deutschlandfunk.de/mo nika-gruetters-zum-einheitsdenkmal-brandenburger-tor-ist.691.de.html? dram:article_id=365238 (accessed 21 October 2016).
10. Young, 'The Memorial's Arc', p. 330.

Bibliography

Archival and Document Sources

The archives used in this study are listed below; individual documents are referenced with catalogue information (where available) in the Notes.
Archiv der Stiftung Gedenkstätten Buchenwald und Mittelbau-Dora
Museum Pankow Archiv (formerly Prenzlauer Berg Museum)
Stadtarchiv Chemnitz
Stadtarchiv Dessau
Stadtarchiv Halle
Stadtarchiv Hennigsdorf
Stadtarchiv Neubrandenburg
Stadtarchiv Schwerin

Unpublished documents and papers from the following public and private organisations were also used, and are detailed in the Notes:
Arbeitsgemeinschaft Fünfeichen e.V.
Bezirksamt Pankow
Bezirksamt Treptow
Bürgerschaft der Hansestadt Greifswald (Büro des Oberbürgermeisters)
Büro für Kunst im öffentlichen Raum, Berlin (Kiör-Büro)
Gedenkstätte Berliner Mauer
Initiativgruppe Buchenwald 1945–1950 e.V.
Kulturbüro der Landeshauptstadt Magdeburg
Kulturbüro der Landeshauptstadt Schwerin
Kulturbüro der Stadt Halle/Saale
Kulturstiftung Leipzig
Museum Treptow-Köpenick

Newspaper and Other Primary Sources

References to all newspaper articles appear in the Notes, as well as to documents of the Deutscher Bundestag and Abgeordnetenhaus Berlin (published online). Other primary sources include:

'17. Juni in Leipzig', brochure published by Bürgerkomitee Leipzig e.V. and Stiftung zur Aufarbeitung der SED-Diktatur, 2003.
Aktives Museum Faschismus und Widerstand in Berlin and NGBK (eds), *Erhalten – Zerstören – Verändern? Denkmäler der DDR in Ost-Berlin: Eine dokumentarische Ausstellung* (Berlin: Aktives Museum Faschismus und Widerstand in Berlin, 1990).
Apelt, Andreas (ed.), *Der Weg zum Denkmal für Freiheit und Einheit* (Schwalbach: Wochenschau, 2009).
'Architektonisch-künstlerischer Ideenwettbewerb. Gedenkstätte Berliner Mauer in der Bernauer Straße. Ausschreibung', Deutsches Historisches Museum (Berlin, April 1994).
Bundesministerium für Verkehr, Bau- und Wohnungswesen (ed.), *Kunst am Bau: Die Projekte des Bundes in Berlin* (Bonn: VG Bild-Verlag, 2002).
Denk Mal Positionen. Dokumentation zur Ausstellung vom 14. Juli–13. August 1993 im Prenzlauer Berg Museum (Berlin: Kulturamt Prenzlauer Berg / Prenzlauer Berg Museum, 1993).
'Denkzeichen. Für die Opfer der ehemaligen Haftstätte Prenzlauer Allee, Berlin-Pankow. Auslobung' (Berlin, October 2004).
'Empfehlungen der Expertenkommission zur Schaffung eines Geschichtsverbundes "Aufarbeitung der SED-Diktatur"', 15 May 2006, https://www.bundesstiftung-aufarbeitung.de/uploads/pdf/sabrow-bericht.pdf (accessed 15 December 2017).
'Erläuterungsbericht zum Wettbewerb "Gestaltung eines Denkmals zum 17. Juni 1953 / Herbst 1989" in Hennigsdorf', document kindly provided by Heidi Wagner-Kerkhof.
'Gesamtkonzept zur Erinnerung an die Berliner Mauer: Dokumentation, Information und Gedenken' (Berlin: Senatsverwaltung für Wissenschaft, Forschung und Kultur, 12 June 2006), http://www.berliner-mauer-gedenkstaette.de/de/uploads/allgemeine_dokumente/gesamtkonzept_berliner_mauer.pdf (accessed 15 December 2017).
Gestaltungswettbewerb für ein Freiheits- und Einheitsdenkmal Berlin. Auslobungstext – 1. Stufe (Berlin: Bundesamt für Bauwesen und Raumordnung, 2008).
Gestaltungswettbewerb für ein Freiheits- und Einheitsdenkmal in Berlin. Dokumentation des offenen Wettbewerbs 2009 (Berlin: Bundesamt für Bauwesen und Raumordnung, 2009).
Gestaltungswettbewerb für ein Freiheits- und Einheitsdenkmal in Berlin – 2010. Protokoll der Preisgerichtssitzung (Berlin: Bundesamt für Bauwesen und Raumordnung, 2010).
Greifswald 1945: Kampflose Übergabe und Kriegsende. Reden und Beiträge anlässlich des 60. Jahrestags am 29. und 30. April 2005 (Greifswald: Universitäts- und Hansestadt Greifswald, 2005).

Hans Böckler Stiftung (ed.), *17. Juni, von der ungewöhnlichen Entstehung eines kleinen Denksteins vor dem Rosengarten in der Karl-Marx-Allee, der ehemaligen Stalinallee, 17. Juni 2003* (Berlin-Friedrichshain: Oktoberdruck AG, 2005).

Hildebrandt, Alexandra (ed.), '17. Juni 1953: Ein sichtbares, aussagekräftiges und stolzes Denkmal ist längst überfällig', collection of documentation for 149th press conference of the Arbeitsgemeinschaft 13. August e.V., June 2007.

Jarausch, Konrad H., Martin Sabrow and Hans-Hermann Hertle, 'Die Berliner Mauer – Erinnerung ohne Ort? Memorandum zur Bewahrung der Berliner Mauer als Erinnerungsort' (Potsdam: Zentrum für Zeithistorische Forschung, 2005), hsozkult.geschichte.hu-berlin.de/daten/.../2005_mauer_memorand um.doc (accessed 26 July 2011).

Kommission zum Umgang mit den politischen Denkmälern der Nachkriegszeit im ehemaligen Ost-Berlin, 'Bericht' (Berlin, 15 February 1993).

Kreißler, Frank (ed.), *Runder Tisch Dessau: Beratungsprotokolle, Anträge und Vorlagen* (Dessau: Stadtarchiv, 2000)

'Künstlerische Lichtinstallation – Nikolaikirchhof Leipzig. Ausschreibung' (Leipzig, 2002).

'Kunstwettbewerb Denkmal 17. Juni 1953: Begrenzter zweiphasiger Realisierungswettbewerb – Ausschreibung' (Berlin: Senatsverwaltung Für Bauen, Wohnen und Verkehr, 1997).

Markierung des Mauerverlaufs. Hearing am 14. Juni 1995. Dokumentation (Berlin: Senatsverwaltung für Bau- und Wohnungswesen, 1995).

'Nikolaikirchhof Leipzig. Ausschreibung' (Leipzig, 1992).

'Reichtagsflagge über Buchenwald? Eine zweite Rudolf-Heß-Walhalla in Vorbereitung', in *Die Glocke vom Ettersberg*, Mitteilungsblatt der Lagergemeinschaft Buchenwald-Dora/Freundeskreis e.V., IV/1993.

Übergänge. Ausschreibung (Berlin: Senatsverwaltung für Bauen, Wohnen und Verkehr, 1996).

Verlorene Inhalte, Verordnetes Denkmal: Beiträge zum Wettbewerb '17. Juni 1953' (Berlin: Neue Gesellschaft für Bildende Kunst, 2000).

Volkskammer der DDR and Deutscher Bundestag (eds), *Gedenkstunde anläßlich des 17. Juni, Schauspielhaus Berlin, 17. Juni 1990* (Berlin, 1990).

Weber, Stefan, *Chemnitz – Ein Stadtzentrum sucht sein Gesicht* (Limbach-Oberfrohna: Bildverlag Thomas Böttger, no date [prob. late 1993/early 1994]).

'Zur Neuorientierung der Gedenkstätte Buchenwald: Die Empfehlungen der vom Minister für Wissenschaft und Kunst des Landes Thüringen berufenen Historikerkommission' (Weimar-Buchenwald, 1992).

Secondary Sources

Adam, Hubertus, 'Erinnerungsrituale – Erinnerungsdiskurse – Erinnerungstabus: Politische Denkmäler der DDR zwischen Verhinderung, Veränderung und Realisierung', *kritische berichte*, 20 (1992) 3, 10–35.

Adam, Hubertus, 'Zwischen Anspruch und Wirkungslosigkeit: Bemerkungen zur Rezeption von Denkmälern der DDR', *kritische berichte*, 19 (1991) 1, 44–64.

Adams, Paul C., Steven Hoelscher and Karen E. Till (eds), *Textures of Place: Exploring Humanist Geographies* (Minneapolis, MN; London: University of Minnesota Press, 2001).

Adorno, Theodor W., 'Was bedeutet: Aufarbeitung der Vergangenheit?', in *Gesammelte Schriften*, vol. 10/2, Kulturkritik und Gesellschaft II, ed. by Rolf Tiedemann (Frankfurt am Main: Suhrkamp, 1977), pp. 555–72.

Ahbe, Thomas, *Ostalgie: Zum Umgang mit der DDR-Vergangenheit in der 1990er Jahren* (Erfurt: Landeszentrale für politische Bildung Thüringen, 2005).

Aly, Götz et al. (eds), *Demontage... revolutionärer oder restaurativer Bildersturm? Texte und Bilder* (Berlin: Karin Kramer Verlag, 1992).

Anderson, Benedict, *Imagined Communities* (London; New York: Verso, 1983).

Andrews, Molly, 'Grand National Narratives and the Project of Truth Commissions: A Comparative Analysis', *Media, Culture & Society*, 25 (2003), 45–65.

Anz, Thomas (ed.), *Es geht nicht um Christa Wolf: Der Literaturstreit im vereinten Deutschland* (Munich: Edition Spangenberg, 1991).

Apitz, Bruno, *Nackt unter Wölfen* (Halle: Mitteldeutsche Verlag, 1958).

Arndt, Karl, 'Die NSDAP und ihre Denkmäler', in *Denkmal-Zeichen-Monument: Skulptur und öffentlicher Raum heute*, ed. by Ekkehard Mai und Gisela Schmirber (Munich: Prestel-Verlag, 1989), pp. 69–81.

Assmann, Aleida, 'Canon and Archive', in *A Companion to Cultural Memory Studies*, ed. by Astrid Erll and Ansgar Nünning (Berlin: de Gruyter, 2010), pp. 97–107.

Assmann, Aleida, 'Europe: A Community of Memory?' Twentieth Annual Lecture of the GHI, 16 November 2006, *GHI Bulletin*, 40 (2007) Spring, 11–25.

Assmann, Aleida, *Der lange Schatten der Vergangenheit: Erinnerungskultur und Geschichtspolitik* (Munich: Beck, 2006).

Assmann, Jan, 'Communicative and Cultural Memory', in *A Companion to Cultural Memory Studies*, ed. by Astrid Erll and Ansgar Nünning (Berlin: de Gruyter, 2010), pp. 109–18.

Assmann, Jan, *Das kulturelle Gedächtnis* (Munich: Beck, 1999).

Azaryahu, Maoz, 'Zurück zur Vergangenheit? Die Straßennamen Ost-Berlins 1990–1994', in *Denkmalsturz: Zur Konfliktgeschichte politischer Symbolik*, ed. by Winfried Speitkamp (Göttingen: Vandenhoeck & Ruprecht, 1997), pp. 137–54.

Bach, Jonathan, 'The Berlin Wall after the Berlin Wall: Site into Sight', *Memory Studies*, 9 (2016) 1, 48–62.

Baker, Frederick, 'The Berlin Wall: Production, Preservation and Consumption of a 20th-Century Monument', *Antiquity*, 67 (1993), 709–33.

Bakhtin, Mikhail M., 'The Problem of Speech Genres', in *Speech Genres and Other Late Essays*, trans. Vern W. McGee (Austin, TX: University of Texas Press, 1986), pp. 60–102.

Bartlett, Frederic, *Remembering: A Study in Experimental and Social Psychology* (Cambridge: Cambridge University Press, 1932).

Baumann, Tobias, 'Das Speziallager Nr. 9 Fünfeichen', in *Sowjetische Speziallager in Deutschland 1945 bis 1950*, vol. 1: *Studien und Berichte*, ed. by Sergej

Mironenko, Lutz Niethammer and Alexander von Plato (Berlin: Akademie Verlag, 1998), pp. 426–44.
Bavidge, Eleanor, 'The "When" of Memory: Contemporary Memorials to Distant and Violent Pasts', *International Journal of Cultural Studies*, 16 (2012) 4, 319–34.
Beattie, Andrew H., *Playing Politics with History: The Bundestag Inquiries into East Germany* (New York; Oxford: Berghahn Books, 2008).
Becker, Daniel, 'Coming to Terms with *Vergangenheitsbewältigung*: Walser's *Sonntagsrede*, the Kosovo War, and the Transformation of German Historical Consciousness', in *Victims and Perpetrators: 1933–1945. (Re)Presenting the Past in Post-Unification Culture*, ed. by Laurel Cohen-Pfister and Dagmar Wienroeder-Skinner (Berlin: de Gruyter, 2006), pp. 337–61.
Beiersdorf, Leonie, *Die doppelte Krise: Ostdeutsche Erinnerungszeichen nach 1989* (Berlin: Deutscher Kunstverlag, 2015).
Benjamin, Walter, *Illuminations*, ed. by Hannah Arendt, trans. Harry Zorn (London: Pimlico, 1999).
Benz, Wolfgang, 'Authentische Orte: Überlegungen zur Erinnerungskultur', in *Der Nationalsozialismus im Spiegel des öffentlichen Gedächtnisses: Formen der Aufarbeitung und des Gedenkens*, ed. by Petra Frank and Stefan Hördler (Berlin: Metropol Verlag, 2005), pp. 197–203.
Berdahl, Daphne, '"(N)Ostalgie" for the Present: Memory, Longing, and East German Things', *Ethnos*, 64 (1999) 2, 192–211.
Berlin-Brandenburgische Geschichtswerkstatt (ed.), *Prenzlauer, Ecke Fröbelstraße* (Berlin: Lukas Verlag, 2006).
Berliner, David, 'The Abuses of Memory: Reflections on the Memory Boom in Anthropology', *Anthropology Quarterly*, 78 (2005) 1, 197–211.
Betts, Paul, 'The Twilight of the Idols: East German Memory and Material Culture', *The Journal of Modern History*, 72 (2000) September, 731–65.
Beuchel, Karl Joachim, *Die Stadt mit dem Monument: Zur Baugeschichte 1945–1990*, Aus dem Stadtarchiv Chemnitz, vol. 9 (Chemnitz: Druckerei Dämmig, 2006).
Bickford, Louis and Amy Sodaro, 'Remembering Yesterday to Protect Tomorrow: The Internationalization of a New Commemorative Paradigm', in *Memory and the Future: Transnational Politics, Ethics and Society*, ed. by Yifat Gutman, Adam D. Brown and Amy Sodaro (Basingstoke: Palgrave Macmillan, 2010), pp. 66–86.
Blum, Martin, 'Club Cola and Co.: Ostalgie, Material Culture and Identity', in *Transformations of the New Germany*, ed. by Ruth A. Starkman (New York; Basingstoke: Palgrave Macmillan, 2006), pp. 131–54.
Blum, Martin, 'Remaking the East German Past: Ostalgie, Identity, and Material Culture', *Journal of Popular Culture*, 34 (2000) 3, 229–53.
Blume, Eugen, 'Hans Haacke', in *Die Endlichkeit der Freiheit. Berlin 1990: Ein Ausstellungsprojekt in Ost und West*, ed. by Wulf Herzogenrath, Joachim Sartorius and Christoph Tannert (Berlin: Hentrich, 1990), pp. 102–4.
Bodnar, John, *Remaking America: Public Memory, Commemoration, and Patriotism in the 20th Century* (Princeton, NJ: University of Princeton Press, 1992).
Bourdieu, Pierre, *Outline of a Theory of Practice*, trans. Richard Nice (Cambridge: Cambridge University Press, 1977).

Boym, Svetlana, *The Future of Nostalgia* (New York: Basic Books, 2001).
Brockmeier, Jens, 'Remembering and Forgetting: Narrative as Cultural Memory', *Culture & Psychology*, 8 (2002) 1, 15–43.
Buske, Norbert (ed.), *Die kampflose Übergabe der Stadt Greifswald im April 1945: Dokumentation* (Schwerin: Landeszentrale für politische Bildung Mecklenburg-Vorpommern, 2000).
Calle, Sophie, *Die Entfernung* (Dresden: Verlag der Kunst, 1996).
Camphausen, Gabriele, 'Das Denkmal "Gedenkstätte Berliner Mauer"', in *Berliner Mauer: Gedenkstätte, Dokumentationszentrum und Versöhnungskapelle in der Bernauer Straße*, ed. by Verein "Berliner Mauer – Gedenkstätte und Dokumentationszentrum" (Berlin: Jaron, 1999), pp. 18–22.
Camphausen, Gabriele and Manfred Fischer, 'Die Bürgerschaftliche Durchsetzung der Gedenkstätte an der Bernauer Straße', in *Die Mauer: Errichtung, Überwindung, Erinnerung*, ed. by Klaus-Dietmar Henke (Munich: dtv, 2011), pp. 355–76.
Carrier, Peter, *Holocaust Monuments and National Memory Cultures in France and Germany since 1989* (New York; Oxford: Berghahn Books, 2005).
Caspar, Helmut, *Marmor, Stein und Bronze: Berliner Denkmalgeschichten* (Berlin: Berlin Edition, 2003).
Confino, Alon, 'Collective Memory and Cultural History: Problems of Method', *The American Historical Review*, 102 (1997) 5, 1,386–403.
Connerton, Paul, 'Seven Types of Forgetting', *Memory Studies*, 1 (2008) 1, 59–71.
Cooke, Paul, *Representing East Germany since Unification: From Colonization to Nostalgia* (New York: Berg, 2005).
Cottin, Markus, Karl-Heinz Kretzschmar, Dieter Kürschner and Ilona Petzold, *Leipziger Denkmale*, vol. 2 (Beucha: Sax-Verlag, 2009).
Crownshaw, Richard, *The Afterlife of Holocaust Memory in Contemporary Literature and Culture* (Basingstoke: Palgrave Macmillan, 2010).
Crownshaw, Richard, 'The German Countermonument: Conceptual Indeterminacies and the Retheorisation of the Arts of Vicarious Memory', *Forum for Modern Language Studies*, 44 (2008) 2, 212–27.
Dale, Gareth, *Popular Protest in East Germany, 1945–1989* (London; New York: Routledge, 2005).
Detjen, Marion, 'Die Mauer als politische Metapher', in *Die Mauer: Errichtung, Überwindung, Erinnerung*, ed. by Klaus-Dietmar Henke (Munich: dtv, 2011), pp. 426–39.
Dewey, John, *Experience and Education* (New York: Kappa Delta Pi, 1938).
Dickel, Hans and Uwe Fleckner (eds), *Kunst in der Stadt: Skulpturen in Berlin 1980–2000* (Berlin: Nicolaische Verlagsbuchhandlung, 2003).
Diedrich, Torsten, *Der 17. Juni 1953 in der DDR: Bewaffnete Gewalt gegen das Volk* (Berlin: Dietz, 1991).
Diedrich, Torsten, *Waffen gegen das Volk: Der 17. Juni in der DDR* (Munich: Oldenbourg Wissenschaftsverlag, 2003).
Diers, Michael, 'Die Mauer: Notizen zur Kunst- und Kulturgeschichte eines deutschen Symbol(l)Werks', *kritische berichte*, 20 (1992) 3, 58–74.
Diers, Michael, *Schlagbilder: Zur politischen Ikonographie der Gegenwart* (Frankfurt am Main: Fischer, 1997).

Diers, Michael and Kasper König, *Der Bevölkerung: Aufsätze und Dokumente zur Debatte um das Reichtagsprojekt von Hans Haacke* (Cologne: Verlag der Buchhandlung Walter König, 2000).
Dolff-Bonekämper, Gabi, 'Conservation as Found – Erhalten wie vorgefunden?', in *Denkmalpflege für die Berliner Mauer: Die Konservierung eines unbequemen Bauwerks*, ed. by Axel Klausmeier and Günter Schlusche (Berlin: Ch. Links Verlag, 2011), pp. 82–92.
Dolff-Bonekämper, Gabi, 'Denkmalschutz für die Mauer', *Die Denkmalpflege*, (2000) 1, 33–40.
Doss, Erika, *Memorial Mania: Public Feeling in America* (Chicago, IL; London: University of Chicago Press, 2010).
Eckert, Rainer, 'Gegen die Wende-Demagogie – für den Revolutionsbegriff', *Deutschland Archiv*, 40 (2007) 6, 1,084–86.
Ehrentraut-Daut, Hans-Peter, Daniel Gaede, M. Gräfe et al., *Das sowjetische Speziallager Nr. 2: Buchenwald 1945 bis 1950*, 'Materialien' Series, vol. 61 (Bad Berka: ThILLM, 2001).
Eisenfeld, Bernd, Ilko-Sascha Kowalczuk and Eberhart Neubert, *Die verdrängte Revolution: Der Platz des 17. Juni 1953 in der deutschen Geschichte* (Bremen: Edition Temmen, 2004).
Elfert, Eberhard, 'Die Chronologie zum Abbau des Lenin-Denkmals', *Kunst am Bau: Kunst im Stadtraum*, 35–36 (1992), 60–62.
Elfert, Eberhard, 'Monumentalplastik im Widerstreit der politischen Systeme in Ost- und West-Berlin', in *Enge und Vielfalt – Auftragskunst und Kunstförderung in der DDR*, ed. by Paul Kaiser and Karl-Siegbert Rehberg (Hamburg: Junius, 1999), pp. 353–72.
Elfert, Eberhard, 'Die politischen Denkmäler der DDR im ehemaligen Ost-Berlin und unser Lenin', in *Demontage... revolutionärer oder restaurativer Bildersturm? Texte und Bilder*, ed. by Götz Aly et al. (Berlin: Karin Kramer Verlag, 1992), pp. 53–58.
Elfert, Eberhard, 'Unsere Fachkommission für "Sozialistische Denkmäler"', *Kunst am Bau: Kunst im Stadtraum*, 35/36 (1992), 63.
Elfert, Eberhard, 'Was wird aus dem Thälmann-Denkmal?', *Kunst + Stadt. Stadt + Kunst*, 37 (1993), 6–8.
Erll, Astrid, *Kollektives Gedächtnis und Erinnerungskulturen* (Stuttgart: Metzler, 2005).
Erll, Astrid and Ann Rigney (eds), *Mediation, Remediation, and the Dynamics of Cultural Memory* (Berlin; New York: de Gruyter, 2009).
Falser, Michael S., *Zwischen Identität und Authentizität: Zur politischen Geschichte der Denkmalpflege in Deutschland* (Dresden: Thelem, 2008).
Feindt, Gregor, Félix Krawatzek, Daniela Mahler, Friedemann Pastel and Rieke Trimçev, 'Entangled Memory: Toward a Third Wave in Memory Studies', *History and Theory*, 53 (2014) February, 24–44.
Feist, Peter, 'Denkmalplastik in der DDR von 1949 bis 1990', in *Denkmale und kulturelles Gedächtnis nach dem Ende der Ost-West-Konfrontation*, ed. by Akademie der Künste (Berlin: Jovis Verlag, 2000), pp. 189–98.
Fell, Herbert, 'Tempel des Goldenen Traumes', *kunststadt – stadtkunst*, 38 (1993), 10–11.

Fentress, James and Chris Wickham, *Social Memory* (Oxford: Blackwell, 1992).
Feversham, Polly and Leo Schmidt, *Die Berliner Mauer heute: The Berlin Wall Today* (Berlin: Verlag Bauwesen, 1999).
Finn, Gerhard, *Die politischen Häftlinge in der Sowjetzone 1945–1959* (Pfaffenhofen: Ilmgauverlag, 1960).
Flemming, Thomas, *Kein Tag der deutschen Einheit: 17. Juni 1953* (Berlin: be.bra, 2003).
Flierl, Bruno, *Gebaute DDR – Über Stadtplaner, Architekten und die Macht – Kritische Reflexionen 1990–1997* (Berlin: Verlag Bauwesen, 1998).
Flierl, Thomas, *Berlin: Perspektiven durch Kultur. Texte und Projekte* (Berlin: Theater der Zeit, 2007).
Flierl, Thomas, 'Denkmalstürze zu Berlin: Vom Umgang mit einem prekären Erbe', *kritische berichte*, 20 (1992) 3, 45–52.
Foucault, Michel, *Language, Counter-Memory, Practice: Selected Essays and Interviews*, trans. and ed. by Donald F. Bouchard (Ithaca, NY: Cornell University Press, 1977).
Frank, Sybille, *Der Mauer um die Wette gedenken* (Frankfurt am Main: Campus, 2009).
Frank, Sybille, 'Der Mauer um die Wette gedenken', *Aus Politik und Zeitgeschichte*, 61 (2011) 31–34, 47–54.
Fricke, Karl Wilhelm, *Politik und Justiz in der DDR: Zur Geschichte der politische Verfolgung 1945–1968* (Cologne: Verlag Wissenschaft und Politik, 1979).
Fricke, Karl Wilhelm, '"Konzentrationslager, Internierungslager, Speziallager": Zur öffentlichen Wahrnehmung der NKWD/MWD-Lager in Deutschland', in *Instrumentalisierung, Verdrängung, Aufarbeitung: Die sowjetischen Speziallager in der gesellschaftlichen Wahrnehmung 1945 bis heute*, ed. by Petra Haustein, Anna Kaminsky, Volhard Knigge und Bodo Ritscher (Göttingen: Wallstein, 2006), pp. 44–62.
Fricke, Karl Wilhelm and Roger Engelmann, *Der 'Tag X' und die Staatssicherheit: 17. Juni 1953 – Reaktionen und Konsequenzen im DDR-Machtapparat* (Bremen: Edition. Temmen, 2003).
Friedlein, Ingrid, 'Arbeitsgemeinschaft Fünfeichen', in *Die Opfer von Fünfeichen: Erlebnisberichte Betroffener und Angehöriger*, ed. by Sprecherrat der Arbeitsgemeinschaft Fünfeichen (Schwerin: Stock & Stein Verlag, 1996), pp. 10–47.
Friedlein, Ingrid, 'Die Arbeitsgemeinschaft Fünfeichen – eine Rückbesinnung', in *Die Opfer von Fünfeichen: Gedanken und Erinnerungen*, ed. by Sprecherrat der Arbeitsgemeinschaft Fünfeichen (Bozen: Athesiadruck, 2000), pp. 55–64.
Friedrich, Jörg, *Der Brand: Deutschland im Bombenkrieg 1940–1945* (Munich: Propyläen Verlag, 2002).
Fukuyama, Francis, *The End of History and the Last Man* (New York: Free Press, 1992).
Fulbrook, Mary, 'Historiografische Kontroversen seit 1990', in *Views from Abroad: Die DDR aus britischer Perspektive*, ed. by Peter Barker, Marc-Dietrich Ohse and Dennis Tate (Bielefeld: Bertelsmann, 2007), pp. 41–51.
Fulbrook, Mary, *The People's State: East German Society from Hitler to Honecker* (New Haven, CT: Yale University Press, 2005).

Gamboni, Dario, *The Destruction of Art: Iconoclasm and Vandalism since the French Revolution* (London: Reaktion Books, 1997).
Gerlach, Honika and Ute Mirea (eds), *denk' mal! Eine Dokumentation zum Lenin-Denkmal* (Berlin: Kulturverein Prenzlauer Berg e.V., 1992).
Gillis, John R., *Commemorations: The Politics of National Identity* (Princeton, NJ: Princeton University Press, 1994).
Glaser, Gerhard, 'Das Karl-Marx-Forum in Chemnitz', in *Verfallen und vergessen oder aufgehoben und geschützt? Architektur und Städtebau der DDR – Geschichte, Bedeutung, Umgang, Erhaltung*, Schriftenreihe des deutschen Nationalkomittees für Denkmalschutz, vol. 51 (Bonn: Deutsches Nationalkomitee für Denkmalschutz, 1997), pp. 52–60.
Göring-Eckardt, Katrin, 'Für ein kritisches Geschichtsbewusstsein', in *Jahrbuch für Kulturpolitik 2009. Thema: Erinnerungskulturen und Geschichtspolitik*, ed. by Bernd Wagner (Essen: Klartext Verlag, 2009), pp. 95–99.
Grass, Günter, *Im Krebsgang: Eine Novelle* (Göttingen: Steidl, 2002).
Greiner, Bettina, *Verdrängter Terror: Geschichte und Wahrnehmung sowjetischer Speziallager in Deutschland* (Hamburg: Hamburger Edition, 2010).
Großbölting, Thomas, 'Eine zwiespältige Bilanz: Zwanzig Jahre Aufarbeitung der DDR-Vergangenheit im wiedervereinigten Deutschland', in *Das Ende des Kommunismus: Die Überwindung der Diktaturen in Europa und ihre Folgen*, ed. by Thomas Großbölting, Raj Kollmorgen, Sascha Möbius and Rüdiger Schmidt (Essen: Klartext, 2010), pp. 61–74.
Großbölting, Thomas, Raj Kollmorgen, Sascha Möbius and Rüdiger Schmidt (eds), *Das Ende des Kommunismus: Die Überwindung der Diktaturen in Europa und ihre Folgen* (Essen: Klartext, 2010).
Halbwachs, Maurice, *Les cadres sociaux de la mémoire* (Paris: Alcan, 1925).
Halbwachs, Maurice, *La mémoire collective* (Paris: Presses universitaires de France, 1950).
Hamann, Christoph, 'Berliner Erinnerungsorte und Denkmäler', in *Der 17. Juni 1953: Eine Handreichung für den Unterricht*, ed. by Elena Demke, Christoph Hamann and Falco Werkentin (Berlin: Berliner Landesbeauftragte für die Unterlagen des Staatssicherheitsdienstes der ehemaligen DDR / Berliner Landesinstitut für Schule und Medien, 2003), pp. 68–76.
Harrison, Hope M., 'The Berlin Wall and Its Reconstruction as a Site of Memory', *German Politics and Society*, 29 (2011) 2, 78–106.
Hechler, Daniel and Peel Pasternack, *Deutungskompetenz in der Selbstanwendung: Der Umgang der ostdeutschen Hochschulen mit ihrer Zeitgeschichte* (Halle-Wittenberg: Institut für Hochschulforschung Wittenberg, 2011).
Henke, Klaus-Dietmar, *Revolution und Vereinigung 1989/90: Als in Deutschland die Realität die Phantasie überholte* (Munich: dtv, 2009).
Herf, Jeffrey, *Divided Memory: The Nazi Past in the Two Germanys* (Cambridge, MA; London: Harvard University Press, 1997).
Herlt, Günter, *Birne contra Historie* (Berlin: Spotless Verlag, 1993).
Hertle, Hans-Hermann and Maria Nooke (eds), *Die Todesopfer an der Berliner Mauer 1961–1989: Ein Biographisches Handbuch* (Berlin: Ch. Links, 2009).
Herz, Rudolf, *Lenin on Tour* (Göttingen: Steidl, 2009).

Herzogenrath, Wulf, Joachim Sartorius and Christoph Tannert (eds), *Die Endlichkeit der Freiheit: Berlin 1990. Ein Ausstellungsprojet in Ost und West* (Berlin: Hentrich, 1990).

Hildebrandt, Alexandra, *Die Freiheit verpflichtet: Das Freiheitsmahnmal am Platz Checkpoint Charlie*, Sozialwissenschaften 34 (Berlin: Technische Universität, 2005).

Hirsch, Marianne, 'The Generation of Postmemory', *Poetics Today*, 29 (2008) 1, 103–28.

Hirst, William and David Manier, 'The Diverse Forms of Collective Memory', in *Kontexte und Kulturen des Erinnerns: Maurice Halbwachs und das Paradigma des kollektiven Gedächtnisses*, ed. by Gerald Echterhoff and Martin Saar (Konstanz: UVK, 2002), pp. 37–58.

Hobsbawm, Eric, 'Foreword', in *Art and Power: Europe under the Dictators 1930–45*, ed. by Dawn Ades et al. (London: Thames and Hudson, 1995), pp. 11–15.

Hobsbawm, Eric and Terence Ranger, *The Invention of Tradition* (Cambridge: Cambridge University Press, 1983).

Hoffmann-Axthelm, Dieter, 'The Demise of Lenin Square', *Daidalos*, 'Denkmal/Monument', 49 (1993), 122–29.

Hogwood, Patricia, 'After the GDR: Reconstructing Identity in Post-Communist Germany', *Journal of Communist Studies and Transition Politics*, 16 (2000) 4, 45–67.

Hoskins, Andrew, 'Television and the Collapse of Memory', *Time & Society*, 13 (2004) 1, 109–27.

Hübner, Holger, *Das Gedächtnis der Stadt: Gedenktafeln in Berlin* (Berlin: Argon, 1997).

Hutton, Patrick H., *History as an Art of Memory* (Hanover, NH; London: University Press of New England, 1993).

Huyssen, Andreas, *Present Pasts: Urban Palimpsests and the Politics of Memory* (Stanford, CA: Stanford University Press, 2003).

Huyssen, Andreas, *Twilight Memories: Marking Time in a Culture of Amnesia* (New York; London: Routledge, 1995).

Jankowski, Martin, *Der Tag, der Deutschland veränderte: 9. Oktober 1989* (Leipzig: Evangelische Verlagsanstalt, 2007).

Janzing, Godehard, 'National Division as a Formal Problem in West German Public Sculpture: Memorials to German Unity in Münster and Berlin', in *Figuration / Abstraction: Strategies for Public Sculpture in Europe 1945–1968*, ed. by Charlotte Benton (Aldershot: Ashgate, 2004), pp. 127–46.

Jarausch, Konrad H., 'Realer Sozialismus als Fürsorgediktatur: Zur begrifflichen Einordnung der DDR', *Aus Politik und Zeitgeschichte*, B20 (1998), 33–46.

Jarausch, Konrad H. 'Der Umbruch 1989/90', in *Erinnerungsorte der DDR*, ed. by Martin Sabrow (Munich: Beck, 2009), pp. 526–35.

Jarosinski, Eric, '"Threshold Resistance": Dani Karavan's Berlin Installation *Grundgesetz*', in *Walls, Borders, Boundaries: Spatial and Cultural Practices in Europe*, ed. by Marc Silberman, Karen E. Till and Janet Ward (New York; Oxford: Berghahn Books, 2012), pp. 61–76.

Jessen, Ralph, 'Die Montagsdemonstrationen', in *Erinnerungsorte der DDR*, ed. by Martin Sabrow (Munich: Beck, 2009), pp. 466–80.

Jochimsen, Lukrezia, 'Die linke Gegenstimme zu: Erinnerungskultur und Geschichtspolitik', in *Jahrbuch für Kulturpolitik 2009, Thema: Erinnerungskulturen und Geschichtspolitik*, ed. by Bernd Wagner (Essen: Klartext Verlag, 2009), pp. 89–94.

Jordan, Jennifer, 'A Matter of Time: Examining Collective Memory in Historical Perspective in Postwar Berlin', *Journal of Historical Sociology*, 18 (2005) 1/2, 37–71.

Jordan, Jennifer, *Structures of Memory: Understanding Urban Change in Berlin and Beyond* (Stanford, CA: Stanford University Press, 2006).

Kaiser, Alexandra, '"We Were Heroes." Local Memories of Autumn 1989: Revising the Past', in *Remembering and Rethinking the GDR: Multiple Perspectives and Plural Authenticities*, ed. by Anna Saunders and Debbie Pinfold (Basingstoke: Palgrave Macmillan, 2013), pp. 179–94.

Kaiser, Paul and Andreas Kämper, 'Gestützte Helden, gestützte Welten', in *Enge und Vielfalt*, ed. by Paul Kaiser and Karl-Siegbert Rehberg (Hamburg: Junius, 1999), pp. 375–82.

Kaminsky, Anna, 'Gedenkstätten für die Opfer des Stalinismus als "Stiefkinder" der deutschen Erinnerungskultur?', in *'Asymmetrisch verflochtene Parallelgeschichte?' Die Geschichte der Bundesrepublik und der DDR in Ausstellungen, Museen und Gedenkstätten*, Geschichte und Erwachsenenbildung, vol. 19, ed. by Bernd Faulenbach and Franz-Josef Jelich (Essen: Klartext, 2005), pp. 93–110.

Kaminsky, Anna, '"...es gibt gute Gründe, den 13. August nicht aus dem Auge zu verlieren"', *Deutschland Archiv* (2011) 7, http://www.bpb.de/geschichte/zeitgeschichte/deutschlandarchiv/53543/erinnerung-an-die-berliner-mauer?p=all (accessed 29 September 2016).

Kaminsky, Anna (ed.), *Orte des Erinnerns: Gedenkzeichen, Gedenkstätten und Museen zur Diktatur in SBZ und DDR* (Bonn: Bundeszentrale für politische Bildung, 2007).

Kantsteiner, Wulf, 'Memory, Media and *Menschen*: Where is the Individual in Collective Memory Studies?', *Memory Studies*, 3 (2010) 1, 3–4.

Kaplan, Brett Ashley, '"Aesthetic Pollution": The Paradox of Remembering and Forgetting in Three Holocaust Commemorative Sites', *Journal of Modern Jewish Studies*, 2 (2003) 1, 1–18.

Kassner, Jens, *Chemnitz. Architektur. Stadt der Moderne* (Leipzig: Passage-Verlag, 2009).

Keubke, Klaus-Ulrich, *Schwerin: Kontinuität im Wandel* (Schwerin: APH, 1992).

Kiele, Ingvild, 'Ein Denkmal in Ehren: Lenin – Was tun?', *Kommune*, 11 (1991), 62–64.

Klausmeier, Axel, 'Die Gedenkstätte Berliner Mauer an der Bernauer Straße', in *Die Mauer: Errichtung, Überwindung, Erinnerung*, ed. by Klaus-Dietmar Henke (Munich: dtv, 2011), pp. 394–406.

Klein, Kerwin Lee, 'On the Emergence of Memory in Historical Discourse', *Representations*, 69 (2000) Winter, 127–50.

Klemke, Rainer, 'Das Gesamtkonzept Berliner Mauer', in *Die Mauer: Errichtung, Überwindung, Erinnerung*, ed. by Klaus-Dietmar Henke (Munich: dtv, 2011), pp. 377–93.

Klother, Eva-Maria, *Denkmalplastik nach 1945 bis 1989 in Ost- und West-Berlin* (Münster: LIT, 1998).
Knabe, Hubertus, *17. Juni 1953: Ein deutscher Aufstand* (Munich: Propyläen Verlag, 2003).
Knigge, Volkhard, 'Buchenwald', in *Das Gedächtnis der Dinge: KZ-Relikte und KZ-Denkmäler 1945–1995*, ed. by Detlef Hoffmann (Frankfurt; New York: Campus, 1998), pp. 94–173.
Knigge, Volkhard, 'Die Umgestaltung der DDR-Gedenkstätten nach 1990: Ein Erfahrungsbericht am Beispiel Buchenwalds', in *Woran erinnern? Der Kommunismus in der deutschen Erinnerungskultur*, ed. by Peter März and Hans-Joachim Veen (Cologne: Böhlau, 2006), pp. 91–108.
Knigge, Volkhard, 'Zweifacher Schmerz: Speziallagererinnerung jenseits falscher Analogien und Retrodebatten', in *Instrumentalisierung, Verdrängung, Aufarbeitung: Die sowjetischen Speziallager in der gesellschaftlichen Wahrnehmung 1945 bis heute*, ed. by Petra Haustein, Anna Kaminsky, Volkhard Knigge and Bodo Ritscher (Göttingen: Wallstein, 2006), pp. 250–64.
Knischewski, Gerd and Ulla Spittler, 'Remembering the Berlin Wall: The Wall Memorial Ensemble Bernauer Straße', *German Life and Letters*, 59 (2006) 2, 280–93.
Koop, Volker, *Der 17. Juni 1953: Legende und Wirklichkeit* (Berlin: Siedler Verlag, 2003).
Koshar, Rudy, *From Monuments to Traces: Artifacts of German Memory, 1870–1990* (Berkeley, CA: University of California Press, 2000).
Kowalczuk, Ilko-Sascha, *17 Juni 1953. Volksaufstand in der DDR. Ursachen – Abläufe – Folgen* (Bremen: Edition Temmen, 2003).
Kowalczuk, Ilko-Sascha, *Endspiel: Die Revolution von 1989 in der DDR* (Munich: Beck, 2009).
Kowalczuk, Ilko-Sascha, 'Die Vorgeschichte und die Revolution 1989 in der DDR', in *Zwanzig Jahre friedliche Revolution*, ed. by Martin Hermann (Jena: IKS Garamond, 2010), pp. 37–48.
Kowalczuk, Ilko-Sascha, Armin Mitter and Stefan Wolle (eds), *Der Tag X – 17. Juni 1953: Die 'innere Staatsgründung' der DDR als Ergebnis der Krise 1952/54* (Berlin: Ch. Links, 1995).
Krüger, Dieter and Gerhard Finn, *Mecklenburg-Vorpommern 1945 bis 1948 und das Lager Fünfeichen* (Berlin: Verlag Gebr. Holzapfel, no date [1990/91?]).
Krüger, Dieter and Egon Kühlbach, *Schicksal Fünfeichen – Versuch einer Ermittlung: Stand 1991* (Neubrandenburg: Regionalmuseum Neubrandenburg, 1991).
Kuhn, Ekkehard, *Der Tag der Entscheidung: Leipzig, 9. Oktober 1989* (Berlin: Ullstein, 1992).
Kuhn, Ekkehard, *'Wir sind das Volk!' Die friedliche Revolution in Leipzig, 9. Oktober 1989* (Berlin: Ullstein, 1999).
Küttler, Thomas and J. Curt Röder, *Die Wende in Plauen: Eine Dokumentation* (Plauen: Vogtländischer Heimatverlag Neupert, 1991).
Ladd, Brian, 'East Berlin Political Monuments in the Late German Democratic Republic: Finding a Place for Marx and Engels', *Journal of Contemporary History*, 37 (2002) 1, 91–104.

Ladd, Brian, *The Ghosts of Berlin* (Chicago, IL: University of Chicago Press, 1997).
Lambert, Ladina Bezzola and Andrea Oschner (eds), *Moment to Monument: The Making and Unmaking of Cultural Significance* (Bielefeld: transcript Verlag, 2009).
Landsberg, Alison, *Prosthetic Memory: The Transformation of American Remembrance in the Age of Mass Culture* (New York: Columbia University Press, 2004).
Langenbacher, Eric, 'The Mastered Past? Collective Memory Trends in Germany since Unification', in *From the Bonn to the Berlin Republic: Germany at the Twentieth Anniversary of Unification*, ed. by Jeffrey J. Anderson and Eric Langenbacher (New York; Oxford: Berghahn Books, 2010), pp. 63–89.
Langenbacher, Eric, Bill Niven and Ruth Wittlinger, 'Introduction: Dynamics of Memory in Twenty-First Century Germany', *German Politics and Society*, 26 (2008) 4, 1–8.
Langenohl, Andreas, *Erinnerung und Modernisierung: Die öffentliche Rekonstruktion politischer Kollektivität am Beispiel des Neuen Rußland* (Göttingen: Vandenhoeck und Ruprecht, 2000).
Langner, Johannes, 'Denkmal und Abstraktion', in *Denkmal-Zeichen-Monument: Skulptur und öffentlicher Raum heute*, ed. by Ekkehard Mai und Gisela Schmirber (Munich: Prestel-Verlag, 1989), pp. 58–68.
Lee, Mia, 'GDR Monuments in Unified Germany', in *Memorialization in Germany since 1945*, ed. by Bill Niven and Chloe Paver (Basingstoke: Palgrave Macmillan, 2010), pp. 308–17.
Leggewie, Claus and Erik Meyer, 'Shared Memory: Buchenwald and Beyond', *Tr@nsit online*, 22 (2002).
Le Goff, Jacques, *History and Memory*, trans. Steven Rendall and Elizabeth Claman (New York: Columbia University Press, 1992).
Lemmons, Russel, '"Imprisoned, Murdered, Besmirched": The Controversy Concerning Berlin's Ernst Thälmann Monument and German National Identity, 1990–1995', in *Memory Traces: 1989 and the Question of German Cultural Identity*, ed. by Silke Arnold-de Simine (Bern: Lang, 2005), pp. 309–34.
Leo, Annette, 'Spuren der DDR', in *Demontage... revolutionärer oder restaurativer Bildersturm? Texte und Bilder*, ed. by Götz Aly et al. (Berlin: Karin Kramer Verlag, 1992), pp. 59–66.
Lipinsky, Jan, 'Gefängnisse und Lager in der SBZ/DDR als Stätten des Terrors im kommunistischen Herrschaftssytem', in *Materialien der Enquete-Kommission: 'Überwindung der Folgen der SED-Diktatur im Prozeß der deutschen Einheit'*, vol. VI, ed. by Deutscher Bundestag (Frankfurt; Baden Baden: Nomos Verlagsgesellschaft, 1999), pp. 490–566.
Loeb, Carolyn, 'The City as Subject: Contemporary Public Sculpture in Berlin', *Journal of Urban History*, 35 (2009) 6, 853–78.
Lowe, David and Tony Joel, *Remembering the Cold War: Global Contest and National Stories* (New York; London: Routledge, 2013).
Lowenthal, David, *The Past Is a Foreign Country* (Cambridge: Cambridge University Press, 1985).

Lupu, Noam, 'Memory Vanished, Absent, and Confined: The Countermemorial Project in 1980s and 1990s Germany', *History & Memory*, 15 (2003) 2, 130–64.

Lyotard, Jean-François, *The Postmodern Condition: A Report on Knowledge*, trans. Geoff Bennington and Brian Massumi (Minnesota: University of Minnesota, [1979] 1984).

MacGregor, Neil, *Germany: Memories of a Nation* (London: Allen Lane, 2014).

Mählert, Ulrich (ed.), *Der 17. Juni 1953: Ein Aufstand für Einheit, Recht und Freiheit* (Bonn: Dietz, 2003).

Mai, Joachim (ed.), *Spurensicherung. Greifswald 1945. Neue Dokumente und Materialien* (Berlin: FIDES Verlag, 1995).

Maier, Charles S., 'Hot Memory... Cold Memory: On the Political Half-Life of Fascist and Communist Memory', *Tr@nsit online*, 22 (2002).

Maier, Charles, 'A Surfeit of Memory? Reflections on History, Melancholy, and Denial', *History & Memory*, 5 (1993) 2, 136–52.

Major, Patrick, *Behind the Berlin Wall: East Germany and the Frontiers of Power* (Oxford: Oxford University Press, 2010).

Manghani, Sunil, *Image Critique and the Fall of the Berlin Wall* (Bristol: intellect, 2008).

Marcuse, Harold, 'Holocaust Memorials: The Emergence of a Genre', *American Historical Review*, 115 (2010) February, 53–89.

Matenklott, Gert, 'Denkmal / Memorial', *Daidalos*, 49 (1993) September, 28–35.

Maur, Hans, *Arbeiterbewegung – Gedenkstätten* (Berlin: Gedenkstättenverband e.V., 1999).

Maur, Hans, *Sowjetische Ehrenmale: Schutz und Erhalt – Abriss und Verfall* (Berlin: Gedenkstättenverband, 1999).

Mausbach, Florian, *Über Sinn und Ort eines nationalen Freiheits- und Einheitsdenkmals* (Berlin: Bundesamt für Bauwesen und Raumordnung, 2008).

McAdams, A. James, *Judging the Past in Unified Germany* (Cambridge: Cambridge University Press, 2001).

Meier, André and Ludwig Rauch, 'Kulturbetrieb im Niemandsland', *Bildende Kunst*, 10 (1990), 19–26.

Michalski, Sergiusz, *Public Monuments: Art in Political Bondage 1970–1997* (London: Reaktion, 1998).

Mitter, Armin and Stefan Wolle, *Untergang auf Raten: Unbekannte Kapitel der DDR-Geschichte* (Munich: Bertelsmann, 1993).

Mittig, Hans-Ernst, 'Das Denkmal', in *Kunst: Die Geschichte ihrer Funktionen*, ed. by Werner Busch and Peter Schmoock (Weinheim; Berlin: Quadriga Verlag, 1987), pp. 457–89.

Mittig, Hans-Ernst, 'Gegen den Abriß des Berliner Lenin-Denkmals', in *Demontage... revolutionärer oder restaurativer Bildersturm? Texte und Bilder*, ed. by Götz Aly et al. (Berlin: Karin Kramer Verlag, 1992), pp. 41–45.

Mittig, Hans-Ernst, 'Politische Denkmäler und "Kunst am Bau" im städtischen Kontext', in *Verfallen und vergessen oder aufgehoben und geschützt? Architektur und Städtebau der DDR – Geschichte, Bedeutung, Umgang, Erhaltung*, Schriftenreihe des deutschen Nationalkomittees für Denkmalschutz, vol. 51 (Bonn: Deutsches Nationalkomitee für Denkmalschutz, 1997), pp. 23–32.

Moeller, Robert G., 'Germans as Victims? Thoughts on a Post-Cold-War History of World War II's Legacies', *History & Memory*, 17 (2005) 1/2, 147–94.

Moeller, Robert G., 'On the History of Man-Made Destruction: Loss, Death, Memory, and Germany in the Bombing War', *History Workshop Journal*, 61 (2006), 103–34.

Moeller, Robert G., *War Stories: The Search for a Usable Past in the Federal Republic of Germany* (Berkeley, CA: University of California Press, 2001).

Morré, Jörg, 'Geschichte des NKWD-Speziallagers Nr. 9 in Fünfeichen', in *Streng verboten: Das Tagebuch des Pastors Bartelt*, ed. by AG Fünfeichen (Neubrandenburg: Henryk Walther, 2008), pp. 5–15.

Mosse, George L., *Fallen Soldiers: Reshaping the Memory of the World Wars* (New York; Oxford: Oxford University Press, 1990).

Mühlberg, Dietrich, 'Vom langsamen Wandel der Erinnerung an die DDR', in *Verletztes Gedächtnis: Erinnerungskultur und Zeitgeschichte im Konflikt*, ed. by Konrad H. Jarausch and Martin Sabrow (Frankfurt am Main: Campus, 2002), pp. 217–51.

Mumford, Lewis, *The Culture of Cities* (London: Secker & Warburg, 1938).

Münchow, Michael, *Die friedliche Revolution 1989/1990 in Magdeburg: Eine Analyse der Ereignisse* (Kremkau: Block Verlag, 2007).

Mundus, Doris, *Leipzig 1989: Eine Chronik* (Leipzig: Lehmstedt Verlag, 2009).

Musil, Robert, *Nachlaß zu Lebzeiten* (Hamburg: Rowohlt, 1957).

Muther, Richard, 'Die Denkmalseuche', in *Aufsätze über bildende Kunst*, vol. 2: *Betrachtungen und Eindrücke* (Berlin: J. Ladyschnikow Verlag, 1914), pp. 59–68.

Nadkarni, Maya, 'The Death of Socialism and the Afterlife of Its Monuments: Making and Marketing the Past in Budapest's Statue Park Museum', in *Memory, History, Nation: Contested Pasts*, ed. by Katherine Hodgkin and Susannah Radstone (New Brunswick, NJ: Transaction Publishers, 2007), pp. 193–207.

Navrud, Ståle and Richard C. Ready, *Valuing Cultural Heritage: Applying Environmental Valuation Techniques to Historic Buildings, Monuments, Artifacts* (Cheltenham: Edward Elgar, 2002).

Neubert, Erhart, 'Intellektuelle Bewältigung in Politik, Wissenschaft und Literatur', in *Volkserhebung gegen den SED-Staat: Eine Bestandsaufnahme zum 17. Juni 1953*, ed. by Roger Engelmann and Ilko-Sascha Kowalczuk (Göttingen: Vandenhoeck & Ruprecht, 2005), pp. 378–413.

Neubert, Ehrhart, *Unsere Revolution: Die Geschichte der Jahre 1989/90* (Munich: Piper, 2008).

Nipperdey, Thomas, 'Nationalidee und Nationaldenkmal in Deutschland im 19. Jahrhundert', *Historische Zeitschrift*, 206 (1968), 529–85.

Niven, Bill, *The Buchenwald Child: Truth, Fiction, and Propaganda* (Rochester, NY: Camden House, 2007).

Niven, Bill, *Facing the Nazi Past: United Germany and the Legacy of the Third Reich* (London; New York: Routledge, 2002).

Niven, Bill, 'From Countermonument to Combimemorial: Developments in German Memorialization', *Journal of War and Culture Studies*, 6 (2013) 1, 75–91.

Niven, Bill (ed.), *Germans as Victims: Remembering the Past in Contemporary Germany* (Basingstoke: Palgrave, 2006).
Niven, Bill, 'On the Use of "Collective Memory"', *German History*, 26 (2008) 3, 427–36.
Niven, Bill and Chloe Paver (eds), *Memorialization in Germany since 1945* (Basingstoke: Palgrave Macmillan, 2010).
Nooke, Günter, 'Ein Denkmal für die Einheit in Freiheit? Formen der Auseinandersetzung mit der DDR', in *Woran erinnern? Der Kommunismus in der deutschen Erinnerungskultur*, ed. by Peter März and Hans-Joachim Veen (Cologne: Böhlau, 2006), pp. 111–22.
Nora, Pierre, 'Between Memory and History: Les Lieux de Mémoire', *Representations*, 26 (1989) Spring, 7–24.
Nora, Pierre (ed.), *Les Lieux de Mémoire*, 7 vols (Paris: Gallimard, 1984–92).
Nora, Pierre, 'The Reasons for the Current Upsurge in Memory', *Transit – Europäische Revue*, 22 (2002), Tr@nsit online.
Ohse, Marc-Dietrich, 'Aufarbeitung und Gedenken', *Deutschland Archiv*, 40 (2007) 6, 965–67.
Olick, Jeffrey K., '"Collective Memory": A Memoir and Prospect', *Memory Studies*, 1 (2008) 1, 23–29.
Olick, Jeffrey K., 'Collective Memory: The Two Cultures', *Sociological Theory*, 17 (1999) 3, 333–48.
Olick, Jeffrey K., 'From Collective Memory to the Sociology of Mnemonic Practices and Products', in *A Companion to Cultural Memory Studies*, ed. by Astrid Erll and Ansgar Nünning (Berlin: de Gruyter, 2010), pp. 151–61.
Olick, Jeffrey K., 'Genre Memories and Memory Genres: A Dialogical Analysis of May 8, 1945 Commemorations in the Federal Republic of Germany', *American Sociological Review*, 64 (1999) 3, 381–402.
Olick, Jeffrey K., *The Politics of Regret: On Collective Memory and Historical Responsibility* (New York; London: Routledge, 2007).
Olick, Jeffrey K. (ed.), *States of Memory: Continuities, Conflicts, and Transformations in National Retrospection* (Durham, NC; London: Duke University Press, 2003).
Olsen, Jon Berndt, *Tailoring Truth: Politicizing the Past and Negotiating Memory in East Germany, 1945–1990* (New York; Oxford: Berghahn Books, 2015).
Pampel, Bert, *'Mit eigenen Augen sehen, wozu der Mensch fähig ist.' Zur Wirkung von Gedenkstätten auf ihre Besucher* (Frankfurt; New York: Campus Verlag, 2007).
Pearce, Caroline, *Contemporary Germany and the Nazi Legacy: Remembrance, Politics and the Dialectic of Normality* (Basingstoke: Palgrave Macmillan, 2008).
Pearce, Caroline, 'An Unequal Balance? Memorializing Germany's "Double Past" since 1990', in *The GDR Remembered: Representations of the East German State since 1989*, ed. by Nick Hodgin and Caroline Pearce (Rochester, NY: Camden House, 2011), pp. 172–98.
Pessard, Gustave, *La Statuomanie parisienne: Etude critique sur l'abus des statues, liste des statues et monuments existants* (Paris: H. Daragon, 1912).
Petershagen, Rudolf, *Gewissen in Aufruhr* (Berlin: Verlag der Nation, 1957).

Pinfold, Debbie, '"Das Mündel will Vormund sein": The GDR State as Child', *German Life and Letters*, 64 (2011) 2, 283–304.
Plato, Alexander von, 'Sowjetische Speziallager', in *Erinnerungsorte der DDR*, ed. by Martin Sabrow (Munich: Beck, 2009), pp. 90–97.
Plato, Alexander von, 'Sowjetische Speziallager in Deutschland 1945 bis 1950: Ergebnisse eines deutsch-russischen Kooperationsprojektes', in *Speziallager in der SBZ: Gedenkstätten mit 'doppelter Vergangenheit'*, ed. by Peter Reif-Spirek and Bodo Ritscher (Berlin: Links, 1999), pp. 124–48.
Plato, Alexander von, 'Zur Geschichte des sowjetischen Speziallagersystems in Deutschland: Einführung', in *Sowjetische Speziallager in Deutschland 1945 bis 1950*, vol. 1: *Studien und Berichte*, ed. by Sergej Mironenko, Lutz Niethammer and Alexander von Plato (Berlin: Akademie Verlag, 1998), pp. 19–75.
Reichel, Peter, *Politik mit der Erinnerung: Gedächtnisorte im Streit um die nationalsozialistsiche Vergangenheit* (Frankfurt am Main: Fischer, 1999).
Richter, Michael, 'Ebenfalls gegen die Wende-Demagogie und für den Revolutionsbegriff', *Deutschland Archiv*, 40 (2007) 6, 1,086–87.
Richter, Michael, *Die Friedliche Revolution: Aufbruch zur Demokratie in Sachsen 1989/90* (Göttingen: Vandenhoeck & Ruprecht, 2009).
Richter, Michael, 'Die Wende: Plädoyer für eine umgangssprachliche Benutzung des Begriffs', *Deutschland Archiv*, 40 (2007) 5, 861–68.
Richter, Sebastian, 'Die Mauer in der deutschen Erinnerungskultur', in *Die Mauer: Errichtung, Überwindung, Erinnerung*, ed. by Klaus-Dietmar Henke (Munich: dtv, 2011), pp. 252–66.
Riegl, Alois, 'Der moderne Denkmalkultus: Sein Wesen und seine Entstehung', in *Gesammelte Aufsätze* (Vienna: WUV-Univ.-Verl., [1903] 1996), pp. 139–84.
Robin, Régine, 'Das Verschwinden der DDR im kollektiven Gedächtnis', in *Vom kritischen Gebrauch der Erinnerung*, ed. by Thomas Flierl and Elfriede Müller (Berlin: Karl Dietz Verlag, 2009), pp. 49–66.
Rödder, Andreas, *Deutschland einig Vaterland: Die Geschichte der Wiedervereinigung* (Munich: C.H. Beck, 2009).
Roettig, Petra, 'Sprechende Denkmäler', *kritische berichte*, 20 (1992) 3, 75–82.
Rosenfeld, Gavriel D., 'The Controversy That Isn't: The Debate over Daniel J. Goldhagen's *Hitler's Willing Executioners* in Comparative Perspective', *Contemporary European History*, 8 (1999) 2, 249–73.
Rosenfeld, Gavriel, *Hi Hitler! How the Nazi Past Is Being Normalized in Contemporary Culture* (Cambridge: Cambridge University Press, 2014).
Rosenfeld, Gavriel, 'A Looming Crash or a Soft Landing? Forecasting the Future of the Memory "Industry"', *Journal of Modern History*, 81 (2009), 122–58.
Rosenfeld, Gavriel D., *Munich and Memory: Architecture, Monuments, and the Legacy of the Third Reich* (Berkeley, CA: University of California Press, 2000).
Rosenfeld, Gavriel D. and Paul B. Jaskot (eds), *Beyond Berlin: Twelve German Cities Confront the German Past* (Ann Arbor, MI: University of Michigan Press, 2008).
Roth, Heidi, *Der 17. Juni in Sachsen* (Cologne: Böhlau, 1999).
Rothberg, Michael, *Multidirectional Memory: Remembering the Holocaust in the Age of Decolonization* (Stanford, CA: Stanford University Press, 2009).
Rüger, Maria, 'Das Berliner Lenin-Denkmal', *kritische berichte*, 20 (1992) 3, 36–44.

Sabrow, Martin, 'Erinnerung als Pathosformel der Gegenwart', in *Der Streit um die Erinnerung*, Helmstedter Kolloquien, vol. 10, ed. by Martin Sabrow (Leipzig: Akademische Verlagsanstalt, 2008), pp. 9–24.
Sabrow, Martin (ed.), *Erinnerungsorte der DDR* (Munich: Beck, 2009).
Sabrow, Martin, '"Wende" oder "Revolution"? Der Herbstumbruch 1989 und die Geschichtswissenschaft', paper presented at Forum Neuer Markt, 2 April 2009, p. 5, www.zzf-pdm.de/Portals/images/default/09_04_02_Vortrag_Wende oder Revolution (Potsdam).pdf (accessed 31 August 2011).
Sabrow, Martin et al. (eds), *Wohin treibt die DDR-Erinnerung? Dokumentation einer Debatte* (Göttingen: Vandenhoeck & Ruprecht, 2007).
Sachs, Angeli, *Erfindung und Rezeption von Mythen in der Malerei der DDR: Analysen* (Berlin: Akademie Verlag, 1993).
Sachse, Christian, 'Denkzeichen für die Inhaftierten im NKWD-Haftkeller. Ein Bericht', *Zeitschrift des Forschungsverbundes SED-Staat*, 17 (2005), 179–81.
Samuel, Raphael, *Theatres of Memory*, vol. 1: *Past and Present in Contemporary Culture* (London; New York: Verso, 1994).
Saunders, Anna, 'Challenging or Concretising Cold War Narratives? Berlin's Memorial to the Victims of 17 June 1953', in *Memorialization in Germany since 1945*, ed. by Bill Niven and Chloe Paver (Basingstoke: Palgrave Macmillan, 2010), pp. 298–307.
Saunders, Anna, 'The Ghosts of Lenin, Thälmann and Marx in the Post-Socialist Cityscape', *German Life and Letters*, 63 (2010) 4, 441–57.
Saunders, Anna, 'The Luxemburg Legacy: Concretising the Remembrance of a Controversial Heroine?', *German History*, 29 (2011) 1, 36–56.
Saunders, Anna, 'The Politics of Memory in Berlin's *Freiheits- und Einheitsdenkmal*', in *Remembering and Rethinking the GDR: Multiple Perspectives and Plural Authenticities*, ed. by Anna Saunders and Debbie Pinfold (Basingstoke: Palgrave Macmillan, 2013), pp. 164–78.
Saunders, Anna, 'Remembering Cold War Division: Wall Remnants and Border Monuments in Berlin', *Journal of Contemporary European Studies*, 17 (2009) 1, 9–19.
Scharnowski, Susanne, 'Heroes and Victims: The Aesthetics and Ideology of Monuments and Memorials in the GDR', in *Memorialization in Germany since 1945*, ed. by Bill Niven and Chloe Paver (Basingstoke: Palgrave Macmillan, 2010), pp. 267–75.
Schasler, Max, 'Ueber moderne Denkmalswuth', *Deutsche Zeit- und Streit-Fragen*, 7 (1878) 103, 253–92.
Schittenhelm, Karin, *Zeichen, die Anstoß erregen: Mobilisierungsformen zu Mahnmalen und zeitgenössischen Außenskulpturen* (Opladen: Westdeutscher Verlag, 1996).
Schlie, Ulrich, *Die Nation erinnert sich: Die Denkmäler der Deutschen* (Munich: Verlag C.H. Beck, 2002).
Schlör, Joachim, '"It Has to Go Away, but at the Same Time It Has to be Kept": The Berlin Wall and the Making of an Urban Icon', *Urban History*, 33 (2006) 1, 85–105.

Schmid, Hans-Dieter, 'Denkmäler als Zeugnisse der Geschichtskultur', in *Geschichte und Öffentlichkeit: Orte-Medien-Institutionen*, ed. by Sabine Horn and Michael Sauer (Göttingen: Vandenhoeck & Ruprecht, 2009), pp. 51–60.
Schmidt, Leo, 'The Architecture and Message of the "Wall", 1961–1989', *German Politics and Society*, 29 (2011) 2, 57–77.
Schmidt, Leo, 'The Berlin Wall: A Landscape of Memory', in *On Both Sides of the Wall: Preserving Monuments and Sites of the Cold War Era*, ed. by Leo Schmidt and Henriette von Preuschen (Berlin: Westkreuz, 2005), pp. 11–17.
Schmidt, Leo, *Einführung in die Denkmalpflege* (Darmstadt: Wissenschaftliche Buchgesellschaft, 2008).
Schmidt, Leo, 'Vom Symbol der Unterdrückung zur Ikone der Befreiung: Auseinandersetzung, Verdrängung, Memorialisierung', in *Die Berliner Mauer: Vom Sperrwall zum Denkmal* (Bonn: Deutsches Nationalkomitee für Denkmalschutz, 2009), pp. 169–86.
Schmitz, André, '20 Jahre Mauerfall', in *Jahrbuch für Kulturpolitik 2009. Thema: Erinnerungskulturen und Geschichtspolitik*, ed. by Bernd Wagner (Essen: Klartext Verlag, 2009), pp. 117–22.
Schneider, Richard, Johannes Hildebrandt, Helmut Trotnow and Gabi Dolff-Bonekämper, 'Grenzanlage Bernauer Straße – Friedhof, Museum, Denkmal', in *Verfallen und vergessen oder aufgehoben und geschützt? Architektur und Städtebau der DDR – Geschichte, Bedeutung, Umgang, Erhaltung* (Bonn: Deutsches Nationalkomitee für Denkmalschutz, 1997), pp. 93–99.
Schönfeld, Martin, 'Erhalten – Zerstören – Verändern? Diskussionsprozess um die politischen Denkmäler der DDR in Berlin', *kritische berichte*, 19 (1991) 1, 39–43.
Schönfeld, Martin, *Gedenktafeln in Ost-Berlin* (Berlin: Aktives Museum Faschismus und Widerstand in Berlin e.V., 1991).
Schönfeld, Martin, 'Kritisches Denkzeichen und restauratives Denkmal', in *Vom kritischen Gebrauch der Erinnerung*, ed. by Thomas Flierl and Elfriede Müller (Berlin: Karl Dietz Verlag, 2009), pp. 141–74.
Schug, Alexander (ed.), *Palast der Republik: Politischer Diskurs und private Erinnerung* (Berlin: BWV, 2007).
Schwartz, Barry, 'Christian Origins: Historical Truth and Social Memory', in *Memory, Tradition, and Text: Uses of the Past in Early Christianity*, ed. by Alan Kirk and Tom Thatcher (Atlanta: Society of Biblical Literature, 2005), pp. 43–56.
Schwartz, Barry, 'Introduction: The Expanding Past', *Qualitative Sociology*, 19 (1996) 3, 275–82.
Schwartz, Barry, 'The Social Context of Commemoration: A Study in Collective Memory', *Social Forces*, 61 (1982) 2, 374–402.
Skriebeleit, Jörg, '"Orte des Schreckens": Dimensionen verräumlichter Erinnerung', in *Der Nationalsozialismus im Spiegel des öffentlichen Gedächtnisses: Formen der Aufarbeitung und des Gedenkens*, ed. by Petra Frank and Stefan Hördler (Berlin: Metropol Verlag, 2005), pp. 205–20.
Speitkamp, Winfried (ed.), *Denkmalsturz: Zur Konfliktgeschichte politischer Symbolik* (Göttingen: Vandenhoeck & Ruprecht, 1997).

Stadtarchiv Chemnitz (ed.), *Karl-Marx-Stadt 1989 – Chemnitz 2009. Eine Stadt im Wandel. Chronik in Wort und Bild* (Erfurt: Sutton Verlag, 2009).

Staiger, Uta, 'Cities, Citizenship, Contested Cultures: Berlin's Palace of the Republic and the Politics of the Public Sphere', *Cultural Geographies*, 16 (2009), 309–27.

Stedtler, Andreas, *Die Akte Lenin: Eine Rettungsgeschichte mit Haken* (Halle: Mitteldeutscher Verlag, 2006).

Steinbach, Peter, 'Der 9. November in der Erinnerung der Bundesrepublik', *Deutschland Archiv*, 41 (2008) 5, 877–82.

Steininger, Rolf, *17. Juni 1953: Der Anfang vom langen Ende der DDR* (Munich: Olzog, 2003).

Strom, Elizabeth A., *Building the New Berlin: The Politics of Urban Development in Germany's Capital City* (Lanham, MD: Lexington Books, 2001).

Stude, Sebastian, 'Halle/Saale 1989', *UTOPIE kreativ*, 201/202 (2007), 764–82.

Sturken, Marita, *Tangled Memories: The Vietnam War, the AIDS Epidemic, and the Politics of Remembering* (Berkeley, CA: University of California Press, 1997).

Süß, Walter, 'Von der Ohnmacht des Volkes zur Resignation der Mächtigen: Ein Vergleich des Aufstands 1953 mit der Revolution von 1989', in *Volkserhebung gegen den SED-Staat: Eine Bestandsaufnahme zum 17. Juni 1953*, ed. by Roger Engelmann and Ilko-Sascha Kowalczuk (Göttingen: Vandenhoeck & Ruprecht, 2005), pp. 426–62.

Symposium zum Denkmal für die Ereignisse des 17. Juni 1953 – Dokumentation (Berlin: Senatsverwaltung für Bauen, Wohnen und Verkehr, 1996).

Taberner, Stuart and Paul Cooke (eds), *German Culture, Politics, and Literature into the Twenty-First Century: Beyond Normalization* (Rochester, NY: Camden House, 2006).

Tetzner, Reiner, *Leipziger Ring. Aufzeichnungen eines Montagsdemonstranten. Oktober 1989 bis 1. Mai 1990* (Frankfurt am Main: Luchterhand Literaturverlag, 1990).

Thamer, Hans-Ulrich, 'Von der Monumentalisierung zur Verdrängung der Geschichte', in *Denkmalsturz: Zur Konfliktgeschichte politischer Symbolik*, ed. by Winfried Speitkamp (Göttingen: Vandenhoeck & Ruprecht, 1997), pp. 109–36.

Thießen, Malte, *Eingebrannt ins Gedächtnis: Hamburgs Gedenken an Luftkrieg und Kriegsende 1943 bis 2005* (Munich: Dölling und Galitz Verlag, 2007).

Tietz, Jürgen, *Berliner Verwandlungen: Hauptstadt / Architektur / Denkmal* (Berlin: Verlag Bauwesen, 2000).

Till, Karen E., *The New Berlin: Memory, Politics, Place* (Minneapolis, MN: University of Minnesota, 2005).

Till, Karen E. 'Reimagining National Identity: "Chapters of Life" at the German Historical Museum in Berlin', in *Textures of Place: Exploring Humanist Geographies*, ed. by Paul C. Adams, Steven Hoelscher and Karen E. Till (Minneapolis, MN; London: University of Minnesota Press, 2001), pp. 273–99.

Till, Karen E., 'Staging the Past: Landscape Designs, Cultural Identity and Erinnerungspolitik at Berlin's Neue Wache', *Ecumene*, 6 (1999) 3, 251–83.

Tomberger, Corinna, *Das Gegendenkmal: Avantgardekunst, Geschichtspolitik und Geschlecht in der bundesdeutschen Erinnerungskultur* (Bielefeld: transcript Verlag, 2007).
Trotnow, Helmut, 'Sag mir, wo die Spuren sind... Berlin und der Umgang mit der Geschichte der Berliner Mauer', in *'Asymmetrisch verflochtene Parallelgeschichte?' Die Geschichte der Bundesrepublik und der DDR in Ausstellungen, Museen und Gedenkstätten*, ed. by Bernd Faulenbach and Franz-Josef Jelich (Essen: Klartext Verlag, 2005), pp. 157–67.
Varvantakis, Christos, 'A Monument to Dismantlement', *Memory Studies*, 2 (2009) 1, 27–38.
Verheyen, Dirk, *United City, Divided Memories? Cold War Legacies in Contemporary Berlin* (Lanham, MD: Lexington Books, 2008).
Ward, Janet, *Post-Wall Berlin: Borders, Space and Identity* (Basingstoke: Palgrave Macmillan, 2011).
Ward, Simon, *Urban Memory and Visual Culture in Berlin: Framing the Asynchronous City, 1957–2012* (Amsterdam: Amsterdam University Press, 2016).
Webber, Andrew, *Berlin in the Twentieth Century: A Cultural Topography* (Cambridge: Cambridge University Press, 2008).
Wemhoff, Matthias, *Der Berliner Skulpturenfund: 'Entartete Kunst' im Bombenschutt*, Staatliche Museen zu Berlin – Stiftung Preussischer Kulturbesitz (Regensburg: Schnell & Steiner, 2011).
Wentker, Hermann, 'Arbeiteraufstand, Revolution/Die Erhebungen von 1953 und 1989/90 in der DDR: ein Vergleich', *Deutschland Archiv*, 34 (2001) 3, 385–97.
Wertsch, James V., *Voices of Collective Remembering* (New York: Cambridge University Press, 2002).
White, Hayden, *Metahistory: The Historical Imagination in Nineteenth-Century Europe* (Baltimore, MD; London: Johns Hopkins University Press, 1973).
White, Hayden, 'The Question of Narrative in Contemporary Historical Theory', *History and Theory*, 23 (1984) 1, 1–33.
Widrich, Mechtild, *Performative Monuments: The Rematerialisation of Public Art* (Manchester; New York: Manchester University Press, 2014).
Wierling, Dorothee, 'Das Ende der DDR erinnern', in *Bewältigte Diktaturvergangenheit? 20 Jahre DDR-Aufarbeitung*, Helmstedter Colloquien vol. 12, ed. by Martin Sabrow (Leipzig: Akademische Verlagsanstalt, 2010), pp. 37–57.
Wiese, Rüdiger and Klaus Joachim Albert (eds), *2. Bildhauer-Symposium Metall, Schwerin 1990* (Lübeck: Kaiser & Mietzner, 1990).
Williams, Paul, *Memorial Museums: The Global Rush to Commemorate Atrocities* (Oxford; New York: Berg, 2007).
Winter, Jay, 'The Generation of Memory: Reflections on the "Memory Boom" in Contemporary Historical Studies', *Bulletin of the German Historical Institute*, 27 (2000) 3, 69–92.
Winter, Jay, *Remembering War: The Great War between Memory and History in the Twentieth Century* (New Haven, CT; London: Yale University Press, 2006).
Winter, Jay, 'Sites of Memory and the Shadow of War', in *A Companion to Cultural Memory Studies*, ed. by Astrid Erll and Ansgar Nünning (Berlin: de Gruyter, 2010), pp. 61–74.

Winter, Jay, *Sites of Memory, Sites of Mourning: The Great War in European Cultural History* (Cambridge: Cambridge University Press, 1995).
Wippermann, Wolfgang, *Denken statt Denkmalen: Gegen den Denkmalwahn der Deutschen* (Berlin: Rotbuch, 2010).
Wise, Michael Z., *Capital Dilemma: Germany's Search for a New Architecture of Democracy* (New York: Princeton Architectural Press, 1998).
Wittiber, Günter and Irma Emmrich, *Die keramische Säule*, Schweriner Reihe (Rat der Stadt Schwerin, Abteilung Kultur, 1986).
Wodiczko, Krzysztof, 'Leninplatz-Projektion', in *Die Endlichkeit der Freiheit: Berlin 1990. Ein Ausstellungsprojet in Ost und West*, ed. by Wulf Herzogenrath, Joachim Sartorius and Christoph Tannert (Berlin: Hentrich, 1990), pp. 205–11.
Wolf, Christa, *Was bleibt: Erzählung* (Munich: Luchterhand, 1990).
Yates, Frances, *The Art of Memory* (London: Routledge and Kegan Paul, 1966).
Yoder, Jennifer, 'Truth without Reconciliation: An Appraisal of the Enquete Commission on the SED Dictatorship in Germany', *German Politics*, 8 (1999) 3, 59–80.
Young, James, 'Berlin's Holocaust Memorial: A Report to the Bundestag Committee on Media and Culture, 3 March 1999', *German Politics and Society*, 17 (1999) 3, 54–70.
Young, James E., 'The Biography of a Memorial Icon: Nathan Rapoport's Warsaw Ghetto Monument', *Representations*, 26 (1989) Spring, 69–106.
Young, James E., 'The Counter-Monument: Memory against Itself in Germany Today', *Critical Inquiry*, 18 (1992) 2, 276–96.
Young, James E., 'The Memorial's Arc: Between Berlin's *Denkmal* and New York City's 9/11 Memorial', *Memory Studies*, 9 (2016) 3, 325–31.
Young James E., *At Memory's Edge: After-Images of the Holocaust in Contemporary Art and Architecture* (New Haven, CT; London: Yale University Press, 2000).
Young, James E., *The Texture of Memory: Holocaust Memorials and Meaning* (New Haven, CT; London: Yale University Press, 1993).
Zerubavel, Eviatar, *Time Maps: Collective Memory and the Social Shape of the Past* (Chicago, IL; London: University of Chicago Press, 2003).
Zerubavel, Yael, *Recovered Roots: Collective Memory and the Making of Israeli National Tradition* (Chicago, IL; London: University of Chicago Press, 1995).
Zibler, Barbara, 'Kinder als Opfer der Mauer', in *Thomas Brussig. Am kürzeren Ende der Sonnenallee. Lehrerheft*, ed. by Günther Gutknecht and Brigitte Rapp (Biberach: Krapp & Gutknecht, 2001), pp. 71–77.
Zimmer, Hasko (ed.), *Der Buchenwald-Konflikt* (Münster: agenda Verlag, 1999).

 Index

Adenauer, Konrad, 160–61
AG. *See Arbeitsgemeinschaft Fünfeichen*
Alexanderplatz, 59, 252, 253, 255
Alltag. *See* everyday
Andersdenkende, 69, 134
Animal Farm (Orwell), 294
anniversaries. *See also specific anniversaries*
  of Dessau bombing, 284
anti-church policies, of GDR, 325
antifascism, 57–58, 110, 111–12, 114, 118, 316, 319
antimonumentalism, 39, 266
anti-Soviet memorial, 63–64, 99n39
Arbeitsgemeinschaft (AG) *Fünfeichen*, 129–30, 133, 135
art, 267, 323
  projects, 63, 66, 197–201
  socialist icons relating to, 58, 60, 66
Arts Advisory Board, of Berlin Senate, 219
Assmann, Aleida, 29–30, 34
Assmann, Jan, 29–32, 36, 239, 322
Association for a Monument to the People's Uprising of 17 June 1953, 179
Association of Central Germans, 222, 223

Association of Victims of Stalinism (VOS), 123
atheist policies, of SED, 111
Aufarbeitung, 5, 9, 10, 11, 15, 57, 140
  process of, 16, 218, 240, 321
Augustusplatz, 268, 269, 274
Axel-Springer-Haus, 248n177, 258

Bautzen, 112
BBK. *See* Berlin's Professional Association for Fine Artists
bells
  Democracy Bell, 269, 274, 276, 297, 307n126
  Dessau peace bell, 281–86, 310n160, 319
  at Fünfeichen, 118, 130–33, 135, 148
Berlin, 65. *See also* Eastern Berlin; *specific monuments*
  Alexanderplatz in, 59, 252, 253, 255
  anti-Jewish laws in, 7
  deportation sites in, 7
  East Side Gallery in, 1, 198–99
  Neue Wache in, 4, 6, 8, 42, 265
  Potsdamer Platz in, 3, 66, 166, 198, 199
  750th anniversary of, 9
  Television Tower in, 9

352 • *Index*

Berlin-Brandenburg History Workshop, 142
Berlin Citizens Association, 195, 218–20
Berlin City Parliament, 200
Berlin Republic, 251, 263, 264
Berlin Senate, 65, 69, 169, 231, 232, 266
   Arts Advisory Board of, 219
   Freedom Memorial and, 225, 227, 230
   funding of, 165
   Lenin Monument and, 71–72
   Prenzlauer Allee and, 142
   Übergänge and, 201–2
   Wall remembrance and, 197, 199, 208–9, 211, 225
Berlin's Professional Association for Fine Artists (BBK), 170–71
Berlin Wall, 18, 55, 160
   Bernauer Straße, *Gesamtkonzept* and, 231–36, 240
   Bernauer Straße Wall Memorial, 195, 199, 201, 207–14, 218, 223, 225, 227, 233–35, 237, 324
   commodification of, 197–201
   early post-*Wende* years, 197–201
   Eastern and Western visions of, 196
   Eastern side of, 199
   Freedom Memorial, at Checkpoint Charlie, 172, 221, 224–31, 238, 239, 323
   history of, 194–95
   image of, 195
   at Niederkirchnerstraße, 199
   private projects associated with, 214
   symbolism of, 236
   Treptow child victims, 214–18
   Übergänge, 201–7
   as UNESCO heritage site, 199
   vandalism to, 62
   wall-peckers at, 199
   white crosses in duplicate, 195, 218–24
Berlin Wall, fall of, 17, 19n1, 251, 269, 318
   auction of pieces of, 196–97
   9 November linked to, 163, 194, 254, 257–58, 284
   10th anniversary of, 200, 256, 287, 314
   15th anniversary of, 225
   20th anniversary of, 3, 252, 257, 262, 281, 292
   25th anniversary of, 223, 328
   30th anniversary of, 257, 258
Berlin Wall Association, 212
Berlin Wall Foundation, 233, 235
Bernauer Straße, *Gesamtkonzept* and, 213, 222, 236, 240
   approval of, 231
   authenticity of, 233, 249n202
   commemoration with, 235
   concept of, 231–32
   development of, 232, 233, 234, 238
   as Wall remembrance, 231
Bernauer Straße Wall Memorial, 195, 199, 201, 207–18, 223–27, 237, 324
   competition for, 209–10
   construction of, 211–12
   controversial debates over, 207–11
   criticism of, 212
   death strip associated with, 195, 201, 207, 212
   extension of, 233–35
   financial difficulties for, 211
   by Kohlhoff & Kohlhoff, 210, 211, 233, 235
   reconstruction *vs*. preservation with, 211
   role of, 214
   tunnels associated with, 207
   white crosses at, 218, 223
Betriebskampfgruppen (workers' militia groups), 59, 65
Der Bevölkerung, 4
Birthler, Marianne, 142
Board of Trustees for the Magdeburg Citizens Monument, 286–87
Bohley, Bärbel, 70, 227
bombing anniversary, of Dessau, 284

border guards, 174, 195, 196, 327
  killed in action, 59, 73, 235, 239
  trial of, 215
Der Brand (The Fire), 8
Brandenburg Gate, 19n1, 161, 208, 230, 266, 326
Brandt, Willy, 46, 79, 208
Buchenwald, 2, 6, 74, 110, 112, 114, 321
  commemoration at, 117–28, 153n39, 325
  crosses at, 120, 126–27
  mass graves at, 129
Buchenwald Memorial Site, 6, 59, 118, 119–26, 135, 148–49, 152n37
  architects of, 121–23
  design of, 121–22
  exhibition phases of, 119–20
  Knigge and, 122–24, 126, 135, 148
  steel poles used in, 125–26, 154n70
Bundesstiftung zur Aufarbeitung der SED-Diktatur (Federal Foundation for the Reappraisal of the SED Dictatorship), 11, 162, 229
Bundestag
  Freedom and Unity Monument and, 230, 254, 256, 257–58, 267
  special enquiry commission of, 6, 11, 116, 119, 168
Bundeswehr, 4, 5, 130, 321

capsules, in monuments, 294, 296, 320
CDU. *See* Christian Democratic Union
CDU/CSU coalition, 11, 223, 236
CDU/SPD coalition, 11, 165, 211
Central European Development Corporation, 225
Central Investigation Office for Government and Unification Criminality, 215
Centre against Expulsions in Berlin, 8, 21n30
Centre for Political Beauty, 223, 240

Ceramic Column, in Schwerin, 279–81
Chapel of Reconciliation, 213, 234, 324
Chausseestraße memorial (Sachse), 206–7
Checkpoint Charlie, 7, 162, 195, 203, 204–5. *See also* Freedom Memorial, at Checkpoint Charlie; Haus am Checkpoint Charlie Museum
Chemnitz, 322, 326
  Karl Marx Monument in, 77, 78–79, 80, 81–84, 96
  redevelopment of, 81
  renaming of, 80
  unemployment in, 80
child victims. *See* Treptow child victims
Chipperfield, David, 273
Christian Democratic Union (CDU), 116, 128, 138, 171–72
  coalition of CSU and, 11, 223, 236
  coalition of SPD and, 11, 165, 211
  Freedom Memorial and, 227, 228
  monument activity and, 71, 75, 87, 141, 165, 174, 186, 213, 222, 227, 230, 254, 265–66, 276, 316
  representatives of, 69, 93–94, 168, 223, 256, 283, 287, 297
Christianization, 148
Christian Social Union in Bavaria (CSU), 11, 116, 233, 236, 267
Christo, 4, 68
Citizens' Monument, in Magdeburg, 286–91
City Palace, 13, 69, 70, 96, 265, 267, 326
civil rights activists, GDR relating to, 253
Cold War, 3, 8, 39, 115, 144
  end of, 26, 46, 196
  ideology of, 33
  monuments relating to, 1, 73, 172, 194, 196, 221, 226–27, 228, 231
  museum for, 231
collective amnesia, 56

collective memory, 16, 18, 30–36, 240
  cultural context of, 28–29
  within groups, 28–29
  individual embodied memory and, 28
  process of, 27
collective remembrance, 18, 27, 323
column, for Nikolaikirchhof, 270, 271, 277, 326
'combimemorial', 320
commemoration, 212, 252
  with Bernauer Straße, *Gesamtkonzept* and, 235
  at Buchenwald, 117–28, 153n39, 325
  of Treptow child victims, 216
  of victimhood, 213, 255
commemorative marker, at Greifswald, 136, 137, 138, 148, 150
commemorative practices, 17, 325
Commission for Dealing with Postwar Political Monuments in Former East Berlin, 72–73, 235
communicative memory, 17, 27, 206, 258, 277, 322
  of Assmann, Jan, 29–30
  cultural memory and, 15, 29, 97, 149, 171, 239, 297, 321
  of GDR, 61, 140, 174, 177
  socialist, 60
Communist Party of the Soviet Union (CPSU), 56, 169
communist self-liberation, 118
concentration camp victims, memorialization of, 118
Confederation of German Trade Unions, 173
Conscience in Turmoil (Petershagen). *See Gewissen in Aufruhr*
countermemorial. *See* countermonuments
counter-memory, 40, 84
countermonuments, 17, 27, 162, 239, 298–99, 320, 324
  audience participation with, 41–42
  concept of, 40
  fascism relating to, 40–41
  material presence of, 42–44, 53n113
  termination relating to, 255
CPU, CSU, SPD, coalition of, 116
Cremer, Fritz, 59, 114, 118
'Crimes of the Wehrmacht', 5
crosses, 161, 324. *See also* white crosses
  at Buchenwald, 120, 126–27
  at Freedom Memorial, 225
  at Fünfeichen, 131, 132, 133, 135
CSPU. *See* Communist Party of the Soviet Union
CSU. *See* Christian Social Union in Bavaria
cultural memory, 17, 27, 35, 187, 322
  of Assmann, Jan, 29–32, 36
  of Berlin Republic, 263, 264
  communicative memory and, 15, 29, 97, 149, 171, 239, 297, 321

DAAD. *See* German Academic Exchange Service
Day of German Unity, 3 October 1990 as, 160, 251
death strip, 195, 201, 207, 212
decolonization, 26
de Maizière, Lothar, 256
democracy, 318, 328n2
  concept of, with Plauen *Wende* monument, 291, 296
  in GDR, 17
  speech, 254
Democracy Bell, 297
  egg with, 274, 307n126
  in Leipzig, 269, 274, 276
democratization, of memory, 26
demolition, 4, 13–14
  debates about, 68–70, 77–84
  of monuments, 57, 63, 65, 66, 68–71
  of socialist icons, 56–57, 63
demonstrations, 77, 162, 176
  in Dessau, 281
  in Leipzig, 178
  in Nikolaikirchhof, 268
  1989, 2, 14, 43, 55, 68, 79, 81–82, 84, 86, 89, 94–95, 163, 178, 251, 254, 262, 265, 268, 318

1990, 55, 251
 in Plauen, 291–92
17 June 1953, 43, 159–60, 165, 179, 181–83
Denkmal, 36, 37, 40, 59, 98
Denk-Stein, 187
Denkzeichen (memorial marker), 40, 140–45, 147, 255
Dessau
 bombing anniversary of, 284
 mass demonstrations in, 281
 Museum for Town History in, 282
 Square of German Unity in, 284
Dessau, magnetic tape factory in, 281
 armoury housed in, 282
 6 December 1989 initiative relating to, 282, 283
 swords into ploughshares slogan, 283, 299, 310n173
 workers votes relating to, 282
Dessau, peace bell in, 281–82, 285–86, 310n160
 casting of, 284
 competitions for, 283
 in Market Square, 283
 Peace Bell Board of Trustees for, 283
 steel for, 283, 319
destalinization, 56
Deutsche Mark (DM)
 arrival of, 251
 buying power of, 253
 monument costs in, 68, 70, 75, 165, 270, 273
 return of, 184
Deutschland '83, 3
Dewey, John, 35
DHM. *See* German Historical Museum
diachronic memory, 36
dialogism, 315, 322
 memory with, 34–35
dictatorship, 6, 9, 10
 of SED, 11–12, 17, 39, 69–70, 74–75, 80, 94, 96, 114, 117, 124, 130, 173, 186, 199, 213, 230

Diepgen, Eberhard, 9, 69, 164, 168, 211
Disneyfication, 208, 228, 234
DM. *See* Deutsche Mark
documentation, 199, 224
 of monuments, 71–73
Dolff-Bonekämper, Gabi, 45, 208–9, 239, 321
Dresden. *See also* 17 June 1953 uprisings, Dresden memorial to
 Museum of Military History in, 179
 Postplatz in, 181–82
 tank tracks in, 181–85
Dresden1706, 184
Dreßel, Heidemarie, 182, 186–87
dual past
 at Fünfeichen, 133, 134, 148
 of Soviet special camps, 115–16

Eastern Berlin, 60, 62, 65–72, 72–77, 140–47, 165–74, 194–240, 256–77
Eastern Europe, 26, 267
Eastern side, of Berlin Wall, 199
East German demonstrators, 262
East Germany. *See* German Democratic Republic
East Side Gallery, 1, 198–99, 327
Ebertstraße, white crosses on, 219, 220, 221
egg, with Democracy Bell, 274, 307n126
Ehm, Lothar, 283, 286–87, 297, 315
Einheitswippe (unity seesaw), 267
election fraud, of GDR, 252
Die Endlichkeit der Freiheit (The Finiteness of Freedom), 66, 197–98
Engel, Carl, 136–37
entangled memories, 6, 18, 31, 35–36, 93, 96, 231, 322–28
Erinnerungsmal (sign of remembrance), 287
Evers, Rudolf, 286–87, 288, 290, 291, 315
everyday, 13, 14, 30, 42
Experience and Education (Dewey), 35

fascism, 58–59, 131, 160
  countermonuments relating to, 40–41
Faulenbach, Bernd, 6
Faulenbach formula, 6, 116
FDJ. *See* Free German Youth
FDP. *See* Free Democratic Party
Fechter, Peter, 195, 214
Federal Budget Committee, 257
Federal Committee for Culture and Media, 263, 264
Federal Foundation for the Reappraisal of the SED Dictatorship. *See* Bundesstiftung zur Aufarbeitung der SED-Diktatur
Federal Republic of Germany (FRG), 6–7, 35, 39, 136
Federation of Central Germans, 221
Federation of Victims of Stalinism, 181
Festival of Lights, in Leipzig, 269
15th anniversary, of Berlin Wall fall, 225
50th anniversary, of 17 June 1953 uprisings, 162, 173, 180
The Finiteness of Freedom. *See Die Endlichkeit der Freiheit*
The Fire (Der Brand), 8
Fischer, Manfred, 199, 208, 233, 239
Flag Monument, in Halle, 85–89, 90
  colouring of, 85
  discussion about future of, 87–88
  renovation of, 88–89
  Revolutionary Flame as official title of, 86
  site of, 85
  symbolism of, 86–87, 88
Fliegel, Siegbert, 85, 89, 90
Flierl, Thomas, 74, 143–44, 147, 200, 213, 228–29, 232
40th anniversary, of GDR, 252, 268, 291
Forum for Contemporary History, 269
fountain, at Nikolaikirchhof monument, 272–74

4 November 1989 demonstrations, 251
Frankfurt Constitution, 3
Eine Frau in Berlin (A Woman in Berlin), 8
Free Democratic Party (FDP), 11, 69, 71, 75, 87, 181–82, 230
Freedom and Unity Monument, 4, 5, 7, 12, 15, 230, 252–68, 296–99, 319–26
  Bundestag and, 230, 254, 256, 257–58, 267
  citizen initiative of, 256
  construction of, 261, 268
  democratic credentials for, 259, 260
  design of, 256–57, 262–66, 298, 299, 302n28, 302n39, 304n59, 305nn80–81, 319–20, 323
  funding of, 257, 261, 266, 267, 303n49
  German Society adoption of, 256
  Holocaust remembrance relating to, 323–24, 326
  location of, 261, 262, 263, 265
  peaceful revolution and, 256–68, 296, 297–98
  positive historical connotations of, 259
  public hearings on, 257
  termination of, 259
  timing of, 257–58, 262
Freedom Memorial, at Checkpoint Charlie, 172, 221, 224–32, 238, 239, 315, 321–23
  Berlin Senate and, 225, 227, 230
  CDU and, 227, 228
  criticism of, 224, 229
  on Friedrichstraße, 225, 230–31, 323
  Hildebrandt associated with, 172, 224–31, 248n181, 315, 321
  installation of, 225, 227–28, 230, 232
  legitimization of, 227, 247n153
  location of, 229
  removal of, 225–26, 227, 228, 229, 248n177
  symbolism of, 226
  wooden crosses at, 225

Free German Youth (FDJ), 74, 75, 222
French national memory, 29
Freudenmal (mark of joy), 260
FRG. *See* Federal Republic of Germany
Friedrich, Jörg, 8
Friedrichshain, 63, 66, 68, 71, 72, 173
Friedrichstraße, 225, 230, 323
Führer, Christian, 93, 94, 270
Fünfeichen, 325
   AG Fünfeichen, 129–30, 133, 135
   dual past at, 133, 134, 148
   German internees at, 128–29
   Greifswald relating to, 135, 137, 138
   mass graves at, 129, 132
   near Neubrandenburg, 128, 133
   POWs at, 129, 130, 133, 134
   Soviet special camps at, 110, 128–35
Fünfeichen memorial site, 118, 129–35, 148–49
   bells at, 118, 130–33, 135, 148
   bronze plaques at, 132, 133
   crosses at, 131, 132, 133, 135
   Grimm with, 131, 132, 134
   identification of, 132–33
   Lüdtke with, 130, 133, 135
   public funding for, 130
   stelae at, 131, 133, 135
   symbolism of, 134

GDR. *See* German Democratic Republic
Gedenkstättenkonzeption. *See* Memorial Sites Concept
Gegendenkmal. *See* countermonument
Generation War, 2013. *See Unsere Mütter, unsere Väter*
German Academic Exchange Service (DAAD), 66
German Conservative Party, 223
German Democratic Republic (GDR), 9, 19n4, 27, 198, 262. *See also* memorialization, of GDR
   anti-church policies of, 325
   citizen's rights movement of, 11
   civil rights activists relating to, 253
   communicative memory of, 61, 140, 174, 177
   cultural sphere of, 12–13
   demise of, 2, 110, 328
   election fraud of, 252
   40th anniversary of, 252, 268, 291
   Greifswald and, 136–37, 140
   leadership crimes of, 6
   legacy of, 3–4, 5, 12–14, 16
   legitimacy of, 237
   memory of, 5, 10, 15, 17–19, 33
   monument role in, 57–62, 65, 238, 314, 320
   Museum for German History of, 199
   remembrance of, 3, 6, 14, 16, 18, 164
   Round Table associated with, 277–79
   Rust as prisoner of, 222
   17 June 1953 uprisings relating to, 159–60, 161, 164
   victims of, 266, 316
   working through past of, 5, 10–15
German Historical Museum (DHM), 199, 207, 208, 263, 282
German national anthem, 267, 305n92
German Society, 256, 266, 267
German unification, on 3 October 1990, 251, 262
German War Graves Commission, 125
Gesamtkonzept zur Erinnerung an die Berliner Mauer (Integrated Concept for Memory of the Berlin Wall), 14, 197, 213, 222, 231–33, 238, 240, 316, 319, 327
Gestapo, 4, 113, 129
Gewissen in Aufruhr (Conscience in Turmoil) (Petershagen), 136
Goetheplatz, 118
Goldberg, Thorsten, 203–4, 206
Goldhagen, Daniel, 5
Gorbachev, Mikhail, 56, 252, 253
GPU-cellars, 113, 140

graffiti, 14, 42, 62, 69, 70, 71
  on Karl Marx Monument, 81
  on Marx Engels Monument, 46
  on Thälmann Monument, 76–77
grand narratives, 26
Grass, Günter, 8
graves. *See* mass graves
Green government, SPD and, 71, 227–28, 256, 258
Greifswald
  commemorative marker at, 136, 137, 138, 148, 150
  Fünfeichen relating to, 135, 137, 138
  GDR and, 136–37, 140
  legacy of, 136
  Petershagen and, 136, 138, 140
  stelae at, 135, 138–40
GRH. *See* Society for Legal and Humanitarian Support
Grimm, Uwe, 131, 132, 134
Grotewohl, Otto, 58–59
Grundgesetz 49, 4
Gueffroy, Chris, 214

Haacke, Hans, 4, 198
Haftstätte, on Prenzlauer Allee, 140, 316, 321, 324
Halbwachs, Maurice, 28–29, 31, 32, 38
Halle. *See* Flag Monument, in Halle
Hartmann, Jörg, 215, 216, 217
Haus 3, at Prenzlauer Allee, 140, 143, 146, 148–49, 161–62, 232
Haus am Checkpoint Charlie Museum, 161–62, 165, 172, 195, 204, 213, 223, 224, 228
Hennig, Lothar, 235, 239
Hennigsdorf. *See* 17 June 1953 uprisings, Hennigsdorf memorial to
Henry the Lion, 280–81
heroization, 2, 122, 323
Heym, Stefan, 16, 70
Hildebrandt, Alexandra, 172, 224–31, 248n181, 315, 321
historical narratives, 2, 16, 26, 31, 32, 34

Historic Monuments Protection Authority, 228
history, 11
  end of, 26
  memory and, 26, 31–32
  of monuments, 37–38
history-light, Freedom and Unity Monument as, 264–65, 266, 298
Hitler's Willing Executioners (Goldhagen), 5
Hobsbawm, Eric, 32
Hohenschönhausen, 115, 227
Holocaust, 4. *See also* Memorial to the Murdered Jews of Europe; memory
  Freedom and Unity Monument relating to, 323–24, 326
  industry of, 7
  memorial in Berlin, 2, 6–7, 8, 17, 39, 41, 45, 165, 166, 168, 187, 230, 238, 255, 260, 265, 266, 298, 326
  memory of, 6–8, 25–26, 33, 39, 40–41, 163
  remembrance of, 7, 127, 149, 168, 230, 238, 258, 298, 323–24, 326, 327
  victims of, 39, 122, 222, 255
Holocaust-centred memory, 6–8
Honecker, Erich, 62, 74–76, 77, 79
House of Democracy, in Schwerin, 280
House of Ministries, 161, 166, 168, 169
Hussein, Saddam, 2, 55

iconoclasm, 55, 56
IKBD. *See* International Committee of Buchenwald-Dora
'Illuminated box' (Thiel), 204–6
IM. *See* unofficial collaborator of Stasi
Im Krebsgang (Crabwalk) (Grass), 8
individual memory, 27, 28, 30, 31, 48n14
Initiative for a Monument to German Unity, 256
Initiativgruppe Buchenwald 1945–1950, 120, 123, 126, 127–28

Integrated Concept for Memory of the Berlin Wall. *See Gesamtkonzept zur Erinnerung an die Berliner Mauer*
International Buchenwald Committee, 121
International Committee of Buchenwald-Dora, 121
internees, in Soviet special camps, 110, 112–16, 128–29
Internierte, 112
interrogation centers, special camps and, 110, 112–17
The Invention of Tradition (Hobsbawm and Ranger), 32

Jena, 14, 18
Jewish Museum, 7
Jews, 4, 7, 114
Jung, Anni, 280, 281
Jung, Burkhard, 93, 274, 275

Kaiser Wilhelm National Memorial, 38, 85, 257, 262, 266, 325
Kapos, 118
Karl-Marx-Allee, 56, 166, 173
Karl Marx Monument, in Chemnitz, 77–84, 96
   artistic installation with, 83–84
   as dual site of memory, 79
   graffiti on, 81
   as icon, 82
   jokes about, 79, 82
   by Kerbel, 77, 78–79
   removal discussions about, 81
   role of, 81–82
   symbolism of, 79, 82–83
Karl Marx Relief, in Leipzig, 64, 91, 97, 325
   debate about, 93–95
   removal and re-erection of, 92–95
Karl-Marx-Stadt, 78, 80. *See also* Chemnitz
Karrenberg, Katharina, 165, 167–69, 170, 172–73, 186, 317, 321
Kerbel, Lev, 84
   Karl Marx Monument by, 77, 78–79
   Thälmann Monument by, 60, 73, 74, 75
Knabe, Hubertus, 115, 227
Knigge, Volkhard, 122–24, 126, 135, 148
Kohl, Helmut, 6, 8, 65, 69, 323
   as Chancellor of Unity, 254
Kohlhoff & Kohlhoff, 210, 211, 233, 235
Kohlhoff Plus, 213, 233
'Kohl-onization', 12
Konrad Adenauer Foundation, 128, 295
Koshar, Rudy, 3, 38, 40, 46
Kristallnacht, 163

Länder, 1
Das Leben der Anderen (*The Lives of Others*), 3
Leipzig, 306n96. *See also* Nikolaikirchhof, demonstrations at; 17 June 1953 uprisings, Leipzig memorial to
   Augustusplatz in, 268, 269, 274
   as birthplace, of peaceful revolution, 269
   Democracy Bell in, 269, 274, 276
   Festival of Lights in, 269
   as Freedom and Unity monument location, 262, 263, 265
   as GDR city of heroes, 269
   monument designs for, 275–77, 308nn136–37
   Nikolaikirche in, 93, 268–69, 272–74
   Paulinerkirche in, 92, 94, 95, 96, 325
   Runde Ecke in, 269
   tank tracks in, 178–81, 319
   Tucker-Frost memorial design for, 275, 276, 297, 307n128
   Wilhelm-Leuschner-Platz in, 275, 307n129
   Young Social Democrats Forum in, 179
Leipzig Cultural Foundation, 269, 270, 273, 274
Leipziger Freiheit, 178
Leipziger Platz, 166, 167, 169

Leipzig Sparkasse Media Foundation, 272
Lenin, Vladimir, 56, 59
  hundredth birthday of, 66
Lenin Monument, in Berlin, 64, 65, 68–72, 96
  Berlin Senate and, 71–72
  demolition of, 68–71
  documentation of, 71–72
Lenin monuments, 52, 57, 62, 66, 72
  re-erection of, 72
  re-evaluation of, 72
Lenk, Peter, 280, 281
Liebknecht, Karl, 39, 58–59, 65, 323
lieux de mémoire, 28, 29
Les Lieux de Mémoire (Nora), 2, 29
light installation, with Nikolaikirchhof fountain, 273
Lingner, Max, 59, 169–70, 172, 325–26
Die Linke, 12, 258, 265, 276, 292. *See also* PDS/Die Linke
Lion Monument, in Schwerin, 280–81
Lions Club, in Plauen, 292
Literaturstreit, 12
Litfin, Günter, 214
The Lives of Others. *See Das Leben der Anderen*
Loest, Eric, 93–94, 179, 272
Luban, Peter, 293–4
Lüdtke, Rita, 130, 133, 135, 315
Luxemburg, Rosa, 39, 58–59, 68–69, 134, 228, 323

Magdeburg, 160, 164, 326
  high unemployment in, 287
  right-wing extremism in, 287
Magdeburg Citizens Monument, 286–91, 326
  Board of Trustees for the Magdeburg Citizens Monument, 286–87
  citizen stones associated with, 290–91
  design competition for, 288–90
  Evers associated with, 286–87
  funding for, 287–88, 290
  location of, 287–88
  9 October 1989 relating to, 287
  unveiling of, 290–91
magnetic tape factory, in Dessau, 281–83
Mahnmal, 37, 39, 93, 260, 261, 300
Market Square
  in Dessau, 283
  in Schwerin, 278–79, 280
mark of joy. *See Freudenmal*
Marx Engels Forum, 60
Marx Engels Monument, 46, 63–65, 99n40
mass graves
  discovery of, 114, 118, 120, 124–25
  of fallen soldiers, 59
  of German internees, 110
  at Soviet special camps, 118, 129, 132
mastering the past. *See Vergangenheitsbewältigung*
Masur, Kurt, 93, 270
Die Mauer - Berlin '61 (*The Wall - Berlin '61*), 3
Mausbach, Florian, 168-69, 256, 259
media, memory and, 32–33
memorialization, 14. *See also specific monuments*
  of concentration camp victims, 118
  of 1989/90, 252, 254
  notion of place with, 42
  of SED, 58–60, 66, 83, 85, 86, 92–93, 315
  of 17 June 1953 uprisings, 164
  of Soviet special camps, 111, 119
memorialization, of GDR, 9, 10, 15, 16, 322
  as palimpsest of memory, 315
  themes for, 314
memorial marker. *See Denkzeichen*
memorial museum, 320
memorials, 6, 10, 13, 33. *See also specific memorials*
  anti-Soviet, 63–64, 99n39
  art for, 146–47
  construction of, 36–40, 211–12, 261, 268, 315, 317

Fünfeichen site of, 129, 130–31, 149
to Holocaust, 2, 7, 8, 17, 39, 41, 45,
  165, 166, 168, 187, 230, 238, 255,
  260, 265, 266, 298, 326
landscape of, 5, 14, 16, 17, 34, 252,
  300, 314, 327–28
shifting memorial culture, 15–19
Soviet special camp sites as, 115–17
SPD support of, 165, 260
Memorial Sites Concept
  (*Gedenkstättenkonzeption*), 6, 12,
  13, 14, 17
Memorial to the Murdered Jews of
  Europe, 4, 7. See also Holocaust
  Memorial
memory, 226, 268. See also collective
  memory
anniversary, 318
communicative, 17, 27, 29–31, 60,
  171, 206, 258, 297, 321, 322
communities of, 172
counter-memory, 40, 84
cultural, 17, 27, 29–31, 32, 35, 171,
  187, 297, 321, 322
debates about, 1, 5–9, 18, 261
definition of, 25, 27
democratization of, 26
diachronic, 36
dialogism with, 34–35
formats of, 30, 34
French national, 29
of GDR, 5, 10, 15, 17–19, 33
history and, 26, 31–32, 198
of Holocaust, 6–8, 25–26, 33, 39,
  40–41, 163
Holocaust-centred, 6–8
homogenization of, 318
individual, 27, 28, 30, 31, 48n14
media and, 32–33
multidirectional, 27, 36
national, 260
of National Socialism, 5
official, 27, 30
palimpsest of, 315
political, 27, 30
prosthetic, 27, 31
ritual, 272

of sites, 2–3, 6, 13, 15, 17, 18, 26, 29,
  79, 183
social, 27, 30
synchronic, 36
vernacular, 27, 30
memory activists, 16, 230, 239,
  286–87, 300, 315–17, 319, 322
memory boom, 18, 25–26, 36
memory epidemic, 25
memory industry, 25
Merkel, Angela, 211, 222, 257
Mies van der Rohe, Ludwig, 39, 58
migration, 26
milieux de mémoire, 29
Milla und Partner, 257, 264, 302n28
M+M / ANNABAU, 276
mnemonic communities, 254, 297
mnemonics, 15, 29, 33
  process of, 9, 27, 32, 43, 45, 111
mnemorials, 41
modernism, 38
monument activity
  of CDU, 71, 75, 87, 141, 165, 174,
    186, 213, 222, 227, 230, 254,
    265–66, 276, 316
  of PDS, 71, 76, 83, 87–88, 137,
    143–45, 146–47, 149, 179, 215,
    280, 287, 321
Monument against Fascism, 41
Monument of the Revolutionary
  Workers' Movement, 162
monuments, 2–3, 16, 18, 25–26,
  33, 163, 313n223. See also
  countermonuments; monument
  activity; *specific monuments*
aesthetics of, 298–99, 322–23
authenticity of, 43
Axel-Springer-Haus, 258
becoming of, 44–45
to Berlin Wall, 37, 64, 194–240
capsules in, 294, 296, 320
Cold War relating to, 1, 73, 172,
  194, 196, 221, 226–27, 228, 231
costs of, 68, 70, 75, 165, 270, 273
demolition of, 57, 63, 65, 66, 68–71
documentation, 72–73
donors for, 297–98, 313n222

monuments (*cont.*)
  GDR role with, 57–62, 314
  history of, 37–38
  location of, 43–44
  mass participation with, 299, 313n224, 319, 320
  memorials and, 36–47
  national, 38–39
  parks with, 57, 64
  performative, 40
  as processual, 44
  Prussian, 56, 325–26
  ritual acts associated with, 60, 61–62
  to 17 June 1953 uprisings, 161, 162, 164
  socialist realist, 17
  as subset of memorials, 37
  toppling of, 55, 65–66
monuments, October 1989–October 1990, 64–65
  exhibitions about, 63, 99n36
  intended and unintended monuments, 62
  vandalism of, 62
Monuments to the Victims of the Communist Dictatorship, in Jena, 14
Monument to the Battle of the Nations. *See Völkerschlachtdenkmal*
multidirectional memory, 27, 36
multiple narratives, 319
Museum for Town History, in Dessau, 282
Museum of German History, 199
Museum of Military History, in Dresden, 179
museums, 3, 11, 13, 14, 16
  Jewish, 7
  Temporary Museum of Modern Marx, 83–84, 97

narratives
  democratic, 16–17
  dominant, 317–21

for Freedom and Unity Monument, 320
  grand, 26
  historical, 2, 16, 26, 31, 32, 34
  memory, 318, 326
  multiple, 319
  for Plauen *Wende* monument, 294–95
National Democratic Party of Germany (NPD), 183–85, 186, 187
Nationalist movements, 33, 268
National People's Army (NVA), 86
National Socialism, 6, 116, 171. *See also* Nazism.
  interpretations of, 124
  memory of, 5
  SED relating to, 230
  victims of, 122
National Socialist regime, 6, 39, 110, 129, 166
  crimes of, 177
  party of, 56
  past of, 3–4, 5, 122, 171
Nazis, 113–16, 119, 137, 144–45, 316
Nazism, 6, 10, 15, 212. *See also* National Socialism.
negative nationalism, 260, 300, 323
Neubrandenburg, 128, 133
Neues Forum, 252
Neue Wache, 4, 6, 8, 42, 265
Neumann, Bernd, 11, 263
New Course, 159
New Society for the Visual Arts (NGBK), 63, 169
Niederkirchnerstraße, 199
Nikolaikirchhof, 271–77
  as central site of memory, of 1989, 268
  demonstrations at, 268
  fountain on, 272–74
  redevelopment of, 269–70
Nikolaikirchhof monument, 270–77
  column for, 270, 271, 277
  competition for, 270
  Stötzner as designer of, 270, 272, 273
  unveiling of, 271–72

Index • 363

9 November 1918, 3, 254–55
9 November 1923, 254–55
9 November 1938, 255, 267
9 November 1989, 3, 194, 253
9 November 2009, 258, 263
9 October 1989, 268–69, 271–76, 287, 290, 299
1989/90
  interpretation of, 255
  memorialization of, 252, 254
1989 role, of Plauen, 292
Nischel, in Chemnitz, 77–84
NKVD. *See* Soviet People's Commissariat for Internal Affairs
Nooke, Günter, 169, 256, 259, 260–1, 266
Nora, Pierre, 2, 28, 29, 31
normalization, 4–5, 13, 19n11, 23n50
NPD. *See* National Democratic Party of Germany
NVA. *See* National People's Army

official memory, 27, 30
Orwell, George, 294
Ostalgie, 12, 13, 213, 287

Palast der Republik, 4, 12, 13–14, 261–62
palimpsest, 17, 35, 36, 43, 150
  concept of, 322
Party of Democratic Socialism (PDS), 69, 186, 222
  monument activity of, 71, 76, 83, 87–88, 137, 143–45, 146–47, 149, 179, 215, 280, 287, 321
  representatives of, 70, 211, 213
PDS. *See* Party of Democratic Socialism
PDS/Die Linke, 186, 223, 232, 240, 254, 316
Peace Bell Board of Trustees, 283
peaceful revolution, 251–55, 314
  Citizens' Monument, 286–91
  concrete legacy of, 296–300
  in cultural memory of Berlin Republic, 263, 264
  Dessau peace bell, 281–86, 319

Freedom and Unity Monument, 256–68, 296, 297–98
Leipzig, as birthplace of, 269
Nikolaikirchhof and beyond, 268–77
Plauen *Wende* monument, 291–96
Round Table, 277–81
performative monuments, 40
perpetrators, 111, 148, 319, 327
Petershagen, Rudolf, 136, 138, 140
Pieck, Wilhelm, 58, 59
Pionierorganisation Ernst Thälmann, 74
plaques
  at Fünfeichen, 132, 133
  at Prenzlauer Allee memorial, 141
  for 17 June 1953 uprisings, 162, 180, 182
  for Treptow child victims, 215–16
Platz des 17. Juni, 177
Platz des Aufstandes (Square of the Uprising), 172
Plauen
  demonstrations in, 291–92
  Lions Club in, 292
  1989 role of, 292
Plauen *Wende* monument, 291–96, 319, 326
  capsule in foundation of, 294, 296
  design competition for, 293
  exhibition of, 293
  funding for, 292–93
  location of, 292
  narrative for, 294–95
  peaceful revolution and, 291–96
  unveiling of, 295
  vote for, 293
political memory, 27, 30
postmodernism, 26, 39
Postplatz, in Dresden, 181–82
post-unification era, 315, 325
Potsdamer Platz, 3, 66, 166, 198, 199
POWs. *See* prisoners of war
Prenzlauer Allee
  Berlin Senate and, 142
  GPU-cellar on, 140
  Haftstätte on, 140, 316, 321, 324

Prenzlauer Allee (*cont.*)
  Haus 3, 140, 143, 146, 149, 161–62
  history of, 147
  NKVD associated with, 140, 142, 148
  Stasi associated with, 141, 142, 143–44
Prenzlauer Allee memorial, 141–47
  art for, 146–47
  controversy about, 143–45
  key principles for guidelines of, 145–46
  plaque, 141
  questions for, 142–44, 146–47
  Sachse design of, 142–44, 146, 147
Prenzlauer Berg museum, 142, 147
preservation
  of Berlin Wall, 197, 236
  of Bernauer Straße Wall Memorial, 211
  of socialist icons, 57, 63–64
prisoners of war (POWs), 112, 128, 131, 136
  at Fünfeichen, 129, 130, 133, 134
prosthetic memory, 27, 31
Prussian monuments, 56, 325–26

Radeloff, Thomas, 138–39
Ranger, Terence, 32
Ravensbrück, 114
Reconciliation Church. *See*
  Versöhnungskirche
Red Army, 8, 59, 65, 128, 136
Regional Office for the Protection of the Constitution, 183
Reichstag
  Dem deutschen Volke on, 4
  white crosses at, 218–19, 222
religious symbolism, 148, 325
remembrance, 36, 275, 326
  archive relating to, 34
  of Berlin Wall, 197, 236
  canon relating to, 34
  collective, 18, 27, 323
  dialogic, 322–28
  forgetting and, 34
  of GDR, 3, 6, 14, 16, 18, 164

  of Holocaust, 7, 127, 149, 168, 230, 238, 258, 298, 323–24, 326, 327
reunification. *See* unification
Revolutionary Flame, in Halle, 86
Roehl, Rüdiger, 216
Round Table, in Schwerin, 296, 297
  GDR associated with, 277–79
  in Market Square, 278–79, 280
  relocation of, 279
  sculptures with, 278
  by Steinbrüggen, 277–81
Runde Ecke, in Leipzig, 269
Rüppel, Wolfgang, 165, 169, 170, 171–74, 228
Rust, Gustav, 222

Sabrow, Martin, 10, 11, 15, 117, 231, 254–55
Sachs, Wolfgang, 292, 293, 297, 315
Sachse, Karla, 142–44, 146, 147, 173, 206–7, 317
Sachsenhausen, 110, 112, 114, 116, 129
Schleusener, Lothar, 215, 216, 217
Schröder, Gerhard, 7, 8, 20n21, 213, 266, 271–72, 290
Schultz, Egon, 195, 235
Schweigelager, 114
Schwerin
  Ceramic Column in, 279–81
  Henry the Lion as founder of, 280–81
  House of Democracy in, 280
  Lion Monument in, 280–81
  Round Table in, 277–81
  Symposium of Metal Designers in, 277
Second World War, 3, 4, 25–26
SED. *See* Socialist Unity Party of Germany
self-liberation, 114, 118, 318, 319
7 October 1989, 291, 294–95
750th anniversary, of Berlin, 9
17 June 1953, 316, 317, 318
  demonstrations, 43, 159–60, 165, 179, 181–83

17 June 1953 uprisings, 14, 18, 138, 150, 219, 236, 321
  Berlin and, 161, 163, 164
  as failed fascist putsch, 160
  50th anniversary of, 162, 173, 180
  GDR relating to, 159–60, 161, 164
  interpretations of, 165
  leadership issues with, 160, 163, 166
  memorials to, 170, 171, 180, 182, 326
  monuments to, 161, 162, 164, 174, 175, 176, 181, 228, 238, 316, 323, 325
  New Course associated with, 159
  60th anniversary of, 162, 172
17 June 1953 uprisings, Berlin memorial to, 161, 163
  competition for, 165–67
  criticism of, 168–69, 170–71
  debate over, 168–69, 170–73
  Karrenberg design for, 165, 167–69, 170, 172–73, 186, 317, 321
  at Leipziger Platz, 166, 167, 169
  location of, 166
  Rüppel, 165, 169, 170, 171–74
17 June 1953 uprisings, Dresden memorial to
  Dreßel design for, 182, 186–87
  importance of date with, 183–85
  NPD associated with, 183–85
  unveiling ceremony of, 183–85
17 June 1953 uprisings, Hennigsdorf memorial to
  competition for, 175
  proposals for, 174–75
  symbolism of, 176, 187
  unveiling of, 177–78
  Wagner-Kerkhof design for, 175–77
17 June 1953 uprisings, Leipzig memorial to
  commemorative activity with, 178, 187
  design for, 179–80
  unveiling ceremony of, 181
sign of remembrance. *See* Erinnerungsmal

sites. *See also* Buchenwald Memorial Site
  of deportation, 7
  of Flag Monument, 85
  historic, 9
  Memorial Sites Concept, 6, 12, 13, 14, 17
  of memory, 2–3, 6, 13, 15, 17, 18, 26, 29, 79, 183
  60th anniversary, of 17 June uprisings, 162, 172
Skuin, Jan, 216
slogans, 257, 283, 299, 310n173, 318
SMT-Verurteilte, 112
Social Democratic Party of Germany (SPD), 75, 79, 87, 116, 215
  coalition of CDU and, 11, 165, 211
  coalition of Green government and, 71, 227–28, 256, 258
  coalition of PDS and, 71, 227–28, 256, 258
  fractions of, 69, 83, 165
  memorial support of, 165, 260
  representatives of, 94, 177, 184, 213, 230, 283
socialism
  end of, 3–4, 5, 6, 39, 56, 59
  public art produced under, 323
socialist and post-socialist monument projects, 315
socialist art, 66
socialist communicative memory, 60
socialist icons
  adaptation of, 57
  art relating to, 58, 60, 66
  demolition of, 56–57, 63
  Karl Marx Monument, 78–84
  Karl Marx Relief, 91–95
  Lenin Monument, 65–72, 75
  modern makeover for Halle's flag monument, 85–90
  modification of, 63
  monument role, in GDR, 57–62m314
  October 1989–October 1990, 62–65
  preservation of, 57, 63–64
  relocation of, 57, 63

socialist icons (*cont.*)
  removal of, 55–56, 63, 64
  Thälmann Monument, 72–77
Socialist Unity Party of Germany (SED), 16, 79
  atheist policies of, 111
  dictatorship of, 11–12, 17, 39, 69–70, 74–75, 80, 94, 96, 114, 117, 124, 130, 173, 186, 199, 213, 230
  fall of, 55, 69
  memorialization relating to, 58–60, 66, 83, 85, 86, 92–93, 315
  political bankruptcy of, 161
  with 17 June 1953 uprisings, 160
social memory, 27, 30
Society for Legal and Humanitarian Support (GRH), 144
Sophie Scholl – Die letzten Tage (*Sophie Scholl – The Final Days*), 3
Soviet memorials, 58, 59
Soviet People's Commissariat for Internal Affairs (NKVD), 8, 112–13, 128, 140, 142, 148
Soviet special camps (*Speziallager*), 151n23, 238, 327
  Bautzen, 112
  Buchenwald, 110, 112, 117–28, 153n39
  death rates in, 112
  dual past of, 115–16
  Fünfeichen, 110, 128–35
  Greifswald, 135–40
  internees in, 110, 112–16
  interrogation centers and, 110, 112–17
  mass graves at, 118, 129, 132
  memoirs about, 110
  as memorial sites, 115–17
  perpetrators at, 111
  Prenzlauer Allee, 140–47
  Sachsenhausen, 110, 112, 114, 116, 129
  Schweigelager, 114
  victims at, 110–11, 115–16
SPD. *See* Social Democratic Party of Germany
Speer und Er (*Speer and Hitler*), 3

Speziallager. *See* Soviet special camps
Spree, 3, 4, 198, 203, 218–19, 220
Square of German Unity, in Schwerin, 284
square of mourning. *See* Trauerplatz
Square of the Uprising. *See* Platz des Aufstandes
Stalin, 2, 159
Stalinism, 6, 131, 150, 171
Stasi, 1, 13, 94, 140
  dissolution of, 277
  employees of, 119, 123, 143–44, 147, 160, 235
  headquarters of, 14, 64, 111, 115, 141, 253, 282
  IMs for, 2, 12
  Prenzlauer Allee associated with, 141, 142, 143–44
  victims of, 8, 142
State Council Building, 58, 59
Steinbrüggen, Guillermo, 277–81
stelae, 2, 37, 149, 164, 214, 324
  at Fünfeichen, 131, 133, 135
  at Greifswald, 135, 137–40, 147
  at Hennigsdorf, 175
  at Holocaust memorial, 230
  in Plauen *Wende* monument, 294
St Nicholas Column, in Leipzig, 270, 271, 277, 299, 319
Stolpersteine, 41–42. *See also* stumbling stone
Stone, paper, scissors (Goldberg), 203–6
Stötzner, Andreas, 270, 272, 273
Straße des 17. Juni, 161, 178, 195
Streitwert (dispute value), 45, 321
stumbling stone, 181, 212
Stunde Null (zero hour), 252
swords into ploughshares slogan, 283, 299, 310n173
symbolism
  of Berlin Wall, 236
  of Flag Monument, in Halle, 86–87, 88
  of Freedom and Unity Monument, 259, 260

of Freedom Memorial, at
  Checkpoint Charlie, 226
of Fünfeichen memorial site, 134
of Karl Marx Monument, in
  Chemnitz, 79, 82–83
religious, 148, 325
traditional, 239
West German, 132
Symposium of Metal Designers, in
  Schwerin, 277
synchronic memory, 36

tank tracks
  in Dresden, 181–85
  in Leipzig, 178–81, 319
technological progress, 26, 32
Temporary Museum of Modern
  Marx, 83–84, 97
10th anniversary, of Berlin Wall fall,
  200, 256, 287, 314
Thälmann, Ernst, 57, 59, 74
Thälmann Monument, in Berlin,
  72–77, 90, 97
  discussions about, 75–76
  graffiti on, 76–77
  by Kerbel, 60, 73, 74, 75
  restoration of, 97
  survival of, 72–77
Thiel, Frank, 204–6
Thierse, Wolfgang, 10, 15, 219, 221,
  260–61, 267
Third Reich, 6
13 August Association, 223, 228, 229
30th anniversary, of Berlin Wall fall,
  257
3 October 1990
  as Day of German Unity, 251
  German unification on, 251
  as national holiday, 251
3 October 2010, 258
Tiefensee, Wolfgang, 179, 180, 181,
  272, 273
Tillich, Stanislaw, 292, 295–96
Tomski, Nikolai, 60, 66-68
Trabant Monument, 14
Trauerplatz (square of mourning), 119,
  120, 126

Treptow child victims
  at border, 214–15
  bullet holes in memorial to,
    216–18
  commemoration competition for,
    216
  GDR coverup of, 215
  Hartmann as, 215, 216, 217
  memorial plaque for, 215–16
  monument to, 216–18, 319
  Schleusener as, 215, 216, 217
Treuhandanstalt, 166
Trotnow, Helmut, 199, 207–8
Tucker-Frost, Miley, 275, 276, 297,
  307n128
tunnels, Bernauer Straße Wall
  Memorial and, 207
20th anniversary
  of Berlin Wall fall, 3, 252, 257, 262,
    281, 292
  of unification, 258, 292
25th anniversary, of Berlin Wall fall,
  223, 328

Übergänge
  Berlin Senate and, 201–2
  as border crossings and transitions,
    201–7
Übergänge memorial designs, 239
  at Chausseestraße, 206–7
  communicative memory with, 206
  competition for, 201–2
  Illuminated box, 204–6
  seven designs for, 202–3, 242n46
  Stone, paper, scissors, 203–6
Ulbricht, Walter, 58, 66
UNESCO heritage site, Berlin Wall
  as, 199
unification, 3–4, 13, 87, 113, 327
  German, 251, 262
  Holocaust memory intensification
    with, 6–7
  Lenin's Fall and, 65–72, 75
  memory debates relating to, 1, 5–9,
    18
  20th anniversary of, 258, 292
unity seesaw. *See Einheitswippe*

unofficial collaborator of Stasi (IM), 2, 12, 235
Unsere Mütter, unsere Väter (*Generation War*, 2013), 3
Der Untergang (*Downfall*), 3
'Unveiled: Berlin and Its Monuments', 71

vandalism, 62
Vergangenheitsbewältigung (mastering the past), 5
vernacular memory, 27, 30
Versöhnungskirche (Reconciliation Church), 207, 213
victimhood, 229, 238
　commemoration of, 213, 255
　concept of, 2, 33
　experiences of, 8
　visibility and, 214–18
victims
　of communism, 325
　of concentration camps, 118
　of fascism and communist resistance movement, 58–59
　of GDR border regime, 266, 316
　of Holocaust, 39, 122, 222, 255
　of Nazism, 212
　perpetrators and, 148, 319, 327
　at Soviet special camps, 110–11, 115–16
　of Stalinism, 150
　of Stasi, 8, 142
Vietnam Veterans Memorial, 38, 43
das Volk (people), 187, 268
Völkerschlachtdenkmal (Monument to the Battle of the Nations), 275, 326
VOS. See Association of Victims of Stalinism

Wagin, Ben, 198
Wagner-Kerkhof, Heidi, 175–77
Waldfriedhof (woodland graveyard), 121, 125

The Wall - Berlin '61. See *Die Mauer - Berlin '61*
Warsaw Ghetto Monument, 46
Was bleibt (*What Remains*, 1990) (Wolf), 12
Waterloo Column, 37
Wehrmacht, 128
Weimar, 37, 118, 120, 136
　Constitution, 3, 262
Wende, 94, 129, 253, 269, 297
　in Leipzig, 269
　of 1989, 274
　period of, 81, 87, 88, 130, 274
　Plauen *Wende* monument, 292–96, 319, 326
　term of, 255, 301n23
Wende monuments, 291–96, 315, 319
Werwölfe, 113, 116, 129
West Berlin, 63, 66, 70, 73, 160–61, 165, 174
What Remains, 1990. See *Was bleibt*
white crosses, 195, 238
　at Bernauer Straße, 218, 223
　on Ebertstraße, 219, 220, 221
　political function of, 219–20, 223
　at Reichstag building, 218–19, 222
　removal and return of, 223–24
　on Western side of Wall, 218–19
Wilhelm-Leuschner-Platz, in Leipzig, 275, 307n129
Window of Commemoration, 234, 235, 238
Wodiczko, Krzysztof, 60, 66, 68
Wolf, Christa, 12
woodland graveyard. See *Waldfriedhof*
working through the past. See *Aufarbeitung*
Wowereit, Klaus, 1, 173, 213, 266

Young Social Democrats Forum, 179

Zagel, Norbert, 288–89

www.ingramcontent.com/pod-product-compliance
Lightning Source LLC
Chambersburg PA
CBHW072142100526
44589CB00015B/2045